RHEA COUNTY TENNESSEE

Circuit Court Minutes

September 1815–March 1836

Carol Wells

HERITAGE BOOKS
2010

HERITAGE BOOKS
AN IMPRINT OF HERITAGE BOOKS, INC.

Books, CDs, and more—Worldwide

For our listing of thousands of titles see our website
at
www.HeritageBooks.com

Published 2010 by
HERITAGE BOOKS, INC.
Publishing Division
100 Railroad Ave. #104
Westminster, Maryland 21157

Copyright © 1996 Carol Wells

All rights reserved. No part of this book may be reproduced or transmitted in any form or by any means, electronic or mechanical, including photocopying, recording or by any information storage and retrieval system without written permission from the author, except for the inclusion of brief quotations in a review.

International Standard Book Numbers
Paperbound: 978-0-7884-0468-9
Clothbound: 978-0-7884-8405-6

CONTENTS

Foreword v
Abbreviations vi

1815
   September 1
1816
   March 4
   September 7
1817
   March 10
   September 13
1818
   March 15
   September 17
1819
   March 20
   September 22
1820
   March 23
   September 26
1821
   March 29
   September 33
1822
   March 39
   September 45
1823
   March 49
   September 52
1824
   March 55
   September 58
1825
   March 61
   September 64
1826
   March 67
   September 71
1827
   March 75
   September 79
1828
   March 84
   September 88

1829
- March 92
- September 97

1830
- March 103
- September 107

1831
- March 111
- September 116

1832
- March 121
- September 124

1833
- March 128
- September 133

1834
- March 136
- September 139

1835
- March 143
- September 146

1836
- March 150

INDEX 152

FOREWORD

Rhea County was created in 1807 from Roane County. In 1819 Hamilton County was cut from Rhea. Through Rhea came families intending to settle, travelers spending a season or two before heading west, and renters hoping eventually to own their own farms. A dearth of material about early Rhea County makes Circuit Court minutes useful to genealogists. Besides the names of residents and transients, names of people in other counties and other states appear in the minutes.

One of the difficulties in doing genealogy is the struggle to read puzzling handwriting. While some Rhea minutes were beautifully written, the work of some clerks was nearly impossible to decypher. Add to those scrawls the variety of spelling as well as the problems associated with transcribing from microfilm. The reader will please use all the imagination in searching for family names that the clerks and judges used in writing those names.

Carol Wells

ABBREVIATIONS

A&B	Assault & Battery
ac	acres
ackd	acknowledged
addl	additional
admr	administrator
agt	against
appt	appoint
atty	attorney
compl/compt	complainant
compy	company
cr	creek
CSC	Clerk Sumner County
dam	damages
decd	deceased
depo	deposition
dft	defendant
D/G	deed of gift
DS	deputy sheriff
exd	excused
exn	execution
exr	executor
judgt	judgment
P/A	power of attorney
plf	plaintiff
rd	road
recd	received
respt	respondant
retd	returned
sec	security
secy	security
shff	sheriff
TAB	trespass assault & battery
will	last will and testament
wit	witness

SEPTEMBER 1815

p.1   Be it remembered that on Monday the 18th day of September 1815 a Circuit Court was open and holden for the County of Rhea in the Court House in Washington. Present the Honorable Thomas Stuart, Judge &c.

Miller Francis Sheriff by his Deputy Woodson Francis returned the venire facias: Charles Ryon, Edward Cox, Robert Bell, David Parkhill, Robert Gamble, Joseph Johnson, James Galbreath, John Jack, Robert Love, Ezekiel Henry, Henry Collins, John Sapp, Marston Mead, Samuel Logan, James Mitchell, Col William Johnson, Richard G Waterhouse, George Gillespie, James Preston, James Rodgers, George Starns, James Snelson, James Bailey, Mathew Hubbert, Richard Paris.

Grand jury: Richard G Waterhouse foreman, James Bailey, James Preston, Robert Love, Charles Ryon, David Parkhill, Henry Collins, Ezekiel Henry, Joseph Johnson, George Starns, Robert Bell, Edward Cox.

p.2   Excuse James Snelson from further attendance as a juror at this Term.

Vincent Bennet v George Walker. Appeal. Plf recovered judgmt in County Court April 1815 for $198 deft and $15.84 damages besides costs. Dft granted appeal with Seymour Catching security. Judgment of Court below in all things affirmed. Plf recovers agt dft and his security debt, damages and costs.

p.3   Lucy Robinson v John Robinson. Power/attorney 13 Sept 1815 proven by John Corby[Corley?] and Wm K Kulbeth.

Charles McClung to Thos N Clark. Deed 2800 acres 11 Sept 1815 proven by Robert H Adams and William Lyon.

Henry Owens v David Crum. Cause continued until next term.

Ramseys Heirs v Thos Kelly. Plfs not ready; postponed until tomorrow; plf pays costs accrued during this day.

Charles McClungs lessee v George Starnes. Plf orders suit dismissed; dft
p.4   recovers against plf his costs of defence.

Robert Bell & wife v Azariah David. Cause continued until next term.

Francis Smith v Willis Morgan and others. Sheriff awarded a Plurius returnable to next term.

Alexr McCall & wifes lessee v Archd Roane. Cause continued until next Term.

Thomas Brown v Polly Hopkins. Plf granted leave to file a new declaration.
p.5   Thomas Brown v Mary Morgan. Plf granted leave to file a new declaration.

Richard G Waterhouse lessee v James Callison. Suit dismissed; dft pays all costs not exceeding $14; plf pays balance.

Robert Purdy trustee v Thomas J Vandyke & John Love. Suit revived agt heirs at law of Thos J Vandyke viz Alexander O Vandyke, Jefferson C Vandyke, Nixon Vandyke, Mary H Vandyke and Eliza Vandyke. Continued.

Court adjourned until tomorrow morning 9 Oclock.   Thos Stuart

p.6   Tuesday September 19th. Present the Honorable Thomas Stuart, Judge &c.

Richard G Waterhouses lessee v Charles Gamble. Suit dismissed; dft pays all costs except the attendance of the plaintiffs witnesses which plf will pay.

Richard G Waterhouses lessee v Mary Brooks. Dismissed; [worded as above].
p.7   Richard G Waterhouses lessee v John Russell & Thomas Ackman. Suit dismissed and dfts pay all costs that have accrued thereon.

Richard G Waterhouses lessee v Robert Meany. [worded as above]

Richard G Waterhouses lessee v Heirs of James Russell decd. Suit dismissed; Andrew Russell executor of deceased pays all costs accrued in this case.
p.8   Richard G Waterhouses lessee v Robert Gamble. Suit dismissed; dft pays all

SEPTEMBER 1815

costs except the attendance of the plaintiffs witnesses, which plf pays.
    Richard G Waterhouses lessee v Robert Gamble. Dismissed [worded as above].
p.9   Excuse Wm Johnson & George Gillespie from attending as jurors at this term.
    George Starns to Richd G Waterhouse. Deed 28 Aug 1815 200 acres ackd.
    Richd G Waterhouse to Polly Waterhouse. Deed 14 Jan 1814 166½ acres ackd.
    Jacob Bayson v Cain Abel. Depositions of Richard Langston, William Booker, Solomon Marshal esq, John Belcher, Basil Neal esq, Joseph Marshal esq and Jefferson
p.10   Pitman of Columbia County, Georgia, to be taken on behalf of defendant. Depositions of Abraham Marshal and John Willingham of Columbia County, Georgia, and Benjamin Williams of Jasper County, GA, and Freeman Walker, Robert Walker, & Ferdinand Finvice[Tinvice?] of Richmond County, GA, to be taken on behalf plaintiff.
    Jonathan Walker v Joseph Frost. Jury: Matthew Hubbert, James Galbreath,
p.11   James Green, Thomas Woodward, John A Smith, John Macoy, John Jack, John Martin, James Lauderdale, John Shell, Charles Gamble, Richard Walker cannot agree. Cause continued until next term for a new trial to be had thereon.
    John Williams's lessee v Lyon & French[Finch?]. Continued until next term.
    Carters Heirs lessee v Clark & Rawlings. Continued until next term. Deposition to be taken of Alexander McMillen in Knoxville before John N Gamble or James Ponk[Porck?] and deposition of John Cotten of Indiana, Kentucky or Illinois Territory to be taken before two justices in benefit of plf. Willis Breazeale and
p.12   George Gordon summponed as witnesses in this cause failed to appear; they forfeit according to act of assembly.
    Jesse White v William Robison. On affidavit of Alexander S Winford the defendant's agent, the cause is continued. John B Hood summoned as a witness failed to appear; forfeits according to act of assembly.
    Court adjourned until tomorrow morning 9 Oclock.   Thos Stuart

p.13   Wednesday Sept 20th. Present the Honorable Thomas Stuart, Judge.
    Heirs of Landon Carter v George Gordon. Forfeiture entered against dft for failing to attend as witness at this term in suit Carters Heirs lessee agt Thomas N Clark and Daniel Rawlings be set aside; dft pays costs in this behalf expended.
    Carters Heirs lessee v Clark & Rawlings. Deposition of Alexander Outlaw to be taken before Judge Stuart at the house of Mrs. Campbell in this town within this evening in benefit of dft. John Williams attorney for plfs and John McCampbell atty for dft agree notices to take depositions may be served upon themselves.
p.14   State v Esaias Bowman. Plurias issued to Sheriff returnable next term.
    State v Randolph Smith. Forfeited recognizance. Defendant not appearing, on motion of James C Mitchell solicitor general, an execution issued against goods &c of Randolph Smith for $250 and also costs of writ.
    Thomas Hopkins lessee v David Stuart. Cause continued until next term.
p.15   Robert Bell & wife v Azariah David. Deposition of Thomas Noton of Mississippi Territory to be taken; should sd deposition be taken in Huntsville plf must give defendant twenty days notice, if in any other part of sd Territory forty days notice. Also depositions of Martha Howard, John Howard and John Shell of this County before James Campbell & Abram Howard esqrs in benefit of plaintiff.
    State v John Thompson. Dft in proper person pleads not guilty. Cause continued. John Thompson, James Thompson, Jesse Thompson & Joseph Thompson securities.
p.16   John Thompson to appear to answer charge of passing counterfeit money.
    Thomas Brown v Polly Hopkins and v Mary Morgan. To plead at next Term.

SEPTEMBER 1815

p.17   Richard G Waterhouses lessee v John Murphy. Jury Matthew Hubbert, John Jack, James Callison, Hugh Berry, Richard Philpot, Willam Hyde, Jackson Howerton, Martin Mahaffee, James Stuart, Joseph Paine, Thomas Hudson, Jesse Sherill find dft guilty of trespass and ejectment; assess plfs damage to 6¢ and costs. Plf granted writ to issue to cause him to have his possession.

Thomas N Clarks lessee v Azariah David. Cause continued until next Term.

p.18   Charles McClungs lessee v James Thompson. John Thompson and Jesse Thompson the defendants securities.

George Williams v William Henry. Cause dismissed by plf. John Henry confesses judgment for $3 of costs; plaintiff pays the balance.

Lewis Bledsoe for the use of Joseph Thompson v Allen Johnson. Jury James Mitchell, James Baily, James Preston, Robert Love, Charles Ryon, David Parkhill, Henry Collins, Ezekiel Henry, Joseph Johnson, George Starns, Richard G Waterhouse, Jeremiah Duncan find dft hath paid the debt by delivering to plf a sorrel horse

p.19   with $100 in full satisfaction for same. Dft recovers agt plf his costs.

Richard G Waterhouses lessee v John Thompson & others. Jury Matthew Hubbert, John Jack, Jackson Howerton, Joseph Pain, Thomas Hudson, Martin Mahaffe, James Stuart, Jesse Sherill, James Bailey, James Preston, Robert Love, James Mitchell. Continued tomorrow.

John Skidmore v Jacob Wassom[Wassinn?]. Cause continued until next term.

Court adjourned until tomorrow morning 9 Oclock.   Thos Stuart

p.20   Thursday Sept 21st. Present the Honorable Thomas Stuart, Judge &c.

Carters Heirs lessee v Clark & Rawlings. Depositions of Stockley Sharp of South Carolina, Little Page Sims of Maddison County, Mississippi Territory in behalf plf.

Jonathan Walker v Joseph Frost. Deposition of John Stapleton of Ohio to be taken in behalf dft.

p.21   Richard G Waterhouses lessee v William Murphree. Cause continued next term.

Charles McClungs lessee v Isaac West. Cause continued until next term.

Andrew Campbells lessee v York and Dunlap. Cause continued to next term.

Richard G Waterhouses lessee v John Thompson & others. Jury consulting.

Court adjourned until tomorrow morning 9 Oclock.   Thos Stuart

p.22   Friday Sept 22d. Present the Honorable Thomas Stuart, Judge &c.

Stephen Blythe and John Love v Samuel Erwin. Sci Fa. Parties in person agree scire facias be dismissed and dft pay costs.

Richard G Waterhouses lessee v John Thompson and others. Jury sworn on Wednesday could not agree. Cause continued until next term.

Charles McClung v. Return J Meigs & Timothy Meigs. Continued to next term.

p.23   Robert Fergusons lessee v Richard G Waterhouse. John Moore deft's security.

Heirs of John Ramsey's lessee v Thomas Kelly. Jury Charles Ryon, Robert Bell, David Parkhill, Henry Collins, Ezekiel Henry, Joseph Johnson, George Starns, John D Jones, Frederic Fulkerson, Henry Tuttle, Jacob Bryson, Samuel Logan respited until tomorrow.

William Murphrees lessee v Alexander Burns, James Cannon & Mary Gravelly. Peter Bennett agent for Charlotte Lewis, William B Lewis and his wife Margaret heirs at law of William T Lewis filed petition praying writs issue to bring this

MARCH 1816

cause into Court so far as it respects James Cannon & Mary Gravelly; writs issue. Court adjourned until tomorrow morning 8 Oclock. Thos Stuart

p.24 Saturday Sept 23d. Present the Honorable Thomas Stuart, Judge &c.
John Ramseys lessee v Thomas Kelly. Jury sworn yesterday could not agree. Cause continued until next term for a new trial to be had thereon.
James Rodgers v William S Leuty. Apl. Grant plaintiff leave to amend his declaration; plf pays costs.
Order causes now pending not otherwise disposed of to be continued until next term. Court adjourned until court in course. Thos Stuart

p.25 Monday 18th March. Present the Honorable Edward Scott, Judge &c.
Miller Francis Sheriff returned venire facias: Warham[Wacham?] Easly, Henry Ayrheart, Jesse White, William Thomas, Jesse Davidson, Cumberland Rector, John Robinson, Henry Taylor, Thomas Moore, Hugh Rhea, James Blackley, John Thompson, John Rice, Lemuel Reed, Frederick Fulkerson, George Lewis, Turner Harwood, Henry Collins, William Lewis.
Grand Jury: John Rice foreman, Hugh Rhea, John Thompson, Lemuel Reed, George Lewis, Henry Ayrheart, James Blackley, William Lewis, Henry Collins, Warham Easley, John Robison, Jesse White, Cumberland Mountain[sic].
John Lewis a constable sworn to attend the Grand Jury.
p.26 Ordered following suits: Carters Heirs less v Clark & Rawlings, Jesse White v William Robinson, Thomas N Clarks less v Azariah David, John Williams less v Lyon and French, McCall & wife less v Archibald Roane, Charles McClung v Return T Meigs & Timothy Meigs be continued until next term for want of a competent Court.
William Robinson v John B Hood. Dft in person; parties agree that scire facias be dismissed, defendant pays costs.
Jesse White v William Robinson. Parties agree to take depositions of John B Hood & David Haley this evening at John Love's house in this town before Wm Smith.
p.27 Excuse Thomas Moore from further attendance as a Juror at this term.
Francis Smith v Willis Morgan & others. Charles Gamble bail for William Lauderdale one of the defendants surrendered him; Jesse Day dft's special bail.
George Walker v Vincent Bennett. Equity. Rule granted defendants attorney.
Court adjourned until tomorrow morning 9 Oclock. Edw Scott

p.28 Tuesday March 19th. Present the Honorable Edward Scott, Judge &c.
Richard G Waterhouses lessee v John Thompson & others. Motion of dfts atty and it appearing to Court from affidavit of John Thompson that a fair & impartial trial of this cause cannot be had in this County, order cause adjourned for trial to Circuit Court for Roane County in Kingston on first Monday of September.
Jonathan Walker v Joseph Frost. On motion of dft's atty and it appearing that fair & impartial trial of this cause cannot be had [worded as above]
p.29 Frederick Fulkerson, Turner Harwood, and William Thomas were duly summoned; they not appearing, they are to pay State $5 each unless they shew sufficient cause

4

MARCH 1816

to contrary at the next term of this Court.
It appearing that Sheriff had summoned George Winton and Major Gillihan to serve as jurors for the day and they not appearing, for their contempt they make their fine by payment of $2.50 each.
Jonathan Walker v Joseph Frost. Deposition of John Stepleton to be taken in behalf of the defendant.
p.30   Den on demises of Thomas Hopkins v Richard Fen with notice to Geo Winton and Vallentine Shoolls. On motion of Carlisle Humphreys by atty and its appearing to Court that tenants are living on the land in question as tenants of Carlisle Humphreys, order Carlisle Humphreys admitted deft. Whereupon Jacob Wassinn[Wapin?] undertakes for dft Humphreys to pay condemnation or render him to prison.
Den on demise of Thomas Hopkins v Fen with notice to Lemuel Reed. On motion of Carlisle Humphreys by atty and upon its appearing to Court that the tenant in possession lives on land in question as tenant of Carlisle Humphreys [as above].
p.31   Robert Purdy trustee v Heirs of Thomas J Vandyke decd and John Love. Jury: Henry Saylor, James Kelly, John Handy, James Nail, George Winton, Robert Ferguson, James Thompson, Major Gillihan, Samuel Murphy, John Gillihan, Thomas Moore, Joseph Payne find debt not paid and assess plfs damage by detention of debt $67.54 besides costs. Dfts by attorney say judgment ought not be against them because action was brought upon a joint contract in writing entered into by Thomas J Vandyke and John Love, and by death of original dft Vandyke, suit abated and could not by law be revived agt heirs of sd Thomas J Vandyke; pray arrest of judgment.
p.32   James Rodgers assignee of Alexander Outlaw v William York. Cause continued.
Jacob Bryson v Cain Abel. Cause continued; depositions of Richard Langston, William Booker, Solomon Marshal esq, John Belcher, Basil Neal esq, Joseph Marshall esq, and Jefferson Pitman residents of Columbia County, Georgia, to be taken in behalf of the defendant.
Following causes are continued until next term: Thomas Brown collector v Polly Hopkins, Same v Mary Morgan, and Aquilla Johnson v Isaac S Memems[?] and Abner Underwood.
p.33   Thomas Hopkins lessee v David Stuart. Cause continued until next Term.
Ramseys lessee v Thomas Kelly. Cause continued until next Term.
Richd G Waterhouses lessee v William Murphree. Cause continued next Term.
Charles McClungs lessee v Isaac West. It appearing to Court from affidavit of Abner Underwood that a fair trial cannot be had in this county, cause adjourned to Circuit Court for Blount County in Maryville on first Monday of August.
p.34   Taylor Townsend to Charles McClung. Deed 19 Aug 1814 8000 acres proven by Thomas L Williams and John McClellan two of subscribing witnesses thereto.
Court adjourned until tomorrow morning 9 Oclock.   Edw Scott

Wednesday March 20th. Present the Honorable Edward Scott, Judge &c.
Robert Bell & wife v Azariah David. Cause to determination of Thomas L Williams, Enoch Parsons and Col. John Brown whose award is to be the judgment of
p.35   this Court. Further agreed that deposition of Martha Howard as now taken shall be read as evidence on the trial of this cause.
State v John Thompson. It appearing to Court that a fair trial cannot be had in this County, order this cause to Circuit Court for Roane County first Monday of September. Whereupon John Thompson, James Thompson, Moses Thompson, and Joseph
p.36   Thompson recognizance, condition John Thompson's appearance. Also Richard G

5

MARCH 1816

Waterhouse, Alexander Ferguson and Woodson Francis recognizance, condition they appear to give evidence on behalf State on a charge against John Thompson for passing counterfeit money.

p.37   Josiah Danforth v John Brown. Deed. Daniel Rawlings one of the subscribing witnesses saith he saw Josiah Danforth sign sd deed and that he saw John McClellan sign said deed as a concurring witness.

    Richard G Waterhouse v Jacob Wapum. Cause continued until next term.

    John Skidmore v Jacob Wassum. Cause continued until next term.

    James Rodgers v William S Leuty. Appeal. Plaintiff no further prosecutes; Defendant recovers against plf his costs by him in this behalf expended.

p.38   James Rodgers v William S Lenty. Jury Henry Taylor, Jesse Davidson, Hezekiah Johnson, Jacob Bryson, Edward Cox, James Callison, Alexander Forbes, James Rodgers, Valentine Shoolls, Seymour Catchings, John Ferguson, Thomas Woodward Assess plfs damages by reason of nonperformance to $21 besides costs.

    Thomas Brown collector v Polly Hopkins. Parties attornies dismiss suit at defendants cost.

p.39   State v John Runnion. Recognizance, John Runnion, Samuel Murphey, John Gillihan, Nimrod Pentergrass, condition John Runnion appear at next term. Also Charles Gamble, Thomas Laman, William McAlister & David Parkhil, condition they appear to give evidence on behalf State. Wilson Nivens was bound in recognizance to appear this term to give evidence behalf State agt John Runnion and sd Nivens p.40   not appearing, he forfeits to State $150.

    Robert Fergusons lessee v Richd Waterhouse. Jury John Rice, Hugh Rhea, Lemuel Reed, Geo Lewis, Henry Ayrheart, James Blackley, William Lewis, Warkum Easley, John Robison, Jesse White, Cumberland Rector, Jesse Rody find dft not guilty.

    Ramseys lessee v Thomas Kelly. John Moore bail for William Ramsey surrendered him; whereupon James Campbell & James Callison special bail.

p.41   William Murphrees lessee v John Hill. John Thompson and Seymour Catchings securities for William Murphree.

    Charles McClungs lessee v James Thompson. Parties by attornies agree that this suit be dismissed, defendant to pay all costs except attorneys tax fee.

    George Walker v Vincent Bennett. On motion of dfts attorney, injunction is dissolved.

    William Murphrees lessee v John Hill; Richard G Waterhouses lessee v William Murphree; and William Murphrees lessee v Alexander Burns. Depositions of p.42   Elisha Jones of Burk County, North Carolina, of Abraham Swaggerty of Roane County, Tennessee, of James Peace of sd county, of James Hubbert of Rhea County to be taken in benefit of William Murphree.

    Court adjourned until tomorrow morning 9 Oclock.   Edw Scott

p.43   Thursday March 21st. Present the Honorable Edward Scott, Judge &c.

    Enoch Parsons to John D Jones & George W Hall. Deed 21 March 1816 for Lot 2 in Washington ackd by Enoch Parsons the grantor.

    Isaac S McMeans to Carlisle Humphreys. Deed 11 March 1816 Lot 26 in Washington proven by Wm L Bradley and Isaac Roddy subscribing witnesses.

    Den on demise of Thomas Hopkins v Fen with notice to Margaret Gillihan. Major Gillihan is admitted defendant in lieu of the casual ejector. Whereupon William Lewis undertakes for defendant.

    Carters Heirs lessee v Clark & Rawling. On affidavit of Thomas L Williams,

MARCH 1816

plaintiffs to take deposition of Jane Starns of Green County Tennessee.
p.44   James Callison v James Rodgers. Jury John Rice, Hugh Rhea, Lemuel Reed, George Lewis, Harry Ayrheart, James Blackley, William Lewis, Henry Collins, Warham Easly, Cumberland Rector, Jesse Davidson, Major Gillihan. By consent of parties, jurors are discharged; on motion of dft, plf is nonsuited, and dft recovers agt plf his costs by him in this behalf expended.

William Murphrees lessee v Alexander Burns, James Cannon, & Mary Gravelly. On affidavit of Wm B Lewis, Charlotte Lewis, and Maryann Lewis by her guardian Wm B Lewis are admitted defendants in lieu of casual ejector. Also from affidavit of sd Wm B Lewis, an impartial trial cannot be had in this county, order cause to Circuit
p.45   Court for nearest County being free from like exceptions, Knox, in Knoxville, on second Monday of August next.

Henry Owens v David Crum. Cause is continued until next term.

Francis Smith v Willis Morgan & others and Daniel McPherson v Mary Brooks and Thos Brown collector v Mary Morgan. In these causes by consent time is given parties to plead so as not to delay the trial at next term.

Robert Purdy trustee v Heirs of Thos J Vandyke and John Love. Plf recovers agt dft $187.46 debt, $67.54 damages assessed by jury, and also his costs.
p.46   Matthew Nail to John Henry. Deed 23 Oct 1806 300 acres on Piney River proven by Woodson Francis and Ezekiel Henry who say they are acquainted with the hand writing of Charles Henry whose signature appears as a subscribing witness and they believe it to be his and that sd Charles Henry is dead.

State v Randolph Smith. Forfeiture agt Smith on his recognizance is set aside upon his giving security for the costs, George White, security.

Daniel McCally assignee v John Skidmore. Plaintiff by attorney dismissed suit. Dft recovers agt plaintiff his costs in this behalf expended.
p.47   Charles McClung v Return J Meigs & Timothy Meigs. Dfts attorney suggests that since last continuance of this cause sd Timothy Meigs dft departed this life.

Court adjourned until Court in Course.   Edw Scott

p.48   Monday 16th September. Present the Honorable Thomas Emmerson, Judge &c.
Excuse Jacob Riggel and John Robinson from attendance as jurors this term.
Remit fines against William Thomas, Turner Harwood and George Winton for non attendance as jurors at the last term of this Court.

Following suits continued untill next term, the Court having been engaged therein as Counsel: White v Robinson; Ramseys lessee v Kelly; Waterhouse v Wassum; Hopkins lessee v Stuart; Smith v Morgan and others; Waterhouses lessee v Murphree; Skidmore v Wassum; Owens v Crum; McPherson v Mary Brooks; Hopkins lessee v Moore & Murphy; Hopkins lessee v Gillihan; Ramseys lessee v Caldwell; Murphrees lessee v Hill.
p.49   Miller Francis sheriff returned venire facias: John Murphree, Robert Cozby, John Robinson, Robert Bell, William French, John Hill, Frederick Fulkerson, Roswell Hall, William S Linly, Rezin Rawlings, Thomas James, Charles Gamble, Patrick Martin, Joseph Johnson, George White, James Wilson, Joseph Harwood, David Bush, Jacob Riggel, Joshua Atckley, Nichodemus Hackworth, Seymour Catchings, Robert Moore, Thomas Anderson.

SEPTEMBER 1816

Grand Jury: Robert Bell foreman, Nichodemus Hakworth, Robert Cozby, William French, John Hill, Thomas James, Charles Gamble, Patrick Martin, Joseph Johnson, Joseph Harwood, Joshua Atckly, Seymour Catchings, Robert Moore.
Constable John Hannah sworn to attend the Grand Jury.
Remit fine entered against Frederick Fulkerson for nonattendance as a juror at the last term of this court.
Jos Hopkins lessee v Carlisle Humphreys. Two suits. Continued to next term.

p.50 Hugh Malony v George White and George Walker & John D Jones his security. Appeal. Plf recovered judgment in July County Court for $45 damage for nonperformance of an assumption besides costs. Defendant obtained appeal to this Court and entered into bond with George Walker and John D Jones his security to prosecute appeal. Failing to bring record of proceedings in Court below and file same with Clerk of this Court 15 days before commencement of term. Therefore judgment of Court below is in all things affirmed and plf recovers agt dft and his security sd sum with 12½% interest thereon from 23 July 1816 until present term and 6% thereafter until paid, and also his costs in this behalf expended.

p.51 Heirs of Landon Carter decd v Willis Breazeale. Sci fa. Forfeiture agt Willis Breazeale for failing to attend as witness in suit Carter Heirs lessee v Clerk & Rawlings Sept 1815 is set aside upon defendant paying costs of forfeiture.
Court adjourned until tomorrow morning 9 oclock.   Thos Emmerson

Tuesday September 17th Present the Honorable Thomas Emmerson Judge &c.
Thomas Brown collector v Mary Morgan. Parties in proper person dismissed suit; defendant pays costs.

p.52 Andrew Campbells lessee v William York and Hugh Dunlap. It appearing a fair trial cannot be had in this County, and it being agreed that Knox County is the nearest County free from the like exception, order this cause to Circuit Court to be holden for Knox County second Monday of February next.
Fine Frederick Fulkerson and Henry Taylor and John Caywood fined $2.50 each for failing to attend as jurors this day.
Byrum Breeden v George White. Cause is continued until next term.

p.53 Carters Heirs lessee v Clark & Rawlings. Cause continued until next term. Also on affidavits of Thomas L Williams and John Williams. deposition of James Glasgow, Davidson County, and John Howard of Rhea County to be taken in behalf the plaintiff, giving dft's atty John McCampbell twenty days previous notice. Depositions of Hon Edward Scott of Knox County and of General Andrew Jackson of Davidson

p.54 County to be taken in behalf defendants to be read in evidence in cause Thos N Clarks lessee against Azariah David and John Williams lessee against Wm Lyon & Wm Frank which two causes are continued until next term.
Richd G Waterhouses lessee v William Murphree and William Murphrees lessee v John Hill. On affidavits of Richard G Waterhouse and John Hill, deposition of James Cunningham to be taken at house of Mistress Campbell in this town before Daniel Rawlings esq.
Michael Stoner v Robert Hopkins. Hugh Berry bail for dft surrenders him. Henry Tuttle and Joseph Thompson undertake he shall satisfy condemnation or be delivered to prison or sd Tuttle & Thompson will do it for him.

p.55 Thomas Hudson v Alexander Outlaw. Plurius issued returnable at next Term.
Joseph C Strong v James Mitchell. Als. Caps. ad Rasp. issued.
Jacob Bryson v Cain Abel. Jury John Murphy, Jacob Brown, Richard Philpot,

8

SEPTEMBER 1816

William Long, Philip Paine, Thomas Bolton, William McAlister, Isaac Love, Reuben Truman, Moses Roddy, Henry Owings, Hugh Murphy assess plfs damages to $150 besides costs together with his costs. William Hyde and Jesse Sherill summoned as witnesses failed to appear; they forfeit according to act of Assembly.

p.56   James Rodgers v William S Luty. Als issued returnable here at next Term.

It appearing from Sheriffs return on Venire facias that William S Leuty, Rezin Rawlings and Thomas Anderson were summoned as Jurors this term and they not appearing, they forfeit $5 each unless cause shewn to contrary at next Term.

Court adjourned until tomorrow morning 9 oclock.   Thos Emmerson

p.57   Wednesday September 18th. Present the Honorable Thomas Emmerson, Judge &c.

Thomas N Clark v Robert Bell. Deed 16 Sept 190 acres in three tracts on Richland creek ackd by Thomas N Clark the grantor.

Aquilla Johnson v Isaac S McMeans & Abner Underwood. Jury Robert Bell, Nichodemus Hackworth, Abraham Bryson, Jacob Bryson, Abijah Harris, Moses Roddy, David Ragsdale, William Luis, William Baldwin, William McAllister, James McCarty, Thomas Drinon say dfts have not performed their covenant; assess plfs damage to $10.78¼ besides costs.

p.58   State v John Runnion. Samuel Murphy, Major Gillihan and Nimrod Pendergrass surrender dft whereupon William Lewis special bail.

Jacob Bryson v Cain Abel. Rule granted dft's atty to shew cause why a new trial should be had; discharged by order of dft's attorney.

Robert Bell & wife v Azariah David. Cause continued until next term.

p.59   State v John Runnion. Dft in person; solicitor no further prosecutes and prosecution is dismissed.

Mary Gravelly v Peter Bennett. Parties in person agree suit be dismissed and plaintiff pays all costs except attorney's tax fee.

State v Major Gillihan. Major Gillihan, Hugh Berry and James Kelly recognizance, condition Major Gillihan attend day to day during present term.

p.60   State v Jacob Wassum. Jacob Wassum, William Murphree and John Thompson recognizance, condition Jacob Wassum attend day to day during present term.

Waterhouses lessee v William Murphree and Wm Murphrees lessee va John Hill. Deposition of Elisha Jones of Lincoln County, North Carolina, to be taken in benefit of sd William Murphree.

p.61   Remit fine of John Cawood entered against him for failing to attend as a juror yesterday.

Joseph Frost for the use of Rowland Childs v John Thompson. Grant dft leave to amend his second plea by adding "nor did the sd Joseph Frost, nor the said Rowland Childs demand the property in the said Plaintiffs Declaration mentioned at the place of residence of the said Defendant."

Isaac S McMeans to David Parkhill. Deed 14 June 1816 for Lot 36 in Kingston proven by Robert Bell and Elisha Parker subscribing witnesses thereto.

Alexander McCall & wifes lessee v Archibald Roane. Jury: John Murphy, Abijah Harris, Moses Roddy, David Ragsdale, William Lewis, William Baldwin, James McCarty, Thomas Drinon, Hugh Berry, Adam Caldwell, Samuel Murphy, Hugh Murphy; from rendering their verdict are respited until tomorrow.

Court adjourned until tomorrow morning 9 oclock.   Thos Emmerson

SEPTEMBER 1816

p.62 Thursday September 19th. Present the Honorable Thomas Emmerson, Judge &c.
Joseph C Strong v James Mitchell. Plfs atty & dft in person agree that suit be dismissed; defendant pays costs.
Charles McClung to Richd G Waterhouse. Two deeds, 9th July for 3000 acres, 25 March for 400 acres each proved by Thomas L Williams and William P Hackett.
Alexander McCall & wifes lessee v Archibald Roane. Jury say defendant is guilty of trespass and ejectment. Plf recovers his term in the premesis and his damages assessed together with his costs about his suit expended.
p.63 Alexander McCall & wifes lessee v Archibald Roane. Abraham Smith who was summoned as a witness for defendant failed to appear; forfeits according to law.
Remit fine of Henry Taylor who was fined for failing to attend as juror.
State v Major Gillihan. Solicitor for State & dft in proper person who says he is guilty; fined $5 and costs. Dft with Robert Looke confess judgment.
Court adjourns until tomorrow morning 9 Oclock.   Tho Emmerson

p.64 Friday 20th September. Present the Honorable Thomas Emmerson, Judge &c.
State v Jacob Wassum. Solicitor being unwilling further to prosecute.
Following item X'd out: Hugh Saint for use of Kings Extrs v John B Haynes. Constable John Lewis attended five days, receives certificate accordingly.
p.65 Charles McClung v Return J Meigs & Timothy Meigs. Plaintiff's demurers heard. Trial at next Term.
Francis Smith v Willis Morgan & al. Dfts by Robert A Adams their attorney; plaintiff came not. Dfts recover agt plf their cost about their defence expended.
p.66 Ramsas[Racusus?] Heirs lessee v Thomas Kelly. Deposition of David Murphree Esq of Rhea County to be taken in behalf Thomas Kelly.
Hugh Stewart for use Knoxs Executors v John B Haynes. Debt. Agreed by parties that original writ was executed by Sheriff within limits of Rhea and within
p.67 Cherokee Country to which the Indian title has never been extinguished. Dft can plead in abatement, otherwise judgmt in favour of plf for $120 with interest at 6% from 6 August 1811. Case is adjourned to Supreme Court of Errors and Appeals.
Court adjourned Until Court in Course.   Tho Emmerson

p.68 Monday 17th March. Present the Honorable Edward Scott, Judge &c.
Sheriff Woodson Francis returned venire facias: William Smith, Robert Patterson, Richard G Waterhouse, James Cannon, George Gillespie, Jacob Riggel, James Wilson, Henry Riggel, Charles Brady, Col William Johnson, Azariah David, Martin Wyrick, James Snelson, George W Riggel, Daniel Walker, George W Lewis, Jesse Roddy, James Preston, Roswell Hall, Frederick Fulkerson, William Barclay, Abraham Howard, Barton McPherson.
Grand Jury: Richd G Waterhouse foreman, William Smith, Robert Patterson, James Cannon, George Gillespie, Jacob Riggel, James Wilson, Henry Riggel, Charles Brady, Col William Johnson, Azariah David, Martin Wyrick, James Snelson.
Constable William Lewis sworn to attend the Grand Jury.
p.69 Richd G Waterhouse v John Moore. Deed 3 Oct 1815 ackd by grantor.
Set aside forfeiture agt Fredk Fulkerson for not attending as juror Sept.

MARCH 1817

    Daniel McPherson v Mary Brooks. Jury George W Riggel, Daniel Walker, George W Lewis, Jesse Roddey, Roswell Hall, Frederick Fulkerson, William Brady, Thomas Jack, John Macoy, Jacob Wassum, Martin Shoolls, Major Gillihan find dft is guilty of the trover & conversion; assess plfs damage to $424 and his costs.
p.70   Richd G Waterhouse to Major Gillihan. Deed 23 Feb 1816 70 acres ackd.
    Following causes continued until next Term, the Court having heretofore concerned therein as counsel: Carters lessee v Clark & Rawlings. White v Robison. Clerks lessee v David. Williams Lessee v Lyon & French. McClung v Meigs.
    George Walker v Vincent Bennett. In Equity. Complainant made no replied to dfts answer; on motion of dfts attorney, cause is dismissed at complainants cost.
    Court adjourned until tomorrow morning 9 Oclock.   Edw Scott

p.71   Tuesday March 18th. Present the Honorable Edward Scott, Judge &c.
    James Rodgers assignee of Alexander Outlaw v William York. Cause continued.
    Richd G Waterhouse v Jacob Wassum. Trespass. Jury George W Riggel, Daniel Walker, Geo W Lewis, Jessy Roddey, Roswell Hall, Frederick Fulkerson, William Barclay, Barton McPherson, John D Jones, Thomas Jack, Thomas Johnson, Michael Stoner. Plf recovers against defendant damages $60 together with his costs of suit.
p.72   Thomas Hopkins lessee v David Stuart. Cause continued until next Term.
    Richd G Waterhouses lessee v William Murphree. An impartial trial of this cause cannot be had in this County; trial to be in Roane County on first Sept next.
    William Murphrees lessee v John Hill. [worded as above]
p.73   Robert Bell & wife v Azariah David. [worded as above]
p.74   Byrum Breeden v George White. Dft's death being suggested, parties agree that suit be revived agt Daniel McPherson admr of estate of George White decd.
    Joseph Frost for the use of Rowland Childs v John Thompson. Continued.
    John Skidmore v Jacob Wassum. Deposition of Peter White to be taken at house of Warham Easley in this Town. And it appearing on affidavit of dft that an impartial trial of this cause cannot be had in this County, and it being agreed by the parties that Roane is nearest adjoining County free from the like exception,
p.75   order trial at Circuit Court for Roane County first Monday Sept next.
    Lilburn L Henderson executor &c of William Trigg deceased v Isaac S McMeans. Debt. Jury George W Riggel, Daniel Walker, George W Lewis, Jesse Roddey, Roswell Hall, Frederick Fulkerson, William Barclay, Barton McPherson, Abraham Howard, John D Jones, Thomas Jack, Thomas Johnson. Plf recovers agt dft $570.14¾ the ballance of debt unpaid, also damages $92.82 together with his costs of suit.
p.76   Charles McClung v Roswell Hall. Jury Geo W Riggel, Danl Walker, George W Lewis, Jesse Roddy, Fredk Fulkerson, Wm Barclay, Abraham Howard, Barton McPherson, Wm Smith, Robt Patterson, Jas Cannon, Geo Gillespie. Plf recovers agt dft damages by reason on nonperformance of assumption $100 together with his costs of suit.
    State v John Freels. Murder. Cause is a change of venue from Roane County.
    Court adjourned until tomorrow morning 9 Oclock.   Edw Scott

p.77   Wednesday March 19th. Present the Honorable Edward Scott, Judge &c.
    John A Smith to Richd G Waterhouse. Deed 15th Dec 1815 188 acres ackd.
    State v John Freels. Murder. Prisoner remanded to prison.
    Charles McClung to Evan Evans. Deed 17th March 1817 220 acres ackd.
    Shff Miller Francis to Robt Bell. Bill/sale 23 Jan 1817 negro boy Jack ack.

MARCH 1817

        Henry Owens v David Drum. Cause continued until next term.
p.78   Carters lessee v Clark & Rawlings. Deposition of Major General Andrew Jackson to be taken in behalf defendants.
        Thos N Clarks lessee v Azariah David. Deposition of Major General Andrew Jackson to be taken in behalf the plaintiff.
        John Williams lessee v Lyon & French. Deposition of Major General Andrew Jackson to be taken in behalf the defendants.
p.79   Charles McClung v Warham Easley. Parties in person agree that this suit be dismissed, defendant paying the costs.
        Charles McClung v Adam Caldwell. [worded as above]
        Heirs of John Ramseys lessee v Thomas Kelley. Jury William Smith, Robert Patterson, Geo Gillespie, Jacob Riggel, Henry Riggel, Chas Brady, Martin Wyrick, Jas Snelson, Geo W Riggel, Geo W Lewis, Jesse Roddey, Abraham Howard; jury from rendering their verdict are respited until tomorrow.
        Court adjourned until tomorrow morning 9 Oclock.   Edw Scott

p.80   Thursday March 20th. Present the Honorable Edward Scott, Judge &c.
        Charles McClung to James Snelson. Deed 22 Apr 1816 300 acres ackd.
        State v John Freels. Murder. Prisoner again remanded to prison. John Leftwich, William Wall, Samuel Hall, Wm T L Davidson recognizance, condition they appear third day next term to give evidence behalf State against John Freels.
        State v William L Hornbuckle. Writs of certiorari & supercedas dismissed, Wm L Hornbuckle paying costs in this behalf expended. Whereupon Thomas L Williams
p.81   attorney for sd Hornbuckle that error committed in judgmt agt sd Hornbuckle as prosecutor of Samuel Williams on indictment in County Court for $31.84. Order record of sd cause transmitted to this Court.
        Thomas Hudson v Alexander Outlaw. Plf by atty directed suit be dismissed, plaintiff paying costs.
        Cain Abel v William Hyde. Sci fa. Alias issued returnable here next Term.
        Ramsey Lee v Thomas Kelly. Jury sworn yesterday were again respited from rendering their verdict until tomorrow.
        Court adjourned until tomorrow morning 9 oclock.   Edw Scott

p.82   Friday March 27. Present the Honorable Edward Scott, Judge.
        John Love to William Love. Bill/sale 20th March 1817 ackd.
        Joseph Frost for the use of Rowland Childs v John Thompson. Grant plf leave to amend his Replication so as not to delay the trial of this cause.
        Thomas Hopkins Lessee v Carlisle Humphreys. Jury Roswell Hall, Frederick Fulkerson, Wm Barclay, Barton McPherson, John Condly, James Kelly, Wm McCormick, Joseph Johnson, Wm Long, John Robinson, Andw Wilhelms, John McAndlass find dft guilty of trespass and ejectment; assess plfs damage to 6¢ besides costs.
p.83   Thomas Hopkins lessee v John Moore & Samuel Murphy. Plf by attorney directed his suit be dismissed, dft recovers agt plf his costs.
        Thomas Hopkins lessee v Major Gillihan. Plf by atty dismissed suit; dft recovers agt plf his costs about his defence expended.
        Warham Easley v James Stuart. Parties in person agree suit be dismissed; dft pays clerks fees and half the State tax.
p.84   Ramseys lessee v David Caldwell. from affidavit of William Ramsey, an

MARCH 1817

impartial trial of this cause cannot be had in this County, cause adjourned to Knox County, second Monday of August next.

Michael Stoner v Robert Hopkins. Jury Roswell Hall, Wm Barclay, Barton McPherson, John Conolly, James Kelly, Wm McCormick, Joseph Johnson, John Robinson, Andw Wilhelms, John McAndlass, John Moore, Valentine Shoolls find dft not guilty. Defendant recovers against the plaintiff his costs about his defence expended.

p.85   Heirs of John Ramseys lessee v Thomas Kelly. Jury sworn on Wednesday find dft guilty of trespass and ejectment, assess plfs damages to 6¢ and costs. Motion of dfts atty rule granted to show cause why a new trial should be had.

William L Hornbuckle v State. Writ of Error. Record of Court below having been read and argument heard thereon, and Court being sastisfied that error was committed by Court below, judgment of County Court is reversed. County pays costs.

Court adjourned until tomorrow morning 9 oclock.   Edw Scott

p.86   Saturday March 22d. Present the Honorable Edward Scott, Judge &c.

State v John Freels. Murder. Prosecution continued until next term; prisoner remanded to prison.

Martin Shootts v The State. Appeal in nature of writ of error. Record of Court below having been read and argument held thereon, Court is satisfied error hath been committed, judgment of County Court reversed.

Michael Stoner v Robert Hopkins. Affidavit of plf, trial granted him at next Term of this Court.

p.87   Ramseys lessee v David Caldwell. Deposition of Andrew Wilhelms of Rhea County and Jacob Gibson of Bledsoe County to be taken in behalf plaintiff.

Ramseys lessee v Thomas Kelly. Continued.

George Christian v Richard T Gains. Motion of George Christian by J C Mitchell his attorney who produced record from Superior Court of Hamilton District by which David Ross recovered a judgment by scire facias against said George Christian special bail for sd Richard T Gains for $420 damages with interest from 15 March 1815 till paid, together with $32.90 costs. Also from receipt of Thomas

p.88   Hopkins here shown, sd judgment with interest & costs was paid by George Christian 22 January 1810 which amounted to $576.80. Therefore, sd George Christian recovers agt sd Richard T Gains sd sum with interest thereon from 22 Jany 1810 untill paid together with costs of this motion and judgment.

State v John Freels. Murder. Jail of this County is not sufficient for safe keeping of the prisoner, order Sheriff convey John Freels to jail of Roane County there to remain untill demanded by order of Court for Trial or untill he is otherwise discharged by due course of Law.

Court adjourns till Court in Course.   Edw Scott

p.90   Monday 15th September 1817. Present the Honorable Thomas Emmerson, Judge.

Sheriff Woodson Francis returned Venire facias: Alexander Russell, Nicholas Starnes, Jessee White, Nicholas Nail, Jessee Thompson, John Sapp, Abraham Smith, James Rodgers, Matthew McClellan, James W Cozby, John Robinson, Jeremiah Johnes, John Rice, John Cozby, James Riddle, Alexander Ferguson, Robert Gamble, Joseph

SEPTEMBER 1817

Johnson, Robert Parks, William Henderson, James Coulter, Miller Francis, Robert Means, John S Parker.

    Grand Jury: Alexr Ferguson foreman, Nicholas Starns, Nicholas Nail, Jessee Thompson, John Sapp, Matthew McClellan, James W Cozby, John Robinson, John Corly, James Riddle, Robert Parks, Robert Means, John S Parker.

p.91   Constable Spillsby Dyre sworn to attend the Grand Jury.

    Following causes continued until next Term, the Court having been previously concerned therein as counsel: White v Robinson, Ramseys lessee v Kelly, Hopkins lessee v Stuart, Owens v Crum.

    Court adjourned until tomorrow morning 9 Oclock.   Tho Emmerson

Tuesday Sept 16th. Present the Honorable Thomas Emmerson, Judge &c.
    John Rhea esq took oath prescribed for attornies and is admitted.
    From Sheriffs return on Venire facias, Alexander Russell, Jesse White, Abraham Smith, James Rodgers, Jeremiah Jones, John Rice, and William Francis had been summoned; they not appearing, forfeit $5 each to State unless they can show sufficient cause to the contrary at next term of this Court.

p.92   Carters lessee v Clark & Rawlings. On affidavit of Thomas N Clark one of the defendants, this cause is continued until next term.

    James Rodgers v William York. Certiorari. Deposition of Alexander Outlaw to be taken in behalf plaintiff.

    Following causes were continued by consent: Thomas N Clarks lessee v Azariah David, John Williams lessee v Lyon & French, Frost for the use of Childs v Thompson, Cain Abel v Jessee Sherill, George Walker v James Collins, James Rodgers v Wm S Leuty.

    Josiah Danforth to Hezekiah Lord. Deed 16 Sept 1809 for 8500 acres proven by John Wilkinson & John Wallace two of the subscribing witnesses thereto.

p.93   Michael Stoner v Robert Hopkins. AB. Jury Joseph Johnson, Hugh McClung, James C Reed, Carson Caldwell, James Lewis, Robert Taylor, Robert Locke, Jacob Brown, Hiram A Defreese[Depreese?], Charles Woodward, Edmund Dyre, William Ramsey. Plf recovers against deft damages $35 and his costs. Henry Tuttle bail for dft surrendered defendant who was ordered into custody of the sheriff.

    Henry Owens v David Crum. Deposition of William Millican to be taken tomorrow evening before Daniel Rawlings at house of sd Rawlings in behalf plaintiff.

p.94   Byrum Breeden v Daniel McPherson. Depositions of Miner Porter and John Collins of Madison County, Alabama, to be taken in behalf defendant.

    William Murphrees lessee v Whitfields heirs & Richd G Waterhouse. Cause continued until next term. Deposition of Abraham Swaggerty of Roane County and of Littlepage Sims of Alabama Territory to be taken in behalf of plaintiff.

p.95   Charles McClung v Return Meigs. Cause continued to next Term.

    Court adjourned until tomorrow morning 9 Oclock.   Tho Emmerson

Wednesday Sept 17th. Present the Honorable Thomas Emmerson, Judge &c.
    Michael Stoner v Robert Hopkins. Henry Tuttle, Providence L W Brooks and William Beerman confess judgment in conjunction with defendant for costs. Plaintiff recovers costs confessed as afsd.

    State v Jasen Jacks. Solicitor general no further prosecutes.

p.96   State v James Cresup, John Cresup & Fletcher Cresup. Horse stealing.

MARCH 1818

Solicitor general no further prosecutes.
State v John Freels. Murder. John Freels had broke custody and made his escape; capias on indictment is awarded agt him returnable here next term.
Owen David v Benjamin Allison. Cause transmitted from Circuit Court of Bledsoe County; respited until next term.
p.97   James F Foster v Samuel Riley. Trial at next term of this Court.
James F Foster v Willie Tuten. Alias awarded sheriff returnable next Term.
State v Moses Lewis. Passing counterfeit bank note. Jury John Taylor, Moses Roddy, Joseph Keeler, Thomas James, Ludwin Brooks, William Ingle, Henry Taylor, George Gillespie, John A Smith, Ezekiel Henry, Mark Robinson, Jeremiah Howerton find dft not guilty.
p.98   Cain Abel v William Hyde. Sci fa. Parties in proper persons agree that cause be dismissed; plaintiff recovers against defendant his costs.
Court adjourned until tomorrow morning 9 oclock   Tho Emmerson

Thursday Sept 18th. Present the Honorable Thomas Emmerson, Judge, &c.
John Gardiner v Mumford Smith. Plaintiff came not. Dft recovers agt plf his costs in this behalf expended.
p.99   Court adjourned untill Court in Course.   Tho Emmerson

p.100   Monday 16th March. Present the Honorable Edward Scott, Esq, Judge, &c.
Woodson Francis Sheriff returned Venire facias: John Birdsong, John Day, Edmund Bean, Carlisle Humphreys, James C Reed, Adam W Caldwell, William Gamble, Robert Bell, William French, Matthias Benson, Charles Gamble, William McGill, Patrick Martin, Robert McMillen, Robert Parks, James Varner, Hugh McClung, Jacob Bryson, James Coulter, John Henry Jr, John Woodward, Thomas Woodward, Grief Howarton, Robert Love.
Grand Jury: Robert Bell foreman, Thomas Woodward, William French, Grief Howarton, John Birdsong, John Woodward, James Varner, Robert McMillen, Adam W Caldwell, James Coulter, Mathias Benson, Robert Love, James C Reed.
Constable Philip Abel sworn to attend the Grand Jury.
Excuse Patrick Martin, unable to attend as a juror this term
p.101   Excuse Hugh McClung, Wm Gamble, John Day, extremely inconvenient to attend as jurors this term.
William Smith clerk of this court produced treasurers receipt for tax by him collected in virtue of his office for year 1817.
Richard G Waterhouse to Moses Paul. Deed 23 Nov 1815 230 acres on east side Piney River acknowledged by conveyor.
James Rodgers assignee of Alexander Outlaw v William York. Certiorari. Deposition of Alexr Outlaw of Alabama Territory to be taken in behalf plaintiff.
James Rodgers v William S Leuty. Trespass on case. Deposition of Elizabeth Campbell of Alabama Territory to be taken in behalf plaintiff.
p.102   Polly Morrison by next friend Absalom Majors v Edward C Morrison. Petition for divorce. Next friend of plf with Woodson Thomas entered bond. Subpoena defendant to next court.

MARCH 1818

William Smith Clark of this Court resigned sd office.
Court adjourned until tomorrow morning nine oclock.   Edw Scott

p.103   Tuesday 17th March. Present the Honorable Edw Scott, Judge, &c.
To fill the vacancy occasioned by resignation of William Smith former clerk of this Court; appoint to that office Asahel Rawlings. Asahel Rawlings, Daniel Rawlings, William Smith and Richard G Waterhouse bound unto Joseph McMinn governor in sum $10,000. Condition Asahel Rawlings shall keep safe the records and faithfully discharge duties of his office.

p.104   Bond of Asahel Rawlings, Richd G Waterhouse, Wm Smith, D Rawlings.
p.105   Bond of Asahel Rawlings and his securities.
p.106   Order following causes continued until next term of this court, Court having been concerned therein as counsel: Carters lessee v Clark & Rawlings; White v Robinson; Clarks lessee v David; Williams lessee v Lyon & French; McClung v Meigs.

James F Foster v Samuel Riley. Appoint John McCampbell to take depositions of Thomas N Clark & Susan Clark his wife. Dft to take depositions of John Gilchrist, Marcum McGhee & Benjamin Allen before agent of Chickasaw Nation. Plf to have deposition taken of Robert Marlin & George W Foster of Green County, Georgia.

p.107   Sheriff summoned Robert Parks and John Henry Jr to attend as jurors this term but they came not; they forfeit $25 each unless cause be shewn to contrary.

Cain Abel v Jesse Sherrell. Scire facias. Dft confessed judgment for costs.

Order Edmund Bean, Wm McGill, Robt Parks, John Henry Jr, John Condley, Robt Ferguson and John Locke pay State $2.50 each for failure to attend as jurors.

Thomas Hopkins lessee v David Stuart. Ejectment. Plf by his attorney James C Mitchell. Sheriff returns that James King was summoned to attend this Court as
p.108   witness for plf but came not; fined $125 unless he shew satisfactory reasons to the contrary at next term of this court.

Owen David v Benjamin Allison. On motion of James C Mitchell and Azariah David heretofore bound as prosecution bail they are released; Thomas Kelly and Woodson Francis undertook for plf that they would pay for him should he fail.

Frederick Washington to Richard G Waterhouse. Letter/attorney relative to a landed interest duly proven by John Thompson a subscribing witness thereto.

Richard G Waterhouse to Asahel Rawlings. Deed 137½ acres dated 17 March 1818 acknowledged.

p.109   Asahel Rawlings to Robert Locke. Deed 7 acres dated this day acknowledged.

Byram Breeden v Daniel McPherson admr of George White decd. Debt. Jury: Edmund Bean, Charles Gamble, Jacob Bryson, Absalom Majors, William Woodward, Elias Ferguson, Isaac Love, John Condley, Thomas Kelly, John Knox, Robert Ferguson, John Locke. Plf recovers of dft his debt $69, damages $21.39 to be levied on estate of sd deceased in the hands of the administrator.

Remit fines of $2.50 each assessed this day against Edmond Bean, Wm McGill, Jno Condley, Robert Parks, John Henry Jr, Robert Ferguson, John Locke; forfeiture against Robert Parks and John Henry Jr not remitted.

p.110   James Rogers assignee of Alexander Outlaw v William York. Continued.
James Rogers v William S Leuty. Continued on affidavit of plaintiff.
Henry Owens v David Crum. Continued until next Term.
Court adjourned till tomorrow morning 9 Oclock.   Edw Scott

SEPTEMBER 1818

p.111   Wednesday 18th. Present the Honorable Edward Scott, Esq, Judge, &c.
        John Ramsey's heirs lessee v Thomas Kelly. Ejectment. Order new trial.
        Permit William E Anderson and Alexander Rembert Esqrs to practice as attornies in this Court on taking oath of admission.
        Joseph Frost for the use of Rowland Childs v John Thompson. Continued.
        George Walker v James Collins. Cause is continued until next Term.
        William Murphree's lessee v Whitfields heirs & Richard G Waterhouse. Ejectment. Order to take Deposition of Abraham Swaggerty of Roane County and of Little Page Sims of Madison County, Alabama Territory, in behalf plaintiff is revived with the alteration that notice be served on Thomas J Campbell Esq agent of Whitfields heirs. Cause continued until next Term.
p.112   Owen David v Benjamin Allison. Cause is continued until next Term.
        Order that all forfeitures entered this Term against jurymen be set aside generally without costs.
        State v John Frields. Murder. Plurias capias awarded returnable next Term.
        Thomas Hopkins lessee v David Stuart. Ejectment. Plf no further prosecutes. Dft recovers against plaintiff his costs about his defence expended.
        Thomas Hopkins v James King. Forfeiture. Plf by his attorney James C Mitchell set aside forfeiture taken against defendant yesterday on payment of clerk.
        Court adjourned until Court in Course.   Edw Scott

p.113   Monday Sept 21st. Present the Honorable Thomas Emmerson, Esq, Judge, &c.
        Sheriff Woodson Francis returned Venire facias: William Smith, Robert Gamble not found, Charles Ryon not found, John Cozby, George Winton, Robert Locke, John Moore Senr, Roswell Hall, John Jack, John Martin, Isaac Love, Thomas Huddleston, William Henderson, Jesse Day not found, William Alexander not found, John Russell, Robert Parks, William Woodward, Henry Collins, James Neal not found, Geo W Riggle, Jonathan Fine, Thomas Blakeley, Daniel Walker, John Wasson not found.
        Grand Jury: Jonathan Fine foreman, Daniel Walker, John Moore, William Woodward, George W Riggle, George Winton, Thomas Huddleston, John Martin, Robert Locke, John Jack, John Russell, Isaac Love, Robert Parks.
        Constable William Lewis sworn to attend the Grand Jury. Certificate issued to Lewis for 4 days.
p.114   Following persons were summoned but came not: Russell Hall, William Henderson, William Smith. Forfeit $25 each unless at next Term of this Court they shew sastisfactory reasons for such failure.
        Thomas J Campbell to Edmund Been. Deed Lots 5 & 6 in Washington dated 14 December 1817 ackd.
        John Martin to David Parkhill. Deed 200 acres Sale Creek 2d Apr 1818 ackd.
        John Ramsey's heirs lessee v Thomas Kelly. Court being incompetent to try this cause, continued until the next Term of this Court.
p.115   On application of Spencer Jarnigen and John Fulton Esqrs they were admitted to practice as attorneys on taking required oath.
        Polly Morrison by her next friend Absalom Majors v Edward Morrison. Divorce. Plf by attorney John M Campbell Esq; Sheriff returned that Edward Morrison was not to be found. Order publication be forthwith made for four weeks in

SEPTEMBER 1818

Knoxville Gazette notifying Edward Morrison to appear at next Term to answer petition of plaintiff.

Polly Morrison by her next friend Absalom Majors v Edward Morrison. Divorce. Alias subpoena issued against defendant returnable next term of this Court.

Court adjourned until tomorrow morning nine Oclock.   Thos Emmerson

p.116   Tuesday Sept 22d. Present the Honorable Thomas Emmerson, Esq, Judge, &c.

Thomas N Clark v William Lyon. Deed 386½ acres Richland creek date [blank] 1816 was proven by John McCampbell and John J Fulton.

Excuse Edmund Bean from fine & further attendance as a juror this Term.

James Rogers assignee of Alexander Outlaw v William York. Deposition of Hamilton Bradford of Bedford County to be taken in behalf plf, also of Alexander Outlaw of Alabama Territory.

James F Foster v Samuel Riley. Order of last Term for taking deposition of plf's witness in Georgia is revived.

p.117   Representatives of Landon Carter & lessee v Thomas N Clark & Daniel Rawlings. Depositions of George Gordon, Cornelius Newman, Leonard Starnes, Valentine Sevier, Douglass Hale and others of Greene County, Peter Kenner and Alexander McMillon of Knox County, George Baker of Campbell County and Little Page Sims of Alabama Territory to be taken in behalf plf, on his serving John McCampbell or William Lyon with notice of time and place of taking depositions. Depositions of Andrew Jackson of Davidson County, George W Sevier of Overton County, John Anthony of Knox County, John Gray and Cornelius Newman of Greene County to be taken in behalf of the dft on his giving notice to John Williams or Thomas L Williams.

Remit fine of William Smith for his failure to attend as a juror.

p.118   Thomas N Clarks lessee v Azariah David. Continued until next Term.

John Williams's lessee v William Lyon and William French. Continued.

Henry Owens v David Crum. Appeal. Jury Absalom Majors, James C Reed, Richard Philpot, John Thompson, Samuel Murphey, Willis McClendon, Jacob Hunter, John Myers, John Cozby, Henry Collins, Thomas Blakeley, Hugh Murphy. A Majors withdrawn & jury discharged. Grant plf's attorney leave to amend his declaration; cause is continued until next Court.

Landon Carter's lessee v Thomas N Clark and Daniel Rawlings. Depositions of William Dixson, James Galbreath, Joseph Holt, Jesse Lincoln, Robert McClure, James Gutherie and John Gass of Greene County to be taken in behalf plaintiff.

p.119   Charles McClung v Return J Meigs. Trespass. Jury[above except Jonathan Fine, Daniel Walker, William Woodward for John Myers, Saml Murphey, John Thompson] From rendering verdict are respited until tomorrow.

William H Standefer v Rice Humphreys & Co. Trespass. Deposition of Hugh L White of Knox County and of John McKenney, David Duncan, Robert Hoge, Samuel Terry & Samuel McReynolds Jr of Bledsoe County to be taken in behalf plaintiff.

James F Foster v Willis Tulen. Plf no further prosecutes. Dft recovers agt plf his cost of defence.

Court adjourned until tomorrow morning nine Oclock.   Tho Emmerson

p.120   Wednesday 23d Sept. Present the Honorable Thomas Emmerson, Esq, Judge.

Thomas N Clark's lessee v Azariah David, and John Williams's lessee v William Lyon and William French. Depositions to be taken in the case of Landon

SEPTEMBER 1818

Carters heirs lesse against Thomas N Clark and Daniel Rawlings are to be read in evidence on the trial of these causes so far as they may be applicable.

Deed Charles McClung to Thomas Thompson, 100 acres Muddy Creek date 7 March 1817 ackd by said Charles McClung.

Charles McClung v Return J Meigs. Jury elected yesterday find dft guilty; assess plaintiffs damages to $37.50 besides costs.

p.121 Jesse Garland v Ruthey Garland. Petition for divorce. William Ramsey his security; subpoena awarded against defendant returnable at next Term of this court.

Appoint John S Fulton Esq to officiate in stead of Attorney General.

Henry Owens v David Crum. Deposition of Daniel Clayton of this county to be taken in behalf plaintiff.

George Walker v James Collins. Continued until next Term of this Court.

p.122 John Ramseys heirs' lessee v Thomas Kelly. Deposition of John Black of Alabama Territory to be taken in behalf plaintiff.

State v John Freelds. Murder. [X's out]

Joseph Frost for use of Roland Childs v John Thompson. Covenant. Jury John Moore, George W Riggle, George Winton, Thomas Huddleston, Jno Martin, Robert Locke, John Jack, John Russell, Isaac Love, Robert Parks, Wm Smith, John Locke. Plf recov-
p.123 ers agt dft $242 damages and his costs in this behalf expended.

John Williams's lessee v William Lyon & William French. James S Gains to take deposition of Berry Green of Cherokee Nation near Fort Deponte in behalf dft William Lyon.

William Murphree's lessee v Whitfields heirs & Richard G Waterhouse. Deposition of Alexander Outlaw of Alabama Territory to be taken in behalf plf.

p.124 James Rogers v William S Leuty. Jury Jas C Reed, Richd Philpot, Robt Ferguson, Hugh Murphey, Thomas Blakeley, Henry Collins, Jonathan Fine, Daniel Walker, Wm Woodward, Thomas Coulter, Henry Walton, Absalom Majors respited until tomorrow.

Thomas Blakeley and William Woodward Junr failed to attend as jurors; fined $5 each and costs.

Joseph Martin & the State v Cain Abel. Plf no further prosecutes. Dft recovers agt plf his costs of defence.

William H Standefer v Rice Humphreys & Co. Depositions to be taken; notice
p.125 to be given by plf is to be served on John Rice one of the defendants.

Court adjourned until tomorrow nine Oclock.   Tho Emmerson

Thursday 24 September. Present the Honorable Thomas Emmerson Esq, Judge, &c.

Jesse White v William Robinson, & Owen David v Benjamin Allison. Continued.

James Rogers v William S Leuty. Jury sworn yesterday say dft assumed as plf
p.126 hath complained. Plf recovers agt dft $12 besides costs.

Remit fines agt Thos Blakeley & Wm Woodward for nonattendance as jurors.

State v Hannah Stoner. Appeal. Dismissed; remanded to court below.

Jurors are discharged.

p.127 John Ramseys heirs lessee v Thomas Kelly. On affidavit of William Ramsey subpoena Richard G Waterhouse to next Term of this Court to produce field notes of John Hacket decd, particularly field notes of a survey of 1000 to Stockley Donelson in fourth bend of Tennessee River below mouth of Piney River.

Joseph Frost for use of Roland Childs v John Thompson. Covenant. New trial to be had at next Term, defendant pays costs that have accrued in this cause since the term at which it was put to issue.

MARCH 1819

p.128 James F Foster v Samuel Riley. Depositions of George Griffith, Malcum McGhee, James Allen, John Kilcrease, and James Gunn of Chickasaw Nation to be taken in behalf Defendant.

Joseph Frost for the use of Roland Childs v JOhn Thompson. Covenant. Plf no further prosecutes. Dft recovers agt plf his costs of defence.

Court adjourned until Court in Course.   Tho Emmerson

p.129 Monday 15th March. Present the Honorable Edward Scott, Esq, Judge.

Sheriff Woodson Francis returned venire facias: William McCray, John B Swan, Arthur Fulton, Jeremiah Howarton, William Thomas, William Kennedy, Jesse Roddye, Richard G Waterhouse, James Coulter, Evan Evans, John Russell, Azariah David, William McGill, John Locke, John Cozby, Robert Cozby, John Hill, Joseph Williams, William Smith (yellow creek), Abraham Howard, Joshua Atchley, Joseph Harwood, Robert Gamble, James Kelly, Joseph Johnson.

Grand jury: John Cozby foreman, Azariah David, Joseph Johnson, Evan Evans, William Kennedy, John Hill, James Coulter, Jesse Roddye, John Locke, Joseph Williams, Arthur Fulton, James Kelly, William Smith.

Constable James Upton sworn to attend the Grand jury this Term.

p.130 Jurors who came not: Jeremiah Howarton, Joseph Harwood, Wm McGill, Robert Gamble, John Russell, Richard G Waterhouse, Abraham Howard.

Representatives of Landon Carters heirs lessee v Thomas N Clark & Daniel Rawlings. Thomas N Clarks lessee v Azariah David. John Williams's lessee v Wm Lyon & William French. In these causes came parties by attornies; causes continued.

Polley Morrison by her next friend Absalom Majors v Edward Morrison. Petition for divorce. Plf by attorney John McCampbell Esq; defendant came not.

David Parkhill to Chrisstian[?] E Shelton. Deed 200 acres Sale Creek 27th Feb 1819 proven by John Russell and Patrick Martin.

p.131 Henry Owens v David Canon. Decision referred to James Preston, Elias Ferguson, Jesse Roddye, and John Cozby with power to choose an umpire.

Court adjourned until tomorrow morning nine oclock.   Edw Scott

Tuesday 16th March. Present the Honorable Edward Scott, Esquire, Judge, &c.

Polly Morrisson by her next friend Absalom Majors v Edward Morrisson. Dft came not.

Jesse White v William Robertson. Jury Jeremiah Howerton, Joseph Harwood, William McGill, Robert Gamble, John Russell, James Preston, Thomas Kelly, George Walker, Jacob Wassum, James Bailey, William Ramsey, Hugh Murphey assess plaintiffs
p.132 damage to $698.75. Defendant is granted a new trial.

Nicholas Starns to Moses Thompson. Deed 60 acres Muddy Creek 15 March 1819 proven by John Rice and Richard G Waterhouse.

James Rogers assignee of Alexander Outlaw v William York. Representatives of David Ross decd & Thomas Hopkins lessee v John Moore. Continued to next Term.

Roswell Hall to Edward Varner. Deed lot in Washington, 15 March 1819. Proven by John Rice and James C Mitchell.

Excuse juror James Preston from further attendance at present Term.

MARCH 1819

p.133   William Murphree's lessee v Whitfields heirs & Richard G Waterhouse. Jury: Robert Garrison, Jacob Wassum Jr, Henry Owens, Richard Rafferty, Hugh Berry, Edmund Bean, Frederick Fulkerson, Hiram A Defriese, David McPhadden, James Edington, James Collins, Owen David. Plaintiff came not. Dfts recover agt plf costs of suit.

Owen David v Benjamin Allison. Jury[above, but James Berry for Owen David]. Dft guilty; plf recovers $60.43¾ and his costs of suit.

p.134   George Walker v James Collins. Deposition of Patsy Walker of Kentucky or Tennessee to be taken in behalf plaintiff.

William H Standefer v John Rice & Carlisle Humphreys & co. Continued.

John Ramsy's heirs lessee v Thomas Kelly. Continued until next Term.

Asahel Rawlings to James Standefer. Letter of Attonrey dated 16th March 1819 acknowledged by the maker.

William Smith v Samuel Murphey. Debt. At last Term of this Court time was given defendant to plead. Dft by attorney says he has well and truly paid the debt, p.135   signed Mitchell & [illegible]. Dft refused to verify on oath. Plf recovers of dft debt $56, further sum of $2.60 damages of detention, and his costs of suit.

Court adjourned until tomorrow morning nine oclock.   Edw Scott

p.136   Wednesday 17th March. Present the Honorable Edward Scott, Judge.

Carters Heirs lessee v Clark & Rawlings. Depositions of Little Page Sims of Alabama Territory to be taken in behalf plf; dft's attorney John McCampbell or William Lyon to be notified of time and place. Depositions of Matthew Nelson & Alexander McMillion of Knox County and John McClellan of Deb[illegible] and William Murphree of Jefferson County to be taken before any justice/peace of Knox County in behalf of the plaintiff.

William H Standefer v John Rice & Carlisle Humphrey & Co. Permission given to take depositions generally; notice to be given by plaintiff to John Rice, one of the defendants.

Frederick Fulkerson to William L Bradley. Bill/sale goods & lands dated 1 May 1818 proven by James C Mitchell.

p.137   Frederick Fulkerson to William L Bradley. Deed lot 24 in Washington, 16 Mar 1819 proved by John Rice and Edmund Bean.

Polly Morrison by her next friend Absalom Majors v Edward Morrison. Petition for divorce. Plfs by atty John McCampbell Esq; dft came not. Continued.

John Smith T v Robert Bell & wife. Equity. Continued.

Alexander Smith v Carlisle Humphreys. Defendant's demurrer overruled.

Jesse White v William Robertson. New trial granted at next Term.

p.138   John Den lessee of Richard G Waterhouse v Robert Hanna. Affidavit of Silas C Geren attorney in fact of Abner Underwood; Underwood is admitted to defend jointly with sd Hannah pleading lease entry and ouster and relying on the title only at trial who together with Silas C Geren & Benjamin Allison ackd bond.

William Smith v Samuel Murphey. [This item X'd out]

William Murphree & lessee v Whitfields heirs & Richard G Waterhouse. The nonsuit entered yesterday is set aside and plaintiffs paying costs of this Term, and cause is continued until next Term of this Court.

p.139   James Baileys lessee v Asa Rowden. Dft came not. Plf recovers of dft his term yet to come in premises and his costs in this suit expended.

John Locke's lessee v Edward Murphey & Hugh Murphey. On affidavit of Thomas Hopkins he is permitted to defend in Stead of sd Murpheys on entering common

SEPTEMBER 1819

rule confessing lease entry and ouster relying on title only on trial.
Jurors are discharged from further attendance at the present Term.
Constable James Upton has attended three days on Grand Jury for which he is entitled to one dollar per day amounting in all to three dollars.
William Smith v Samuel Murphy. Grant dft leave to file his plea.

p.140   Owen David v Benjamin Allison. Dfts atty offered Bill/exceptions to opinion of Court in charging the jury on 2d day this term which bill Court refused to sign because it does not truly represent the charge given the Jury by the Court. [verbatim copy here omitted].

p.141   The Court adjourned until Court in Course.   E W Scott

At a Circuit Court continued and holden in the 2d Judicial circuit for county of Rhea at the Court House in Washington on the 3d Monday and twentieth day of September 1819 was present on the bench the honorable Samuel Powell Esq. Judge &c.

Sheriff Woodson Francis returned Venire facias: Benjamin Jones, William Alexander, Jonathan Moore, John C Simpson, John Lee, Robert Bell, John Robinson, Allen Murphree, Mumford Smith, Chrispian E Chilton, Thomas Cannon, Peter Moyers, James Rodgers, James Bailey, Thomas Blakeley, Jonathan Fine, Daniel Walker, Henry Collins, William Smith, Jessee Witt, James Henry, James Stuart, James Coulter, William Baldwin, Samuel A Ewin.

p.142   Grand jury: Jonathan Fine foreman, Allen Murphree, Mumford Smith, Henry Collins, Thomas Blakeley, Chrispian E Shelton, Benjamin Jones, James Bailey, James Stuart, Samuel A Ewing, William Alexander, Robert Bell, James Coulter. Constable Joseph Rice sworn to attend them. (Certificate issued to Rice 21 Sept 1819)

There remained of the original venire the following persons as traverse jurors: W Smith, Daniel Walker.

John Smith v Robert Bell & wife. Bill in Equity. Continued until next Term.
The following causes were continued until next Term: Landon Carters heirs lessee v Thomas N Clark & Daniel Rawlings; John Williams's lessee v William Lyon & William French; Thomas N Clark's lessee v Azariah David; John Ramsey's heirs lessee v Thomas Kelly; David Ross's heirs & Thomas Hopkins lessee v John Moore; James Rogers v William York.

p.143   Jesse White v Wm Robertson. Continued until next Term.
William H Standefer v John Rice & Carlisle Humphreys. Continued to March.
Excuse juror Thomas Cannon from further attendance this Term.
Alexander Smith v Carlisle Humphreys. [Item X'd out]
Admitted Anderson Hutchison Esq to practice as an attorney in this Court.

p.144   Tuesday 21st September. Present the Honorable Samuel Powell Esq Judge &c.
Alexander Smith v Carlisle Humphreys. Plf recovers agt dft his damages by nonperformance of covenant; writ of inquiry awarded to determine amount of damages.
Henry Owens v David Canon[Croom?]. Cause deferred until next Term.
William Smith v Samuel Murphey. Cause continued until next Term.
William Murphree's lessee v Whitfields heirs & Richard G Waterhouse. Grant change of venue to Anderson County, next Term of sd Court.

22

SEPTEMBER 1819

p.145   Richard G Waterhouse's lessee v Robert Hanna & Abner Underwood. Continued.
George Walker v James Collins. Continued until next Term.
John Locke's lessee v Rosses Heirs & Thomas Hopkins. Continued.
Joseph C Strong v James Mitchell and Thomas Woodward. Sheriff executed writ on James Mitchell and Thomas Woodward, dft, was not found in this county. Alias writ awarded sheriff against Woodward, returnable to next Term of this Court.
p.146   Polly Morrison by her next friend Absalom Majors v Edward Morrison. Divorce. Proclamation and publication having been made, dft not found by sheriff, petitioner resided in Rhea County from 16 Oct 1814 to this time, that she married dft in Oct 1814 and dft Edward Morrison in April 1815 absented himself for more than two years, that he had for some time before the filing of sd petition been living publicly with another woman under the pretense of her being his wife, therefore decreed that bonds of matrimony be dissolved, and dft Edward Morrison pay costs of this cause for which execution may issue. (signed) S Powel.

State by Thomas Tigner prosecutor v John H Williams. Robbery. William E Anderson atty general on behalf state, dft in proper person. Offence was not committed within limits of Rhea County, prisoner was discharged.
p.147   Frederick Washington to Richard G Waterhouse. Deed 100 acres on Muddy Creek proven by John Skidmore and James Campbell.
Court adjourned until Court in Course.   S Powell

p.148   Monday 20th March 1820. Circuit Court holden for Rhea County; Present the Honorable Charles F Keith Judge of the 7th Judicial District.
Office of Clerk of this Court being vacated by appointment of Asahel Rawlings as clerk of the Court of Pleas & Quarter Sessions of Hamilton, Daniel Rawlings is appointed Clerk until sd vacancy be filled.
Sheriff Woodson Francis returned Venire facias: William Johnson, Richard G Woodhouse, Henry Collins, Roswell Hall, Even Evans, Robert W McMillen, John Parker, William Gamble, Wright Smith, George Gillespie, Abraham Smith, Jesse Thompson, Robert Gamble, William McCray, John Birdsong, William T Gillenwaters, James Kelly, Robert Locke, James Montgomery, Arthur Fulton, Abraham Howard, James W Cozby, William French, Azariah David, Charles Gamble. Constables Crispin E Shelton and James Upton summoned to attend as constables.
Release juror John Birdsong from further attendance at his term.
Thomas N Clark's lessee v Azariah David. Continued till next term.
p.149   John Williams' lessee v William French & William Lyon. Plf no further prosecutes, dfts recover agt lessor of plf their costs of defence.
Jesse White v William Robertson. Thomas L Williams the plf's attorney suggests that plaintiff hath departed this life; leave granted sd atty to revive suit in the names of the legal representatives of sd decedent.
Power of attorney Thomas Howet[Howit?] and wife Nancy to Thomas Bolton proved by Tandy James.
Power of Attorney Elisha Parker and wife Patsy to Thomas Bolton proved by Tandy James.
Holderman Pearson & Co v William Morley. Plf by attorney suggest that dft hath departed this life; grant leave to plaintiffs to revive this cause against

23

MARCH 1820

legal representatives of sd decedent.
    Benjamin W Shirley v William Worley. Plaintiff's attorney suggests that since the last continuance of this cause the defendant died; cause is revived against the legal representatives of sd decedent.
p.150   Anderson Hutchison is appointed Clerk of this Court.
    Court adjourned until tomorrow morning 9 o'clock.   Charles F Keith

Tuesday March 21; present the Hon: Charles F Keith, Judge &c.
    Anderson Hutchison yesterday apptd Clerk of Court, takes oaths and with John McCampbell, William Lyon and Wm E Anderson his securities enters bonds.
p.151   Bonds of Anderson Hutchison, John McCampbell, Wm Lyon & Wm E Anderson sec.
p.152   John A Montgomery Solicitor General of 11th district takes oaths.
    Grand jurors: Richard G Waterhouse, Evan Evans, Robert W McMillan, John Parker, Wm Gamble, Jesse Thomson, William T Gillenwaters, James Kelly, Robert Locke, James Montgomery, Arthur Fulton, Azariah David, Roswell Hall. Constable James Upton is sworn to attend Grand Jury.
    William Smith assee v Samuel Murphy. Jury Robt W McMillan, Abraham Howard, Richd G Waterhouse, Jno Woodward, Evan Evans, Jno Parker, Wm Gamble, Jesse Thomson, Wm S Gillenwaters, Jas Kelly, Arthur Fulton, Azariah David find dft hath not paid
p.153   the debt, assess plfs damages for detention to $11.76 besides costs.
    John Den on demise of John Ramsey's heirs v Thomas Kelly. On affidavit of Wm Ramsey one of the lessors of plf, this cause is continued at cost of plf.
    Alexander Smith v Carlisle Humphrey. Plaintiff recovers against defendant $179.20 damages confessed and his costs in this behalf expended.
    Richard G Waterhouse's lessee v Robert Hannah and Abner Underwood. Venue changed to Anderson County 4th August next.
p.154   John Locke's lessee v Edward Murphy & Hugh Murphy. Plf dismissed his suit; dfts by Daniel Rawlings their agent pay half costs.
    James Rodgers assee v Wm York. Henry Owens v David Crum. George Walker v James Collins. John Den on the demise of David Ross's heirs & al v John Moore. By consent of parties by their attornies these causes are continued to next Term.
    George Gillespie, Abraham Smith, William McRae, Abraham Howard and William French being summoned to attend as jurors and not appearing fined each $25 unless they show sufficient reason to the contrary at next term.
    Court is adjourned until tomorrow 9 oclock.   Charles F Keith

p.155   Wednesday March 22nd. Present the Hon: Charles F Keith, Judge &c.
    Richard G Waterhouse's lessee v Richard Fen with notice to James Neal, Jesse Thomson, John Thomson & Levi Lemons. Jesse Thomson is admitted to defend in room of Richard Fen the casual ejector, and also in room of the other tenants on whom notice hath been served on his agreement to confess the lease, entry & ouster in plf's declaration & to rely on title only at trial. Woodson Francis, James Preston and James Upton undertake for dft to pay if dft can't.
    John Den on demise of John Ramsey's heirs v Thomas Kelly. On affidavits of Woodson Francis, John Moor, William Lewis & John Rice, order unless lessors of plf within four months give additional security for payment of costs to be incurred in prosecution which may be adjudged against them, this cause shall be discontinued.
p.156   State v Leonard Bullock, John Everett, Newel Everett & Patsy Bullock.

MARCH 1820

State v John Everett & Newel Everett. Comes John A Montgomery solicitor general; noli prosequies entered in these causes.

Richard G Waterhouse's lessee v Richard Fen with notice to George Maines. By consent of plf William French with sd George Maines are admitted to defend in room of Richard Fen on their agreement to confess the lease, entry & ouster in plff's declaration supposed and to rely on title only at trial.

Abraham Howard & William French exparte. Fines entered against them on yesterday for non attendance as jurors are remitted.

State v John Jackson. John Jackson bound with William T Gillenwaters & Miller Francis his securities for his appearance; no person appears to prosecute & he is discharged.

Richard G Waterhouse's lessee v Jesse Thompson. Depositions of Alexander Outlaw of Dallas County, Alabama, of Littlepage Simms of Cahauba County in sd
p.157 state, and of Abraham Stout of Cotaco County in sd state to be taken in behalf of the defendant.

On motion of Anderson Hutchison Clerk of this Court Daniel Rawlings is permitted to qualify as his deputy; sd Daniel Rawlings takes oath.

Grand Jury is discharged.

Court adjourned till tomorrow 10 oclock.   Charles F Keith

Thursday March 23rd.   Present the Hon: Charles F Keith, Judge &c.

William H Standefer v Rice, Humphrey & Co. Plf by atty; John Rice & Carlisle Humphreys who have been arrested and held to bail, by their attorney moved to quash writ in this cause. Plf moved on affidavit of James Standefer to amend writ
p.158 by adding to the name "Rice" in sd writ the name "John" and in like manner to the name "Humphreys" the name "Carlisle". Both motions argued, order plf have liberty to amend writ, and pay costs of this cause accruing at this term.

John Smith v Robert Bell & Elizabeth his wife. Equity. Decreed that complainant's bill be dismissed; complainant pays costs. Complainant allowed appeal to
p.159 Supreme Court of errors & appeals on having given bond with security.

Robert Bell agt Annanias McCoy for use of John Smith. McCoy for use of John Smith recovers agt Bell $475 debt with $428.68 damages for detention, also his
p.160 costs of suit. Sd Robert Bell obtains appeal to Supreme Court.

Joseph Anderson's lessee v Richard Fen with notice to John Knox. Ejectment. Same v Fen with notice to Isaac Brazelton. In Ejectment. Same v Fen with notice to Daniel Walker. In Ejectment. Plaintiff in these causes by attorney; for reasons from affidavit of Murphey, ordered these causes be consolidated; affidavit of sd Murphree he is admitted to defend in room of Richard Fen, and of sd Knox, Brazelton
p.161 and Walker. Affidavit of Miller Francis agent of lessee of plf commissions awarded him to take deposition of Alexander Outlaw of Dallas County, Alabama, and of David Stuart of Cocke County. Deposition to be taken of James Hubbard of this county who is aged and infirm in behalf dft.

p.162 Wm H Standefer v John Rice and Carlisle Humphreys. Depositions of John Rucker, James W Lamkin, William Lamkin, and John Burton of Georgia to be taken in behalf of defendant.

Richard G Waterhouse's lessee v Richard Fen with notice to Elihu D Armstrong. Richard Fen came not; Elihu D Armstrong came not. Plf recovers his term yet to come in lands with appurtenances and his costs in this behalf expended.

Richard G Waterhouse's lessee v Richard Fen with notice to Daniel D Arm-

MARCH 1820

strong. From affidavit of William Murphree he is admitted to defend on his confessing lease entry and ouster and rely on title only at trial, and on his giv-
p.163 ing security for costs and Daniel Armstrong, Joseph Thomson & William Lewis held unto lessee of plf in sum $1000 condition dft pay all costs against him.

Joseph Anderson's lessee v Richard Fen with notice to George Lewis. Richard Fen came not nor doth George Lewis appear. Plf recovers agt Richard Fen his term yet to come and recovers agt George Lewis his costs of suit.

Carter's heirs lessee v Clark & Rawlings. Continued until next Term.

Joseph C Strong v Mitchell & Woodward. Dft not found. Plurias capias awarded against dft returnable &c.

George Walker v John Hill. Take time to plead until next Term.

p.164 James Kelly v James Cozby & James W Cozby. "Not found" as to dft James W Cozby, alias capias awarded agt him to sheriff of Hamilton County.

Deed Enoch Parsons to Richard G Waterhouse. Thomas L Williams and William Johnson the witnesses thereto being sworn say they heard sd Parsons acknowledge same as his act, and sd deed is admitted to record, it being for conveyance of 1920 acres in this county.

Petition of Alexander Forbes was presented praying a divorce to be decreed between him and his wife Rachel Forbes, and subpoena to notify sd Rachel to appear and answer sd petition, giving bond & security for costs.

Court adjourned till Court in Course.   Charles F Keith.

p.165 At a Circuit Court held for County of Rhea at the Courthouse in Washington on 3rd Monday of September 1820. Present the honorable Nathaniel W Williams Judge.

Sheriff Woodson Francis returns venire facias, summoned as Jurors: Richard G Waterhouse, James Stuart, John Moore, Wm Gamble, Robert Parks, John Locke, James McDonald, Henry Collins, John Cozby, Joseph Thompson, John Hall, Thomas Cox, Jesse Martin, William McCray, Roswell Hall, Randolph Gibson, John Robertson, Beriah Frazier, Robert Gamble, Frederic Fulkerson.

Grand Jurors: Richd G Waterhouse foreman, Jno Moore, Wm Gamble, Robt Parks, John Locke, James McDonald, Henry Collins, John Cozby, Joseph Thomson, John Hall, Thomas Cox, James Stuart, Jesse Martin. Constable Wm Lewis sworn to attend them.

Deed William Good to Richard G Waterhouse land on Clear Creek; David Meloney and Daniel Clayton two of witnesses thereto say they saw Good sign and acknowledge same.

Deed William Murphree to Jeremiah Duncan dated 10 June 1819 2500 acres
p.166 proved by George Walker and James Murphree witnesses thereto.

Following causes continued until next term by consent of the parties: Thos N Clark's lessee v Azariah David. James Rodgers assee v Wm York. Henry Owens v David Cresin.

John Den in demise of John Ramseys heirs v Thomas Kelly. Lessees of plf having failed to give additional security, couse is discontinued.

Richard G Waterhouse's lessee v Jesse Thompson. Depositions of Littlepage Simms, Alexander Outlaw & Abraham Stout of Alabama to be taken in behalf of dft.

Jesse White v Wm Robertson. Death of dft suggested at last term, to wit
p.167 Nelson Robertson admr of decedent; cause revived in name of sd admr.

SEPTEMBER 1820

  Holderman Pearson & Co v Wm Worly. Benjamin Sherly v Same. Suits revived in the names of Elijah Creel and Joseph Nelson, admrs of defendant whose death was suggested at last term.
  Court adjourns till tomorrow 9 oclock.   Nath W Williams

Tuesday Sept 19th. Present hon. Nathaniel W Williams, Judge &c.
  William Arnold produced licence signed by honorable Samuel Powel & Edward Scott authorizing him to practice law, having taken oaths, he is permitted to practice as such in this Court.
  Deed John Rice to Jeremiah Harvey and Michael Dennis Lot 26 in Washington proved by Thomas J Campbell and John A Montgomery witnesses thereto.
  Forfeiture against William McRae at last term is set aside.
  Deed Daniel Rawlings to Isaac Maken 49½ acres proved by Elijah Rice & Cain Abel.
p.168 Richard G Waterhouse's lessee v French and Menas. Continued.
  Richard G Waterhouse's lessee v Jesse Thompson. Venue changed to Knox Cty.
  Henry Owens v David Crum. Deposition of Daniel Clayton of this county to be taken at house of Carson Caldwell in Washington in behalf plaintiff.
  George Walker v James Collins. Jury Wm McRae, Shepherd Brazelton, Andw Wilhelm, Jasper Romine, Alexr Carnahan, Jesse Thompson, Thos Hamilton, Daniel Walker, Hiram Worly, Isaac Brazelton, Robt Garrison, Richd G Waterhouse find dft guilty of the trover in declaration mentioned, assess plf's damage to $2.50 besides costs.
p.169 William H Standefer v Rice & Humphreys. On affidavit of dft John Rice depositions of John Rucker, James W Lamkin, Wm Lamkin and John Burton to be taken; also in behalf plf, depositions of Alexr J Matthews of Marion County, Tennessee, and of Palatial Shelton at house of dft John Rice in Washington.
  Thomas Hamilton v Elias Forgerson. Continued.
  George Walker v John Hill. John Robinson present in Court who hath in possession a covenant between the parties in this cause dated 8 March 1819 is directed to file same with Clerk of this Court.
  Court adjourned till Tomorrow 9 O clock.   Nath W Williams

Wednesday Sept 20th 1820. Present the Hon: Nathaniel W Williams Judge.
  Joseph Anderson's lessee v William Murphree. Grant leave to plaintiff to show why name of Wm Murphree who was admitted to defend at last term in room of sundry tenants shall be stricken from record of this suit as a dft.
p.170 Den on demise of David Ross' heirs &c v John Moore. Continued.
  George Walker v John Hill. Time given dft until next term to plead.
  Josiah Dantforth v Jonathan Fine. Continued.
  State (Jno Lovelady prosr) v John Russell & Jos Francis. Affidavit of John Lovelady and Jonathan Cunningham, cause is continued until next term. Dft Russell bond $1000; William Lauderdale, Wm McRae and David Oats his securities $2000 jointly, condition dft Russell appear at Court next term. John Lovelady bond $500, condition he appear next Term to prosecute and give evidence behalf State agt dfts.
  State (by Jonathan Cunningham prosr) v John Russell and Joseph Francis. Continued. Bond of dft Russell $1000, and Wm Lauderdale, Wm McRae and David Oats, condition Russell appear next Term to answer charge of State. Jonathan Cunningham
p.180 $500, condition he appear to prosecute & give evidence aft dft.

SEPTEMBER 1820

State v Jonathan Crawford. Continued. Recognizance, dft $1000, Samuel Oxshire and Matthias Crawford securities. Richard H Gatewood bond $500 condition he appear to prosecute and give evidence agt dft.

Samuel Oxshire, Jane Miles[Mills?], Samuel R Sherrell, Elizabeth Sherrell, Nancy Benton, Jesse B Sherrell, and Joseph Peters, bond $250, condition they appear at next term to give evidence agt dft.

Court adjourned till Tomorrow 9 O'clock.   Nath W Williams

Thursday Sept 21st. Present the hon: Nathl W Williams Judge &c.

Thomas N Clark's lessee v Azariah David. Deposition of Charles McClung to be taken, Knox County, in behalf defendant.

p.181   Lewis Ross agt State. Transcript of record of this cause is imperfect & is to be sent to Clerk of Court of Pleas to be made a full and perfect transcript and forthwith returned to this Court.

State v Joseph Adams. Attorney general John A Montgomery. Jury Wm McRae, Thos D Pain, Edmd Beane, Wm E Cardwell, John McClannahan, George Henry Senr, Wm Locke, John Gamble, Eustace Humphrey, Jacob Burk, Roger Reece, Richd Manly find dft Joseph Adams not guilty; county pay costs of this cause.

Court adjourned till Tomorrow 9 o'clock.   Nath W Williams

p.182   Friday Sept 22d. Present the Hon Nathaniel W Williams, Judge &c.

Alexander Forbes v Rachel Forbes. Proclamation hath been made according to law that unless dft appear & answer petition of plf, same should be set for hearing exparte at next Term; dft not appearing, cause set for hearing next Term.

Deed George W Riggel to Thomas Hopkins lots 72 & 73 in Washington, ackd.

Richard G Waterhouse's lessee v William Murphree. Dft made application to change the venue; cause continued until next Term, venue not to be changed, motion of plaintiff to strike name of dft from the record as a defendant.

Wm H Standefer v Rice & Humphreys. Depositions of Philip Hooterfils and
p.183   Alexander Colter of Bledsoe County to be taken in behalf defendant.

Lewis Ross plf in error agt State dft in error. Attorney general John A Montgomery in behalf State. Court finds no error in proceedings of Court of Pleas; therefore sd judgment is affirmed.

Joseph Anderson's lessee v William Murphree. Court will advise on motion to strike out name of dft from record next Term; order for taking depositions for plf is revived, to take deposition of Francis A Ramsey of Knox County, also the order for taking James Hubbart's deposition for dft is revived; also deposition of Job Simms of Blount County, also of Littlepage Simms of Dallas County, Alabama, in behalf dft, giving 30 days notice to Miller Francis agent of plaintiff.

p.184   Richard G Waterhouse's lessee v William Murphree. Deposition of Littlepage Simms of Dallas County, Alabama, to be taken in behalf defendant.

Allow John Parker, jailor, allowed $40 for keeping Joseph Adams in jail.

State v Joseph Francis. Dft not appearing when called, he forfeits his recognizance; scire facias issued. William Shelton, Jesse Jones, Charles Higdon, John Bodley, Jesse Upton, John Allen, Luster Haines, Archibald Haines and Cornelius McCannon for failing to bring sd dft forfeit their recognizance. Austin Brumby [Brennly?] bound in recognizance for appearance of Catharine Brumly his wife to testify behalf State in this cause, Catharine not appearing, said Austin forfeits

MARCH 1821

his recognizance.
p.185 State v Joseph Francis. Dft not appearing, he forfeits his recognizance; scire facias issues. William Shelton, John Higdon, Jesse Upton, Jesse Jones, Charles Higdon, John Bodley, John Allen, Luster Haines, Archibald Haines, Cornelius McCannon jointly bound in recognizance for appearance of dft Jos Francis and failing to produce him forfeit recognizance; scire facias issue. Austin Brownly bound for appearance of Catharine Brownly his wife to testify behalf State, and sd Catharine not appearing, Austin Brownly forfeits his recognizance; scire facias issues.
   State v John Russell. Same v Same. In these cases Austin Brumby bound in recognizance for appearance of Catharine Brumby his wife to testify behalf State, &
p.186 Catharine not appearing, Austin forfeits, scire facias issues.
   Richard G Waterhouse's lessee v William Murphree. Joseph Thompson security for dft together with other securities for costs of this suit now produced dft but Court refused to receive such surrender in order to discharge him.
   State v John Russell. Same v Same. Austin Bramly[Brownly?] bound in recognizance to appear, came not; forfeits his recognizance.
   State v Joseph Francis. Same v Same. Austin Brumly bound in recognizance in these cases came not; forfeits.
   Court adjourned till Court in Course.   Nath W Williams

p.187 Circuit Court for Rhea County, third Monday in March 1821. Presiding the Honorable Charles F Keith Esquire, Judge of the 11th Circuit.
   State v George Gillespie. Set aside forfeiture of George Gillespie for failure to attend at March Term 1820.
   Release John Rice and John Robinson from attendance as jurors at this Term.
   Sheriff Woodson Francis returned venire facias: Moses Paul, James Rogers, Jesse Roddye, Moses Thompson, Elias Ferguson, Thomas Woodward, James C Mitchell, Daniel Walker, James Wilson, Isaac Lewis, John Robinson, William Smith, John Rice, Frederick Fulkerson, John Holland, Thomas Price, Samuel McDaniel, Jonathan Fine, George Gillespie, William Johnson, James Snelson, Thomas Cox.
p.188 Grand Jury: Willliam Smith foreman, Samuel McDaniel, Moses Paul, James Rogers, Jesse Roddye, Moses Thompson, Elias Ferguson, James C Mitchell, James Wilson, Isaac Lewis, John Holland, Jonathan Fine, Thomas Cox. Constable William Lewis sworn to attend them.
   Traverse jurors: George Gillespie, Thomas Woodward, James Snelson, Thomas Price, William Johnson, Frederick Fulkerson, Daniel Walker.
   Court adjourned until tomorrow morning 10 Oclock.   Charles F Keith

p.189 Tuesday 20th March. Present the Honl Charles F Keith Esqr.
   Landon Carters heirs lessee v Thomas N Clark & Daniel Rawlings. Ejectment. Plaintiff no further prosecutes; defendant pays costs.
   W H Standefer v Rice & Humphreys. Continued.
   H N Clarks lessee v Azariah David. Deposition of Charles McClung, Knox County, to be taken in behalf defendant, giving plaintiff or William Lyon of Knox County ten days previous notice of time and place of taking same.

MARCH 1821

p.190 James Rodgers assee v William York. Continued on affidavit of plaintiff.
p.191 State v Isaac Brazelton. Isaac Brazelton, summoned to attend as a juror, is fined $5 for failure to attend, and is to pay costs of this judgment.

James Kelly v James W Cozby & James Cozby. Jury George W Riggle, Thomas Jack, John Ferguson, Lewis Wilkerson, Robert Garrison, Thomas Hamilton, Samuel Ferguson, Aron Ferguson, Moses Ferguson, Joseph Thompson, Isaac Brazelton, John Locke find dfts guilty. Plf recovers of dfts his damages $30 besides his costs.
p.192 Deed, Charles McClung to Richard G Waterhouse, land between Waltons Ridge, Tennessee River, & North Chickamauga Creek dated 22 Nov 1820 proven by William Smith and William P Hackett.

Deed, James Cozby, Hugh Dunlap & Alexander Ferguson to Richd G Waterhouse, land between Waldons ridge, Tennessee River and mouth of North Chickamauga Creek proven by William Smith and William P Hackett.
p.193 Henry Owens v David Crum. Continued.

W H Standefer v Rice & Humphreys. Change of venue to Roane County.
p.194 George Walker v John Hill. Continued.

David Ross's heirs & Thomas Hopkins lessees v John Moore. Plaintiff came not; dft recovers of the lessors of the plaintiffs his costs of defence.

Joseph C Strong v James C Mitchell & Thomas Woodward. Debt. Dfts agree they owe plf his debt $144.84 and damage of detention $34.76, and his costs.
p.195 R G Waterhouses lessee v William French & George Menas. Ejectment. Lessee of plf by atty suggests that since last continuance, William French one of dfts hath departed this life leaving his heirs under age. William Smith is appointed guardian for sd heirs to defend sd cause; declaration to be served on sd William Smith three months before next term of this Court.

Josiah Denforth v Jonathan Fine. Continued.

Deed, Isaac West to John Jackson 200 acres ackd by grantor.

W C Dunlop Esqr took oath for attorneys and is admitted to practice in this Court.
p.196 Lewis Ross's lessee v John Spear, James McGee, James Cowan & Jno L McCarty. Eject. On affidavit of James Cowan & John L McCarty two of dfts they are admitted to defend jointly in room of Richard Fen whereupon William Smith comes and undertakes for sd defendants.

Holderman Pearson & Co v Wm Worleys admrs. Shirley v Admrs of Wm Worley. These suits are continued until next September Term of this Court.
p.197 Alexander J Matthews v Robert H Davis. Plf came not. Dft recovers of plf his costs about his defence in this behalf expended.

James F Foster v Samuel Riley. Cause long since abatted by death of dft and no steps having been taken by plf to revive suit, plf pays accrued costs.

Court adjourned until tomorrow morning 9 Oclock.   Charles F Keith

p.198 Wednesday 21st March. Present the Honl C F Keith Esqr Judge &c.

Thomas Hamilton v Elias Ferguson. Deposition of Abraham Sevier of Overton County to be taken in behalf defendant. Deposition of Thomas Hamilton Senr and Pleasant B Coffee of Overton County to be taken in behalf plaintiff.

State v Joseph Francis. Forfeiture entered at last term is set aside upon defendant paying costs in this behalf expended.
p.199 State v William Shelton. Forfeiture entered agt Wm Shelton set aside, condition he pay costs in this behalf expended.

MARCH 1821

        State v Jesse James. [same wording as the previous item]
        State v Charles Higdon. [as above]
        State v John Bodley. [as above]
p.200   State v John Allen. [as above]
        State v Luster Haynes. [as above]
        State v Archibald Haynes. [as above]
        State v Cornelius McCannon. [as above]
p.201   State v Joab Blackwell. Defendants security bring dft who is placed in custody of the Sheriff. Afterwards dft with Richard Philpot undertake as follows: that dft ack himself indebted to Tennessee in sum $500 and sd Richard Philpot in like sum, condition Joab Blackwell attend day to day at present Term.

        Henry Owens v David Crum. Deposition of Daniel Clyton of Jackson County, Alabama, to be taken in behalf plaintiff.

        State v John Russell. Two cases. Continued. Recognizance of John Russell, James C Mitchell Esq and William Lauderdale securities. Also recognizances of John
p.202   Lovelady, Jonathan Cunningham, Austin Tilly and Catherine Tilly, condition they appear next term to give evidence on part of the State.

        William T Lewis's heirs lessee v Richd Fen, Elizabeth Lewis, & James Lewis. On affidavit of Richard G Waterhouse these suits are consolidated, and he is permitted to defend in room of Richard Fen, Elizabeth Lewis & James Lewis on agreeing to confess lease entry and ouster; Daniel Walker his security.

p.203   State v Joseph Francis. Two causes. Continued till next Court.

        State v Austin Brumley. Forfeiture entered last term set aside with costs to be paid by Rhea county.

        Grand jurors discharged.

        State v Austin Brumly. Forfeiture entered here at last Term agt Austin Brumley is set aside without costs, Rhea County to pay same.

p.204   State v Austin Brumley. [as above]
        State v Austin Brumley. [as above]
        State v Austin Brumley & wife. [as above]
        State v Austin Brumley & wife. [as above]
p.205   State v Austin Brumley & wife. [as above]
        State v Austin Brumley & wife. [as above]

        State v Jonathan Crawford. Continued to next Court on defendant's paying cost of this Term; dft's recognizance $500, John Narremore & Samuel Oxsheer securities. Richardson H Gatewood, Samuel C Low & Elly Ormes recognizance, condition Gatewood shall appear and give evidence on behalf State.

p.206   State v Jonathan Crawford. It appearing from return of J Norrimore Sheriff of Bledsoe County, that Polly Orme & Nancy Nelson have been summoned here to give testimony behalf dft but failed to appear; they forfeit according to subpoena unless they shew sufficient cause at next Term; sci fa issued to Bledsoe County.

        William T Lewis's heirs lessee v Richard Fen with notice to Christopher Coats. Continued to next Court.

        State v Joseph Francis. Forfeiture entered last term is set aside on defendant's payment of costs.

p.207   State v Joseph Francis. Dft's securities bring dft; in custody of sheriff.

        State v William Shelton. Forfeiture entered at last Term set aside; sd Shelton paying costs in this behalf expended.

        State v Jesse Jones. [as above]
p.208   State v Charles Higdon. [as above]

MARCH 1821

        State v Charles Bodly. [same wording as previous item]
        State v John Allen. [as above]
        State v Luster Haynes. [as above]
p.209   State v Archibald Haynes. [as above]
        State v Cornelius McCannon. [as above]
        State v Thomas Humphrey. Johnson A Montgomery Esqr who prosecutes for the State. Nolle presequi entered. Dft recovers agt State the costs, and Clerk of this Court certify Bill of cash in this case to Bledsoe County whence this case came by change of venue.
p.210   State v Jesse Upton. Alias sci fa is ordered to issue.
        State v Jesse Upton. Alias sci fa is ordered to issue.
p.211   State v Joab Blackwell. Defendant in person. Jury Thomas Woodward, James Snelson, Thomas Price, William Johnson, Frederick Fulkerson, Daniel Walker, Hiram Worley, Richard G Waterhouse, John Park[blot], George W Riggle, Shepherd Brazelton, Carson Caldwell find dft not guilty. Rhea County pays costs.
p.212   Jesse White v Nelson Robinson admr of William Robinson decd. Jury George Gillespie, Thomas Woodward, James Snelson, Thomas Price, William Johnson, Frederick Fulkerson, Daniel Walker, Henry Collins, John Gillian, Walton Edwards, Allen Kennedy, Isaac Rush assess plaintiff's damages by nonperformance of assumption to $500 besides his costs. Plf recovers agt dft damages and his costs of suit.
p.213   Jesse Garland v Ruth Garland. Petitioner came not; suit discontinued and plf pays costs.
        Court adjourns until tomorrow morning 8 Oclock.   Charles F Keith

p.214   Thursday 22d March. Present the Honl Charles F Keith, Judge &c.
        It appearing that the declaration in case John Ramseys heirs lessee against Thomas Kelly who was admitted defence in room of Richard Fen, has been lost from the files when some difficulty hath occurred with the Clerk of this Court as to the proper names of sd heirs; Court also being satisfied that by referring to declaration in case of John Ramseys heirs against David Caldwell their names may be ascertained. Therefore ordered Clerk upon execution against sd heirs in their proper names as by law required, but because it is possible that some error may intervene the clerk is further ordered to endorse on sd executions that sd heirs have leave at next Term to shew cause why these executions should be quashed.
        Wm T Lewis's heirs lessee v Richard G Waterhouse. Depositions of Valentine Shelby, Kinason Shultz, and George Winton of Cahaba County, Alabama, Little P Sims of Dallas County, James Cunningham of St Clair County and Job Sims of either St Clair or Jefferson County, Alabama, and Jacob Shultz of Illinois to be taken in behalf defendant, giving notice to Thomas Hopkins, it appearing from affidavit of James C Mitchell that sd Hopkins is interested in this suit.
p.215   State v Isaac Brazelton. Fine against Brazelton is set aside.
        J Andersons lessee v William Murphree. Plea of plf's lessee to strike name of Murphree as dft being argued, order rule be discharged.
        Andrew Erwin v Edd Verner. Attachment. Dft is not an inhabitant of this State; proceedings stayed until next Term of this Court, publication to be made in the Knoxville Register.
        Waterhouse's lessee v Wm Murphree. Rule of plfs lessee to strike name of Murphree from rolls as dft being argued, rule discharged.
p.216   Alexander Forbes v Rachel Forbes. Dft is not found; publication to be made

SEPTEMBER 1821

in Knoxville Resister and cause to be held for hearing at next Term.
    Alexander Smith v John Rice & James C Mitchell. Defendants in person confess judgment for plaintiffs demand. Plf recovers of dfts $179.20 and his costs.
p.217   J Andersons lessee v William Murphree. Deposition of Valentine Shautz, Kineson Shautz and George Newton of Cahaba County, Little Page Sims of Dallas County, James Cunningham of St Clair and Job Sims of St Clair or Jefferson Counties all of Alabama and Jacob Shautz of Illinois to be taken in behalf defendant on giving Miller Francis agent of plaintiff 30 days notice of time and place.
p.218   State v John Laby. Nolle prosequi entered.
    Court adjourned until third Monday in September next.   Charles F Keith

p.219   Circuit Court in Washington, the third Monday in Sept and 17th day of the month. Presiding the honorable Charles F Keith Esquire Judge &c.
    Grand Jury: Joseph Love foreman, George W Riggle, James Wilson, John Robinson, David Leuty, William Kennedy, James McGonery, John Cozby, Eli Ferguson, Jesse Thompson, Isaac Holland, Carson Caldwell, Joseph Rice.
    Traverse jurors: Robert Bell, James C Mitchell, Roger Rees, Asa Rowden.
    Excuse Moses Thompson, Robert Elder, and Arthur Fulton from further attendance at this Term as jurors.
    Clarks lessee v A David. Continued until next Court.
p.220   James Rodgers assignee v William York. Cause continued to next Court.
    Henry Owens v David Crum. Cause continued till next Court.
    Pryor Lea and Richard Dunlap Esqrs took oath of attorney and are permitted to practice at the Bar of this Court.
    Deed, Elias Ferguson to James Ferguson & Robt Ferguson, 83½ acres ackd.
    State v Jacob Wassum Jr. William Floyd who was bound for appearance of defendant surrenders dft & he is in custody of sheriff.
    George Walker v John Hill. Cause is continued till next Court.
    Holderman et al v Creel & al. Cause is continued till next Court.
p.221   Sherley & al v Creel et al. Cause is continued till next term.
    Robert Gamble v H Robinson & al. Cause is continued till next Court.
    Waterhouses lessee v W Umphrie. Dft in person, cause continued.
    Thomas N Clarks lessee v Azariah David. Deposition of Charles McClung of Knox County to be taken in behalf the defendant.
p.222   State v Jacob Wassum Jr. Recognizance of Jacob Wassum Jr; Jacob Wassum Senr his security, condition Jacob Wassum Jr attend from day to day to answer a bill of Indictment against him by grand jurors.
    Court adjourned until tomorrow morning 9 Oclock.   Charles F Keith

p.223   Tuesday 18th Sept. Present the Honorable Charles F Keith, Judge &c.
    Resignation of Anderson Hutchison Clerk of Court was accepted, whereupon John Locke was appointed Clerk, took oaths, and entered bonds unto Joseph McMinn governor of Tennessee and his successors in office, with Daniel Rawlings, Rezin Rawlings, Woodson Francis and Robert Locke his security.
p.224   [bonds of John Locke are continued]

SEPTEMBER 1821

p.225   William T Lewis lessee v Richard G Waterhouse. Lessee of plaintiff came not; defendant recovers of the lessee of the plaintiff his costs of defence.
   Same v Same. Defendant recovers of the lessee of plf his costs of defence.
   William T Lewis's heirs lessee v Christopher Coats. Lessee of plaintiff failing to appear, dft recovers of sd lessee his costs in his defence expended.
p.226   John Millers lessee v Robert Gamble et al. From affidavit of Thomas C Hindman, order that unless lessor of plf give additional security for payment of costs to be incurred in prosecution of this cause, cause shall stand discontinued.
   John Spears lessee v Thos C Hindman, William Blackwood & Benjamin Bond. On motion of dfts, unless lessor of plfs give additional security [worded as above]
   Lewis's heirs lessee v Waterhouse. From affidavit of lessor of plffs agent Thomas Hopkins a rule is made to shew cause why this suit should be reinstated.
p.227   Lewis's heirs lessee v Waterhouse. [worded as above]
   Lewis's heirs lessee v Christopher Coats. [worded as above]
   Thomas Hamilton v Elias Ferguson. Venue changed to Bledsoe County.
p.228   James G Martin &c lessee v Isaac Baker, Samuel Baker & John Baker. Ejectment. Plf's atty directs suit be dismissed; dfts recover of lessors of plf their costs by them in this behalf expended.
   James G Martin &c lessee v William Johnson, Charles Brady & James Snelson. Ejectment. Plf's atty dismissed suit as to Wm Johnson and James Snelson who recover of lessors of plaintiff their costs by them in this behalf expended.
   James G Martin &c lessee v Isaac Rush, James Gallant & Edward Stuart. Ejectment. Plf's atty directed suit be dismissed as to Edward Stuart; Edward Stuart recovers of lessors of plaintiff his costs in this behalf expended.
p.229   James G Martin &c lessee v James Preston, James Bailey, Landon Rector & Cum-berland Rector. Ejectment. Plf by atty directed suit be dismissed as to James Preston, James Bailey and Cumberland Rector; sd dfts recover of plf their costs.
   Same v Thomas McKeddy, James Moore & John Woodward. Ejectment. Plfs atty dismissed suit as to Thomas McKeddy who recovers of lessors of plf his costs.
   Same v James Rogers, Peter Majors & Abraham Majors. Ejectment. Plf by atty dismissed suit as to James Rogers; sd Jas recovers of lessors of plf his costs.
p.230   James G Martin &c lessee v Robert Beard, Peter Daniel & William Kelly. Ejectment. Plf's atty dismissed suit as to Wm Kelly who recovers of plf his costs.
   Same v Charles Ryon, James Thompson & Charles Mitchell. Ejectment. Plf by atty dismissed suit as to James Thompson who comes in person and confesses judgment for all costs that have accrued against him; sd Thompson pays costs as aforesaid.
   Same v Frederick Fulkerson, Thomas Thompson, Moses Thompson. Ejectment. Plf by atty dismissed these suits whereupon Thos Thompson and Moses Thompson confess judgment for all costs in this behalf expended.
   Court adjourned until tomorrow morning 9 oclock.   Charles F Keith

p.231   Wednesday Sept 19th.
   State v Joseph Francis. Dft in person; cause continued until next term; recognizance of dft $1000 with William H K Shelton and Samuel Francis securities. And John Lovelady and Austin Tilly bond condition they appear next Term to prosecute and give evidence on part of State.
p.232   State v Joseph Francis. Cause continued until next Term; dft's recognizance [as above]; prosecution recognizance [as above]
p.233   State v John Russell. G.L. Dft in person; cause continued till next Term;

SEPTEMBER 1821

dft's recognizance $1000, Wm Lauderdale, George Maghee, Benjamin Allison & David Oats his security; John Lovelady and Austin Tilly bond to appear next Term to prosecute and give evidence on the part of the State against said Russell.

State v John Russell. [as above]

p.234 Anderson[Alexander?] Erwin v Edward Varner. Attachment. Publication has been three times made in Knoxville Register and agreeably to order of last term, dft not appearing nor replevying the property attached, it is considered same be condemned in the hands of the sheriff for satisfaction of plaintiffs demand of $525.75 besides his costs.

p.235 Excuse Daniel Stockton from further attendance as juror at this term.

John Spears lessee v Thos C Hindman. Eject. Plf by atty dismissed suit; dft recovers of lessor of plf his costs in this behalf expended.

John Spears Lessee v William Blackwood. Eject. Plf's atty dismissed suit; dft recovers agt lessor of plf his costs in this behalf expended.

John Spears lessee v Benjamin Bond. Eject. Plf's atty dismissed suit; dft recovers agt lessor of plf his costs of suit.

p.236 State v Jacob Wassum. Dft in proper person; cause continued untill next term; recognizance of dft $500, Jacob Wassum and Coonrod Wassum securities; dft pays costs of this prosecution at this term; Andrew Evins bond, condition he appear next Term to prosecute and give evidence on part of State vs dft.

State v Polly Orm. From affidavit of Elly Orms, forfeiture entered at last Term vs sd Polly is set aside without costs.

James G Martin & al lessee v Rezin Rawlings & Daniel Rawlings. Dfts admitted in room of Richard Fen the casual ejector.

p.237 State v Jonathan Crawford. Dft in person; cause continued; dfts recognizance $500, John Narremore & Samuel Oxshire securities. Recognizance of Richardson H Gatewood to prosecute and give evidence behalf State, Samuel C Low his security.

State v Martin Pharrow[Phanon?] Dft in person; cause is continued; recognizance of dft $500, Richard G Waterhouse and Lewis Wilkerson his securities. And Andrew Evens's recognizance to appear & prosecute and give evidence behalf State.

p.238 State v James Callison. Murder. John A Montgomery solicitor general and defendant at the Bar. Jury Waller Edwards, John Lavender, Charles Brady, Joseph Harwood, David Hannah, George Gillespie, John Thompson, Charles Mitchell, Robert Gamble, William Johnson, Samuel Craig, James Snelson from verdict are respited until tomorrow; prisoner remanded to jail.

Joseph Andersons lessee v William Murphree. Cause is continued.

p.239 Court adjourned until tomorrow morning 9 oclock.   Charles F Keith

Thursday 20th Sept. Present the honorable Charles F Keith, Judge &c.

State v James Callison. Murder. Jury find dft not guilty; prisoner is discharged.

John Miller's lessee v Robert Gamble & John Moore. Grant plf's atty leave to consolidate the writs in this cause so as to correspond with original declaration; same is done on payment of costs of the amendment.

Court adjourned until tomorrow morning 9 O'clock.   Charles F Keith

p.240 Friday 21st Sept. Present the honorable Charles F Keith, Judge &c.

State v Nancy Nelson. Forfeiture entered at last Term for failure to attend

SEPTEMBER 1821

as witness State v Jonathan Crawford is set aside on payment of costs.
    John Miller's lessee v Robert Gamble & John Moore. Cause continued.
    John Miller's lessee v John Moore. Dft came not; plf recovers his term in the premises for which he may have a writ of possession and further, he recovers of defendant his costs about his suit in this behalf expended.

p.241   State v James Barns. Recognizance of Michall W Bustard $500, condition he appear next Term to prosecute and give evidence behalf state against James Barns.
    James G Martin et al lessee v Richard Fen with notice to James Ferguson. From affidavit of Alexander Ferguson, he is admitted to defend in room of sd Fen & James Ferguson tenant in possession, Robert Bell his security.
    Joseph Danforth v Jonathan Fine. Continued till next Court.
    On motion of John Locke Clerk of this Court Daniel Rawlings is permitted to qualify as his deputy; sd Daniel takes oath of office.

p.242   James G Martin et al lessee v Benjamin Erwin. Richard G Waterhouse is admitted to defend jointly with tenant in possession, Daniel Rawlings security.
    Same v Samuel Ferguson. Richard G Waterhouse is admitted to defend jointly with the tenant in possession, Daniel Rawlings security.
    Same v Charles Brady. Richard G Waterhouse is admitted to defend jointly with the tenant in possession, Daniel Rawlings security.

p.243   James G Martin et al lessee v Isaac Rush. Richard G Waterhouse is admitted to defend jointly with the tenant in possession, Daniel Rawlings security.
    James G Nowlin et al lessee v James Gallent. Richd G Waterhouse [as above]
    James G Martin et al lessee v Charles Ryan, tenant. Richard G Waterhouse is admitted to defend jointly with tenant in possession, Daniel Rawlings his security.
    James G Martin &c Lessee v Landon Rector. Richd G Waterhouse [as above]

p.244   Same v James Moore. Richard G Waterhouse [as above]
    Same v John Barnett. Richard G Waterhouse [as above]
    Same v James Montgomery. Richard G Waterhouse [as above]
    Same v Thomas Scott. Richard G Waterhouse [as above]
    Same v Josiah Earp. Richard G Waterhouse [as above]
    Same v James C Mitchell. Richard G Waterhouse [as above]

p.245   James G Martin & others v James Willson. Richard G Waterhouse [as above]
    Same v Thomas Jack. Richard G Waterhouse [as above]
    Same v Lewis Wilkinson. Richard G Waterhouse [as above]
    Same v Arthur Fulton. Richard G Waterhouse [as above]
    Same v Isaac Love. Richard G Waterhouse [as above]
    Same v James McConel. Richard G Waterhouse [as above]

p.246   James G Martin & others v Moses Furguson. Richard G Waterhouse [as above]
    Same v Henry Walton. Richard G Waterhouse [as above]
    Same v Bermilian Holoway. Richard G Waterhouse [as above]
    Same v Jeremiah Howarton. Richard G Waterhouse [as above]
    Same v John Wasson. Richard G Waterhouse [as above]

p.247   James G Martin et al lessee v Wm Floyd. Richard G Waterhouse [as above]
    Same v John Knight. Richard G Waterhouse [as above]
    Same v Spilsby Dyer. Richard G Waterhouse [as above]
    Same v David Hanna. Richard G Waterhouse [as above]

p.248   Same v James Swan. Richard G Waterhouse [as above]
    Same v John Lavender. Richard G Waterhouse [as above]
    Same v Archibald McEntire. Richard G Waterhouse [as above]
    Same v Martin O Harrow. Richard G Waterhouse [as above]

SEPTEMBER 1821

p.249   James G Martin et al lessee v Joshua Hanna. Plfs by atty dismiss suit; dft recovers of plf his costs about his suit in this behalf expended.

J G Martin et al lessee v Bryant Breeding. Grant leave to plffs to amend declaration so that name of Byrum Breeding be inserted in room of Bryant Breeding.

James G Martin et al lessee v Palatiah Chilton & John McClure. Admit Palatial Chilton to defend for himself and John McClure in lieu of Richard Fen the causual ejector.

Grand and traverse jury discharged.

p.250   State v James Calison. Solicitor general moved judgment against dft for costs in this cause; it being opinion of Court that there exists strong presumption of guilt of defendant, it is considered that he pay costs in this behalf expended, whereupon William Gillespie confesses judgment with defendant for sd costs.

James G Martin et al lessee v John Ferguson. Same v Charles Woodward. Same v John Woodward. Same v Jacob Beck. Same v Peter Daniels. Same v Peter Majors. Same v Charles Mitchell. Same v William Hornsby. Same v Lewis Collins. Same v Saml Apple-gate. Same v Robert Beard. Same v John Conley & Ann Conley. Same v Roger Rees. Same v Wm Kennedy. Same v Wm Noblet. Same v Walter Edwards. Same v John McCory. Same v Jonathan Fine. Same v Thomas Kelly. Same v David Oatswell. Same v William Johnson. Same v John Moore. Same v John Hill. Same v Thomas Godbehere. Same v Moses Paul. Each of aforenamed defendants on whom notice served by Sheriff on their motion are admitted to defend separately in room of Richard Fen the casual ejector.

James G Martin et al lessee v Benjamin Erwin & Richard G Waterhouse. Dfts by counsel tendered Bill/exceptions to opinion of Court.

p.251   Jas G Martin et al lessee v Saml Ferguson & Richd G Waterhouse. [as above]
          Same v Charles Brady & Richard G Waterhouse. [as above]
          Same v Isaac Rush & Richard G Waterhouse. [as above]
          Same v James Gallent & Richard G Waterhouse. [as above]
          Same v Charles Ryan & Richard G Waterhouse. [as above]
p.252   Jas G Martin et al lessee v Landon Rector & Richd G Waterhouse. [as above]
          Same v James Moore & Richard G Waterhouse. [as above]
          Same v John Barnett & Richard G Waterhouse. [as above]
          Same v James Montgomery & Richard G Waterhouse. [as above]
          Same v Thomas Scott & Richard G Waterhouse. [as above]
          Same v Josiah Earp & Richard G Waterhouse. [as above]
p.253   Jas G Martin et al lessee v Jas C Mitchell & Richd G Waterhouse. [as above]
          Same v James Wilson & Richard G Waterhouse. [as above]
          Same v Thomas Jack & Richard G Waterhouse. [as above]
          Same v Lewis Wilkinson & Richard G Waterhouse. [as above]
          Same v Arthur Fulton & Richard G Waterhouse. [as above]
          Same v Isaac Love & Richard G Waterhouse. [as above]
p.254   Jas G Martin et al lessee v Jas Wallace[?] & Richd G Waterhouse. [as above]
          Same v Moses Furguson & Richard G Waterhouse. [as above]
          Same v Henry Walton & Richard G Waterhouse. [as above]
          Same v Bremillian Holloway & Richard G Waterhouse. [as above]
          Same v Jeremiah Howarton & Richard G Waterhouse. [as above]
          Same v William Floyd & Richard G Waterhouse. [as above]
          Same v John Wasson & Richard G Waterhouse. [as above]
p.255   James G Martin et al lessee v John Knight & Richd G Waterhouse. [as above]
          Same v Spilsby Dire & Richard G Waterhouse. [as above]

SEPTEMBER 1821

       Same v David Hannah and Richard G Waterhouse. [as above]
       Same v James Swan & Richard G Waterhouse. [as above]
       Same v John Lavender & Richard G Waterhouse. [as above]
       Same v Archibald McEntire & Richard G Waterhouse. [as above]
p.256 Jas G Martin et al lessee v Martin OHarra & Richd G Waterhouse. [as above]
       W T Lewis's heirs lessee v Richd G Waterhouse. Same v Same. Same v Christopher Coats. Agent of plaintiff Thomas Hopkins; these suits are set aside and as to case against Christopher Coats, costs of which that have accrued Daniel Rawlings confesses judgment for, considered by Court that lessor of plf pay to defendants their costs about their defence at this term expended.

       James G Martin et al lessee v William Noblet. From affidavit of John Knight he is admitted to defend jointly with the tenant in possession, John Holland security in sum of $500.

p.257 Alexander Forbes v Rachel Forbes. For Divorce. It appearing that proclamation and publication had been made, and subpoena had been returned not found by sheriff, that petitioner has resided in Rhea County about ten years, that he intermarried with dft on 4 January 1804 in Rockbridge County, Virginia, that the dft Rachel Forbes has for a few years past given herself up to lewd practices and at last eloped with William Goodwin, that petitioner pursued sd dft and found her in Wilson County residing with sd Goodwin in adultery, that petitioner desired dft to return with him to his home but she refused to do so and went away with Goodwin, whereupon it is ordered by Court that the bonds of matrimony be dissolved.

       In the following causes at the suits of James G Martin and others before the defendants John Conley and Ann Conley jointly & Richard G Waterhouse separately for himself upon whom notice appears to have been served, come into Court and on motion are admitted to defend in thse suits in room of Richard Fen:

p.258 James G Martin et al lessee v Ptiah Chilton.
       Same v Rezin & Daniel Rawlings.
       Same v William Noblet & John Knight.
       Same v John Ferguson.
       Same v Jacob Beck.
       Same v Lewis Collins.
       Same v John Conley & Ann Conley.
       Same v William Kennedy.
       Same v Alexander Ferguson.
       Same v Charles Mitchell.
       Same v John Woodward & Charles Woodward.
p.259 James G Martin et al lessee v Peter Majors.
       Same v John Moore.
       Same v Walter Edwards.
       Same v John Macoy.
       Same v David Caldwell.
       Same v Robert Beard.
       Same v Peter Daniel.
       Same v Samuel Applegate.
       Same v William Johnson.
       Same v John Hill.
       Same v Jonathan Fine.
p.260 James G Martin et al lessee v William Hornsby.
       Same v Roger Ruse[Rual?]

MARCH 1822

Same v Richard G Waterhouse.
Same v Moses Paul.
Same v Thomas Kelly. In the progress of the last twenty eight causes the defendants by attorneys took Bills of exception to the opinion of the Court which were signed and ordered to be made part of the record.
Court adjourned till tomorrow morning 7 Oclock. Charles F Keith

p.261 Saturday 22d Sept. Present the honor Charles F Keith, Esqr, Judge, &c.
James G Martin et al lessee v Charles Woodward and [blank] Same v John Woodward. Dfts by attorneys agree with Court, suits are consolidated and sd defendants permitted to defend jointly, cause continued till next Term.
Ordered all causes in this Court stand continued.
Court adjourned until third Monday in March next. Charles F Keith

p.262 Circuit Court in Court House in Washington on third Monday in March 1822 and 18th day of said month. Present the Honorable Charles F Keith, Judge &c.
Sheriff Woodson Francis returned he hath summoned John Hill, Matthias Benson, William Alexander, John Cozby, Jacob Glover, Jesse Poe, Samuel Gamble, Benjamin Bond, Jesse Roddy, Robert Walker, Robert Locke, Adam W Caldwell, Edmund Bean, John Barnett, Isaac Brazleton, Joseph Williams, Elihu D Armstrong, Abraham Howard, Edward Gray, Isaac Love, Martin Atchly, William Kennedy, James Coulter, Richard G Waterhouse.
Grand Jury: Richard G Waterhouse foreman, James Coulter, Martin Atchly, William Kennedy, Isaac Brazleton, John Hill, Jacob Glover, John Cozby, William Alexander, Robert Walker, Jesse Poe, Edward Gray, John Barnett.
Constable Orvell Pain is sworn to attend the Grand Jury.
Excuse Abraham Howard from further attendance as a juror.
p.263 Deed Charles McClung to Alexander Ferguson dated 10th October 1821 land north of Tennessee River and west of Watson Ridge acknowledged.
Commission signed by Governor William Carroll at Murfreesboro 29 December 1821 wherein Thomas G Campbell is apptd solicitor general until the end of next session of the General Assembly for the 11th solicitorial district of sd State was produced in open court and sd Thomas G Campbell took the oaths of office.
Samuel Gamble and Matthias Benson summoned as jurors came not; fined $5 each unless sufficient cause to contrary be shewn at next term of this Court.
Traverse jurors: Robert Locke, Jesse Roddy, Edmund Bean, Isaac Love, Joseph Williams, Adam W Caldwell, Benjamin Bond, Elihu D Armstrong.
Court adjourned untill Tomorrow 9 O'Clock. Charles F Keith

p.264 Tuesday 29th March 1822. Present the honorable Charles F Keith, Judge.
Isaac Love, Adam W Caldwell, Benjamin Bond, Elihu D Armstrong, jurors of original panel came not; fined $5 each.
Thomas N Clarks lessee v Azariah David. Eject. Jury Adam W Caldwell, Joseph Williams, Grief Howarton, Cumberland Rector, Jesse Roddy, George Gilespie, John

MARCH 1822

Moore, Edmund Bean, John Parking, Thomas Piper, Jacob Brown, Robert Locke who retired to consult of their verdict.

Deed William McCrary to Irby Holt[Hoth?] dated 18 Jan 1821 for 200[?] acres proven by Peter Donnell and Robert Walker.

Deed James Upton to Irby Holt dated 29 January 1821 for 160 acres proven by Peter Donnell.

The sheriff summoned John Parker as a juror for the day; called but came not; fined $5 for contempt.

p.265 Josiah Danforth v Jonathan Fine. Cause is continued till next term.

Lewis Ross's lessee v James Cowan & John L McCarty. Parties in person; the lessor of the plf directed this suit be dismissed; dfts pay half the costs.

Hugh Beaty v Pleasant Dawson. On affidavit of Robert S Mahan, the defendant's agent, this cause is continued until next term.

Excuse Elihu D Armstrong for fine assessed this morning for nonattendance.

p.266 James G Martin et al lessee vs John Ferguson. Same v Benjamin Erwin and Richard G Waterhouse. Same v Charles & John Woodward. Same v James Gallant & Richd G Waterhouse. Same v Alexander Ferguson. Same v James Moore & Richd G Waterhouse. Same v Jacob Beck. Same v James Montgomery & Richd G Waterhouse. Same v Peter Daniel. Same v John Barnett & Richard G Waterhouse. Same v Peter Majors. Same v Archibald McIntire & Richard G Waterhouse. Same v James C Mitchell & Richard G Waterhouse. Same v Thomas Scott & Richd G Waterhouse. Same v Henry Walton & Richd G Waterhouse. Same v Charles Mitchell. Same v James McCanse & Richd G Waterhouse. Same v William Hornsby. Same v Charles Ryon & R G Waterhouse. Same v Lewis Collins. Same v Josiah Earp and Richard G Waterhouse. Same v Saml Applegate. Same v Arthur Fulton & Richd G Waterhouse. Same v Robert Beard. Same v Lewis Wilkenson & Richd G Waterhouse. Same v John & Anne Condley. Same v William Floyd & Richd G Waterhouse. Same v Roger Rees. Same v Charles Brady & Richdard G Waterhouse. Same v William Kenedy. Same v Spilsby Dyre & Richd G Waterhouse. Same v William Noblet & John Night. Same v Jeremiah Howerton & Richd G Waterhouse. Same v Walter Edwards. Same v Isaac Love & Richard G Waterhouse. Same v John Macoy. Same v James Wilson & Richard G Waterhouse. Same v Jonathan Fine. Same v John Night & Richd G Waterhouse. Same v Palatiah Chilton. Same v Rezin Rawlings & Daniel Rawlings. Same v Samuel Ferguson & Richd G Waterhouse. Same v Thomas Kelly. Same v Isaac Rush & Richard G Waterhouse. Same v David Caldwell. Same v Landon Rector & Richd G Waterhouse. Same v William Johnson. Same v Moses Ferguson & Richd G Waterhouse. Same v John Moore. Same v Bermilian Holloway & Richd G Waterhouse.

p.267 James G Martin et al lessee v John Hill. Same v Thomas Jack & Richard G Waterhouse. Same v Thos Godbehere. Same v John Wassen & Richd G Waterhouse. Same v Moses Paul. Same v James Swan & R G Waterhouse. Same v David Hannah & R G Waterhouse. Same v Martin Oharow & Richard G Waterhouse. Same v John Lavender & Richd G Waterhouse. Same v Richard G Waterhouse; came the parties by attornies, and for reasons appearing to Court from the affidavit of James G Martin one of the lessors of the plaintiff commissions are awarded sd plaintiffs in each of the foregoing causes to take the depositions of Littlepage Sims of Dallas County, Alabama, Armsteed Moorhead of Warren County, Kentucky, Berry Green of Alabama, Alexander McMillen, John Dudley, Robert Smith, William B Reese, James Craig, Hugh L White, Charles McClung and Edward Scott of Knox County, James Trimble of Davidson County, Hugh Dunlap and Thomas Brown of Roane County, Samuel Gantt of Blount County, Woodson Francis of Rhea County, Micha Taul of Wayne County, and John E King of Cumberland County, Kentucky.

MARCH 1822

p.268   Carters heirs lessee v Robert Benson[Barson?]. Dft will give in evidence on the trial of this cause the title[?] of his improvement in payment of the costs.
   John Millers lessee to Robert Gamble. Return J Meigs undertakes for the lessor of the plaintiff to pay costs if the lessor fail to.
   Court adjourned untill Tomorrow morning 9 O'Clock.   Charles F Keith

p.269   Wednesday 20th March. Present the Honorable Charles F Keith, Esq.
   Deed Joshua Smith to Colonel James C Mitchell lot 2 in Washington proved by James Berry and Miller Francis.
   John Spears' lessee v William Blackwood. From affidavit of Lewis Ross that he is landlord of the sd Blackwood on whom notice has been served, sd Ross is admitted to defend in room of casual ejector George Gillespie and Thomas C Hindman in person undertake to pay costs & condemnation for Ross.
   Thomas N Clarks lessee v Azariah David. Jury sworn yesterday find dft guilty of trespass and ejectment in plfs declaration; assess plfs damages to 6¢ besides his costs.
   Fine of Edward Dean assessed yesterday for not attending as juror when summoned by the sheriff is set aside.
   John Spears lessee v Benjamin Bond. Notice of ejectment served on Bond.
   State v Robert H Prine. Continued to next term. Recognizance of sd Prine $100, George Arnold and Isaac L Hurnbose[?] each in person acknowledged securities.
p.271   And John Leftwich recognizance, to prosecute and give evidence on part of the State, John R Garland and Benjamin Konner[Karsner?] his securities.
p.272   State v Jacob Wassum. Thomas J Campbell solicitor general of 11th district; Jacob Wassum in proper person says he is guilty. Fined $10 and ordered into custody untill the fine and costs are paid. Conrad Wassum confesses judgment conjointly with defendant for fine and costs whereupon judgment entered for same.
   State v Joseph Francis. Defendant in proper person. Jury William Noblet, James Stewart, Cumberland Rector, Isaac Brazleton, Azariah David, Daniel D Armstrong, John Moore, Thomas Kelly, John Woodward, Adam W Caldwell, Robert Walker, James Swan find dft not guilty.
p.273   Josiah Danforth v Jonathan Fine. Time given them to plead.
   State v Jonathan Crawford. Dft in proper person. Jury Jonathan Fine, James Coulter, Daniel Walker, William Kennedy, Edward Gray, John Cozby, Thomas Thompson, Byrum Breeding, Jesse Roddy, George Gilespie, Jesse Thompson, Benjamin Bond; jury retired from Bar under care of an officer until tomorrow.
   James G Martin et al lessee v John Ferguson. Same v Charles & John Woodward. Same v Alexander Ferguson. Same v Jacob Beck. Same v Peter Donel. Same v Peter Majors. Same v Charles Mitchell. Same v William Hornsby. Same v Lewis Collins. Same v Samuel Applegate. Same v Robert Beard. Same v John Conley & Ann Conley. Same v Roger Reese. Same v William Kennedy. Same v William Noblet & John Knight. Same v Walter Edwards. Same v John McCoy. Same v Jonathan Fine. Same v
p.274   Betiah Hilton. Same v Rezin Rawlings & Daniel Rawlings. Same v Thomas Kelly and David Caldwell. Same v William Johnson. Same v John Moore. Same v John Hill. Same v Thomas Godbehere. Same v Moses Paul. Same v [blank] From affidavit of James G Martin one of the lessors of the plaintiff in above causes a fair trial cannot be had in this county. Venue changed to Bledsoe County.
   Court adjourned untill tomorrow morning 9 OClock.   Charles F Keith

41

MARCH 1822

p.275　Thursday 21 March. Present the Honorable Charles F Keith Judge.

James G Martin et al lessee v Benjamin Erwin & Richard G Waterhouse, James Gallent & Richard G Waterhouse. Same v James Moore & Richard G Waterhouse. Same v James Montgomery and Richard G Waterhouse. Same v John Barnett & R G Waterhouse. Same v Archibald McEntire & R G Waterhouse. Same v James P Mitchell & R G Waterhouse. Same v Thomas Scott and R G Waterhouse. Same v Henry Walton & R G Waterhouse. Same v James McCanse & R G Waterhouse. Same v Charles Ryan and R G Waterhouse. Same v Josiah Earp & R G Waterhouse. Same v Arthur Fulton & R G Waterhouse. Same v Lewis Wilkinson and R G Waterhouse. Same v William Floyd & R G Waterhouse. Same v Charles Brady & R G Waterhouse. Same v Spile B Dyre & R G Waterhouse. Same v Jeremiah Howerton & R G Waterhouse. Same v Isaac Love & R G Waterhouse. The same v James Willson & R G Waterhouse. Same v John Knight & R G Waterhouse. Same v Samuel Ferguson & R G Waterhouse. Same v Isac Rush and R G Waterhouse. Same v Landon Rector and R G Waterhouse. Same v Moses Ferguson & R G Waterhouse. Same v Barnett Holloway & R G Waterhouse. Same v Thomas Jack & R G Waterhouse. Same v John Wassum & R G Waterhouse. Same v James Swan & R G Waterhouse. Same v David Hannah and R G Waterhouse. Same v Martin O Barrow & R G Waterhouse. The same v John Lavender & R G Waterhouse. Same v R G Waterhouse. It appearing to Court from affidavit of James G Martin and of lessors of plaintiffs that an impartial trial cannot be had in Rhea County, and on affidavit of Richard G Waterhouse that he cannot have an impartial trial in Bledsoe County, Marion, Blunt or any county of West Tennessee, and farther appearing from affidavit of said James G Martin that he cannot have an impartial
p.276　trial in Roan, McMinn, Monroe, Hambleton, Knox, & Morgan, the trial is to be held in Anderson County.

Joseph Andersons lessee v William Murphree. Continued untill next Term.

State v Joseph Francis. Solicitor general moved Court to tax defendant with costs of prosecution of which he was yesterday acquitted by verdict of jury but the Court refused so to do.

State v Joseph Francis. Nolle prosequi entered. County pays costs.
p.277　There is no page 277. Next page is
p.278　State v John Russell. Grand larceny, horse stealing. Solicitor general T F Campbell Esq. Nolle prosequi entered; clerk to pay costs.

State v John Russell. Grand larceny, horse stealing. [as above]
p.279　Robert Gamble v Alexander Robinson and Andrew Cowan. Parties in person; plf dismisses his action; dft recovers of plf one half of costs of suit.

State v Jesse Upton. Thomas F Campbell solicitor general. Dft failed to comply with conditions of his recognizance whereby he was bound with William Shelton, Jesse Jones, Charles Higdon, John Boddy, John Allen, Lester Hains, Archibald Hains and Cornelius McCannon; condition- to bring into Court at a day long past Joseph Francis to answer charge of state agt him of horse stealing found by the Grand Jury of Marion County. State recovers agt sd Jesse Upton $250 and costs.
p.280　State v Jesse Upton. Dft failed to comply with conditions of his recognizance heretofore made whereby he was bound with William Shelton, Jesse Higdon, Jesse Jones, Charles Higdon, John Bodely, John Allen, Luster Hains and Archibald Hains and Cornelius McCannon to bring into court at a day long past Joseph Francis to answer charge of horse stealing exhibited against him by the State in bill of indictment found by Grand Jury of Marion County. State recovers agt Jesse Upton $250 & costs.

State v Martin O Harrow. Alias Capias awarded.
State v James Barns. Plurius Capias awarded.

MARCH 1822

p.281   State v Jonathan Crawford. Jury yesterday respited, say dft Jonathan Crawford did feloniously take and carry away goods and chattels as charged; value of sd goods is under $10. Dft ordered in to custody of sheriff.
          State v James Stewart. Recognizance of James Stewart, James C Mitchel and William Alexander security, condition Stewart appears at September court.
p.282   James G Martin and others lessee v John Ferguson. Same v Benjamin Erwin and R G Waterhouse. Same v Charles & John Woodward. Same v James Gallant & R G Waterhouse. Same v Alexander Ferguson. Same v James Moore and R. G. Waterhouse. Same v Jacob Beck. Same v James Montgomery & R G Waterhouse. Same v Peter Daniel. Same v John Barnett & R G Waterhouse. Same v Peter Majors. Same v Archibald McEntire & R G Waterhouse. Same v James C Mitchell and R G Waterhouse. Same v Thomas Scott & R G Waterhouse. Same v Henry Walton and R G Waterhouse. Same v Charles Mitchell. Same v James McCanse & R G Waterhouse. Same v William Hornsby. Same v Charles Ryan & R G Waterhouse. Same v Lewis Collins. Same v Josiah Carp & R G Waterhouse. Same v Samuel Applegate. Same v Arthur Fulton & R G Waterhouse. Same v Robert Beard. Same v Lewis Wilkenson & R G Waterhouse. Same v John Conley & Ann Conley. Same v William Floyd & R G Waterhouse. Same v Roger Ruse. Same v Charles Brady & R G Waterhouse. Same v William Kennedy. Same v Spels B Dyer & R G Waterhouse. Same v William Noblet & John Knight. Same v Jeremiah Howarton & R G Waterhouse. Same v Walter Edwards.
p.283   Same v Isaac Love & R G Waterhouse. Same v John McCoy. Same v James Willson & R G Waterhouse. Same v Jonathan Fine. Same v John Knight & R G Waterhouse. Same v Peletiah Chilton. Same v Rezin Rawlings & Daniel Rawlings. Same v Samuel Ferguson & R G Waterhouse. Same v Thomas Kelly. Same v Isaac Rush & R G Waterhouse. Same v David Catsworth. Same v Landon Rector & R G Waterhouse. Same v William Johnson. Same v Moses Ferguson & R G Waterhouse. Same v John Moore. Same v Bermillion Holloway & R G Waterhouse. Same v John Hill. Same v Thomas Jack & R G Waterhouse. Same v Thomas Godbehast. Same v John Wassun & R G Waterhouse. Same v Moses Paul. Same v James Swan & R G Waterhouse. Same v David Hannah & R G Waterhouse. Same v Martin O Harrow & R G Waterhouse. Same v John Lavender & R G Waterhouse and the same against Richard G Waterhouse. Came the parties by attorneys. On affidavit of James G Martin one of the lessors of plaintiffs to take depositions from all above causes of Elias Ferguson a citizen of Mississippi State but now in Rhea County, also depositions of Azariah David, John Thompson, James Nail, George W Riggle, Miller Francis of Rhea County, Alexander Ferguson of Marion, John Smith[?] & Samuel McClelland of Bledsoe County, and Robert Gamble of Rhea County.
p.284   James W[?] Rogers v William York. Jury Richard G Waterhouse, James Coulter, Martin Atchley, Isaac Brazleton, John Hill, Jacob Stover, John Cozby, William Alexander, Robert Walker, Jesse Poe, Edward Gray, John Barnett. Jury discharged; plf no further prosecutes his suit. Dft recovers agt plf his costs of defence.
          Richard G Waterhouse lessee v Frenchs representatives & George Menes. From affidavit of William Smith guardian for French's representatives, cause continued.
          George Walker v John Hill. Continued untill next term.
p.285   Richard G Waterhouse lessee v William Murphree. Continued.
          Charles McClung & James Cozby to Miller Francis. Deed dated 7 Sept 1820 for 400 acres in Hambleton County ackd by Charles McClung one of the grantors.
          William McCray to Erby Holt. Deed William McCray to Erby Holt for 200 acres in Rhea County proved on Monday by Peter Daniel is this day fully proved by Jesse Thompson the other subscribing witness.
          State v Jonathan Crawford. Dft's recognizance, Samuel Low and Samuel Oxsheer securities.

MARCH 1822

p.286　Lewis Ross's lessee v John Spears. Plf to take deposition of George Gillespie and others, giving time and place to James Williams or J L McCarly.
　　Lewis Ross's lessee v John Spears. Cause ordered to Knox County for trial.
　　John Millers lessee v Robert Gamble. Venue changed to Knox County.
　　John Spears's lessee v Lewis Ross. Venue changed to Knox County.
p.287　John Spears's lessee v Benjamin Bond. Venue changed to Knox County.
　　Court adjourned until tomorrow morning 10 oclock. Charles F Keith.

p.288　Friday 22d March. Present the Honourable Charles F Keith, Judge.
　　John A Smith to Miller Francis. Bill/sale for five Negro slaves proven by William S Leuty and Woodson Francis.
　　Richd G Waterhouse lessee v Richard Fen with notice to John A Smith. From affidavit of Thomas Campbell, William Whitfield, Needham Whitfield, Hepzibah Whitfield, Edmund Whitfield, Edith Whitfield, Elizabeth Whitfield, Gains & Bons Whitfield, John T Bryan, Rachel Bryan, Lucy Wooton, Benjamin Hatch and Sally Hatch heirs of Needham Whitfield are admitted to defend in lieu of tenant in possession, line heretofore run between land of sd heirs and Richard G Waterhouse, time given until next Term to plead and give security.
　　Joseph Andersons lessee v William Murphree. From affidavit of Miller Francis commissions awarded to plf to take depositions of David Stuart, Isaac Allen, John Stuart, William Garret of Cocke County, & John Winlow of Roane County.
p.289　Also commission awarded dft to take deposition of Thomas Hopkins of Warren County, giving Miller Hains notice of time and place, also deposition of Samuel Walker of Roane County and Abraham Swaggerty of Monroe County.
　　Waterhouses lessee v William Murphree. Dft to take depositions of Samuel Walker of Roane County, Abraham Swaggerty of Munroe County, and Thomas Hopkins of Warren County.
　　Richd G Waterhouse for himself & others v James G Martin, William Cocke and others. Equity. William Cocke one of the dfts is not an inhabitant of this State but resides in Mississippi, ordered that sd William appear and file his answer to bill of complaint.
p.290　Roper & Hopkins lessee v John Moore. Robert Locke undertakes for dft.
　　Holderman et al v Creel & Neilson admrs. Change of venue. Continued.
　　Thomas N Clarks lessee v Azariah David. New trial awarded, dft pays costs. Dft to take depositions of Charles McClung & John Williams of Knox County and
p.291　William Brazeale of Roane County giving notice to William Lyon of time and place and to Thomas N Clark of taking sd Breazeale's deposition.
　　State v Jonathan Crawford. New trial is granted to dft, Jonathan Crawford, Matthias Crawford & Samuel Oxsheer securities. Also Richardson H Galewood's recog-
p.292　nizance, condition he appear to give evidence agt Jonathan Crawford. Also recognizance of Jesse B Sherrell to appear next term to give evidence agt Jonathan Crawford.
　　Fine Sheriff Woodson Francis $10 for contempt in letting jury sworn in suit of State agt Jonathan Crawford disperse after they were committed to his charge.
　　Lewis's heirs lessee v Richd G Waterhouse. Two cases. From affidavit of Thomas Hopkins plf to take depositions of Alexander Outlaw of Dallis County Alabama, David Stuart, Isaac Allen, John Stuart, William Garret of Cocke County and John Winton of Roane County.
p.293　James G Martin et als lessee v Byrum Breeden. From affidavit of James G

SEPTEMBER 1822

Martin one of the lessors of plf that impartial trial cannot be had in this County, order cause be held in Bledsoe County. Lessors of plf take depositions of Berry Greene, State of Alabama, Little Page Simms of Dallas County, Alabama, giving dft thirty days notice, Armstead Moorehad, John E King, Micha Taul of Kentucky; Alexander McMillan, John Dutley, Robert Smith, William B Reese, James Craig, Hugh L White, Charles McClung, Edward Scott of Knox County; James Kimble of Davidson Co, Hugh Dunlap & Thomas Brown of Roane County, Samuel M Gantt of Blount County; Azariah David, John Thompson, James Nail, George W Riggle, Miller Francis, Woodson Francis, Robert Gamble of Rhea County; Elias Ferguson of Rhea County.

p.294 John Rentfrow v John H Rodes. Attachment. Dft not inhabitant of this State; prosecution stayed untill next term. Publication to be made in Knoxville Register.
    Fine of Woodson Francis for letting jury disperse is set aside.
    Order all fines assessed agt jurors to be set aside.
p.295 Thomas Kelly ads Heirs of John Ramsey. Order of March Term 1821 revived.
Pending causes continued.
    Court adjourned.   Charles F Keith.

p.296 Monday, Septr 16th. Present the Honourable Charles F Keith, Judge.
    Sheriff Woodson Francis summoned Robert Parks, William Kennedy, Henry Walton, John Ferguson Senr, Beriah Frazier, Robert Bell, Matthias Benson, Samuel Gamble, William Johns, Edward Templeton not found, James McDonnald, Patrick Martin, Cain Able, William Howard, Samuel McDaniel, Robert Faris, Arthur Fulton, John Robinson, Jesse Reese, Lewis Wilkerson, John Hill, Jonathan Fine, [illegible] Gibson not found, John Lea, Robert Gamble, William Hornsby.
    Grand Jury: Robert Parks foreman, William Johns, John Lea, Robert Gamble, Samuel McDonnell, Cain Able, John Hill, James McDonald, Beriah Frazier, Samuel Gamble, William Howard, Jonathan Fine, Matthias Benson.
    Constable Shepherd Brazelton sworn to attend the Grand Jury.
p.297 Traverse Jurors. Answered: Patrick Martin, Willliam Kennedy, Robert Bell. Failed to answer: John Ferguson, Henry Walton, Arthur Fulton, John Robinson, Jesse Reese, Lewis Wilkerson, William Hornsby.
    Thomas F Campbell Esqr Solicitor General for the 11th solicitorial district takes oath to support the constitution of the United States, to support the constitution of Tennessee, oath to prohibit duelling, and oath of office.
    Fine against Samuel Gamble for not attending as a Juror at last term set aside on Gambles paying costs.
    Richard Waterhouse to Charles McClung. Deed dated 1 August 1814 for land in Rhea County acknowledged by grantor.
    Andrew Ramsey v Thomas Kelley. Plf by atty orders Feiri Facias quashed.
p.298 George Starns to Charles McClung. Deed dated 28 August 1816 is proved by Richard G Waterhouse a subscribing witness who saw George Starns acknowledge same; Miller Francis swears Nicholas Starns, the other witness, resides in Alabama.
    Forfeiture against Matthias Benson for failure to attend as a Juror at last Term is sett aside without costs.
    Thomas N Charles lessee v Azariah David. Plf to take deposition of Daniel Rawlings this evening or tomorrow morning at his own house.

SEPTEMBER 1822

Richd G Waterhouse to Alexander Ferguson. Deed dated 20 July 1822 for 45 acres on Clear Creek in Rhea County was acknowledged in open court.

p.299 William Henry to Miller Francis. Deed dated 16 May 1808 for two tracts of land, one in Roane County of 1000 acres on Poplar Creek; the other in Anderson County on east fork of Poplar Creek 200 acres; Col James P Mitchell, Azariah David and Woodson Francis, acquainted with signature of William Henry the grantor and also with the handwriting of John Henry the subscribing witness, say the signatures are those of grantor and witness; likewise the attestation of Charles Henry the other witness, and that sd grantor and witnesses are dead.

Daniel Rawlings and others to John Kennedy. Deed dated 16 Sept 1822 for 90 acres in Green County proved by James Berry and Samuel White subscribing witnesses as to Daniel Rawlings, Rezin Rawlings, William Kennedy, Allen Kennedy, George Kennedy, and John McClure.

Commission issued to take examination of Mary Rawlings, Polly Ann Rawlings, and Peggy McClure femme coverts before William Anderson & Thomas J Campbell Esqrs touching execution of a deed for land in Green County.

p.300 Court adjourned.

Tueday Septr 17th. Present the honourable Charles F Keith, Judge.

Thomas N Clarks lessee v Azariah David. Ejectment. Continued.

Henry Owens v David Crun. Continued.

Richard G Waterhouses lessee v Frenches Heirs and George Mainas. Suit dismissed whereupon Thomas N Clarke by William Lyon confessed judgment for costs.

p.301 George Wather v John Hill. Cause continued.

Holderman et al v William Worley. Benja Sherly v William Worley. In these causes parties by attornies by mutual consent continue cause until next term.

Richd G Waterhouses lessee vs William Murphree. Jury Isaac Love, John Rice, David S Williams, John Gillihan, John A Smith, George Henry, James Smith, William Long, Robert Parks, John Lea, William Johns, James McDonald find the defendant not guilty. Dft recovers of lessor of plf his costs in this behalf expended.

Release John Robison from further attendance as a juror at this term.

p.302 Daniel Rawlings and others to John Kenedy. Deed dated 16 Sept 1822 for 90 acres land in Green County. William E Anderson and Thos J Campbell esqrs yesterday apptd to take examination of Polly Rawlings wife of Daniel Rawlings, Polly Anne Rawlings wife of Rezin Rawlings, and Peggy McClure wife of John McClure touching execution of sd deed said execution of deed was done freely & without constraint.

Charles McClung & James Cozby to Richd G Waterhouse. Deed proven by Robert Garrison and Josiah Earp subscribing witnesses thereto and ackd by James Cozby.

John Collins to John Knight Junr. Deed for 62¼ acres dated 24 March 1817. John Johnson a subscribing witness saith the handwriting of both subscribing

p.303 There is no page numbered 303.

p.304 witnesses is his own; believes he subscribed his own name and was authorised to subscribe the name of John Knight Senr as witness though he does not distinctly recollect the fact. He recollects that such a deed was made & he believes at the time it bears date, and he believes sd John Knight is dead.

Thomas N Clarks lessee v Azariah David. Plf to take depositions of William Kelly and George Smith of Madison County, Alabama. Also depositions of Daniel Rawlings and Abraham Howard on tomorrow morning at house of sd Rawlings.

Court adjourned.   Charles F Keith

SEPTEMBER 1822

p.305 Wednesday 18th Sept. Present the honourable Charles F Keith, Judge.
Thomas N Clerk lessee v Azariah David. Revive order to take depositions of Daniel Rawlings and Abraham Howard. Also order of last March for taking deposition of John Williams on part of dft.
State v Robert H Prine. On motion of Thomas J Campbell solicitor general a Nole prosequi is entered. Whereupon Robert H Prine and John Leftwick confess judgment jointly for costs.
Joseph Andersons lessee v William Murphree. Ejectment. Continued.
p.306 Josiah Danforth v Jonathan Fine. Jury John Lea, Robert Gambell, Samuel McDaniel, John Hill, Jas McDonnald, Beriah Frazier, Samuel Gamble, Patrick Martin, Robert Bell, John Ferguson, Henry Walton, Lewis Wilkinson find dft not guilty.
State v Thomas James. Thos F Campbell solicitor genl orders dft discharged.
State v Joseph Thompson. Robbery. Solicitor genl refuses to prefer bill of indictment against sd Joseph Thompson; dft discharged.
p.307 State v John Barns. On motion of Solicitor general, defendant discharged.
State v James Stewart. Stabbing. Thomas F Campbell solicitor genl; James Stewart in proper person. Jury William Hornsby, William Johns, Cain Able, William Howard, Jonathan Fine, William Kennedy, Matthias Benson, Mumford Smith, George W Riggle, Allison[Mison?] Howard, Thomas Woodward, Jos Montgomery find dft guilty of trespass, assault, battery, and stabbing.
p.308 Excuse Arthur Fulton from further attendance as a juror at this term.
State v Martin O Harrow. Nolle prosequi entered.
State v James Barns. Nolle prosequi entered.
Court adjourned.   Charles F Keith

p.309 Thursday Septr 19th. Present the honourable Charles F Keith, Judge.
State v James Stewart. On motion of dft by atty a rule is granted him to shew cause for a new trial to be had thereon.
State v Jonathan Crawford. Cause continued. Recognizance Jonathan Crawford and Matthias Crawford, charge of Grand Larceny. Also came Richard H Gatewood, Nancy Benton, Jesse B Sherrell, John Narimore, Joseph Peters, Samuel C Lowe bond on condition they appear and give evidence against Jonathan Crawford.
p.310 William Bayles v Sion Price. Given time to plead at next Term.
Roger Reese to John Alexander. Deed for 75 acres dated 5 January 1822 proven by Luis Wilkerson.
Miller Francis to Robert Locke. Transfer of Certificate 351 for land in Hiwassee District ackd by Miller Francis.
Carter's heirs lessee vs Robert Patterson. Jury John Lea, Samuel McDaniel, Robert Parks, Beriah Frazier, Henry Walton, William Howard, William Hornsby, Robert Faris, John Moore, Cain Abel, John Hill, James McDonald respited until tomorrow.
Court adjourned.   Charles F Keith

p.311 Friday Sept 20th. Present the Honourable Charles F Keith, Judge.
James P. Mitchell to Thomas Hopkins. Deed dated 3 March 1822 for 150 acres in Rhea County acknowledged by the grantor.
Thomas Hopkins to William S Luty. Deed dated 3 March 1822 for 150 acres in Rhea County acknowledged by the grantor.
Landon Carters heirs lessee v Robert Patterson. Ejectment. Plaintiffs no

SEPTEMBER 1822

further prosecute this suit.
p.312   Excuse John Lea from further attendance as a juror at this term.
    Hugh Batey v Pleasant Davison. Jury Patrick Martin, Wm Kennedy, Robt Bell, John Ferguson, Henry Walton, Lewis Wilkerson, John Hill, Wm Hornsby, Robert Gamble, Saml McDanniell, Cain Able, Robert Parks assess plfs damage to One Dollar & costs.
    Rosses Heirs & Thomas Hopkins lessee v John Moore. Ejectment. Continued.
    Grand jurors discharged from further attendance at this Term.
p.313   Joseph Andersons lessee v William Murphree. Ejectment. Dft to take deposition of Samuel Walker and William Holland of Roane County, also deposition of James Green of Jackson County, Alabama, giving Miller Francis, agent for lessors of plf, ten days previous notice.
    State v Thomas James. State by Thomas J Campbell Esqr solicitor generall refuses to prefer bill/indictment against dft.
    State v Joseph Thompson. Thos J Campbell refusing to prefer bill/indictment agt dft, Thompson is discharged.
p.314   State v John Barns. State by Thos J Campbell who refuses to prefer bill of indictment against the defendant; sd John Barns discharged.
    Court adjourned.   Charles F Keith

Saturday Sept 21st.
    William T Lewis's heirs lessee v Richard G Waterhouse. Ejectment in two causes. Depositions to be taken in behalf dft, giving notice to William E Anderson attorney for lessors of plf.
p.315   Orvill Paine v James Stewart. Case. Dft in person confesses judgment for $12.50 damages besides costs.
    John Rentfrow v John H Roades. Attachment. Thomas Hopkins undertakes for defendant.
    State v James Stewart. Stabbing. Rule for new trial. Defendant in proper person. Defendant fined $15 and confined to common jail of this county 24 hours; dft taken into custody of sheriff; defendant pays all costs of this prosecution.
p.316   Josiah Danforth v Jonathan Fine. Rule for new trial made absolute.
    Thomas Hopkins v John Moore. Ejectment. Plf to take depositions of John H Rodes of Virginia, Robert Moore of Alabama, Samuel Murphey of McMinn County, and Roswell Hale of Marion County, giving defendant notice.
    Richard G Waterhouse v William Murphree. Attendance proven by John Gamble excluded from being taxed in the bill of costs.
p.317   Carters heirs lessee v Robert Patterson. Ejectment. Plf to take deposition of Charles McClung of Knox County, giving dft notice.
    Richard G Waterhouse lessee v John A Smith. Ejectment. On motion of Thomas J Campbell agent for heirs of Needham Whitfield, order that Edmond Whitfield one of sd heirs be admitted to defend in room of tenant in possession in lieu of Richard Fen. Thomas F Campbell undertakes for defendant.
p.318   Richard G Waterhouses lessee v Edmond Whitfield. Dft to take deposition of Alexander Outlaw of Alabama.
    Reuben Callett v Duke Ward. Dft by attorney; plf failing to appear, order plaintiff be nonsuited.
    A Ramsey v Thos Kelley. Motion to quash executions made at this term. Exns quashed; defendants pay all costs in this behalf expended.
p.319   Richd G Waterhouse v James Martin & others. Equity. Publication had been

MARCH 1823

made pursuant to order of last Term of this Court for William Cocke one of the dfts to appear this term & answer complainant, and sd Wm Cocke having failed to answer, consider that sd bill be taken for confessed as to sd William Cocke.

Richard G Waterhouse v James G Martin. Demurrer to complainants bill being argued, cause continued.

Den lessee of Carters Heirs v Robert Patterson. Nonsuit sett aside, cause continued untill next Term.

p.320 Causes not acted on are continued to next Term of this Court.

Court adjourned untill 3d Monday of March Next.   Charles F Keith

Monday March 17th. Circuit Court was opened and held in the courthouse in Washington on third Monday of March, the 17th day of this Instant. Present the honourable Charles F Keith, Judge.

Woodson Francis high sheriff for sd county returned Venire facias: Carson Caldwell, William Long, Robert Taylor, David Caldwell, William Alexander, William Johnson, John Cozby, John Gamble, James McCanse, George W Riggle, William Gamble, Benjamin Marberry, John Mahone, Edward Stuart, Moses Thompson, Wm Kennedy, James Smith, David Campbell, Arthur Fulton, Stephen Winton, John Rice, Beriah Frazier, James Kelley, Robert Locke, Wright Smith, Jesse Poe.

Grand jury: William Kennedy foreman, Arthur Fulton, George W Riggle, Moses
p.321 Thompson, James Kelley, William Johnson, John Cozby, Wm Alexander, William Long, Carson Caldwell, Wright Smith, David Caldwell, James McCanse.

Constable David Shelton sworn and sent to attend the Grand Jury.

Traverse jurors: Edward Stewart, Jesse Poe, Robert Taylor, John Gamble, John Mahone, Stephen Winton, John Rice, Arthur Fulton.

Failed to appear: Robert Locke, Benjamin Marberry, William Gamble.

Den on demise of James Roane et all lessee v Mathew Allen. Same v John Smith. Ejectment. These two suits consolidated, and defendants have leave to plead thereto jointly.

Excuse John Rice from further attendance as a juror at this Term.

Thomas N Clarkes lessee v Azariah David. Ejectment. Jury Robert Taylor, John Gamble, John Mahan, Stephen Winton, Joseph McCall, John H Taber, James Hannah, Thomas Anderson, Elihu D Armstrong, William Walker, William Lewis, Verdingberg
p.322 Thompson respited until tomorrow.

Court adjourned.   Charles F Keith

Tuesday March 18th. Present the Honourable Charles F Keith.

Clerk of this Court produced receipt of Treasurer of East Tennessee for State Tax with which he is chargeable from 1st Octr 1821 to Octr 1822 inclusive; allso a receipt of the Trustee of Rhea County for fines and forfeitures with which he is chargeable from 1st March 1822 up to March 1823 inclusive.

Landon Carter's heirs lessee v Robert Patterson. Agreement of George T Gillespie and Robert Patterson; suit dismissed; costs equally paid by parties except George Gillespies's attendance which is to be paid by George T Gillespie, and James Riddle's attendance to be paid by Robert Patterson. Attest Chas McClung.

MARCH 1823

p.323　Therefore considered by Court that cause be dismissed.

John K Taber and John Mahan jurors who were yesterday sworn to try the issue between Thomas N Clark's lessee and Azariah David and being respited from rendering their verdict until this morning, being solemnly called came not. Fined $5 each for their contempt.

Thomas N Clerks lessee v Azariah David. Jury retires to consider verdict. Richard G Waterhouse to trustees of Monmeth Church & Tennessee Accadamy. Deed dated 6 Nov 1821 for two lots in Suthern liberties of Washington 29 and 30 proven by John Locke and Woodson Francis.

Trustees of Monmuth Church to Trustees of Tennessee acadamy. Deed dated 9 Feb 1822 for one of 2 lots in southern liberties of town of Washington ackd.

p.324　Trustees of Tennessee Acadamy to Trustees of Monmuth Church. Deed dated 9 February 1822 for three fourths of two lots in Southern liberties of Washington Nos 29 & 30 ackd by Benj C Stout Abraham Howard John Rice Azariah David George Gilespie & Thomas J Campbell part of the grantors therein named.

Henry Owens v David Crum. Cause passed for the present.

Joseph Anderson's lessee v William Murphree. Jury William Kenedy, George W Riggel, Arthur Fulton, Moses Thompson, James Kelly, William Johnson, William Alexander, Carson Caldwell, David Caldwell, James McCanse, Allen Kenedy, William Locke respited until tomorrow morning 9 oclock.

Court adjourned.　　　　　　　　　　　　　　　　　　　　　　Charles F Keith

p.325　Wednesday 19th March. Present the Honourable Charles F Keith, Judge.

Joseph Andersons lessee v William Murphree. Ejectment. Trial progressed.

State v Jonathan Crawford. Grand Larceny. On affidavit of dft and allso of John Harimore this cause is continued untill next September. Jonathan Crawford's recognizance, Samuel P[?] Low and Elly Arms securities.

Josiah Danforth v Jonathan Fine. Case. Cause is continued.

p.326　State v Jonathan Crawford. Grand Larceny. Bond of Richard H Gatewood, Joseph Peters, John Harrimore, Samuel C Low and Nancy Benton, condition above Richard, Joseph, Peter[sic], John, Samuel and Nancy appear September next to give evidence on behalf State against Jonathan Crawford.

Thomas N Clarks lessee v Azariah David. Ejectment. Jury elected on Monday find defendant guilty of trespass and ejectment and assess plaintiffs damage to six cents besides his costs. Plf recovers his term yet to come in the lands and tennaments in plfs declaration mentioned together with damages and costs.

Solomon Riggle v William Murphree. Appeal. Cause is continued.

p.327　William Murphree v Samuel Murfree. Exparte. Samuel Murfree was summoned as a witness on behalf deft in cause wherein Joseph Anderson lessee is plf and William Murphree is dft, but Samuel came not. Therefore William Murphree by atty recovers agt dft $125 unless cause of disability to attend be shown at next Term.

Court adjourned.　　　　　　　　　　　　　　　　　　　　　　Charles F Keith

Thursday 20th March. Present the Honourable Charles F Keith.

Isaac Baker James Preston & others adversus James G Martin & others lessee. On motion of James G Martin by Thomas C[?] Williams his attorney a rule is granted him to shew cause why taxation of costs in these causes should be corrected, so that there shall be no attorneys fee taxed therein.

MARCH 1823

  Den on demise of Richd G Waterhouse v Edmd Whitfield. Ejectment. Continued.
p.328 Den on demise of William B Lewis & others lessee v Richard G Waterhouse. Ejectment in two causes. Causes are continued untill next Term.
  Thomas N Clarks lessee v Azariah David. Dft by his atty is to shew cause for new trial.
  William Bayles v Sion Price. Cause is continued.
  Richard G Waterhouse & others complainants v James G Martin & others respondents. Demurrer of respondents heretofore argued is now sustained. Respondants recover agt complainants their costs about their defence expended. Complain-
p.329 ants are granted appeal to next Superior Court.
  Holderman & others v Creel & Nelson adms. Benjamin Sherley v William Worley. In these causes by mutual consent causes are continued.
  Carlisle Humphries to heirs of William T Lewis. Deed of release dated 3 February 1816 for 2500 acres north side of Tennessee River in Rhea County proven by oaths of Fredrick Fulkerson and John Love subscribing witnesses thereto.
  Joseph Thompson v Robert Brabson. Case. Daniel Walker bail for defendant surrendered him; dft ordered into custody of sheriff there to remain untill he find other bail or pay the condemnation in this suit. John McClure and William Buster
p.330 undertake for defendant.
  Joseph Andersons lessee v William Murphree. Jurors heretofore sworn on this issue are respited untill Tommorrow.
  Court adjourned untill Tommorrow morning.   Charles F Keith

Friday 21st March 1823. Present the Honourable Charles F Keith, Judge &c.
  George Walker v John Hill. Covenant. Cause is continued.
  State v --rdon Gibson. Larceny. Noll prosequi entered.
p.331 Jurors not now on trial discharged.
  William York exparte. Upon his application for a pension. The truth of sd Yorks declaration as to his insolvency & reliance on his children, who are in very limited circumstances, for a sustenance appeared to the satisfaction of the court by the testimony of Joseph McDaniel and Stephen Wharton who are men of credit and appeared to have no interest in sd matter. Same is certified.
  Joseph Andersons lessee v William Murphree. Ejectment. Jurors impanelled on Tuesday are respited untill Tommorrow morning 9 Oclock.
  Court adjourned untill lTomorrow.   Charles F Keith.

Saturday 22d March. Present Charles F Keith.
  James Roane & others v Mathew Allen & John Smith tenants in possession. Ejectment. Time given to plead so as not to delay.
p.332 Richard G Waterhouse lessee v Edmond Whitfield. Ejectment. Order to take deposition of Alexander Outlaw is revived.
  Frederick A Ross to Thomas Hopkins. Deed dated 12 Oct 1822 for 300 acres, the island at the mouth of Hiwassee river, proven by James Berry & Miller Francis.
  Thomas N Clarks lessee v Azariah David. Rule for new trial made absolute. Plf to take deposition of William Panque[?] of Fluvanah County, Virginia. Former order to take deposition of John Willliams on part of dft revived.
p.333 R G Waterhouse lessee v Edmond Whitfield. Dft's attorney given leave to amend the plea on payment of costs of the amendment.

51

MARCH 1823

Rosses heirs & Thomas Hopkins lessee v John Moore. Depositions to be taken.
From affidavits of John H[?] Tabor & John Mahone against whom fine entered for failing to attend as jurors, fine is set aside on payment of costs.
Thos N Clarks lessee v Azariah David. Dft to take deposition of Charles McClung of Knox County.

p.334 Wm B Lewis et al lessee v Rhd G Waterhouse. Depositions to be taken, notice to be given by dft to Thomas Hopkins and by plf to Richard G Waterhouse.
Thomas Hughs v Polly Hughs & others. George Brown one of the defendants not being found, order publication made in Knoxville Register.
Wm B Lewis & others v Daniel D Armstrong. Lessors of plf take exceptions to security taken by sheriff.
William B Lewis et al v William Lewis. Isaac Lewis is admitted to defend in stead of William Lewis, and the casual ejector and Adam W Caldwell, Shepherd Brazelton James Hannah and Barefoot Armstrong agree for Isaac and he shall satisfy

p.335 all cost that may be awarded against him.
Joseph Andersons lessee v William Murphree. Jurors heretofore sworn say defendant is guilty of trespass. Plf recovers agt dft his term yet to come in messuage lands hereditaments together with his damages and allso his costs.
Den on demise of Wm B Lewis & others v Richd Fen with notice to Isaac Lewis. Dfts came not; plf recovers agt Richd Fen his term yet to come in the land and his costs by him about his suit in this behalf expended.

p.336 Den on demise of Wm B Lewis et all lessee v Richd Fen with notice to Elihu D Armstrong. Elihu D Armstrong tenant in possession on whom notice served came not nor any other person to answer the plf's declaration. Plf recovers agt sd tenant in possession his term yet to come and allso his costs of suit.
Joseph Andersons lessee v William Murphree. Motion for new trial dismissed.
Wm B Lewis et al lessee v Daniel D Armstrong. Same v Isaac Lewis. Deposi-

p.337 tions of witnesses to be taken by both parties, each giving other notice.
All causes not disposed of are continued until next term of this court.
Court adjourned until Court in Course.

                                                             Charles F Keith

Monday, September 15th 1823. Circuit Court for County of Rhea in courthouse in Washington third Monday of September 1823, being the 15th day. Present the Honourable Nathaniel W Williams, Judge, &c.

Woodson Francis High Sheriff for Rhea County returned Venire facias: Jesse Martin, Samuel Loony, Beriah Frazier, William Alexander, Moses Thompson, Jesse Roddy, Edward Gray, John Hughs, Benjamin Marberry, Benjamin Jones, Gideon Raglin, James Wilson, John Ferguson, John Wasson, Henry Collins, John Lewis, Robert Bell, Robert Gamble, Allen Kennedy, John Lea, Benjamin F Jones, Patrick Martin, Willson Killgore, Samuel Tillery, Joseph Thompson, William Lea.

Grand Jury: Benjamin Jones foreman, Henry Collins, Samuel Tillery, Beriah Frazier, John Wasson, Patrick Martin, Benjamin F Jones, John C Ferguson, James Wilson, Edward Gray, John Hughs, John Lewis, Jesse Martin.

Constable David Shelton sworn to attend the Grand Jury.

John Lea, Robert Gamble, Benjamin Marberry and Jesse Roddy jurors of the original pannell on affidavits are excused from further attendance at this Term.

SEPTEMBER 1823

Den on demise of Wm T Lewis heirs lessee v Richard G Waterhouse. Two causes. By mutual consent these two causes are continued untill next Term.

Josiah Danforth v Jonathan Fine. Case. Parties in person; cause continued.

p.339 Den on demise of James Roane et all lessee v John Smith & Mathew Allen tenants in possession. Ejectment. Came Alexander McCall and Mary Ann Elizabeth his wife; on their motion by attorney Alexander McCall in right of sd Mary Ann Elizabeth claims title to land in question and that sd John Smith and Mathew Allen and John Smith and Mathew Allen upon whom notice was served are their tenants. Alexander and Mary Ann Elizabeth are admitted to defend in stead of sd tenants and in lieu of Richard Fen the causual ejector; George Gilespie their security. Cause is continued untill next Term of this Court.

p.340 Thomas N Clarks lessee v Azariah David. Ejectment. On affidavit of dft that impartial trial of this cause cannot be had in this county, order cause be adjourned to Knox County Circuit Court.

Wm Love to James C Mitchell. Deed for lot 39 in Washington proven by Thomas J Campbell and Edmond Bean the subscribing witnesses thereto.

Henry[?] Owens v David Crum. Cause is continued.

Holderman et al v Creel & Neilsons admr. Benjamin Sherley v Wm Worley. Two causes continued untill next Term of this Court.

p.341 John Rentfrow v John H Roades. Original attachment. Jury Robert Bell, Joseph Thompson, Wm Lea, Robert Love, Mathew Bolejack, George Henry Senr, Owen David, Edmond Bean, John Murphree, George Gilespie, Wm Kennedy, John Gamble who say dft hath not paid debt $308 nor any part thereof, and assess plfs damage of detention of debt to $33.88 besides his costs.

Ross's heirs & Thomas Hopkins lessee v John Moore. Eject. Plf in person dismisses his suit; Dft by his atty James C Mitchell confessed judgment for costs.

p.342 Ross's heirs & Thomas Hopkins compt v John Moore respondent. Equity. Complainant in person dismissed his bill; respondent by James C Mitchell his counsel confessed judgment for costs.

Joseph Thompson v Robert Brabson. Case. Dft surrendered himself in discharge of his bail. Whereupon George Gilespie & Edward Stuart undertake for dft.

William Bayles v Sion Price. Covenant. Cause is continued.

Court adjourned.   Nath W Williams

p.343 Tuesday Sept 16th. Present the Honorable Nathaniel W Williams, Judge &c.

Thomas Hughs v Polly Hughs, George Brown and William Rippite[Rippito?]. In Equity. Complainant recovers of defendants his costs. Further, publication has been made as to George Brown, bill of complaint taken for confessed agt him and set for hearing at next term of this court; dfts have two months in which to file answers.

p.344 John Walkers lessee v Thomas C Clark. Cause is continued.

Excuse juror Allen Kenedy from further attendance at this Term.

Joseph Thompson v Robert Brabson. Cause is continued.

Thos N Clarks lessee v Azariah David. Depositions of witnesses to be taken.

Wm B Lewis & others lessee v Isaac Lewis & Daniel D Armstrong. Ejectment 2 causes. Depositions of witnesses to be taken.

p.345 Isaac Right v George Walker. Cause is continued until next term.

George W Kenedy v Thomas J Campbell. Plf dismissed his suit; dft recovers of plf his costs about his defence expended.

George Walker v John Hill. Jury Robert Bell, Robert Small, William Long,

SEPTEMBER 1823

Owen David, Matthew Bolejack, David S Williams, Joseph Rice, Jacob Groce, Thomas Cox, John Holland, George Henry, Richard Hastrig. Plf recovers agt dft his damages $92.25 besides his costs of suit.

p.346   James Coulter v Even Evens. Parties in proper persons agree to submit matters in dispute to determination of Abraham Howard, David Walker, William Smith, John Rice, and William Kenedy whose award is to be the judgment of the Court.

William Murphree v Samuel Murphey. Dft in proper person; forfeiture entered agt dft at last term for failing to appear and give evidence in cause Joseph Andersons lessee against Wm Murphree is set aside on dft's payment of costs.

Court adjourned untill Tommorrow.   Nath W Williams

Wednesday 17th Septr. Present the honourable Nathaniel W Williams, Judge &c.

State v Joel McCrary. Grand jurors present bill/indictment State agt Joel McCrary for passing an altered and erased bank note which was endorsed thereon as True bill by their foreman.

Court adjourned untill tommorrow Morning.   Nath W Williams

p.347   Thursday Septr 18th 1823.

Daniel Rawlings extrs v James Berry. Debt. Leave granted plf's atty to amend the writ to read "in plea of debt of Three Hundred and forty nine dollars Eighty cents" and the same is amended accordingly.

Den on demise of Richard G Waterhouse v Edmond Whitfield. Ejectment. Deposition of Willis Hines and Robert Collier of Wayne County North Carolina, allso David Stuart of Cocke County Tennessee and Alexander Outlaw of Dallas County, Alabama, to be taken in behalf defendant. Cause adjourned for trial to Circuit
p.348   Court for Bledsoe County in Pikeville in March next.

State v Jonathan Crawford. Samuel C Loe and Elly Ormes bail for dft surrender dft; Jonathan Crawford is ordered into custody of Sheriff. Whereupon came Thomas J Camble solicitor General; dft in propper person pleads not guilty. Jury Isaac West, William Randolph, Robert Taylor, Evan Evans, Jesse Witt, Charles Woodward, James Ferguson, Mathew Hubbard, John Able, Joseph Williams, Robert Parks, John Thompson find dft guilty on two counts and not guilty on third.

Court adjourned untill tommorrow morning.   Nath W Williams

p.349   Friday 19th Septr 1823.

Thomas Hughs compt v Polly Hughs, George Brown & Wm Rippeto. Bill in Equity. Commissions awarded to each party to take depositions of witnesses.

State v Wright Hankins. Grand Jurors present bill/indictment State agt Wright Hankins, a true bill. Grand Jury discharged from further attendance.

State v Joel McCrary. Defendant in propper person says he is not guilty. Trial is postponed untill next Term of this Court, and defendant is remanded to the Jail of this County.

p.350   Thomas York ads James Rodgers. Hugh Dunlap's attendance as a witness taxed illegally; ordered to be expunged from bill of costs.

State v Jonathan Crawford. Petit Larceny. Dft by attorney makes motion for a new trial; rule dismissed. Court pronounces sentence of law: Jonathan Crawford to be forthwith taken from hence to the public whipping post there to receive on

MARCH 1824

his bare back ten lashes well laid on, and pay all costs, and the sheriff to see that this sentence is executed.
    State v Robert Killon. Passing counterfeit money. Nole prosequi entered.
p.351 Mathew Bolejack v Peter Peck. Supercedas. Plf by atty dismised his writ of supercedas; he pays costs.
    Court adjourned untill Tommorrow morning.   Nath W Williams

Saturday 20th Septr 1823.
    Thomas Hughs compt v Polley Hughs, George Brown, Wm Rippito. Equity. On motion of complainant by counsel, order Wm Rippito be enjoined from paying over money in his hands to Polly Hughs and that he have to deposit same with Clerk and master of this Court there to abide the determination of this Court.
    John Walkers lessee v Thomas C Clark. Ejectment. Deposition of John Carr of Marion County to be taken in behalf defendant.
    Richard G Waterhouse assee v Richard Hantrig. Continued to next Term.
p.352 James G Martin et al lessees v James Preston, Wm Johnson & J Baker. Ordered by Court that the tax in these causes be expunged from taxation of costs.
    A Thompson to Benjamin McCanse. Continued untill next term.
    Thos Hopkins compl v James C Mitchell respt. Bill of injunction. Grant rule to respondant to shew cause to disolve complainants injunction; cause continued.
    Court adjourned untill Court in Course.   Nath W Williams

Circuit Court held for Rhea County within the seventh Judicial Circuit in the courthouse in Washington on third Monday and 15th day of March 1824. The Honourable Charles F Keith, Esq, Judge of sd Circuit failing to attend, or any other circuit Judge untill after four Oclock of the evening of this day, whereupon the Clerk of sd Court adjourned the same untill Tommorrow morning 9 OClock.

Tuesday 16th March 1824. Present the Honorable Charles F Keith, Judge &c.
    Woodson Francis Sheriff returned Venire Facias: William Smith, John Robertson, Robert Bell, Isaac Benson, Robert Gamble, William Howard, William Alexander, George Gilespie, John Cozby, James McDonnald, Joseph Love, Jesse Thompson, Frederick Fulkerson, Thomas Price, Samuel McDaniel, Jesse Poe, John Witt, Jonathan Fine, John Bailey, James Preston, Cumberland Rector, Moses Thompson, Moses Ferguson, John Lewis, Henry Collins.
    On being called, following persons appeared in Court: William Smith, Joseph Love, John Robertson, Cumberland Rector, John Lewis, Robert Bell, Samuel McDaniel, James McDonald, Frederick Fulkerson, George Gillespie, Willliam Alexander, Moses Thompson, James Preston, Jonathan Fine, Robert Gamble.
p.354 Grand jury: Joseph Love foreman, John Robinson, Cumberland Rector, John Lewis, Robert Bell, Samuel McDaniel, James McDonald, Fredrick Fulkerson, George Gillespie, William Alexander, Moses Thompson, James Preston, Jonathan Fine.

MARCH 1824

Constable James Smith sworn to attend grand jury.
  Traverse jurors: Robert Gamble, William Howard, John Cozby, Thomas Price, Jesse Poe, John Witt, John Baily, Moses Ferguson, Henry Collins.
  Excuse Jesse Thompson from further attendance as a juror this Term.
  Excuse William Smith from further attendance as a juror this Term.
  William Bayles v Scion Price. Covenant. Parties by attorneys; plf dismisses his suit; defendant confesses judgment for costs.
  Josiah Danforth v Jonathan Fine. Cause is continued untill next Term.
p.355 Den on demise of Wm F Lewis heirs v Richd G Waterhouse. Continued.
  Richd G Waterhouse to Robert Fergusons heirs. Deed dated 22 July 1823 for 33½ acres acknowledged.
  Den on demise of Wm B Lewis & others lessee v Isaac Lewis. Ejectment. Plf by atty dismisses suit; dft recovers agt lessor of plf his costs of defence.
  Holderman & others v Creel & Nelson admrs. Debt. Motion by plf by his attorney, order writ of certiorari to Bledsoe County; cause continued.
  Benjamin Shirly v William Worley. On motion of plf by atty, order alias writ of certiorari awarded to Bledsoe County; cause continued accordingly.
p.356 Henry Owens v David Crum. Cause continued untill next Term. Deposition of William Thomas of McMinn County TN to be taken in behalf plaintiff.
  Clerk of this Court produced receipts for state tax and for fines and forfeitures by him collected.
  Court adjourned untill tomorrow Morning.   Charles F Keith

p.357 Wednesday 17th March. Present the Honourable Charles F Keith, Judge &c.
  State v Joel McCrary. For passing erased or counterfeit bank notes. Solicitor general enters an noll prosequi.
  State v Wm Moor. Assault and Bettery by appeal. Solicitor General Thomas J Campbell prosecutes; dft Wm Moor in proper person. Jury Joseph Love, John Robinson, Cumberland Rector, John Lewis, Robt Bell, Samuel McDaniel, Frederick Fulkerson, George Gillispie, William Alexander, Moses Thompson, James Preston, Jonathan Fine find dft guilty; fined $25; ordered into custody untill fine and cost are paid or
p.358 sufficient security therefor given. Whereupon Jacob Cannon and John Moor confessed judgment with the defendant for fine and costs.
  Ben on demise John Walkers lessee v Thomas C Clark. Ejectment. Cause continued. Depositions of Robert Armstrong and Robert Houston of Knox County and John Carr of Marion County to be taken in behalf of plf.
  Joseph Thompson v Thomas Brabson. [This item appears to be X'd out]. Cause continued. Depositions of Solomon Barnes and John Barnes of Georgia to be taken and William Buster of Green County TN in behalf lessor of plaintiff.
p.359 Thomas James v Robert Brabson. Cause continued untill next term. Depositions of Solomon Barnes and John Barnes of Georgia and William Buster of Green County TN to be taken in behalf plf.
  Den on demise of Wm B Lewis & others v Daniel D Armstrong. Ejectment. Jury William Howard, John Witt, John Baily, Moses Ferguson, Henry Collins, Jacob Runnells, Drury Lykes, William Hill, Orlando Bradly, Samuel Frazier, Alexr Forbush, William Campbell find dft guilty of trespass, asses plfs damage to 6¢ & costs.
p.360 Isaac Wright v George Walker. Plf by atty; dft in proper person says he cannot gainsay plfs action. Plf sustained damages $50 besides his costs.
  Richd G Waterhouse v Richd Haslerig. Debt. Dft not appearing, plf recovers

MARCH 1824

agt dft $118.37½, $18.02½ damages, and his costs.
p.361   Joseph Thompson v Robert Brabson. Cause continued untill next Term. Deposition of Solomon Barnes and John Barnes of Georgia to be taken in behalf plaintiff.
     Court adjourned until tomorrow morning.   Charles F Keith

p.362   Thursday March 18th. Present the Honourable Charles F Keith, Judge &c.
     Den on Demise of James Roane & others v Alexander McCall & wife. Ejectment. Deposition of James Deetlow[?] of Roane County TN and John Thornton of Ohio to be taken in behalf plaintiff. Deposition of John McClelland of Alabama and Thomas Hopkins of Warren County TN and Joshua Masley of Rhea County, also of John Gamble and James Preston of sd county to be taken in behalf defendant.
p.363   [There is no page with this number. The next page is numbered 364]
p.364   Joseph Harwood v John Skilern. Jury Joseph Love, John Robinson, Cumberland Rector, John Lewis, Robert Bell, Samuel McDaniel, James McDonald, Fredrick Fulkerson, George Gillispie, Wm Alexander, Moses Thompson, James Preston find dft not guilty. On motion of plf by atty rule is granted him to shew cause why verdict ought to be set aside.
     Peter Johnson v James Hage. Plaintiff came not. Plf nonsuited; dft recovers agt plf his costs about his defence expended.
p.365   Joseph McDaniel v Townsley Riggs. Certiorari. Cause is continued.
     Grand Jury discharged from further attendance at this term.
     Court adjourned untill tomorrow.   Charles F Keith.

Friday March 19th.
     Joseph Thompson v Robert Brabston. Deposition of William Buster of Green County TN to be taken in behalf defendant.
     Robert Brabston v Joseph Thompson. Deposition of Wm Buster of Greene County TN to be taken in behalf plaintiff.
     Thomas James v Robert Brabston. Deposition of Wm Buster of Greene County TN to be taken in behalf defendant.
p.366   Solomon Riggle v Wm Murphree. Appeal. Dfts demurrer to plfs plea argued. Plf takes nothing by his appeal; judgment of Court below stands; dft recovers agt plf his costs about his defence expended.
     Joseph Harwood v John S Keleru. Rule for new trial discharged.
     State v Wright Hankins. Capias awarded agt dft returnable at next Term.
     Absolum Thompson v Benjamin McKinsie. (item X'd out)
p.367   W B Lewis & others lessee v Danl D Armstrong. Lessors of plf recover agt dft their costs about their suit in this behalf expended. Commission awarded dft to take deposition of Thomas Crutcher, Alfred M Balch and Nathan Ewing of Davidson County TN giving Wm B Lewis one of the lessors of the plf notice. Each party has commissions to take depositions generally giving adverse party 30 days notice.
p.368   Joseph Anderson v Daniel Walker & Isaac Brasleton. Dfts in proper person offer to surrender Wm Murphree their principal; court refused. Plf recovers agt dft $232.40½ his damages and costs and also his costs in prosecuting this writ. To opinion of Court in refusing surrender of Murphey by his bail the dfts by counsel tender bill of exception and appeal to Supreme Court.
     James Coulter v Evan Evans. Rule of reference granted at last Term

SEPTEMBER 1824

discharged, and cause is continued untill next Term.
p.369   Thomas Hughs v Polly Hughs and others. Equity. Deposition of witnesses to be taken.

Den on demise of Richard G Waterhouse v Richard Fen with notice to James G Martin tenant in possession. James G Martin by attorney admitted to defend.

Den on demise of Carters heirs lessee v Clerk and the executors of Daniel Rawlings. Defendants this day save Thomas N Clerk and Rezin Rawlings and John Locke executors of the will of Daniel Rawlings [item illegible]
p.370   Henry Amerine v Miles Vernon & others. Sheriff returns that dft is not found in his county on motion of plf by his atty an alias capias is ordered returnable here next Term of thisCourt.

Absolem Thompson v Benjn McKensie. Time is given plf to reply to dfts plea and file same in three months; cause continued untill next Term.

Richard G Waterhouse v Jacob Wassom & others. Cause continued.

R.G.Waterhouse v C Ryan. Cause continued untill next Term.

Order all causes not specially continued at this term stand continued untill third Monday in September next.   Charles F. Keith

End of this book.

MINUTE BOOK B

p.1   Monday September 20th. Circuit Court held for Rhea County at the courthouse in Town of Washington. Present the Honorable Charles F Keith, Esquire, Judge of and in the 7th Judicial Circuit in the State of Tennessee.

Sheriff Woodson Francis returned venire facias: Edward Stewart, Thomas Henry, Samuel Howard, Wm Noblett, William Harman, Jesse Poe, John Able, John B Swan, James Swan, Adam Cole, Able Arrington, Benjamin Bond, Robert Parks, Robert Phariss, William McDonnald, John Baker, James Rodgers, Absolam Fisher[Foster?], Mathew Hubbard, James Coulter, James Snelson, James Montgomery, John Rody, Caswell Hughs, Samuel Gamble.

Following persons appeared in open Court: Caswell Hughs, John Roddy, James Montgomery, Samuel Gamble, Edward Stewart, Thos Henry, Samuel Howard, William Noblett, William Harmon, Jesse Poe, John Able, Robert Parks, Benjamin Bond, Able Arrington, Adam Cole, James Swan, John B Swan.

Grand jury: Robert Parks, Benjn Bond, Able Arrington, Adam Cole, James Swan, John B Swan, John Able, Jesse Poe, Wm Harmon, Wm Noblett, Samuel Howard, Thos
p.2   Henry, Edward Stewart. Court appoint Robert Parks foreman. Constable George W Riggle sworn to attend the grand jury to consult of their presentments.

Excuse Wm McDonnald from further attendance as a juror at present term.

Josiah Danforth v Jonathan Fine. Cause continued untill next Term.

Henry Owens v David Crum. Jury James Kelley, John Singleton, John Wasson, Landon Rector, Samuel Gamble, James Montgomery, John Roddy, Caswell Hughes, Mathew Hubbard, James Snelson, John Baker, Robert Pharis say dft assumed in manner and
p.3   form as plaintiff against him hath complained; plf's damage $192.50 besides

58

SEPTEMBER 1824

his costs.
      Walter Edwards & wife to Isaac Archey. Deed of relinquishment dated 13th Septr 1824 for 2500 acres in Hambleton County proven by James Snelson and Thomas Snelson subscribing witnesses thereto.
      Rezin Rawlings et al extrs v James Berry. Plf dismissed suit; whereupon dft in person confessed judgment for all costs in this behalf expended.

p.4   Stockley Donelson to John Hackett. Deed dated [blank] 1798 for 14,000 acres in Knox County now in [blank] and [blank] counties offered for probate on oath of the Reverent Mathew Donald who deposeth he signed the deed and a feint recollection of such transaction taking place, as about that time he lived with John Hackett, he does not recolect that he saw Donelson form the letters composing his name but remembers at the time he was called to wtiness sd deed, Donelson and Hackett were setting at a table writing, and that sd witness does not recolect whether sd deed had a day of date or month expressed therein, he thought it expressed the year, witness states he has been a resident of East Tennessee ever since the date or execution of sd deed and in Rhea County about 13 years. Witness states he has no recollection of the locallity or quantity of land conveyed by sd deed; same has allmost left his mind, but when he got hold of sd deed he believed it to be just such a one as it is now; that no inquiry has ever been made of him about sd deed
p.5   untill a few months ago, and the first inquiry made was just as William Smith Esq drew said deed from his pocket and presented it to witness, and that Smith requested himt o attend at the county court to prove sd deed, and Richard G Waterhouse requested his attendance at this. Witness says he recollects witnessing several papers for Hackett and has a distinct recollection of witnessing deed for Hackett and Donalson and believes the deed offered for probate to be the same. Recollects witnessing a paper between Hackett and a man by name of White, either a conveyance or a title bond for a conveyance. Rather thinks a bond for conveyance about the time he lived at Mr. Hacketts.
      Holderman & others v Creel & Neilson admrs. Benjamin Sherley v William Worley. Two causes are continued untill next Term of this Court.
      William P Lewiss heirs lessee v Richard G Waterhouse. Ejectment in two causes. Continued untill next Term of this Court.
      Court adjourned.   Charles F Keith

p.6   Tuesday 21st Sept. Present the honorable Charles F Keith, Judge &c.
      Henry S Purriss Esqr licensed to practice law in Circuit Courts in this state took the usual oath of an attorney and is allowed to practice in this Court.
      James Roane et al lessee v Alexander McCall & wife. Ejectment. On affidavit of Alexr McCall that an impartial trial cannot be had in this county, Court ordered cause adjourned for trial to Roane County in the courthouse in Kingston March next.
      John Walkers lessee v Thomas C Clark. Cause continued. Parties to take depositions of their witnesses.
p.7   Henry Amerine v Miles Vernon & others. Trespass with force & arms. Counterpart alias capias to Hambleton County being returned not executed, on motion of plf by atty a plurias counterpart is awarded him returnable to next Court.
      William B Lewis et all lessee v Daniel D Armstrong. Ejectment. Cause continued. Commissions issue to parties to take depositions of witnesses.
      Joseph Thompson v Robert Brabson. Thomas James v Robert Brabson. These two causes are continued ason special affidavit of the plaintiff.

SEPTEMBER 1824

p.8   Richard G Waterhouse v Charles Ryan. Debt. Jury: Robert Parks, Benjamin Bond, Able Arrington, Adam Cole, James Swan, John Able, Jesse Poe, Wm Harmon, Wm Noblett, Samuel Howard, Thomas Henry, Edward Stewart. Plf recovers agt dft $250 debt, $73.33 damages by detention and also his cost of suit.

John Rice v Joseph McCorcle. Appeal. Jury: Samuel Gamble, James Montgomery, John Roddy, Caswell Hughs, Mathew Hubbard, James Coulter, James Snelson, John Baker, Robert Phariss, William Lea, William Walker, James McCance, say dft doth owe plf $27.25 debt; Plaintiff recovers debt and also his costs.

p.9   James Stewart v John H Tabour. Plaintiff in person dismissed his suit and confesses judgment for the costs.

Rezin Rawlings v Orlando Bradley. Debt. Plaintiff dismisses his suit and confesses judgment for costs.

Stokely Donelson to John Hackett. Deed. Deed from Stockley Donelson to John Hackett presented yesterday in Court, and Mathew Donnald the subscribing witness thereto being sworn and interrogated by James C Mitchell and William E Anderson Esqrs, sd examination ordered to be made of record, and on this day solemn argument being heard by Court, Ordered by Court that sd deed be admitted to Record.

p.10   Absolum Thompson v Benjamin McKinzie. Debt. Plfs demurer to dfts second plea being argued, ordered by Court that cause be continued until next term.

Jeremiah Beshear v David Ragsdale & Samuel Beshear. Case. Plf dismisses suit against Samuel Beshear.

James Coulter v Evan Evans. Case. Cause continued until next term.

Thomas Hughs compl v Polly Hughs and others resps. Equity. Set this cause for hearing at next Term of this Court.

Thomas J Campbell Esqr solicitor General for 11th solicitorial District failing to appear & prosecute in behalf State at present term, Court appointed Spencer Jarnagin Esqr Solicitor Genl pro tem to prosecute in behalf State.

p.11   Joseph McDaniel v Townly Riggs. Cause continued.

Court adjourned untill Tommorrow Morning.   Charles F Keith

James Roane et all lessee v Alexander McCall & wife. Commissions awarded parties to take depositions of their witnesses.

Jeremiah Howerton & Lucy Howarton to James Standefer. Power of attorney from Jeremiah Howarton and Lucy Howarton to James Standefer dated 22d day Septr 1824 ackd by the makers thereof.

p.12   Wednesday 22d September 1824. Present the Honorable Charles F Keith, Judge.

State v John Allen. Charge of passing a counterfeit bank bill and not appearing tho solemnly called; considered by Court that he forfeit his recognizance and that a scire facias issue against him returnable to next Term of this Court, and George Allen, James Stewart, and Ephraim Pregmore bound in recognizance for the appearance of the defendant John Allen failing to bring into Court sd dft, forfeit their recognizances and writs of scire facias to issue against them.

State v John Allen. Recognizance of Thomas Maxwell, condition he appear at next Circuit Court to prosecute and give evidence in behalf State against John Allen; also came Josiah Duff, Jesse Grayson, John Hancock, William Stone, and

p.13   Andrew Still, condition they appear and give evidence in behalf State.

Joseph Thompson v Robert Brabson. Thomas James v Robt Brabson. Commissions

MARCH 1825

awarded plf to take deposition of Solomon Barns and John Barns of Georgia.
State v Wright Hankins. Capias secue returned not executed; alias secue issued returnable at next term.
James G Martin compl v Richard G Waterhouse respt. Respondant by his counsel filed demmurror to complainants bill; set for argument next Term.
p.14 Thomas Hopkins compl v James C Mitchell, respt. Injunction. Order injunction be dissolved for amount of Fifteen hundred dollars. Respondent recovers against complainant his costs about his defence expended.
David Leuty comp v Margarett Leuty resp. Petition for Divorce. It appearing defendant had been repeatedly guilty of drunkenness and adultery as charged in petition, order that the marriage contract be dissolved nullified and cancelled.
p.15 James Stuart v Alexander Coulter. Deposition of John Susenbery[Lissenbry?] of Kentucky to be taken in behalf the defendant.
Court adjourned till court in course.   Charles F Keith

p.16 Monday March 21st. Present the Honorable Charles F Keith, Esq. Judge.
Sheriff Woodson Francis returned Venire Facias: Edward Gray, Benjamin Jones, Jacob Garris, Peter Daniel, Jonathan Fine, George Gilespie, John Lewis, Robert Parks, Carson Caldwell, Joseph Love, John Stewart, Abraham Miller, Robert Gamble, William Baldwin, Robert Cozby, James Stewart, John Cozby, Wright Smith, Richard G Waterhouse, Thomas Atchley, John Hudson, Mumford Smith, James L Cobbs.
Grand jury: Joseph Love, Edward Gray, Benjamin Jones, Jonathan Fine, John Lewis, Robert Parks, Carson Caldwell, John Stewart, Abraham Miller, Robert Cozby, Wright Smith, Thomas Atchley, John Hudson. Joseph Love appointed by Court foreman thereof. Constable Henry Henry sworn to attend afsd Grand Jury.
p.17 Gentlemen appearing in Court of the original pannell--Jacob Garrison, Peter Danniel, Robert Gamble, William Baldwin, James Stewart, John Cozby, Richard G Waterhouse, Mumford Smith, James L Cobb.
George Gilespie of the original pannel failed to appear; from affidavit of James L Cobbs he is released from further attendance as a juror at present Term.
Robert Brabson v Joseph Thompson et al. Thomas James v Robert Brabson. Joseph Thompson v Robert Brabson. Actions on the case. From affidavit of Joseph Thompson for himself and as agent for Thomas James these causes are continued untill next Term; further, commissions awarded sd Thompson and James to take the depositions of Solomon Barns and John Barns of Georgia, giving notice.
William Jones & wife to James Powers. Deed for east half of the North East quarter section 23 in Township 18 range 8 in district of Cahaba containing 79 acres & 60/100 ackd by William Jones one of the grantors. In private examination of Elizabeth Jones wife of Wm Jones she ackd execution of deed or her dower therein to be done by her freely and without constraint.
p.18 George W Churchwell and Wyllys H Chapman Esquires licenced to practice as attornies in Circuit Courts in this State took the usual oaths.
Richard G Waterhouse v John Singleton. Debt. Parties in person produced an agreement; suit dismissed; plf recovers against defendant his costs of suit.
State v John W Lowrie. Grand Larceny. William Hope, Margaret Davis, Drinnen Matthew Wells and James Tucker bail for dft surrendered their principal whereupon

MARCH 1825

on motion of Thomas J Campbell solicitor general dft is ordered into custody of sheriff there to remain until he find other bail or be discharged by law.

Henry Welkes[Wilker?] v James G Martin. Debt. Dft in person says he cannot gainsay plfs action, but oweth debt of $250 with $15 damages of detention. Plf recovers debt, damages and costs.

p.19 Jeremiah W Beshear v David Ragsdale. Cause continued. Plaintiff to take depositions of William J Smith, Cader Felts, Britton Medlen, John Barr, Polly Sulivan of White County and Lewis James of Warren County.

Holderman & others v Creel & Neilson, admrs. Debt. Jury John Cozby, Jacob Garrison, Peter Daniel, Robert Gamble, William Baldwin, Richard G Waterhouse, Mumford Smith, James Stewart, John McClennahan, Martin Ferguson, Leonard Britwell, John Singleton say dft intestate has paid the debt except $2025 and they assess plaintiffs damage of detention to $816.93 besides his costs.

p.20 Benjamin Sherley v William Wooley. Case. Plf, not appearing, is nonsuited; dft recovers against plaintiff his costs of defence.

James Stewart v Alexander Coulter. Abraham Miller, bail for dft, surrenders him. Dft ordered into custody of the sheriff. Deposition of Susan Tindal of Rhea County to be taken tomorrow morning between sun rise and eight oclock at the dwelling house of Joshua Tindle in behalf dft. John Day and Miller Francis undertake for defendant.

Josiah Danforth v Jonathan Fine. Cause is continued untill next Term.

p.21 Andrew Hunter v Thomas York. Appeal. Cause is continued untill next Term.

John Den on demise of John Walker v Thomas C Clark. Jury Joseph Love, Edwd Gray, John Hudson, Benjamin Jones, Jonathan Fine, John Lewis, Robert Parks, Carson Caldwell, Robert Cozby, Thomas Atchley, Abraham Miller, Wright Smith find defendant guilty of trespass and ejectment. Plf recovers agt dft his Term yet to come in the afsd messuage lands & tennements together with his costs of defence.

Townley Riggs v Joseph McDaniel. Certiorari. Jury[above] could not agree; respited untill tomorrow.

Court adjourned.

Charles F Keith

p.22 Tuesday 22d March. Present the Honorable Charles F Keith, Judge &c.
William B Lewis et al lessee v Daniel D Armstrong. Ejectment. Continued.
John B Swan v Andrew Evans. Certiorari. [Item is X'd out]
Den in Demise of William T Lewis heirs lessee v Richard G Waterhouse. Same v Same. Ejectment. Causes stand for trial at the next Term of this Court. Commissions awarded generally to parties to take depositions of witnesses.

Townley Riggs v Joseph McDaniel. Certiorari. Jurors yesterday respited declare they could not agree. Jurors discharged; cause continued to next Term.

p.23 Den on demise of Lewis Ross lessee v Isaac Clement tennant in possession. Ejectment. Charles Gambell admitted to defend jointly with the tennant in possession and in lieu of Richard Fen the causual ejector. Robert Gamble and James Kelly undertake for defendants.

Den on demise of Lewis Ross v Benjamin Bond tennant in possession. Ejectment. Plf by attorney and Benjamin Bond on whom notice appearing to be served came into court and is admitted to defend in lieu of Richard Fen causual ejector.

State v John W Lowrie. P Larceny. Grand jury indictment signed by Joseph Love foreman, true bill.

p.24 Cornelius Melegan v William Blithe. Jury Peter Danniel, William Baldwin,

MARCH 1825

John Cozby, Richard G Waterhouse, Mumford Smith, George Gilespie, John McClennahan, James Kelley, Daniel D Armstrong, Benjamin Bond, Thomas Price, James Preston could not agree and are discharged; cause is continued untill next Court.

 John Robinson assigneee of Samuel Smith v Jesse Scott. Cause is continued.

 James Stewart v Alexander Coulter. Cause is continued untill next Term.

 Thomas Hopkins compl v James C Mitchell dft. Equity. Respondant by counsel moved Court to quash injunction; quashed; complainant by counsel obtained rule to shew cause why original injunction should be reinstated.

p.25 John Rentfrow v Thomas Hopkins. Writ of scire facias. Dft in proper person cannot gainsay plf his debt $356.57½ his debt, damages, costs with further sum $31.16 damages of detention & allso costs in this behalf expended.

 State v John W Lowrie. G Larceny. Thomas J Campbell attorney generall; defendant brought to the bar says he is in no wise guilty & is remanded.

 Scion Price v James C Mitchell. Scire facias. Dft cannot gainsay plfs cost $17.47 and further costs in this behalf expended. Execution issues.

 John B Swan v Andrew Evans. Certiorari. Cause is continued.

 Court adjourned.   Charles F Keith

p.26 Wednesday 23d March. Present the Honorable Charles F Keith, Judge &c.

 State v John Allen. Ephraim Prigmore dfts security surrendered dft; John Allen recognizance with John Allen Jr & George Allen condition John Allen Sr appears Sept next to answer charge against him for passing counterfeit money. Recognizance of Thomas Maxwell, condition he attend Septr next to prosecute & give evidence behalf State against John Allen Sr for passing counterfeit bank bills. Recognizance of William Stone, Jessee Grayson, Josiah Duff, Andrew Still, condition
p.27 they attend Stpr next to give evidence agt John Allen Sr. Cause continued. Forfeiture agt John Allen Sr for failing to attend last Term is set aside, dft in person confessed judgment for the costs.

 State v Ephraim Prigmore & George Allen. Forfeiture agt dfts at last Court is set aside and dfts in person confess judgment for all costs.

 Townley Riggs v William Frazier[?] alias David Campbell. Plaintiff in proper person dismissed his suit; defendant recovers agt plf his costs of defence.

p.28 Thomas Hopkins compl v James C Mitchell resp. Equity. Complainant by atty moved court to reinstate injunction heretofore granted which was dissolved at last term of this court; whereupon rule granted to shew cause why injunction should be reinstated. Upon reasons being shewn and argument; injunction reinstated and remain till respondant shall give security to refund in case final decree be gainst him. Thereupon James C Mitchell, Robert Gamble and Thomas Kelly give bond $3000.

 State v James Stewart. Sci Fa. Forfeiture entered agt dft is set aside. Dft came not. State recovers agt dft costs of sci fa in this behalf expended.

p.29 State v John W Lowrie. P Larceny. From affidavit of prosecutor Thomas McCaller, cause continued untill next Term. Whereupon sd Thos McCallie [McCalled?] gives bond. Recognizance of Jacob Brown, Daniel Walker Esq, David Leuty & Rezin Rawlings, condition they appear Septr court to give evidence agt John W Lowrie.

 Court discharged jurors from further attendance at this Term.

p.30 Thomas Hughs compl v Polly Hughs, George Brown & William Reppito resps. Equity. John Hughs decd made a will in which sd will half of his estate was bequeathed to compl and George Brown was apptd executor and Polly Hughs extx, and she, after death of John Hughs, took whole of his estate, and sd William Reppito

SEPTEMBER 1825

had borrowed of Polly Hughs a sum of money, and if that money be not retained from possession of sd Polly Hughs complainant will be unable to secure one half of the estate to which he is entitled. Ordered by Court that Thomas Hughs have one half of the personal estate of sd John Hughs, & further that this cause be referred to Clerk and master, and that he take on account therein ascertaining the amount of the personal estate of sd John Hughs that he died possessed of, allso the amount of money in the hands of sd William Reppito...further that John Locke Clerk of this Court, be apptd receiver to receive whatever sum of money sd Wm Reppito may pay, subject to final decree of Court, whose receipt shall be good, agt claim of sd
p.31 Polly Hughs; Clerk to make report at next Term of this Court.

Absolam Thompson v Benjamin McKinsie. Demurrer. Plfs demurrer to dfts plea argued & overruled; grant plf time to reply on payment of costs.

John Rice, plaintiff in error v Orville Paine. Dismissed. Dft recovers against plaintiff his costs about his defence in this behalf expended.
p.32 State v John W Lowrie. Grand Larceny. Prisoner in custody failing to give security for his appearance at next Term, and it appearing that Jail of this county is not sufficient for safekeeping of the prisoner, therefore order Shff to convey sd John Lowrie to common jail for McMinn County in town of Athens.

James Coulter v Evan Evans. Plfs demurrer to dfts plea argued, disallowed; defendant recovers against plaintiff his costs of defence.
p.33 Causes not disposed of are continued untill next term.
Court adjourned until Court in course.
                                                                         Charles F Keith

Monday 19th September. Circuit Court, Seventh Judicial Circuit, third Monday of September. Present the Honorable Charles F Keith, Esq, one of the Circuit Judges.

Sheriff Woodson Francis returned the Venire Facias: Cain Able, William Howard, Robert Locke, Mathew English, Moses Thompson, Daniel Walker, John Robinson, Allen Kennedy, Robert Pharis, Gideon Ragland, Cumberland Rector, Jonathan Fine, John Lewis, Henry Collins, Samuel Gamble, John Ferguson, Samuel McDaniel, William M Smith, John Leuty, Daniel M Stockton, William Killgore, Avory Hannah, Robert Parks, Matthew Hubbard, Lewis R Collins.

Grand Jury: John Robinson foreman, Moses Thompson, William M Smith, Samuel McDaniel, Robert Locke, Gideon Ragland, Samuel Gamble, John Ferguson, Henry Collins, William Howard, Avory Hannah, Allen Kennedy, Daniel Walker.
p.34 Remaining of original pannell: Lewis R Collins, Cumberland Rector, Cain Able, John Leuty, Robert Parks, John Lewis, Daniel M Stocton, Jonathan Fine, Mathew Hubbard, Robert Pharis, William Kilgore.

Matthew English failed to appear and answer.

Townley Riggs v Joseph McDaniel. Cause is continued.

William Walker to Mary Walker. Bill of sale from William Walker extr of will of George Walker decd to Mary Walker Negro woman Nelly acknowledged.

John Thompson to Orlando Bradley. Deed for 200 acres on Piney ackd.
p.35 Cornelius Milligan v William Blithe. Jacob Davis security for prosecution is released; whereupon James Kelley undertakes for plaintiff.

Court adjourned untill tomorrow.
                                                  Charles F Keith

SEPTEMBER 1825

Tuesday 20th Septr.   Present the Honorable Charles F Keith, Judge, &c.
    Josiah Danforth v Jonathan Fine. Cause is continued.
    William T Lewis heirs lessee v Richard G Waterhouse. Two causes. Continued.
    Joseph Thompson v Robert Brabson. Robert Brabson v Joseph Thompson et al.
Thomas James v Robert Brabson. [Item is X'd out.]
p.36   Henry Amerine v Miles Vernon & others. Jury John Lewis, Matthew Hubbard, Daniel M Stocton, Matthew English, Cumberland Rector, John Leuty, William Walker, William Kilgore, Robert Pharis, Moses Ferguson, Charles Ryan, Benjamin Bond, say dft is not guilty; dfts recover against plf their costs of defence. Whereupon plf prayed a rule to shew cause why a new trial should be had thereon.
    Jeremiah W Beshear v David Ragsdale.   Plf not appearing, is nonsuited. Dft recovers agt plf his costs of defence in this behalf expended.
p.37   Cornelius Milligan v William Blithe. Cause is continued untill next Term.
    John Robinson assee v Jesse Scott. Plaintiff not appearing, this suit is no further prosecuted; dft recovers agt plf his costs about his defence expended.
    Joseph Thompson v Robert Brabson. Cause is continued untill next term upon plf paying all costs. Dft recovers agt plf his costs of defence. Parties to take depositions of witnesses.
p.38   Robert Brabson v Joseph Thompson & others. Cause continued untill next Term, dft paying all costs. Plf recovers agt dft his costs of suit. Depositions of witnesses to be taken.
    Henry Ammerine v Miles Vernon et all. Plf discharges his rule to shew cause for new trial. Miles Vernon and Joseph McDaniel confess judgment for all costs.
    Robert Parks fined $5 for non appearance as a juror at this Term.
p.39   Thos James v Robert Brabson. On affidavit of Joseph Thompson acting as agent for plf, cause is continued untill next Term on plf paying all costs. Depositions of witnesses to be taken.
    John B Swan v Andrew Evans. Cause referred to final determination of Henry Collins, John Robinson and Moses Thompson.
p.40   William H West v Isaac Baker. Matter is referred to final determination of Gideon Ragland, Elisha Sharp, William C Willson, Stephen Winton and John Redmond.
    Andrew Hunter v Thomas York. Matters in dispute referred to final determination of Benjamin Congacre[?] Senr, Benjamin Congacre[?] Jr, Henry Isam, Absolam Majors, John White Snr, John Jackson and Jesse Roddy.
    William B Lewis et all lessee v Daniel D Armstrong. Jury William M Smith, Samuel McDaniel, Robt Locke, Gideon Ragland, Jno Robinson, Samuel Trimble[Tamble?], John Ferguson, Avary Hannah, Allen Kennedy, Cain Able, John Leuty, Moses Thompson who are respited untill Tommorrow morning.
    Court adjourned untill Tommorrow morning.   Charles F Keith

p.41   Wednesday 21st.   Present the Honbl Charles F Keith, Judge &c.
    Jacob Brown v Thomas McCaller[McCallie?]. Plaintiff by James C Mitchell atty dismissed his suit; dft in person confessed judgment for all costs.
    Charles J Love to George Gordon. Deed for a quarter section in Illinois proven by Matthew English one of the subscribing witnesses.
    James C Mitchell to Marck Johnson. Deed 100 acres on Herrcane fork of Sorce Creek in Rhea County ackd by grantor.
    Lewis Ross lessee v Benj Bond. Cause continued untill next Term, dft paying all costs of this Term.

SEPTEMBER 1825

p.42 James Stewart v Alexander Coulter. Cause referred to final determination of Crispian E Shelton, Robert Bell, William Locke, Robert Locke, Matthew Hubbard, and William Smith of Richland with liberty to choose an umpire if they cannot agree.

State v John Allen Senr. Dft not appearing, he forfeits his recognizance. Writ of scire facias to issue. John Allen Jr & George Allen bound for appearance of dft, to answer charge of passing counterfeit bank bill, made default and forfeit recognizance.

p.43 Waterhouse lessee v Richd Fen with notice to F Fulkerson tennant in possession. On motion of Orlando Bradley by attorney and from affidavit of sd Orlando that the tennnant in possession claims under and is living on the land in question as tennant of sd Orlando Bradley, therefore considered that he be admitted to defend in stead of tennant in possession and in lieu of Richard Fen. Whereupon Jacob Wassum undertakes on part of defence.

William T Lewis heirs lessee v Richd G Waterhouse. Two cases. On motion of dft, notice for taking depositions may be served on Thomas Hopkins.

p.44 State v John W Lowrie. Dft not appearing, forfeits his recognizance $5000; scire facias issues. Charles Lowrie and Wm Lowrie bound in sum $2500 each forfeit.

William B Lewis et all lessee v Daniel D Armstrong. Respited jurors now find defendant not guilty of trespass in ejectment; dft recovers of plf his costs.

p.45 Lewis Ross lessee v Charles Gamble. Permit dft to file notice of improvement and cause is continued untill next Term; plf recovers agt dft his costs.

State v John Allen Sr. Recognizance of Thomas Maxwell, condition he appear next Term to prosecute and give evidence agt John Allen Sr.

James Hogue v James Doran. Scire facias. Plf granted execution agt dft for $134.04 his costs in writ & costs expended; execution may issue.

p.46 Charles Ryan compl v Richard G Waterhouse. Equity. Complainant in proper person dismissed his bill. Dft recovers agt complainant his costs of defence.

Fine against juror Robert Parks for failing to answer is set aside.

Cornelius Milligan v William Blythe. Yesterdays order of continuance is sett aside. Jury Cumberland Rector, Matthew Hubbard, Daniel M Stocton, Robt Pharis, Daniel Walker, John Wassen, William Howard, Matthew English, George Cocke, Richard Lawson, James McDonnald, Roger Reece. Plf recovers agt dft his damages $57 & costs.

p.47 Because of indisposition, excuse juror Saml Gamble for further attendance.

Court adjourned untill Tommorrow.

                  Charles F Keith

Thursday Septr 22. Present the Honl Charles F Keith, Judge &c.

Richard G Waterhouse lessee v Jacob Massum[?]. From affidavit of dft that impartial trial cannot be had in Rhea, Bledsoe, Marion and Hamilton, and on affidavit of plf that an impartial trial cannot be had in Roane and McMinn, order venue changed to Monroe County.

p.48 William McCormick v Jesse Mathews. From affidavit of plf, cause continued untill next Term. Dft recovers agt plf his costs expended this Term. Deposition of William Gavins[?] to be taken behalf plf.

William Carter v James Coulter. Jury Lewis Morgan, Washington Morgan, John Day, John Wassum, William Lewis, Wm McCormick, T F Robinson, Roger Reece, Daniel M Stocton, John Leuty, Robert Pharis, John Lewis. Plf recovers agt dft his debt $25, damages 62½¢ and his costs of suit.

Excuse juror Jonathan Fine & Cumberland Rector from further attendance.

p.49 State v John Burk. Nole prosequi entered.

SEPTEMBER 1825

Jonathan F Robinson v John McClennahan. Jury Lewis Morgan, Washington Morgan, John Wassum, Wm Lewis, Mathw Hubbard, Danl M Stocton, John Leuty, Robert Pharis, John Lewis, Matthew English, Cain Able, Robt Parks. Plf recovers agt dft his damages by reason of nonperformance to $30 and also his costs of suit.

Grand Jurors presentment against Andrew Bolinger for assault and battery.
Grand Jurors are discharged from further attendance at this Court.

p.50 Woodson Francis Shff to John C McLemore. Bill/sale of Negroes and other property now in town of Washington sold as property of James G Martin ackd.

Allison Howard v Orville Paine. Plf by atty dismisses suit. Dft recovers against plaintiff his costs about his defence expended.

Thos Hopkins compl v James C Mitchell respt. Parties in proper person agree injunction heretofore granted be dissolved and bill dismissed. Respondent recovers of complainant $1013.40 the ballance due upon the judgments of respondent against complainant at law after giving to compl a credit of $565 and respondant pays costs. James C Mitchell's securities William Leuty and Rezin Rawlings.

p.51 Thomas Hughes compl v Polly Hughs, George Brown & William Reppito resps. It appearing that $400 came to hands of Polly Hughes of estate of John Hughes decd to one half of which complainant is entitled, further that sd Polly Hughes disposed of sd money to her own use and that interest on sd $200 from Sept 1820 to this time will be $48.50 making the amount $248.50, further sd John Hughs died possessed of personal property $350 to one half of which complt is entitled, and interest

p.52 thereon $ $32.13; further that William Reppeto one of the respondents is indebted to sd Polly Hughs $308.60. Therefore order that Thomas Hughs recover of Polly Hughes and George Brown sd sum of $455.63. Further ordered that unless sd William Reppito shall within one month pay to Clerk of Court sd sum $308.60 for use of complainant Thomas Hughes, execution issue against him therefor in name of complainant. Further, Polly Hughes and George Brown pay costs of this cause for which execution may issue. Further, execution may issue agt sd Polly Hughs and George Brown for $147.03 being ballance due complainant Thomas Hughs after deducting the $308.60 to be paid by sd Rippeto.

James G Martin compl v Richard G Waterhouse respd. Respondents demurrer to
p.53 complainants bill being considered, sd bill and matters therein stated and charged are not sufficient to authorise sd complainant to have his suit, therefore order that demurrer afsd be sustained and sd bill dismissed, and respondent recover of complainant James G Martin his costs about his defence expended.

Causes not disposed of continued until next Court.
Court adjourned until Court in Course.   Charles F Keith

p.54 Circuit Court March Term 1826 held at the courthouse in Washington in Rhea County within the seventh Judicial Circuit being the third Monday [20th day]. Present the Honorable Nathaniel W Williams one of the Circuit Judges of the State.

Sheriff Woodson Francis returned the venire facias: Rodger Reese Moses Paul Robert Bell John Cozby John Roddy Abijah Boggs Patrick Martin Samuel Igo William Moore David Campbell Abraham Miller James Coulter Joseph Love James Montgomery James Lillard Pulaski Poe John Day Archibald Taylor Matthew Hubbard James A Darwin Jonathan Fine William Kennedy Frederick Fulkerson. Also returned as to James

MARCH 1826

Carrell & Robert Bell Jr named in sd writ, not found.

Grand Jury Jonathan Fine foreman, Frederick Fulkerson, William Kennedy, Pulaski Poe, John Day, Robert Bell, Matthew Hubbart, David Campbell, Moses Pall, Abraham Miller, James A Darwin, Archibald Taylor, John Roddy.

Constable David Shelton sworn and sent to attend on sd Grand Jury.

Excuse John Cozby from further attendance as a juror at this Term.

William T Lewis's heirs lessee v Richard G Waterhouse. Two causes in Ejectment. These two causes is continued untill next Term.

p.55 Jacob Stover to Francis Rockhold. Assignment on a certificate for a quarter section of land in Herdford district No 359 made by Jacob Stover to Francis Rockhold proven by Thomas Cox the subscribing witness thereto.

John Huff v John Clack & Jacob Stover. Debt. Jury William Moore, Patrick Martin, James Montgomery, Roger Reece, Samuel Igo, William Lea, Gilbert Kennedy, David Leuty, Isaac Mahone, Townley Riggs, Joseph McDaniel, Allison Howard, who say dft hath not paid debt $115 nor any part thereof, and assess plfs damage of detention to $13.80 besides his costs.

Richard G Waterhouse v Henry Walton. Debt. Dft by atty cannot gainsay plfs action for $111.65¼ debt, $14.79 damages by detention thereof besides costs.

Richd G Waterhouse to Daniel Walker. Deed 280 acres in Rhea County proven by oaths of John Smith and Spills B Dyer.

p.56 Richard G Waterhouse v Spills B Dyer. Debt. Dft by atty cannot gainsay plfs action for $231 debt, $30.60 damages by detnetion besides his costs.

Williams & Carter v Henry Collins. Debt. Dft by atty cannot gainsay plfs action for $100 debt and $43.50 damages of detention and his costs.

Williams & Carter v Henry Collins. Debt. Dft by atty cannot gainsay plfs action for $100 debt, $36.50 damages & his costs of suit.

p.57 Williams & Carter v Henry Collins. Debt. Dft by atty cannot gainsay plfs action for $100 debt, $49.50 damages of detention, and his costs.

Court adjourned untill Tommorrow morning.   Nath W Williams

Tuesday 21st March. Present the Honorable Nathaniel W Williams Judge &c.

Richard G Waterhouse v Peletiah Chelton. Debt. Plf by atty dismissed suit. Dft in proper person confessed judgment for all costs in this behalf expended.

p.58 Richard G Waterhouse lessee v Jesse Thompson & Henry Breakbill tennant in possession. Ejectment. Lessee of plf by his attorney; James Thompson claims title to land in dispute, sd Henry Breakbill is his tennant, therefore he is admitted to defend for himself in in stead of sd Henry Brakebill and in lieu of Richard Fen the causual ejector. From his affidavit together with affidavit of Roger Rice and Frederick Fulkerson that an impartial trial cannot be had in Rhea, Bledsoe, Marion or Hambleton, venue changed to McMinn April next.

Thomas Jack to Allen Kennedy. Deed for lot in southern liberties of Washington No.15 dated 27 Septr 1819 ackd by Thomas Jack the maker thereof.

p.59 Lewis Rosss lessee v Benjamin Bond. Eject. Jury Wm Moore, Patk Martin, Jas Montgomery, Roger Reece, Samuel Igo, Jas Coulter, Townly Riggs, Jos McDaniel, Jacob Moore, Joseph Courson, Thomas B Swan, Moses Ferguson find dft guilty of trespass in ejectment. Plf recovers agt dft his Term yet to come and his costs of suit.

William McCormack v Jesse Matthews. From affidavit of Wm C Dunlop atty for plf, cause is continued untill next Term of this Court. Plf to take deposition of William Givens this evening in Washington.

MARCH 1826

Josiah Dunforth v Jonathan Fine. Cause is continued.
George W Thompson v James P Miller. Cause is continued.
Court adjourned untill Tommorrow morning.   Nath W Williams

p.60   Wednesday 22d March. Present the Hon Nath W Williams, Judge, &c.
Richard G Waterhouse lessee v Orlando Bradley. From affidavit of Frederick Fulkerson agent for respondant, depositions of Little Page Sims of Alabama, John Dudley and James Craig of Knox County TN, John E King of Cumberland County, KY, to be taken. Another affidavit of sd Fredrick Fulkerson as agent for Orlando Bradley, Jesse Thompson and Edmund Bean that an impartial trial cannot be had in Rhea Bledsoe Hambleton or Marion counties, therefore venue changed, and this cause adjourned for trial to McMinn County, April next.
    Townley Rigs v Joseph McDaniel. Cause continued to next Term on dft paying all costs expended at present term. Dft to take deposition of Thomas Powel of
p.61   Georgia Hall County Painsville.
    Hugh Murphy for use of Alexander Ferguson v Benjamin Johnson & Ruben Freeman. Petition. Order writ/certiorari & supercedas issue returnable next Term.
    James Hogue v James Doran. Defendant by attorney to shew cause why plfs execution should be quashed as to costs therein taxed from Circuit Courts of Franklin and Marion counties.
    David Shelton a constable sworn to attend grand jury failing to attend, for his contempt he forfeits $10.
    Whereupon Anson Dearman a constable was sent to attend the Grand Jury.
    William N West v Isaac Baker. Plaintiff by atty dismissed his suit. Dft in proper person confesses judgment for all costs expended.
p.62   John B Swan v Andrew Evans. Jury William Moore, Patrick Martin, James Montgomery, Roger Reece, Wm Lewis, Saml Gamble, Jesse Thompson, Joseph McDaniel, Wm Lea, Townly Riggs, Robt Small, Moses Ferguson. Plf recovers agt dft debt $3.62½ and $1.08¼ damages of detention, and his costs about his suit expended.
    Grand Jurors indictment against William S Leuty and Polly Leuty for murder, true bill indorsed by Jonathan Fine foreman.
    Michael Stiner and Willliam Long, summoned to attend as jurors, came not; forfeit $5 each for contempt.
    State v William S Leuty & Polly Leuty. Murder. Thomas J Campbell attorney general prosecutor for State. Jury Palatial Chelton, Samuel Gamble, James Boran,
p.63   James Taylor, William Moore, Daniel Walker, John Sulivan, John Walker, John Whaley, Thomas Kelly, Thompson Meriot, Thomas Eaves respited under care of a sworn officer until tomorrow morning.
    Court adjourned until tomorrow morning nine oclock.   Nath W Williams

Thursday 23 March 1826. Present the HOnorable Nathaniel W Williams, Esqr, Judge.
    Isaac Wright v William Walker Executor &c. Scire facias. William Walker executor of will of George Walker deceased in proper person says he cannot gainsay plf. Plf granted execution for $10.37½ against assets of estate of decedent.
    Richard Hale v Leroy Ferguson. Cause is continued untill next Term.
p.64   Richard G Waterhouse lessee v Jesse Thompson. Woodson Francis & Roger Reace undertake for deft who is admitted to defend in stead of Henry Breakbill, tenant.
    State v William S Leuty & Polly Leuty. Murder. Jury respited yesterday say

MARCH 1826

the defendants are not guilty of murder.
Court adjourned untill Tommorrow morning.   Nath W Williams

Friday 24th March 1826. Present the Honorable Nathaniel W Williams, Judge.
State v William S Leuty & Polly Leuty. Murder. Dfts discharged.
Remit fines entered yesterday agt Wm Long & Michael Stiner for failing to attend as Jurors.
Remit fine against David Shelton for failing to attend as constable of Grand Jury.

p.65 Joseph Thompson v Robert Brabson. Plaintiff to take deposition of Solomon Barns of Georgia.
Robert Brabson v Joseph Thompson & others. Plaintiff came not; Plaintiff nonsuited. Dft recovers agt plf his costs of defence.
Thomas James v Robert Brabson. On motion of Joseph Thompson agent for plf, order plf take depositions of Solomon Barns and John Barns of Georgia.
Grand and Traverse Jurors discharged from further attendance this Term.

p.66 Richard G Waterhouse lessee v James G Martin. Eject. Jury Jonathan Fine, Frederick Fulkerson, Wm Kennedy, Pulaski Poe, Robert Bell, Matthew Hubbart, David Campbell, Moses Paul, Abraham Miller, James A Darwin, Archd Taylor, John Roddy find dft guilty of trespass and ejectment. Plf recovers against dft his term yet to come in messuage & lands and also his costs of suit.
George S[T?] Gillespie v George Gordon. Cause is continued.
Same v Same. Cause continued as on affidavit of defendant untill next Term.
Absolam Thompson v Benjamin McKinsie. Cause is continued untill next Term.
Richard G Waterhouse v Jacob Wassum & others. Cause is continued.

p.67 James Stewart v Alexander Coulter. Matters of difference between parties are referred to determination of Crespian E Shelton, Robert Bell, William Locke, Robert Locke, Matthew Hubbert, Wm Smith of Richland.
Lewis Ross lessee v Charles Gambel. Cause is continued. Dft to take depositions of Robert Houston and Robert Armstrong of Knox County TN.
John Rutherford v James C Mitchell. Debt. Matters in defendants demurrer not sufficient in law for plaintiff to maintain his action against the defendant. Dft recovers against plf his costs in this behalf expended.
James Hogue v James Doran. Plf recovers agt dft his costs from which opoinion dft prays appeal to next Court of Errors.

p.68 Thomas Hughs v Adam Lamb Shff &c. Ex parte. Writ of fierie facias execution had issued Sept Term 1825 directed to sheriff of Bledsoe County for $541.70½ debt & costs in favour of Thomas Hughs against Polly Hughs George Brown and William Rippeto; also appearing by return made by sd sheriff that he had collected $360.87½ which moneys he hath failed to pay. Plf recovers agt dft Adam Lam sheriff afsd the afsd sum and also his costs in making this motion & judgment.
Andrew Hunter v Thomas York. Arbitrators to whom the determination of matters in dispute were submitted Sept 1825 returned their award. Personally appeared Jesse Roddy, Benjn Longacre, John White, Henry Isam, Absolam Majors, Alexander Brown, John jackson who say that Andrew Hunter to recover judgment against York for $11, and each pay his own witnesses, and York pays court costs.

p.69 James C Haynes compl v Thomas B Swan & Samuel F D Swan respt. Equity. Injunction dissolved. Respondant recovers against James P Haynes and Thomas Kelly and Woodson Francis his securities $100 with interest thereon from 28 Jany last.

SEPTEMBER 1826

James Swan v William Randolph. In Error. Record from Court below being inspected and argument heard thereon, opinion of Court here sitting that judgment of court below in not granting prayer of petitioner there is error. Writs of Certiorari and Supercedas issue returnable next Term of this Court.

State v Jonathan Crawford. Change of venue on a charge of Grand Larceny. Dft has no property whereon to distrain for costs expended. Therefore on motion of Hopkins L Turney atty on part of claimants, costs that accrued on part of State since change of venue be certified to the treasurer of East Tennessee for payment.

p.70 John Rice plf in error v Samuel Hoskins. The record of Court below being argued, judgment of Court below stands in all things affirmed; appeal in error dismissed, dft recovers against plaintiff his costs in defending this appeal.

Court adjourned untill tomorrow morning.   Nath W Williams

Saturday 25th March 1826. Present the Hon Nathaniel W Williams, Judge &c.

James Berry is admitted to quallify as deputy Clerk of Court and was sworn in accordingly.

Morgan & Jacobs v Jacob Slover. Attachment. Defendant came not. A jury next term to inquire of plaintiffs damage.

p.71 George Morgan v Jacob Slover. Attachment. Dft came not. Damages plf has sustained to be determined by a jury at next Term.

Court adjourned till Court in Course.   Nath W Williams

Monday Septr 18th. Circuit Court in Rhea County, Seventh Judicial Circuit of law, third Monday before Nathaniel W Williams one of the Circuit Judges.

Sheriff Woodson Francis returned the venire facias: William Hornsby, John Riggle, Jesse Roddy, Robert Walker, George Gilespie, Micajah Howerton, Jackson Howerton, John Wasson, Vaden H Giles, Jesse Martin, Azariah David, Joseph Williams, David Caldwell, John McClure, Thomas Hunter, John Whaley, Leonard Brooks, James Kelley, John Toff, Robert Elder, John Cozby, Wm C Wilson, Stephen Winton, Peach Taylor, Joseph Love.

p.72 Grand jurors: Azariah David foreman, William Hornsby, Robert Walker, Leonard Brooks, John McClure, James Kelley, Jesse Roddy, John Toff, David Caldwell, Peach Taylor, John Cozby, John Wassum, John Whaley. Constable David Shelton sworn to attend said Grand Jury.

Remaining of original pannel now present Stephen Winton, George Gilespie, Thomas Hunter, Robert Elder, Joseph Love, John Riggle. And Micajah Howerton, Vaden H Giles, Jackson Howerton and Jesse Martin failed to answer to their names.

William C Wilson one of the original pannel is a postmaster in this county and from affidavit of Joseph Williams one of the original venire also, they are excused from further attendance as jurors this present Term.

Lewis Ross lessee v Charles Gamble. Ejectment. Defendants death being suggested, rule is granted to revive this cause in the name of the legal representative of the afsd decedent.

James P[?] Haynes, compl v Thos B & Samuel F C Swan respt. Equity. On motion of complainants counsel time given to take depositions is enlarged untill

SEPTEMBER 1826

last day of this Court and sd cause is continued accordingly.
p.73   Josiah Danforth v Jonathan Fine. Suit is continued untill next Term.
    Morgans & Jacobs v Jacob Slover. Attachment. Plfs by Thos J Campbell their attorney. Jury Stephen Winton, Thos Hunter, Robert Elder, Joseph Love, John Riggle, Miller Francis, Joseph Thompson, Elijah Griffith, Leroy Ferguson, Benjn McKinsie, David Campbell, Townley Riggs say plf hath sustained damage by nonperformance of promise of sd deft to $353.10 besides his costs for which execution may issue.
    George Morgan v Jacob Slover. Attachment. Jury[above] say plf damage by non performance of dfts promise $103.55 besides his costs.
    Court adjourned untill Tommorrow morning.   Nath W Williams

p.74   Tuesday 19th Septr. Present the Honorable Nathaniel W Williams, Judge.
    James Stewart v Alexander Coulter. Trial is respited untill next Term.
    John Spears[?] lessee v John McClennahan & Alexander Mahan tennants &c. Ejectment. Lessor of plf by his attorney. From affidavit of Lewis Ross that he claims title to the land in dispute and sd John McClennahan & Alexander Mahan are his tennants, therefore he is admitted to defend in room of afsd tennants in possession and in lieu of Richd Fen the causual ejector. Whereupon George Gilespie undertakes for defendant.
    Absolam Thompson v Benjamin McKinsie. Cause is continued, commissions generally awarded the parties to take depositions of their witnesses.
p.75   Allison Howard & wife v Orville Paine. Commission awarded dft to take deposition of John Glenn in Kentucky.
    Lewis's heirs lessee v Richd G Waterhouse. Ejectmt, two causes. Continued.
    Joseph Thompson v Robert Brabson. Jury Stephen Winton, Thos Hunter, Robt Elder, Jos Love, John Riggle, Jackson Howarton, Wm Hill, Jas Swan, John Alexander, Jas P Miller[?], Robert Parks, Wm Fowler find dft not guilty. On motion of plf by attorney rule is granted him to shew cause for a new trial to be had thereon.
    Joseph Thompson v Curtis Ritchards. Curtis Richards who before this time was summoned a witness on behalf of Joseph Thompson against Robert Brabson but came not; therefore on motion of plf by atty, plf recovers agt Curtis Richards $125 unless sufficient cause of disability to attend be shewn next Term.
p.76   Allison Howard & wife v Orville Paine. Joseph McDaniel appearance bail surrendered dft into custody of sheriff. Thereupon Henry Collins undertakes for dft.
    Thomas James v Robert Brabson. Plf no further prosecutes his suit. Plf nonsuited, dft recovers agt plf his costs of defence. On motion of plf by atty a rule is granted him to shew cause why the nonsuit should be set aside.
    Townley Riggs v Joseph McDaniel. Jury Stephen Winton, Thos Hunter, Robt Elder, John Riggle, Jackson Howerton, Wm Hill, Jas Swan, John Alexander, Jas P[?] Miller, Wm Fauler, Jas A Darwin, Gilbert Kennedy find dft not guilty. Dft recovers agt plf his costs about his defence expended.
p.77   Richard G Waterhouse to Thomas Underwood. Deed dated 11 May 1826 for 130 acres proven by Richard Waterhouse & Joseph Garrison subscribing witnesses.
    Leroy Ferguson v William Meryman. Wm Merryman summoned a witness behalf plf in a case wherein Richard Hale was plf and Leroy Ferguson was dft, came not but made default. On motion of plf by atty, plf recovers agt sd Wm Meryman $125 unless sufficient cause of his disability to attend be shewn at next Term of this Court.
    Richard Hale v Leroy Ferguson. Jury Azariah David, Wm Hornsby, Robt Walker, Leonard Brooks, John McClure, Jas Kelley, Jesse Roddy, John Toff, David Caldwell,

SEPTEMBER 1826

Peach Taylor, John Whaley, Geo Gilespie find for plf that dft promised to pay the debt $194, damage by detention $17.46 besides his costs for which exn may issue.

Grand Jury returned Bill/Indictment agt Richard Waterhouse for murder endorsed true bill by Azariah David foreman of sd Grand Jury.

p.78   William mcCormack v Jesse Matthews. Jury Stephen Winton, Thomas Hunter, Jos Love, James Swan, Wm Fouler, Joseph Casteel, Andw Casteel, David Leuty, John McCarrel, Thos Price, John Woods, Jackson Howarton. Plf no further prosecuting his suit, jury discharged from rendering verdict. On motion of defendant by attorney, dft recovers against plf his costs about his defence in this behalf expended.

Daniel Walker & Isaac Brazleton v William Murphree. Exparte. Plf had been security for dft in cause Joseph Anderson lessee against sd defendant, and in a scire facias awarded at instance of sd Joseph Andersons lessee against sd Walker & Brazleton execution was awarded thereon for $265.43½; plf had paid. On motion of plf by atty, they recover agt dft afsd amount for which execution may issue.

Thomas Kelley v John Armstrong. Jury[above] to inquire if plf was security and subject to payment of money for dft find plf to be dfts security in one note of hand given to John Locke of Rhea County and on 19 Septr 1826 judgmt was obtained before Carson Caldwell an acting Justice of the peace in Rhea County upon sd note for sum of $85 debt with $3.61¼ damage which plf is convicted & bound to pay. On
p.79   motion of plf by atty, plf recovers agt dft afsd sum, & his costs of suit.

Court adjourned untill Tommorrow morning.   Nath W Williams

Wednesday 20th Septr. Present the Honorable Nathaniel W Williams, Judge, &c.

Robert Brabson v George Gordon. Cause is continued untill next Term.

State v Richard Waterhouse. Murder. Richard Waterhouse in proper person says he is not guilty. Jury Wm Lisenby, Peter Minick, Cornelius Moyers, James Preston, Jeremiah Howerton, James Nail, Thomas M Kinnon, James McCanse, Matthew English, Thomas Price, Wm Noblit, Hugh Ray respited untill Tommorrow and retired under care of the Sheriff charged by Court to keep them together in some convenient room and not to suffer sd jury to disperse nor converse with no other person.

p.80   State v William Hill. Exparte. Wm Hill summoned by Sheriff as a juror but came not is fined $5.

Court adjourned untill Tommorrow.   Nath W Williams

Thursday 21st Septr. Present the Honorable Nathan W Williams Judge &c.

State v William Hill. Sheriff had erred in returning dft as a juror for the day; fine against him entered yesterday is rescinded.

State v Richard Waterhouse. Solicitor Generall prosecutes for State. Dft in custody of sheriff in proper person. Jury afsd from rendering verdict are respited untill Tommorrow morning nine Oclock, said jury to retire under charge of sheriff directed by Court to keep them together in some convenient room and not to suffer sd jurors to disperse nor converse with any other person. Whereupon the prisoner at the bar continued in Custody of Sheriff.

Court adjourned untill Tommorrow morning nine Oclock.   Nath W Williams

p.81   Friday 22d Septr. Present the Honorable Nathan W Williams Judge &c.

State v John W Lowrey. Dft came not; State recovers agt dft $5000 & costs.

SEPTEMBER 1826

        State v William Lowrey. Dft came not; State recovers agt dft $2500 & costs.
        State v Charles Lowrey. Dft came not; State recovers agt dft $2500 & costs.
        State v John Allen Sr. Dft came not; State recovers agt dft $1000 & costs.
p.82   State v John Allen Jr. Dft came not; State recovers agt dft $250 & costs.
        State v George Allen. Dft came not; State recovers agt dft $250 & costs.
        State v John Allen Sr. Permit Atty Genl in proper person to enter nole prosequi in this cause.
        Traverse jurors of original pannel are discharged from further attendance.
        Richard G Waterhouse to John Holland. Deed 12 Jany 1825 for 50 acres on Tennessee River proven by Richard Waterhouse one of the witnesses thereto.
p.83   John Den on demise of Richd G Waterhouse v Richard Fen with notice to John Smith & Henry Henry tennants in possession. Ejectment. Plf by atty; dfts having filed with Clerk of Court a mutual agreement attested between sd lessee of plf and dfts purporting that cause of action was amicably adjusted between parties; that lessee of plf should dismiss his suit and dft should pay all costs.
        State v Richard Waterhouse. Came Solicitor Generall as well as defendant in proper person. Jury heretofore sworn from rendering verdict are again respited untill tommorrow morning, sd jury directed to retire under care of Sheriff; whereupon prisoner is remanded into custody of sheriff.
        Court then adjourned untill Tommorrow morning.   Nath W Williams

p.84   State v John W Lowrie. Nole prosequi.
        Jesse Matthews v Adam Seaboult. Plf directed his suit be dismissed and confessed judgment for all costs.
        State v Richard Waterhouse. Dft in proper person. Jury heretofore sworn say they cannot agree and from rendering their verdict are discharged untill Monday morning, and thereupon retired under charge of the sheriff to be kept together in some convenient room and not to disperse nor converse with any indifferent person.
        State v William Hill. [blank]
p.85   Grand Jury released from further attendance at this present Term.
        Court adjourned untill Monday morning.   Nath W Williams

Monday 25th Septr. Present the Honorable Nathaniel W Williams, Judge, &c.
        State v Richard Waterhouse. Solicitor generall prosecutes for State; dft in proper person. Jury heretofore sworn declare they cannot agree. From rendering verdict are respited untill Tommorrow morning; retired under care of Sheriff who is ordered to keep sd jury together in some convenient room and not suffer them to disperse nor converse with any indifferent person. Prisoner being in custody of the sheriff, the Court then adjourned untill Tommorrow morning.   Nath W Williams

Tuesday 26th Septr. Present the honorable Nathaniel W Williams judge &c.
        State v Richard Waterhouse. Solicitor Generall prosecutor; dft in proper person. Jury heretofore sworn declared they could not agree. They are respited under care of sheriff to some convenient room, not to disperse nor converse with any indifferent person. Court adjourned untill Tommorrow Morning. Nath W Williams.

MARCH 1827

p.86   Wednesday 27th Septr. Present the Hon. Nathaniel W Williams, Judge &c.
State v Richard Waterhouse. Solicitor Generall prosecuted; dft in proper person. Jury heretofore sworn declared they could not agree whereupon they are discharged and a mistrial ordered; cause is continued untill the next Term of this Court. It is also ordered that the sheriff take charge of the prisoner to which the counsell on behalf of the prisoner objected. And the Court then adjourned untill Court in Course.   Nath W Williams

Monday 19th March. Circuit Court for Rhea County, within the Seventh Judicial Circuit of law and Equity, on third Monday, 19th day of March. Present the honorable Charles F Keith, esquire, one of the Circuit Judges for Tennessee.
Sheriff John Lea by his deputy Orville Paine returned venire facias: Wm
p.87 Lauderdale, James Stewart, William Buyse, Benjamin Jones, Richard A McCandless, John Day, Beriah Frazier, Grief Howerton, John Lewis, William Ferguson, James Coulter, Ezekiel Bates, Jno Lillard, Samuel McDaniel, William Smith, Jonathan Fine, Daniel Walker, Thomas Anderson, George Gillespie, Jesse Thompson, John Cozby, Wm Johnson. William Wright was not found in his county.
Grand jurors: Jonathan Fine foreman, John Lewis, George Gillespie, John Cozby, William Johnson, Jas Coulter, Benjamin Jones, Jesse Thompson, Thos Anderson, William Smith, Beriah Frazier, James Stewart, William Lauderdale.
Constable William S Russell sworn to attend on said Grand Jury.
Remaining of the original pannell: Wm Buice, Richd A McCandless, John Day, Ezekiel Bates, John Lillard, Daniel Walker, Grief Howerton. It appearing to Court that Samuel McDaniel is a postmaster, therefore he is excused from further attendance as a juror at this Term.
State v Cornel "Aleas" Colonel Blackwell. Larceny. Same v Daniel Arnold. Larceny. Defendants in these causes have been committed to the common jail of McMinn County for safekeeping. Sheriff to bring dfts to court.
p.88   Richd G Waterhouse v Jacob Wassum et al. Spencer Jernagen Esq attorney suggested that since last continuance of this cause the plf departed this life; rule is granted him to revive suit in name of legal representative of decedent.
Richd G Waterhouse v Thomas Jack. Came Spencer Jarnagin [worded as above]
McDowel & Patten v Haselrig & Berry. Plfs by atty suggested that since last continuance of this cause Richard Haselrig departed this life, rule is granted them to revive this suit against the legal representatives of afsd decedent.
Richd G Waterhouse v James Stewart. Atty Spencer Jarnagin suggested that plf departed this life; rule granted him to revive this cause in the name of the rightfull representatives of said decedent.
William J Standefer Esq licensed to practice as an attorney in the Circuit Courts took usual oaths and is permitted to practice in this Court.
Court adjourned untill Tommorrow.   Charles F Keith

p.89   Tuesday 20th March. Present the honorable Charles F Keith, Judge &c.
George W Thompson v James P[?] Miller. Cause is continued untill next Term.
George T Gillespie v George Gordon. Jury Wm Buice, Richd A McCandless,

75

MARCH 1827

Ezekiel Bates, John Lillard, Daniel Walker, Gilbert Kennedy, Archibald Fitzgerrald, Wm Miller, Anderson Fitzgerrald, Isaac Mahone, John Redmond, Wm Lewis find for plaintiff and assess his damage to $21.03 and also his costs.

Joseph Thompson v Curtis Richards. Plf no further prosecutes. Dft recovers against plaintiff his costs about his defence on this writ expended.

p.90 Absolam Thompson v Benjamin McKenzie. Plf not appearing, is nonsuited. Defendant recovers against plaintiff his costs about his defence expended.

James Stewart v Alexander Coulter. Cause is continued untill next Court.

James Stewart v Wm Walton. Wm Walton before this time was summoned as a witness on behalf plf in cause wherein James Stewart is plf and Alexander Coulter is dft, but came not. Plf recovers against dft $125 unless sufficient cause of his disability to attend be shewn to Court after notice of this judgment.

p.91 John Spear lessee v Lewis Ross. Order proceedings enjoined on dft entering into bond and security according to law.

Lewis Ross lessee v Charles Gamble. The lessor of the plaintiff brings into Court the names of the legal heirs of defendant whose death was suggested at last Term, to wit Robert L Gamble, Margaret J Gamble, David F Gamble, James A Gamble, Charles P Gamble and that said heirs are minors, that Samuel Gamble is their guardian. Whereupon Samuel Gamble in proper person is admitted to defend this cause in behalf minor heirs on his giving security for cost of this suit.

Richard G Waterhouse v Jacob Wassum et al. Plf by attorney saith that afsd plf made his will and appointed Richard Waterhouse & Blackstone Waterhouse executors thereof. Whereupon dft Jacob Wassum in proper person and by consent this cause is revived in name of executors and plfs by attorney directed suit be dismissed on defts confessing costs. Defendant in person confessed judgment for all costs.

p.92 Allison Howard & wife v Orville Paine. Jury Wm Buice, Richd A McCandless, Ezekiel Bates, John Lillard, Danl Walker, Gilbert Kennedy, Archd Fitzgerrald, Wm Miller, Anderson Fitzgerrald, Isaac Mahone, John Redmond, Saml Fitzgerrald say dft is guilty of speaking the words in manner and form as plf hath complained; assess plaintiffs damage to $1000 besides costs.

Mary Randolph admx to Wm N Merrick[?]. Exn of Bill/sale dated 19 March 1827 for negro child slave named Henry proven by Thomas J Campbell & James Berry.

Mary Randolph admx to Jane Merriot[?]. Exn of Bill/sale dated 19 March 1827 for negro slave child Viney proven by Thos J Campbell & Jas Berry.

Eli Sharp v Anderson Fitzgerrald et all. Cause is continued.

p.93 Mary Randolph admx to Mary Ann Merriott[?]. Bill/sale dated 19 March 1827 for negro child Nicholas proven by Thos J Campbell & James Berry.

James L Hayne compl v Thos B & Samuel F D Swans. Cause is continued.

George P Gillespie v George Gordon. Jury Ralph B Locke, Jonathan Fine, John Lewis, John Cozby, Wm Johnson, James Coulter, Benjn Jones, Thos Anderson, Wm Smith, Beriah Frazier, Jas Stewart, Wm Lauderdale assess plfs damage to $21.55 & costs.

Leroy Ferguson v William Merrimon. Plf in proper person dismissed his writ. Dft recovers agt plf his costs in defending sd writ; execution may issue.

Bean et al compl v Roberts & McCalla. Dfts to shew cause why injunction should be dissolved.

p.94 Robert Brabson v George Gordon. Plf not appearing, is nonsuited. Defendant recovers against plf his costs about his defence expended; execution may issue.

Hugh Murphree for use of Alexander Ferguson v Benjamin Johnson & Ruben Freeman. Atty for plf saith that since last Cont of this cause Alexr Ferguson departed this life; rule granted to revive suit in name of his legal representative.

MARCH 1827

Robert Brabson v Joseph Thompson. Dft not appearing, plf granted execution agt dft for $55.67½ and also his cost of suit.

John Walkers lessee v William Arnett & Parson Poe. Sheriff notified Wm Arnett; Parson Poe was not found in his county, did not appear when called. Plf granted execution agt dft for $25.79 the costs in writ specified and costs of writ.

p.95 Townley Rigg v Joseph McDaniel. Jury Geo Gilespie, John Lewis, Wm Johnson, James Coulter, Jesse Thompson, Thos Anderson, Wm Smith, Beriah Frazier, William Lauderdale, Henry Henry, Wm Lowry, Wm Locke assess plfs damages to $20.55½ & costs.

Samuel Hoskins v Elijah C Rice & Wm Johnson. Dfts not appearing, plf granted execution agt dfts for $7.54 costs of writ and also his costs of suit.

James Thompson v Robert Brabson. Cause is continued untill next Term; dft
p.96 to take deposition of Thomas Brabson in Washington County TN.

William C Wilson v David Hounshell & wife. Jno Redmond appearance bail surrenders defendant. George Gillespie undertakes for defendant.

Court adjourned untill Tommorrow.   Charles F Keith

Wednesday 21st March. Present the Honorable Charles F Keith, Judge &c.

State v Wright Hankins. Nole prosequi entered.

State v James Sappington. Passing counterfeit bank notes. Dft not appearing
p.97 forfeits his recognizance $1000; John Lowrie & Wm C Dunlap appearance bail for James Sappington forfeit $500 each. Writs of scire facias issue.

William C Wilson v David Hounshell & wife. Plfs demurrer argued; not sufficient in law to preclude plf from maintaining action against defendant.

Beard et all by their next friend v Henry Henry. Defendant recovers against plaintiff his costs by him about his defence in that behalf expended.

p.98 State v Richard Waterhouse. Homicide. Dft in proper person moved to shew cause why he should be discharged from further prosecution upon bill/indictment found against him because Septr 1826 jury Wm Lisenby, Peter Menick, Cornelius Majors, Jas Preston, Jeremiah Howarton, Jas Nail, Thos McKennon, Jas McCanse, Mattw English, Thomas Price, Wm Noblett, and Hugh Roy could not agree whereupon they were discharged and a mistrial ordered by Hon. Nathaniel W Williams then presiding Judge of Circuit Court contrary to the will and consent of dft, sd dft now avers; which
p.99 jury were elected and sworn in same cause & indictment that he is now required to go to trial upon, & none other or different cause than the one set forth in his plea afsd. To which plea atty generall for state Thomas J Campbell filed a demurrer that state ought not be barred from prosecution afsd against Richd Waterhouse because he says the matters in sd plea contained are not sufficient in law. Argument of counsel heard. Demurrer overruled; plea sustained and dft is discharged from prosecution afsd, & his motion to be discharged be also sustained. From which judgment of Court the attorney generall for State prays appeal in nature of Writ of error to Supreme Court of Errors and appeals to be held at Knoxville on 2 Monday of July next which was granted; defendant ordered to enter recognizance and security for his appearance at sd Court. Whereupon Richard Waterhouse ackd himself indebted $5000, James McCanse, Jesse Thompson, Daniel Walker, John McClure, Robert Parks and
p.100 Moses Thompson his securities. Joseph Kelough recognizance, condition he make appearance at Supreme Court of Errors and Appeals to prosecute on behalf State against Richard Waterhouse on charge of murder.

Lewis Ross lessee v Gambles heirs. Plf by attorney and Daniel Walker and William Kennedy undertake for defendants.

MARCH 1827

Rezin Rawlings v Anson Dearmon. Parties in proper persons by mutual consent; cause is continued untill next Term of this Court.

Edmond Bean plff in error v John & James Obryant. Plff in error as well dft by council; record of Court below argued; opinion of this Court that in judgment of
p.101   Court below there appears no error; judgment affirmed.

Josiah Danforth v Jonathan Fine. Demurrer of plf discharged.

State v Colonel Blackwell & Daniel Arnold. Grand jury bill of indictment, endorsed by foreman Jonathan Fine a true bill.

Richard G Waterhouse to William Johnson. Deed dated 18 April 1825 which has been certified for further probate was duly proven by oath of Blackstone Waterhouse one of subscribing witnesses thereto.

George T Gillispie v George Gordon & Matthew English. Plfs attorney moved for rule to shew cause why a judgment rendered at this Term agt George Gordon alone on appeal from Justice of peace should be extended against sd appallants security; judgment extended against Matthew English his security. Plf recovers agt George Gordon and Matthew English $21.03 and also the costs.

p.102   George T Gillispie v George Gordon & Matthew English. Judgment for $21.55 extended against Matthew English security for appeal.

State v Colonel Blackwell. Thomas J Campbell attorney general prosecutes for State; Colonel Blackwell in proper person. Jury James Moore, Thompson Merriott, George Mainor, William Carter, Thomas Noblett, John McClure, Major Holloway, Geo Cyphers, James Swan, Cornelius Moyers, William Lewis, Thomas Little who find defendant guilty in manner and form as charged in the bill of indictment.

Court adjourned untill Tommorrow.
                                                                Charles F Keith

p.103   Thursday 22d March. Present the Honorable Charles F Keith.

Allison Howard & wife v Orville Paine. Henry Collins bail for defendant surrenders defendant and is discharged from his undertaking.

Richard Hale v Leroy Ferguson. Moses Ferguson undertakes for defendant.

David Leuty & Jesse Poe v Elijah Rice. Plfs no further prosecute their suit. Dft recovers against plfs his costs about his defence expended.

George W Thompson v James P Miller. Dft to take depositions of John Rice Joseph Rice & George Rice of Marion County TN.

William Randolph v James Swan. Alias Writ of Certiorari is awarded dft.
p.104   Jesse Gordon v Woodson Francis. Plaintiff no further prosecutes; dft recovers against plaintiff his costs about his defence in this behalf expended.

Bean et al by next friend v Roberts & McCallie. Motion for disolution of injunction continued, three momnths given dft Roberts to file his answer.

Motion of Thomas J Campbell Esqr atty Generall; clerk of Court produced the Treasurer & Trustees respective receipts for publick monies by him collected for 1826: Received 21 Nov 1826 of Clerk of Circuit Court $77.57 amount of State tax with which he is chargeable....M Nelson. Recd & presented on oath by Clerk of Circuit Court for 1827 certificate from which it appears there is no fines and forfeitures in his hands due. Carson Caldwell, Trustee.

Jurors belonging to Original pannel are discharged from further attendance.
p.105   Eliza White v William White. Petition for Divorce. Decree. Bonds of matrimony annulled, Eliza White restored to rights of a single woman as though no marriage had ever taken place between sd William White and Eliza White; petitioner by her next friend pays costs of this cause for which execution may issue.

78

MARCH 1827

    State v Daniel Arnold. Thomas J Campbell atty generall prosecutes for State; dft in proper person. Jury Geo Henry Jr, John McDonough, Saml Craig, Danl Kennedy, Jas Beck, Geo Groat, Jesse Poe, Wm Hancock, Wm Hornsby, Wm Jackson, Simon
p.106   Jackson, Wm Lewis, could not agree; put in care of Sheriff under charge of not letting them separate or converse with any indifferent person.
    Court adjourned untill Tommorrow morning.   Charles F Keith

Friday 23d March.   Present the Honourable Charles F Keith, Judge &c.
    William Hill v James Stewart. Plaintiff no further prosecutes. Defendant recovers against plaintiff his costs about his defence in this behalf expended.
    Howard & wife v Orville Paine. New trial granted to defendant. On motion of plaintiff dft is ordered into custody of Sheriff untill he find special bail. Whereupon Wm S Luty, Wm Johnson, Cornelius Moyers, Jas P Miller undertake for dft.
p.107   William Johnson presented two accounts against Rhea County. March 1826, jurors and officer trial of William S Leuty, $9.75. Septr 1826 boarding jury of 12 men & officer 8 days, $78.
    State v Daniel Arnold. Jurors sworn yesterday find dft guilty; dft counsel prays rule to shew cause why a new trial should be had. Affidavits of Jesse Davidson & Danl Arnold to shew cause in support of sd rule argued. Rule discharged. On motion of atty genl, Col Blackwell & Danl Arnold brought to bar to hear their sentence: Col Blackwell & Daniel Arnold to be branded in inside left hand with letters
p.108   H.T. in the courthouse this day. That then in their bare backs at some convenient place near the courthouse they receive twenty five lashes each, and that they set in the pillory two hours on thre different days between the hours of 10 oclock A.M and 2 oclock P.M. to wit on Saturday 24th, Monday 26th and Tuesday 27th of March 1827, and that they be confined in the common jail of Rhea County without bail nine callender months computed from day they pay the costs respectively in each of their cases and that they be held in custody also untill sd costs are paid and that the sheriff of Rhea County afsd see this sentence executed.
    Morgans & Jacobs v Jacob Slover. Plfs by attorney moved for alias vinditioni exponas issue which is ordered by court.
    George Morgan v Jacob Slover. Alias vinditioni exponas ordered.
    Court adjourned till court in course.   Charles F Keith

p.109   Monday 17th September. At Circuit Court held for Rhea County in town of Washington, before the honorable Charles F Keith Esquire one of the Circuit Judges.
    Sheriff John Lea returned venire facias: Edward Gray, Cain Abel, Thornton Creed, James Rodgers, Robert Kerr, William Miller, Miles B Davis, Jeremiah Chapman, John Hill, John Miller, Eli Ferguson, Fredrick Fulkerson, James Cowan, John Smith, William Alexander, Joseph Love, Joseph Williams, Daniel D Armstrong, John Miller, John Jack, Jesse Witt, Townley Rigg. Upon William Rice, Samuel Igo and David Roper sd writ was not executed.
    Grand Jury: Joseph Love, Townly Rigg, Robert Kerr, Jesse Witt, Wm Miller, Jos Williams, John Hill, Fredrick Fulkerson, John Smith, Cain Able, Edward Gray, Miles B Davis, Eli Ferguson. Constable Anson Dearmon sworn to attend sd grand

SEPTEMBER 1827

Jury. Joseph Love one of sd Jury was appointed foreman thereof.
Excuse John Jack and John Miller from attendance as jurors at present time.
p.110 Thomas J Campbell solicitor generall of 11th solicitorial district of Tennessee failing to appear and prosecute, Court appoint William L Wilkes atty genl pro tempore who took oath and proceeded to duties of his appointment.

James Stewart v Alexander Coulter. Clerk of Court of pleas and quarter sessions of Rhea County to bring a certain paper into this Court.

Edward McDonalds extr v George Gillispie. Cause is continued.

Richard G Waterhouse v Thomas Jack. Richard Waterhouse and Blackstone Waterhouse by their attorney saith that aforesaid plf made his will and apptd Richd and Blackstone his executors, afterwards he died. Richard and Blackstone took upon themselves the execution of sd will which defendant doth not deny; whereupon this suit stand revived in the name of the executors.

Wright Smith v George Henry Jr & Fleming Manley. Parties in proper person; plaintiff dismisses his writ; defendants confess judgment for all costs.

p.111 William C Wilson v David Houndshell & wife. Jury Joseph Love, Townley Rigg, Jesse Hill, Wm Miller, Jos Williams, John Hill, Fredrick Fulkerson, John Smith, Cain Able, Edwd Gray, Miles D Davis, Eli Ferguson who say defendants are guilty and assess plaintiffs damages to $5 besides his costs.

Court then adjourned untill Tommorrow morning.
                                                    Charles F Keith

Tuesday 18th Septr. Present the Honorable Charles F Keith, Judge &c.

Allison Howard & wife v Orville Paine. Plf by atty directed his suit be dismissed; defendant in proper person confessed judgment for all costs.

The constable appointed to attend this Court failing to appear, order Constable Robert H Jorden now present give his attendance during present Term.

p.112 Waterhouses executors v James Stewart. Plf by atty dismissed his suit; dft in proper person confessed judgment for costs to amount of $5 and plaintiff confesses judgment for the residue.

Josiah Danforth v Jonathan Fine. Plf by atty dismissed suit and confessed judgment for all costs.

William T Lewis' heirs lessee v Richard G Waterhouse. Two causes. Lessee of plf by attorney suggests that dft departed this life; rule granted him to revive cause against the legal heirs of sd defendant.

Thomas Hopkins to Robert Locke. Bond from Thomas Hopkins to Robert Locke for lands lying in Rhea County dated 22 March 1823 proven by James C Mitchell and Spencer Jarnagin subscribing witnesses thereto.

p.113 Joel Blackwell compl v Abraham Davis & David Houndshell respt. Complainant by counsel dismissed his bill whereupon John Redmond in proper person confessed judgment for costs in this behalf expended.

George W Thompson v James P Miller. Plf not appearing is nonsuited; dft recovers agt plf his costs by him about his defence in this behalf expended.

Richd G Waterhouse extrs v Thomas Jack. Dft cannot gainsay plfs action for $302 debt, $118.53 damages besides costs.

Azariah David to James Cowan. Deed of Trust Azariah David to James Cowan dated 18 Septr 1827 ackd by the maker thereof.

p.114 James Thompson v Robert Brabson. Cause is continued untill next term on defendants paying the costs of present Term. Commissions awarded dft to take deposition of Thomas Brabson of Washington County TN.

SEPTEMBER 1827

Rezin Rawlings v Anson Dearmon. From affidavit of Ruben Freeman this cause is continued untill next term upon dfts paying costs of present term.

Samuel Smith v William Snelson. Plaintiffs attorney being absent as a member of the legislature, cause is continued.

James Martin v Josiah Hauser. Power of attorney from sd Martin to sd Hauser dated 19 July 1827 proven by oath of Thomas Cox.

p.115 Eli Sharp v Anderson Fitzgerrald & others. Jury Allison Howard, Jesse Atwood, James Stuart, Jacob Brown, David Leuty, Ruben Freeman, Hezekiah Clements, George Glaze, Daniel D Armstrong, Delmore Chapman, Thornton J Creed, & John Barnett who find dfts are not guilty of trover and conversion as plaintiff complained. Dft recovers against plaintiff his costs of defence in this behalf expended.

State v Nathan S Cole. Grand jurors bill of indictment endorsed thereon a True bill by their foreman Joseph Love.

Samuel Murphey v Major M Gillian. Cause is continued.

Elijah Creel & Joseph Neilson admrs v James C Mitchell and William H Campbell. Sci Fa. James C Mitchell in proper person says he cannot gainsay plaintiffs having execution for $70.46. Plfs granted execution against defendants for amount specified and also their costs of suit and prosecution.

Nathan S Cole v James Montgomery and others. The plaintiff who commenced his suit as a pauper in his own proper person comes into Court and T L Williams Esq in behalf of Cole[interlineation is unclear] and is permitted to dismiss his writ.

p.116 An account against Rhea County by Orville Paine deputy sheriff: To bringing Daniel Arnold & Colonel Blackwell from Athens jail, expenses paid in Athens $4.12, ferrages going and coming $2, To pay self & guard 2 days 6/ per day $6, to one horse for 2 prisoners to ride $1. Guard while in Washington: James Swan 1 day & night $3, James Beck 1 day & night $1, Eli Ferguson 4 do $4, Toliver Ferguson 7 do $7, Jeremiah Howarton 4 do $4, Joshua Little 2 do $2, Elijah Runolds 1 do $1, Moses B Thompson 1 do $1, David Shelton 1 night .50, James Agey 1 do .50, Wm Riddle 1 do .50, Isaac Anderson 1 do .50: [total] $25.00. Sworn in Open Court 18th Sept 1827 John Locke, Clerk. Above account allowed.

p.117 James Rutherford v Henry Henry. On 4 August 1827 appealant field in Clerks office his written dismissal of his appeal and confessed judgment for $25 debt with 62½¢ damages together with .75 the costs of this appeal. Plaintiff recovers agt defendant his debt and damages aforesaid confessed and also his costs of suit.

Account against Rhea County filed: State v Daniel Arnold, Colonel Blackwell and Jesse Mies. Horse Stealing. Robert H Jorden charges for conveying defendants from house of William C Wilson to the jail in Athens, McMinn County, sixteen miles with a guard of 8 men $9. To supper lodging breakfast & of self with 8 others $9. R. H. Jorden clk. Appeared Robert H Jordan before me George Gillespie an acting Justice for Rhea County and made oath above account is just and true. George Gillispie J.P. Said account allowed.

Court adjourned untill tomorrow morning.   Charles F Keith

p.118 Wednesday 19th Septr. Present Charles F Keith, Judge &c.

Thomas Hopkins to John Locke. Deed dated 20 Aug 1825 from Thomas Hopkins to John Locke for 138 acres ackd by the maker thereof.

William T Lewis' heirs lessee v Richard G Waterhouse. Richard Waterhouse and Blackstone Waterhouse executors for Richard G Waterhouse decd; also William Smith is guardian of heirs who are minors: Myra Waterhouse, Cyrus Waterhouse,

SEPTEMBER 1827

Darius Waterhouse, Euclid Waterhouse, Ann Waterhouse, Vesta Waterhouse, Franklin Waterhouse. On 6 March 1827 sd Richard G Waterhouse departed this life, and sd Richard Waterhouse and Blackstone Waterhouse executors of will has had same proven at May Session of Court of pleas and quarter Sessions for Rhea County. By consent of Thomas S Williams attorney for Richard & Blackstone Waterhouse Executors and guardian of sd minors, suit of lessee is revived.

p.119 Allen York v Abijah Baugus. Plf to take deposition of William Upton, Wm Shipley, Josiah York, and Thomas York of Carrol County, Georgia.

Woodson Francis late sheriff presented his account against Rhea County: Conveyence of John W Lowrie to McMinn County jail $4, expenses $3.37½. Sworn in open court by sd Francis, John Locke clerk by his deputy James Berry.

Thompson Minott a juror summoned came not; fine $5.

State v Richard Waterhouse. Cause remanded by Supreme Court to present term of this Court for trial. William L Wilker atty genl pro tem prosecutes for State; dft in proper person says he is not guilty. Jury John Hill, Edward Gray, Thompson Merriot, Joseph Williams, Andrew Casteel, John Rawlings, John Wood, John Walker, Robt Monteeth, Aaron Ferguson, Abraham Wright, Peter Majors. Orville Paine
p.120 Deputy sheriff directed to take charge of jury and keep them together in some comfortable convenient place strictly injoined not to suffer them to disperse nor converse with any other person or persons whatsoever.

Order Isaac Moore forfeit and make fine $2 for contempt of this Court.

Remit fine of $5 against Thompson Merriot for failure to attend as juror.

Court adjourned untill tommorrow morning.   Charles F Keith

Thursday 20th Septr. Present the honorable Charles F Keith, Judge &c.

William T Lewis' heirs lessee v Richard G Waterhouse. [worded as suit above by same parties]

p.121 Lewis Ross lessee v Gambles heirs. Parties to take depositions of their witnesses; notices are to be served on Spencer Jarnagin attorney of plaintiff and Samuel Gamble guardian who defends on behalf sd heirs. Thereupon was produced to Court an application in writing of Hugh L White setting forth the county to which sd White wishes this cause to be removed, to Knox County, under the provisions of an act of general assembly to appoint counsel to attend to suits brought by Indians reserved or their assignees against purchasers of land in Hiwassee district passed at Nashville Decr 9th 1826. Court satisfyed this is a suit brought by an Indian reserve for lands purchased in Hiwassee dist, ordered this cause be removed to Circuit Court of Knox County for trial.

William T Lewis' heirs lessee v Waterhouses heirs. Eject. 2 cases. Lessee of plf to take deposition of witnesses, giving Richard and Blackstone Waterhouse 15 days previous notice.

p.122 John Spears lessee v Lewis Ross. Commissions are awarded parties to take depositions of witnesses, plf giving Spencer Jarnagin and dft giving James Cowan 15 days previous notice. Thereupon was produced an application in writing of Hugh L White setting forth [worded as in suit above Lewis Ross lessee v Gambles heirs]

State v Richard Waterhouse. Dft in proper person. Jury sworn yesterday find Richard Waterhouse not guilty of murder.

Court adjourned untill Tommorrow morning.   Charles F Keith

82

SEPTEMBER 1827

p.123 Friday 21st Septr. Present the honorable Charles F Keith, Judge &c.
Allen York v Abijah Bougers. Continued to next term of this court.
State v Benjn Armstrong. William L Wilker atty genl pro tem enters nole prosequi. Dft & Nathl W Wilson confessed judgment for costs.
James Stewart v William C Walton. Sci Fa. Plf by atty James C Mitchell; dft
p.124 came not. Grant plf execution against goods &c of dft for $125 & costs.
State v Nathan S Cole. Bill amended by grand jury.
Recognizance of Henry Davis, condition he appear to give evidence in behalf State against Nathan S Cole.
p.125 State v Nathan S Cole. William L Wilker atty genl pro tem prosecutes for State; dft pleads he is not guilty. On affidavit of James Montgomery the trial is continued until next term and dft is remanded to prison. Recognizance, Henry Davis March next to give evidence in behalf State against sd Nathan S Cole.
State v James Cahill. Grand Jury indictment agt dft for petit larceny endorsed by Joseph Love their foreman a true bill.
p.126 State v James Cahill. Dft came not but forfeited his recognizance $500.
State v James Cahill. State recovers agt Elisha Cahill $500 agreeable to his recognizance unless he appear at next term and shew cause to the contrary.
p.127 Saml McDowell & others v Richard Hazlerig & others. The death of Richard Hazlerig and of the dfts being suggested, on mention of plf by councel suggesting that John Loeke and James Berry are exrs of will of sd Hazlerig, scire facias is awarded sd plfs to revive sd suit against said executors returnable to next Term.
State v James Cahill. James Newkirk's recognizance, condition he appear next term to prosecute and give evidence in behalf of the State.
James Stewart v Alexr Coulter. Grant dft leave to amend his plea on payment of costs.
p.128 James Stewart v Alexander Coulter. Depositions of witnesses to be taken by parties, giving notice.
State v Will C Dunlap. William C Dunlap in proper person confessed judgment. State recovers of dft costs of scire facias.
William Rodgers v William Howard & Allison Howard admrs of Abraham Howard. Petition of defendants to stay execution until next term of County Court.
Herskel & Brown v same. Grant petition for writ of supersedas.
p.129 James McCance v William Crutchfield. Plf by attorney dismissed his suit; dft recovers of plaintiff all costs of this suit.
James P Haynes v Thos B Swan & Saml F D Swan. On affadavits of parties, time for taking testimony is enlarged five months.
The jurors are all discharged.
Order following account be allowed: 21 Septr 1827 Orville Paine D.S. To self and 12 jurors on trial of Richard Waterhouse 3 diets each at 25 cents pr diet $9.75; lodgings pr two nights at 12½¢ each pr night $3.25.
All causes on docket not otherwise disposed of are continued.
p.130 William T Lewis heirs lessee v Richard G Waterhouse. Same v Same. Death of dft suggested. Myra Waterhouse, Syms Waterhouse, Darius Waterhouse, Euclid Waterhouse, Ann Waterhouse, Vesta Waterhouse, Franklin Waterhouse heirs of decd are minors, on plfs motion, William Smith is apptd guardian to sd minor heirs who agrees that sd suits shall stand revived against him as guardian.
Henry Maneyard v Nancy Maneyard. Petition for divorce. Subpoena issued returned by sheriff Not found, on motion of petitioner by attorney, order publication in Hiwassian & Athens Gazette.

MARCH 1828

Nancey Greenwood v John Greenwood. Petition for divorce. Subpoena returned by sheriff Not found, on motion of petitioner, publication to be made in Hiwassian & Athens Gazette.

p.131 Jacob Slover v Martha Slover. Petition was made known to sd Martha. From testimony of Henry Price, Abraham Cox, John Toff, Miss [blank] Martin, and James Wilson that dft Martha Slover wife of petitioner was guilty of adultery, it is decreed that bonds of matrimony be dissolved; petitioner pays costs.

Court adjourned til Court in Course.

Charles F Keith

p.132 Circuit Court held in the Courthouse in Washington for Rhea County within the Seventh Judicial Circuit in sd State, on fourth Monday of March before the honorable Charles F Keith one of the Circuit Judges of the State.

Sheriff John Lea returned venire facias: Azariah David, Crispian E Shelton, James McDonald, Wm Smith, Carson Caldwell, John Cozby, John McClure, Danl Walker, Jonathan Fine, George Gillispie, Jesse Thompson, Arthur Fulton, Matthew Hubbert, James A Darwin, Saml Gamble, Ezekiel Bates, Thos Cox, Peach Taylor, Robert Cooley, Danl M Stocton, Jas Wilson, Stephen Winton, Josiah Fike.

Grand Jury: William Smith appointed foreman, Azariah David, Samuel Gamble, James McDonald, Carson Caldwell, John Cozby, John McClure, Jesse Thompson, Daniel Walker, Matthew Hubbert, Josiah Fike, Stephen Winton, Daniel M Stocton.

Constable Anson Dearmon sworn to attend on said grand Jury.

Remaining of original pannel Jonathan Fine, George Gillispie, James A Darwin, Ezekiel Bates, Thomas Cox, Peach Taylor, Robert Cooley, James Wilson, Arthur Fulton and Chrispian E Shelton.

p.133 Nancy Greenwood v John Greenwood. Dft called to answer complainants petition or same to be set for hearing exparte.

Henry Mainyard v Edy Mainyard. [worded as above]

Court adjourned untill Tommorrow morning.

Charles F Keith

Tuesday 25th March. Present the honorable Charles F Keith, Judge &c.

Lewis's heirs lessee v Waterhouses heirs & Devisees. Same v Same. Ejectments. Causes continued untill next Term of this Court.

Waterhouses executors to John Locke & John Locke to Waterhouses heirs & devisees. Deed of relinquishment establishing a conditional line dated 9 Octr 1827 acknowledged by the makers thereof.

p.134 Edward McDonalds executors v George Gillispie. Cause continued.

James P Lowrie Esq took usual oaths of Solicitor Generall in this Court.

Azariah David, James McDonald, John Cozby, Jesse Thompson, Daniel Walker, Matthew Hubbert, & Stephen Winton, jurors of the original pannel, came not but made default; fined for contempt $2 each.

Excuse Robert Cooley from further attendance as a juror at this Term.

Rezin Rawlings v Anson Dearmon. Jury Saml Gamble, Josiah Fike, Wm Smith, Danl M Stocton, John H Lea, Wm Rodgers, Wm Lowrie, John Farmer, Jesse Day, David Ragsdale, John Day, Wm Long find dft not guilty. Dft recovers against plaintiff his costs about his defence in this behalf expended.

MARCH 1828

p.135   Arthur Smith v William Snelson. On affidavit of dft cause is continued.
   Henry Mainyard v Eady Mainyard. Dft having failed to make appearance, same taken as proconfesso against her and set for hearing exparte.
   Nancy Greenwood v John Greenwood. [as above]
   James Stewart v Alexander Coulter. Jury Jas McDonald, Jas Wilson, John Cozby, Mattw Hubbert, Jas A Darwin, Carson Caldwell, John McClure, Danl Walker, Stephen Winton, Jonathan Fine, Geo Gillispie, Crispian O Shelton from rendering verdict are respited untill Tommorrow morning.
   Court Adjourned untill Tommorrow morning.   Charles F Keith

p.136   Wednesday March 26th. Present the Honorable Charles F Keith, Judge &c.
   James Swan v William Randolph. On affidavit of James Swan a plurias writ of Certiorari is awarded him returnable to next Term of this Court.
   Nancy Greenwood v John Greenwood. John having failed to appear, on motion of complainant by counsel, this cause is set for hearing exparte.
   Henry Mainyard v Edy Mainyard. On motion of complainant by his counsel this cause is set for hearing exparte.
   Edward McDonalds extrs v George Gillispie. Plfs by attorney dismissed suit and confess judgment for costs.
p.137   Allen York v Abijah Baugus. Cause contd on affidavit of defendant who is to take deposition of Giles Baugus, Carrol County GA, giving Daniel McPherson notice.
   James Stewart v Alexander Coulter. Miller Francis bail surrenders defendant whereupon Wiley Lewis, Jesse Day and James Coulter undertake for dependant.
   Michael W Buster v James Kelley. Cause continued; plaintiff to take depositions of Thomas M Kennon of Carrol County GA and Jacob Derick of McMinn County TN.
   Woodson Francis to John Locke. Deed dated 25 March 1828 for lot #46 in the of Washington acknowledged by the maker thereof.
p.138   State v John C Miller. Defendant came not; forfeits his recognizance $1000; Joseph Dyer and Maleijah Hines jointly bound in sum $1000 for appearance of dft failing to bring dft to Court forfeit recognizance. Scire facias awarded against themm returnable at next Term. Whereupon Joel K Brown gives appearance bond to attend Septr next to prosecute and give evidence in State against John C Miller.
   James Stewart v Alexander Coulter. Jurors respited untill Tommorrow.
   Court adjourned untill Tommorrow morning.   Charles F Keith

p.139   Thursday 27th March. Present the honorable Charles F Keith, Judge &c.
   William Hill v Jerusha Hill. Cause set for hearing.
   Robert Brabson v James C Mitchell & John Thompson. Dfts made default; plf is granted execution against dfts for $52.78½ the amount in writ specified and also his costs by him expended in prosecuting these writs.
   Robert Brabson v Thomas Thompson. On 15 Decr 1827 defendant filed written confession for amount in writ specified & thereupon confessed judgment for $28.56¼ together with costs. Plf granted execution for sums afsd and also for his costs.
   State v Andrew Bolinger. Nole prosequi entered.
p.140   State v James Sappington. Nole prosequi entered.
   State v James Sappington. Dft came not; State granted Execution against defendant for $1000 the amount of his recognizance and also the costs of suit.
   James Stewart v Alexander Coulter. Jurors declare they can not agree. By

85

MARCH 1828

consent, jurors from rendering verdict are discharged and cause is continued untill next Term; grant dft by atty leave to amend his fifth plea on payment of cost of sd amentment. Plf recovers against dft his costs about sd amended plea expended.
Ezekiel Bates a juror of the Original Pannel on his affidavit is excused from further attendance at this time.
p.141   Joseph McDaniel to Thomas Cox. Deed dated 10 March 1827 for fractional quarter in Hiwassee District acknowledged by the maker thereof.
State v Nathan S Cole. Atty Generall James P Lowrie prosecutes for State. Nathan S Cole the prisoner at the bar in proper person says he is not guilty. Jury Wm Carter, Saml Howard, John McCarrol, James P Miller, Wiley Lewis, Allison Howard, Robt McCracken, Caswell Johnson, George Maines, Saml Gamble, Thomas Cox, John Witt retired in care of the sheriff, directed not to suffer said Jury to disperse.
    Court adjourned untill tomorrow morning.   Charles F Keith

p.142   Friday 28th March. Present the Honorable Charles F Keith, Judge, &c.
    Robert Brabson v Thomas Thompson. Dft not appearing, on motion of plf by atty, plf is granted execution against defendant for $28.56¼ his demand in the writ specified and also his costs by him expended in prosecuting his Writ.
    Allen York v Abijah Baugus. On affidavit of plfs agent Daniel McPherson, plf to take depositions of John Looney, James Tipton, Wm Shipley, Josiah York and Thomas York of Carrol County, GA.
    Remit fines assessed this Term against Azariah David, James McDonnald, John Cozby, Jesse Thompson, Daniel Walker, Matthew Hubbert and Stephen Winton.
    Robert Gamble compl v Matthew Nelson. Complainant dismisses his bill and confesses judgment for all costs.
p.143   State v Nathan S Cole. Defendant in proper person. Jury heretofore sworn say defendant is not guilty.
    John H Lea & Orville Paine v Wyllys H Chapman. Plffs by attorney G W Churchwell and on his motion brought into Court writing under seal: six months after date we or either of us promise to pay John Locke & Thomas J Campbell admrs of John Hudson deceased $8.50 for value recd, 8th June 1827. W H Chapman, John H Lea, Orville Paine; judgt 22 March 1828 C Caldwell. Jury Richd Waterhouse, Henry Davis, Wm Hill, John Day, Wm Seymore, John Barnett, Wm Hancocke, James Montgomery, John Whaley, Robt Small, Geo Gillispie, Wm Smith to enquire whether John H Lea and Orville Paine was security for Wyllys H Chapman and as such paid money for sd dft who upon oath say sd plf was security for sd dft and paid therefore the sum of $9.58. John H Lea recovers agt dft the sum of $7.18½ and also his costs and that Orville Paine recover agt sd dft $2.39½ together with his costs.
p.144   James Thompson v Robert Brabson. Jury Azariah David, Carson Caldwell, John Cozby, Jesse Thompson, Daniel Walker, Matthew Hubbert, Josiah Fike, Stephen Winton, James McDonald, Jonathan Fine, Crispian E Shelton, Daniel M Stocton find for plf as ballance due $30.84 and assess plfs damage of detention $8.50½ besides his costs.
    Samuel Murphey v Major M Gillian. Cause is continued on affadavit of deft.
    McDowel & Patten v Haselrigs extrs & Berry. Cause is continued.
    James P Haynes v Thos B & Saml F D Swan. Continued untill the Special Term of this Court to be holden in May next.
p.145   Lewis Knight v Daniel Doxey. Jury Richard Waterhouse, Henry Davis, Wm Hill, John Day, Wm Seymore, John Barnett, Wm Hancocke, Jas Montgomery, John Whaley, Robt Small, Geo Gillaspie, Wm Smith assess plfs damage to $14.70 and his costs.

MARCH 1828

Joseph Anderson v William Murphree. Cause continued until next Court. Jurors from further attendance at this term are discharged.

Nancy Greenwood v John Greenwood. Petition for divorce. It appearing to satisfaction of Court that dft John Greenwood had abandoned petitioner Nancy Greenwood for two years before the filing of her petition without any reasonable cause and had not since taken her under his protection, therefore decreed that bonds of matrimony heretofore entered into and now existing be dissolved.

Henry Mainard v Edey Mainard. Petition for divorce. It appearing to satisfaction of Court that Edey Greenwood(sic) had deserted the petitioner Henry Mainard
p.147 for two years before the filing of his petition without any reasonable cause and had not returned to his bed and board, therefore decreed that bonds of matrimony be dissolved, petitioner paying costs in this behalf expended.

William Hill v Jerusha Hill. Cause is continued untill next regular Term.

Howards admr v James Stewart. Plf in proper person dismissed this cause and confessed judgment for costs.

Wyllys H Chapman to Henry Henry. Transfer of a plat & certificate of survey for [400 or 500, word is written over] hundred acres on Whites Creek in Rhea County was proven by John Locke & Wm Lewis witnesses thereto.
p.148 Louisa G Bean & Leonidas H Bean by their next friend v Thomas McCallie & Samuel Roberts. Complainants by next friend Edmond Bean directed the cause be dismissed and confessed judgment for all costs expended.

State Dr To Sheriff of Rhea County John Lea: to Dinner and Supper to Jurors in case State v N S Cole at 50 pr each $6. To room & attention at night $1. To Breakfast at 25 cts each $3. [Total] $10.

Lewis Knight v Daniel Doxey. Rule entered for new trial made absolute.

Whereupon all Equity Causes is hereby adjourned untill the Fourth Monday of May next and all law causes that have not been acted upon at this Term stands adjourned untill the fourth Monday of Septr next.

Court adjourned untill Court in Course.   Charles F Keith

p.149 Monday May 26th. At a Special Circuit Court held in the Courthouse in Washington for Rhea County within the Seventh Judicial Circuit for Tennessee for the hearing of Equity Causes, present on the bench the honorable Charles F Keith one of the Circuit Judges of the State.

James P Haynes compl v Thomas B Swan & Samuel F D Swan respt. Cause heretofore argued and continued, now decreed by Court that the Clerk & Master ascertain what was the value of the two bay mares at the time of the Sale by Swan to Haynes if they had been sound, also what were their value to complainant in their diseased situation and what complainant received for them when he sold them; additional testimony may be produced.
p.150 William Hill compl v James Stewart & Simeon Given. Defendants by attorney produced in open Court a written compromise wherein complainant undertakes to satisfy and pay attornies tax fee and James Stewart one of dfts undertakes to pay residue of costs in this cause expended.

Court adjourned untill Court in Course.   Charles F Keith

SEPTEMBER 1828

At a Circuit Court held at the Courthouse in Washington in Rhea County within Seventh Judicial Circuit on Fourth Monday of Septr, before the Honorable Charles F Keith Esquire one of the Circuit Judges of the State assigned to hold Circuit Courts.

Sheriff John Lea by his Deputy Orville Paine returned the venire facias:

p.151 Peter Majors, James L Cobb, Palatiah Chilton, Robert McClure, Chrispian E Shelton, James A Darwin, Isaac Roddy, Robert Gamble, Anslen L Dearing, Andrew Kincannon, Peach Taylor, David Caldwell, Joshua Green, James Lillard, Arthur Fulton, Edmund Bean, John Day, David Leuty, William Lowry, Samuel Price, Jonathan Collins, John Stewart, Avard Hanna, James McCanse.

Grand Jury: William Lowry, Anslen L Dearing, John Stewart, Peach Taylor, Avard Hanna, Jas Lillard, Andrew Kincannon, Edmond Bean, Arthur Fulton, Chrispian E Shelton, Joshua Green, Isack Roddy, David Caldwell. Court apptd Wm Lowry foreman.

Remains of the original panal that answered their names Jonathan Collins, David Leuty, and James A Darwin.

Following gentlemen Peter Majors, Jas L Cobb, Pelitiah Chilton, Robt McClure, John Day, Saml Price, James McCanse jurors of the original panel failing to come forfeit $5 each unless sufficient cause of disability be shewn at next Term.

Excuse Robert Gamble from further attendance as a juror at this Term.

Asbury M Coffee licensed as an attorney in the Circuit Courts took the usual oath and therefore is allowed to practice in this Court.

p.152 Simeon Jackson v Micajah Howerton. Cause is continued untill next Term.

Court adjourned untill Tomorrow Morning.   Charles F Keith

Tuesday 23d Septr. Present the Honorable Charles F Keith, Judge, &c.

William P Lawrence v Lewis Howel. Cause is continued untill next term. Dft to take depositions of Archibald B Rodgers and James Rodgers and Alfred Payne of McMinnville Warren County and Blackstone Howel of White County.

Den on Demise of Samuel McDaniel v Miles Vernon. Cause is continued untill the final decree of cause in chancery now depending in Circuit Court, Miles Vernon, Francis Rockhold, Joseph McCorcle are complainants and Samuel McDaniel is respondent, and to abide the decision of that cause.

p.153 Michael W Buster v James Kelley. Plaintiff to take deposition of Anson Dearmon.

William F[?] Lewis heirs lessee v Waterhouses executors et al. Two causes are continued on affidavit of the defendants.

Ansalm L Dearing, Peach Taylor, James Lillard, Andrew Kincannon jurors of the original pannel failing to come into court; they forfeit $5 each.

Order Constable William S Russell be summoned to give his attendance here during the remainder of this present Term.

Orlando Bradley v Fredrick Fulkerson. Power of Attorney from Bradley to Fulkerson dated 22 Septr 1825 proven by Adam W Caldwell & William Locke.

Jackson Howerton v Robert Love. Dft not being found in this county, order attachment awarded plf v goods and lands of defendant.

p.154 Benjamin C Stout to William W Woods. Deed from Stout to Woods dated 3 Septr 1828 for two lots in Washington acknowledged.

James Stewart v Alexander Coulter. Jury Peter Majors, James McCance, Jonathan Collins, David Leuty, John Stewart, Avary Hannah, Joshua S Green, Isaac Roddy, David Caldwell, Edward Templeton, Thomas Price, James Montgomery respited untill

SEPTEMBER 1828

Tommorrow.
  Court adjourned untill Tommorrow morning.   Charles F Keith

Wednesday 24th Sepr. Present the honorable Charles F Keith, Judge, &c.
  On motion of James P Lowrie, Esquire, atty general &c, the clerk produced a receipt from the Treasurer of East Tennessee for revenue claims of sd office, also receipt from Trustee of Rhea County for the fines and forfeitures for 1827.
  Thomas Cary v Pierce McDaniel & others. Plf by atty to shew cause why the appeal should be dismissed.
p.155 John Den on demise of David Hannah v Richard Fen with notice to Rolla Clack & James Powell tennants in possession. Eject. Richard Waterhouse and Blackstone Waterhouse are admitted to defend in the stead of Richard Fen and in lieu of tennants in possession; whereupon Henry Collins and Rezin Rawlings undertake for said defendants.
  James Stewart v Alexander Coulter. Jurors sworn yesterday say defendant is guilty of speaking the words set forth in the plaintiffs declaration. Plf recovers agt dft damages $5 besides his costs about his suit expended; execution may issue.
156 Nathan S Cole v Daniel Walker & Matthew Hubbert. Plf commenced his action as a pauper; court apptd Spencer Jarnagin as counsel for plf whereupon came dfts by atty and pray a rule to shew cause whereby this suit shall be dismissed.
  John McClenahan v John Spears. Dft by atty enter rule to shew cause why proceedings had in County Court in this Cause should be quashed.
  Hugh Murphey for use of Alexander Ferguson v Benjn Johnson & Ruben Freeman. For more than two Terms of this Court last past the plaintiff has departed this life & that no steps have been taken for the two Terms to revive same. Suit abates.
  Court adjourned untill Tommorrow morning.   Charles F Keith

p.157 Thursday 25th Septr. Present the honorable Charles F Keith, Judge &c.
  Samuel Murphey v Major M Gillian. Matters in dispute submitted to final determination of John Crawford and Matthias M Wagner who are to choose an umpire in event of a disagreement between them; if arbitrators refuse, then James C Mitchell and William C Dunlap shall nominate one or two other persons; arbitration to take place in Athens during next term of the Circuit Court of McMinn County.
  Victor Moreau Campbell Esq licensed to practice as an attorney in Tennessee Circuit Courts took oaths and is allowed to practice in this Court.
  McDowel & Patten v Haselrigg extr Berry. Demurrer overruled; writ of inquiry awarded.
  Waterhouses extrs v Howards. Cause is continued untill next term.
p.158 Joseph Anderson v William Murphree. Cause continued. Plf recovers agt dft his costs at this Term expended. Dft to take deposition of James Wilson and Dice Wilson of McMinn County, giving Miller Francis agent for Joseph Anderson notice.
  Grand Jurors return Bill/Indictment State v Jesse Matthews; a bill State Jesse Matthews William Miller & William White not True Bills. Also a Bill of Indictment State v John Madden endorsed thereon a True Bill by William Lowry foreman.
  Allen York v Abijah Baugus. Jury Peter Majors, John Day, James McCance, Jonathan Collins, David Leuty, Jas A Darwin, John Igo, John McDonough, Chase Peper, Barefoot Armstrong, John McCarrol, Wm D Collins are respited untill Tommorrow.

SEPTEMBER 1828

  John McDonough a traverse juror failing to come into Court is fined $5.
p.159 State v John Madden. Recognizance Thomas B Swan and Matthew English, condition they attend March next to testify and give evidence, charge of perjury.
  Court adjourned untill Tommorrow.   Charles F Keith

Friday 26th Septr. Present the honorable Charles F Keith, Judge &c.
  James C Mitchell to Thomas McCallie. Deed dated 26 Septr 1828 for lot #35 in Washington acknowledged.
  Thos Cary v Pierce McDaniel et al. Rule to dismiss heretofore entered is discharged. Jury John Stewart, Jas Lillard, Edmund Bean, Arthur Fulton, Joshua S Green, Thos B Swan, John Wamack, Danl D Armstrong, John Barnett, Wm Howard, James Kelly, John Whaley cannot agree, a juror withdrawn and rest of jurors discharged, cause continued untilll next term.
p.160 Michael W Buster v James Kelley. Cause continued. Dft to take deposition of [blank] Parker of Sulivan County TN; plf to take deposition of Thomas M Kennon of Carrol County, GA.
  Roberts & McCallie. Permit plffs to amend their pleadings.
  Orlando Bradley v James Kelly & John Clack. Cause is continued.
p.161 James Stewart v Alexander Coulter. Dft filed bill of exceptions and prays appeal to Court of Errors and appeals; granted on dfts entering bond & security.
  James Swan plf in Error v William Randolph. Came plf in error by counsel as well dft by atty; record of Court below argued. Judgment of Court below stand in all things affirmed; appeal in error dismissed, and dft recovers agt plf his costs about his defence in this behalf expended.
  John Haynes v Nathaniel W Wilson. Jury Anslen L Dearing, John Stewart, Jas Lillard, Edmund Bean, Arthur Fulton, Chrispian E Chelton, Joshua S Green, Isaac Roddy, Thos B Swan, John Wamach, Jacob Brown, John Clack find for defendant; dft recovers agt plf his costs.
p.162 David Leuty v Elijah C Rice. Cause is continued untill next Term.
  McDowel & Patten v Haselriggs extrs & Berry. Cause is continued.
  Roberts & McCallie v Howards admrs. Jury Henry Johns, Abraham Hughs, Lewis Knight, John Walker, John Parker, Jesse Craft, David Caldwell, Avard Hanna, Benjamin F Locke, Abraham E Rowden, James Montgomery, Daniel D Armstrong find for plaintiff $33.28 besides his costs.
  Allen York v Abijah Baugus. Jurors heretofore sworn declared they could not agree, a juror withdrawn and the rest from rendering verdict are discharged and Daniel McPherson in proper person confessed judgment for costs of plaintiffs witnesses, subpoenas & depositions; dft confessed judgment for residue of costs.
p.163 Roberts & McCallie v James Henry. Plf no further prosecutes his appeal; nonsuited. Dft recovers agt plf his costs of defence.
  John[David Johns] by his next friend [Jonathan]Fry v Anson Dearmon. Cause is continued.
  John A Rodgers v Valentine Houpt. Cause is continued.
  Arthur Smith v William Snelson. Jury Saml Martin, Jas P Miller, Thos Eaves, Abraham Spergin, Chas Goldsby, Henry Johns, Thos Johns, John McCarrol, John Day, Jonathan Collins, Lewis Knight, Levy Griffith respited untill tommorrow.
  Discharge jurors Arthur Fulton & James Darwin.
  Court adjourned untill Tommorrow morning.   Charles F Keith

SEPTEMBER 1828

p.164   Saturday Septr 27. Present the Hon. Charles F Keith, Judge &c.
State v Nathan S Cole. Dft Nathan S Cole heretofore acquitted of charge by a jury, and dft hence discharged by this Court, and it being further ordered at term afsd that the Clerk of Court should tax the costs in this cause for further inspection of this Court, and the sd Clerk, having in compliance taxed the costs, and the Court herehaving inspected same, considered that State pay costs. Bill is as follows: Justice Hubbert .50. O Paine Shff warrant 50 cts, subpoenas 150 cts 34 subp for dft 850 cts. State tax $1 [about half page other items here omitted]

p.165
John Walker 5 days $2.50
Daniel Walker 5 days $2.50
Jeremiah Montgomery 4 days $2
Elizabeth Montgomery 4 days $2
Samuel Montgomery 5 days $2.50
Daniel D Armstrong 4 days $2
Henry Spring 2 days & 40 miles $3.60
James Stewart 2 days $1
Stephen Winton 2 days 25s ferriages $1.25
Thomas Wagner 2 days $1
Anson Dearmon 5 days $2.50
George W Frazier 3 days $1.50
James Wilson 3 days $1.50
James Preston 2 days $1.00
John Farmer 2 days $1.00
Henry Henry 5 days $2.50
Elizabeth Montgomery 4 days $2
Robert Monteith 5 days $2.50
Richd Bradford 5 days $2.50
John Smith 1 day   .50
Matthew Hubbert 5 days $2.50
Jos Smith 2 days $1
John Locke 6 days $3
John McClure 5 days $2.50

State v Colonel Blackwell. Same v Daniel Arnold. Two causes. From sheriff return on Writs of Fiere facias there is none of their property of dfts to be found in this County; Clerk of Court having certified taxation of State costs expended, considered that Clerk certify same to Trustee of Rhea County for payment. In Colonel Blackwells case, Justice Waugh 50 cts, Constable Anderson 75 cts. Witness
p.166   B Holcomb 25 cts. Jail fees in Monroe County 175 cts. State tax $1. [Six lines of miscellaneous expenditures here omitted] Shff John Lea call 4 cts, jury 12½ cts, whipping dft 50 cts, 3 times in pilory 300 cts, commitment 50 cts. Shff Wilson 5 subpoenas 125 cts. Shff Beavers 2 subpoenas 50 cts. Shff J Vaughn 2 subpoenas 50 cts. Witnesses on part of the State George Davis 2 days 25 cts F $1.25, James Pharis 2 days 25 cts F $1.25, H Gaddy 2 days 25 cts F $1.25, R Holcomb 2 days 90 miles 50 cts F $6.10, R McPherson 2 days 44 miles 25 cts F $4.07, S Weaver 2 days 34 m 25 cts F $3.61, R Pharis 2 days 25 cts F $1.25, E Sharp 2 days 25 cts F $1.25, J Davidson 2 days 34 m 25 cts F $3.61. Clerk Writ of Fie Fa & copy of costs .90.
p.167   In the case of Daniel Arnold: Justice Waugh .50, Constable W R Chine $1, State tax $1. [7 lines of miscellaneous expences here omitted] Sheriff John Lea 1 call 4 cts, 2 subp 50 cts, jury 12½ cts, whipping 50 cts; 3 times put in pilory 300 cts, commitment 50 cts. Shff N W Wilson 5 subp 125 cts, Shff S Beavers 2 subp 50 cts, Shff J Vaughn 2 subpoenas 50 cts. Attorney general $5. Witnesses on part of State: [witnesses are same as the Blackwell list, same time, milages & ferriages]

Arthur Smith v William Snelson. Jurors respited yesterday from rendering their verdict this day say dft is not guilty of the trover. Dft recovers against plaintiff his costs about his defence in this behalf expended.
p.168   Lewis Knight v Daniel Doxey. Jury James McCanse, Peter Majors, Wm Lewis, Jesse Matthews, Michael Stiner, Wm D Collins, John Ferrell, Daniel D Armstrong, David Leuty, John Taylor, Philip Harwood, Malacyah Harwood who find for dft.

Remit find of John McDonough a traverse juror to $2.50; all fines entered agt jurors at this Term stand discharged. Grand and Traverse jurors discharged.

Thos McNutt v Orville Paine. Defendants demurrer discharged.

MARCH 1829

William Hill v Gerusha Hill. Attachment to compell the attendance of Martha Armstrong as a witness in this cause awarded the defendant.

p.169   James P Haynes compl v Thomas B & Samuel F D Swan respondents. Report of Clerk set aside, clerk to make an account again and report at next term.
All causes not disposed of are continued.
Court adjourned till court in course.
                                                                Charles F Keith

Monday March 23. At a Circuit Court of Law and Equity for Rhea County at courthouse in Washington before the Honorable Charles F Keith Esqr, one of the Circuit judges of the State, commissioned to hold Circuit Courts of sd county in sd Circuit.

Sheriff Samuel Hackett returned Venire facias: James Coulter, Jackson Howerton, Jacob Beck, Moses Thompson, Jesse Roddy, John Chatten, John Roddy, John Hill, John Walker, Micajah Clack, John Randols, Elijah Blythe, Patrick Martin, Benjamin Jones Sr, Robert Philips, Isaiah R Brown, Archibald Fitzgerrald, James Montgomery, John Chatten, George Keenum, William Ingle, Bryant McDonald, Jesse Tyson, Rodger Reece Junr, James Lauderdale.

Summoned: Jas Coulter, Jackson Howerton, Jacob Beck, Moses Thompson, Jesse Roddy, John Chatten, John Roddy, John Hill, John Walker, Micajah Clack, Jno Randle, Elijah Blythe, Patrick Martin, Benjamin Jones Senr, Robert Philips, Isaiah R Brown, Archibald Fitzgerrald, Jas Montgomery, John Chatten, George Keenum, William Ingle, Bryant McDonald, Jesse Tyson, Roger Reece Junr, James Lauderdale

Attending: James Coulter, Wm Ingle, Jackson Howerton, Jacob Beck, John Hill, Jesse Tyson, James Lauderdale, Robert Philips, Patrick Martin, John Chatten, Archibald Fitzgerrald, James Montgomery, George Keenum, Moses Thompson.

Grand Jury: James Coulter, William Ingle, Jackson Howerton, Jacob Beck, John Hill, Jesse Tyson, James Lauderdale, Robert Philips, Patrick Martin, John Chatten, Archibald Fitzgerrald, James Montgomery, Moses Thompson; Court appointed Moses Thompson foreman.

Constable Samuel Craig was sworn to attend the Grand Jury.
George Keenum remaining of original pannel is of the Traverse Jury.
Jurors who failed to appear: Jesse Roddy, John Roddy, John Walker, Micajah Clack, John Randle, Elijah Blythe, Benjamin Jones Sr, Isaiah R Brown, John Chatten, Bryant McDonald, Roger Reece.

p.171   Lewis heirs lessee v Waterhouses Executors. Cause is continued.
Lewis heirs lessee v Waterhouses Executors. Cause is continued.
McDowel & Patten v Haselrigs Executors & Berry. Plf by George W Churchwell their attorney; dfts in proper person. Dfts relinquishing former pleas say they cannot gainsay plfs action but failed in performing their covenant; parties agree plfs have sustained damage to $116.35 besides his costs, to be levied of goods and lands of James Berry and the assets of estate of Richard Haselrig deceased in the hands of his executors.

Thos McNutt v Orville Paine. Plf on 9 Oct 1828 filed with Clerk a dismissal of this suit. Therefore on motion of dfts attorney, dft recovers agt plaintiff his costs of defence.

p.172   John & Salley Parker to John Cozby. Deed dated 4 March 1829 for one equal undivided third part of 350 acres in Rhea County ackd by John Parker and Salley

MARCH 1829

Parker his wife; Salley Parker formerly Salley Bevely[Revely?] being first examined apart from her husband, said she executed sd deed voluntarily.

James Coulter to James Stewart. Deed dated 15 February 1820 for 35 acres on Richland Creek in Rhea County ackd.

William Smith & James Cowan exrs of William French decd to George Maines. Deed dated 26 Feby 1829 and 4 March 1829 for 183 acres on Richland Creek ackd.

p.173 Mariah Howard & Robert Parks to George Maines. Deed dated 26 Jany 1829 for 50 acres on Richland Creek proven by Allison Howard and Henry Lewis.

Court adjourned untill Tommorrow.   Charles F Keith

Tuesday March 24th. Present on the bench the Honerable Charles F Keith, Judge &c.

Roberts & McCallie v William Howard and Allison Howard admrs of estate of Abraham Howard decd. Jury Wm Ingle, John Hill, Jesse Tyson, Jas Lauderdale, Robt Philips, Patk Martin, John Chatten, Jas Coulter, Benjn Jones Sr, Jas Montgomery, Jackson Howerton, Jesse Roddy. Plf recovers agt dfts $34.65½ together with their costs of suit, to be levied of goods and land of defendants.

p.174 Bill/sale John Bell and Catharine Barns to William Locke for negro girl Leah proven by John Locke and Samuel Craig subscribing witnesses.

Baldwin H Fine complt v John Miller respnt. Dft having filed answer and praying that injunction obtained by complt for staying execution of judgmt agt dft.

Miles Vernon et al complts v Samuel McDaniel dft. On affidavit of plaintiff this cause is remanded to the rules; plf to take depositions of James G Williams Hugh Montgomery and James McDaniel in town of Calhoun.

William Hill complt v Gerusia Hill dft. Divorce. Dft by her counsel and complainant in proper person dismisses his suit; whereupon John Parker confesses judgment jointly with complainant for costs.

p.175 Roberts & McCallie v William Howard & Allison Howard admrs of estate of Abraham Howard decd. Appeal. Jury Jesse Roddy, Geo Keenum, Micajah Clack, Bryant McDonald, Baldwin H Fine, John Day, John Smith, Right Smith, Toliver S Ferguson, Robert Small, Daniel D Armstrong. [Remainder of this suit is X'd out]

Deed John Lea to William S Leuty 160 acres acknowledged.

p.176 Deed John Lea to William S Leuty 160 acres acknowledged.

Thomas Casey v William Pierce. Appeal. Jury Wm Ingle, John Hill, Jesse Tyson, James Lauderdale, Robt Philips, Patk Martin, John Chalten, Jas Coulter, Benjn Jones Sr, Jas Montgomery, Jackson Howerton, Jesse Roddy. Dft recovers of plf his costs about his defence in this behalf expended.

Deed John Lea and Thomas Cox to William Anderson and George W Netherland 640 acres acknowledged.

Orlando Bradley v James Kelly and John Clack. Cause is continued.

Deed Daniel D Armstrong to William S Leuty 100 acres acknowledged.

p.177 Michael W Buster v James Kelly. Cause is continued, dft paying costs of present term.

Deed John Holland to Wm S Leuty 92 acres acknowledged.

David Johns by his next friend Jonathan Fry v Anson De Armon[Dearmon?]. Cause is continued.

John A Rodgers v Valentine Houpt. Cause is continued.

Deed William Howard to heirs and devisees of William S Leuty decd 205 acres proven by Orville Paine and Thomas McCallie.

p.178 Simeon Jackson v Micajah Howerton. Cause is continued.

93

MARCH 1829

David Leuty v Elijah Rice. Parties by attorneys agree that matters in difference referred to consideration and final determination of Thomas J Campbell and Spencer Jarnagin and their award to be judgment of the Court.
Jonathan Fine guardian for heirs of David Duncan decd v William Johnson and John Day. Plf by attorneys and dfts in proper person saith they cannot gainsay plfs action for $253.13½ and his costs.
William P Lawrence v Lewis Howell. Upon affidavit of dft, cause is continued, defendant paying costs of present term.
p.179 David Hannah lesser v Richard Waterhouse & Blackstone Waterhouse extrs of Richard G Waterhouse. Plff came not & is nonsuited; dft recovers cost of defence.
Martha Slover v Jonathan Collins & Miles Vernon. Sci Fa. Plf by atty had warned dft Miles Vernon and that dft Jonathan Collins is not to be found in this county, and sd Jonathan Collins and Miles Vernon came not. Plf recovers agt dfts $28.92¼ costs of scire facias and her costs in suing.
John McAndless v James Stewart. Appeal. Plf by atty dismisses his suit; dft in proper person confesses judgment for costs.
p.180 Court adjourned until tomorrow morning.   Charles F Keith

Wednesday 25th March. Present on the bench the Hon Charles F Keith Judge &c.
State v Joseph Dyer appearance bail for John C Miller dft. Dft in proper person produced his principal who is ordered to custody of the sheriff.
State v John C Miller. Dft's Recognizance, Joseph Dyer his security.
William Hill v John Parker. Deed dated 24 March 1829 Lots 18 & 19 in Washington proven by James Berry and S M McJohnson[illegible] witnesses.
p.181 Grand jurors returned bill of indictment endorsed by Moses Thompson foreman True bill against George Ransom.
David Leuty v Elijah C Rice. Cause is submitted to final determination of Spencer Jarnagin and Thos J Campbell; sd referees having heard testimony, award sd David Leuty recovers agt Elijah Rice $52.05 amount paid for sd Rice as his security in debt, also $8 damages as interest, and also his costs.
State v James Cahill. Dft came not. State has execution for $500 the costs heretofore expended in this cause, also costs in prosecuting writ.
Richard G Waterhouse to John Holland. Deed dated 12 January 1825 for 50 acres on north bank of Tennessee having been proven in part was this day fully proven by oath of Blackstone Waterhouse.
p.182 State v Elisha Cahill. Dft came not. State granted execution against dft for $500 the amount of the recognizance, also costs of suing.
State v John Madden. Dft in proper person saith he is not guilty. From affidavit of Thomas B Swan the prosecutor cause is continued until next Term, John Madden recognizance $1000, William Brown $500 condition sd Madden appear next Term to answer a charge of perjury against him. Recognizance of Thomas B Swan, condition
p.183 he attend next Term to give evidence against John Madden.
John Madden v Thos B Swan. Plf requesting the privilege extended to poor persons, Court appoint G W Churchwell attorney as counsel for sd plf.
John Madden v Matthew English. Defendant not found. On motion of plf, order alias capias awarded him returnable here at next term of this Court.
State v Edward Templeton. Dft in proper person says he is not guilty. Jury Moses Thompson, James Coulter, Wm Ingle, Jackson Howarton, Jacob Beck, John Hill, Jesse Tyson, James Lauderdale, Robert Philips, Patrick Martin, John Chatten, Archd

MARCH 1829

Fitzgerrald find dft not guilty.
Lea & Cox to Anderson & Netherland. Deed heretofore certified for further probate this day was acknowledged by Thomas Cox the other maker.
p.184   State v George Ransom. Dft in proper person says he is not guilty. Jury Wm M Rodgers, Wm Lowrie, Jos McDaniel, Alexr Caldwell, Caswell Johnson, Thos H[illeg], Jesse Roddy, Micajah Clack, Benjamin Jones Sr, John Roddy, Bryant McCarrol, Daniel D Armstrong retire in charge of sheriff.
Court adjourned till tomorrow morning.   Charles F Keith

Thursday 26th March. Present the Hon Charles F Keith, Judge.
State v George Ransom. Jury heretofore sworn say dft is guilty as charged, and that property so feloniously taken to be of value of $8.
p.185   State v John C Miller. Dft came not but forfeited his recognizance. State to recover against dft $1000 unless he appear at next Term and shew cause why this judgment shall not have execution; scire facias awarded accordingly.
State v Joseph Dyer. Dft called to bring with him John Miller as he was bound to do, came not but forfeited his recognizance. State recovers agt dft $500 agreeable to his recognizance unless he appear next Term and shew cause why State may not have execution.
John McClennahan v John Spears. Cause is continued untill next Term.
Silas F Barns v William Locke. Plaintiff not appearing his suit is no further prosecuted. Defendant recovers against plaintiff his costs of defence.
p.186   Carter Brandon v Lewis Brandon. Plf not appearing, is nonsuited. Defendant recovers against plaintiff his costs about his defence expended.
Carter Brandon v Philip Brandon. Plf not appearing, is nonsuited. Defendant recovers against plaintiff his costs about his defence expended.
State v John C Miller. Joel K Brown recognizance, condition he attend next Term to give evidence against John C Miller.
John Love v Waterhouses extrs. Alexander McPherson plaintiffs security.
p.187   Simeon Jackson v Micajah Howarton. Jury George Keenum, John Walker, Samuel Rowden, Geo Frazier, John Miller, Isaac Benson, Jacob Brown, John Hill, Balden H Fine, Henry Davis, James P Miller, James McCanse retire under charge of sheriff.
Cain Able v Leonard Brightwell. Plf by atty; by consent Robert Bell security of dft from his undertaking is discharged, whereupon John Chatten Sr acknowledged himself security for defendant, failure to pay condemnation. Jury Moses Thompson, Jas Coulter, Wm Ingle, Jackson Howarton, Jacob Beck, John Hall Sr, Jesse Tyson, James Lauderdale, Robt Phillips, Archd Fitzgerrald, Jas Montgomery, Abraham Miller. Defendant recovers agt plf his costs about defence expended.
John Madden v Thomas B Swan. Time is given plaintiff to file declaration at next Term.
p.188   Samuel Murphy v Major M Gillian. Referees to whom was refered matters in dispute returned award: Judgment against Major Gillian for $51.63½ together with all other costs. John Crawford. Maths M Wagner.
Grand jury returned presentments against Wright Smith, Edmund Bean & Jacob Brown for gaming. Jurors of the original panel are discharged except Benj Jones, John Chatton, James Montgomery, John Walker.
State v Wright Smith. Dft in proper person says he is guilty. Fined $10 and
p.189   give security for payment of fine and costs. Peletiah Chelton and Robert Locke confess judgment jointly with dft for sd fine and costs.

MARCH 1829

    State v Edmund Bean. Dft in proper person says he is guilty as charged in the presentment of the grand jury against him; fined $10 and give security for payment of sd fine and costs. Robert Locke and Peletiah Chelton confessed judgment jointly with sd defendant for fine and costs.
    State v Jacob Brown. Dft in proper person says he is guilty as charged in the presentment found by the grand jury; fined $10 and give security for payment of fine and costs.
    Court adjourned untill Tommorrow morning.   Charles F Keith

p.190 Friday 27th. Present the Hon. Charles F Keith, Judge &c.
    Simeon Jackson v Micajah Howarton. Jury on yesterday impaneled say dft is not guilty. Defendant recovers against plaintiff his costs of defence.
    State v George Ransom. From affidavits of Richard Waterhouse and Miller Francis a new trial is granted. Attachment awarded against Samuel R Hackett sheriff of this County. Recognizance of George Ransom $1000, Richard Waterhouse $500, condition dft appear September next to answer charge of State. John Miller
p.191 $200 condition he appear and give evidence State against George Ransom.
    State v Jacob Brown. James P Miller, Robert Murphey, John Parker and Isaac Roddy confess judgment jointly with dft for fine of $10 on yesterday entered against him besides costs expended.
    Baldwin H Fine v John Miller & Jesse Atwood. Injunction granted in this cause is dissolved; John Miller one of respondents recovers agt Baldwin H Fine complainant and Palatiah Chilton and David Leuty his securities for the injunction the sum of $124.
    Jackson Howarton v Robert Love. Dft came not. Plf recovers of dft, but a jury to assess the amount.
p.192 Joseph Anderson v William Murphree. Jury John Chilten, Geo Kenum, Wm S Russell, John Roddy, Cain Able, Robt Small, Wm Carter, Thos B Swan, Wm Long, Robt Baulton, Geo W Frazier, Micajah Clack. Plaintiff not further prosecuting his suit, plf is nonsuited, and jury discharged. Dft recovers agt plf his costs of defence.
    Waterhouses executors v William & Allison Howard. Cause is continued.
    John Love v Richard Waterhouse and Blackstone Waterhouse executors of Richd G Waterhouse. Jury Thos B Swan, Allison Howard, Micajah Clack, John Chilton, George Stokes, James Montgomery, Benjamin Jones Jr, Matthias Hains, Henry Shaffer, George Kinnum, Jesse Roddy, John Miller. Nonsuit entered, jury discharged. Dfts recover of plf
p.193 their costs about their defence expended.
    Clerk produced following receipts: Received of John Locke Clerk of Circuit Court his return from 1 October 1827 to 1 Octr 1828 regularly certified by commissioners of said county together with $60.20¼ the amount by him collected. Miller Francis, Treasurer of E. Tennessee.
    Received of John Locke Clerk of Circuit Court of Rhea County his return from 1 March 1828 to 1 Decr 1828 certified by commissioners of county revenue, and by clerk of Rhea County Court in which return he certifies that he has collected no monies in virtue of his office. John Cozby T.R.C.
    All jurors not heretofore released are discharged from further attendance at present term.
    Roberts & McCallie v William & A Howard admr. Order that demurrer of plf to dfts plea be sustained. Plf recovers agt dfts the debt in declaration mentioned

SEPTEMBER 1829

  James P Haynes v Thomas B & Saml F D Swan. Decreed by Court that the report of the Clerk and master be in all things affirmed and that complainant recover against dfts $95.50 according to report of Clerk and Master, and costs in this behalf expended, except the costs of such commissions and depositions taken for complainant as may have been set aside by the Court or clerk and Master. From which
p.195 decree defendants obtained appeal to Supreme Court of Errors and Appeal.
  John A Rodgers v Valentine Haupt. Affidavit of James T Bradford attorney for plaintiff commissions awarded plf to take depositions of Robert Wyly, John Long and Amos Grantham of Hawkins County TN.
  All causes upon docket not specially continued or otherwise disposed of are continued till next term.
  Court adjourned till court in course.   Charles F Keith

p.196 At a Circuit Court of law and equity held for Rhea County, fourth Monday, 28th September, and on the bench the honorable Charles F Keith one of the Circuit Judges commissioned to hold the Circuit Courts of Tennessee and within the Seventh Judicial Circuit.
  Sheriff Samuel R Hackett returned the vensire facias: Asahel Johnston, David Shelton, John Hughes, Samuel Garwood, Rezin Rawlings, Joseph Love, Peter Daniel, James Rodgers, John Lea, Benjamin McKinzie Jr, Samuel Fitzgerrald, Abraham Miller, Orville Paine, Jeremiah Bolin, Vaden H Giles, John Johnson, Isaac Crisman, Robert Pharis, William Miller, William Matlock, Thomas J Haselrig, Kennedy Cooper, William Smith Sr, John Riggle, William Kennedy.
  Grand Jury: Rezin Rawlings foreman, Benjamin McKinzie Jr, Samuel F.Gerrald, Thomas J Haselrig, Kennedy Cooper, William Miller, Samuel Garwood, Joseph Love, Orville Paine, John Riggle, John Hughes, Abraham Miller, Isaac Crisman. The court appointed Rezin Rawlings foreman of sd jury.
p.197 Constable Samuel Craig sworn to attend on the grand jury.
  On affidavits of Robert Pharis, David Shelton and William Kennedy they are excued from further attendance as jurors at this Term.
  Remaining of the original pannel John Johnson, William Matlock, Jeremiah Bolin, Vaden H Giles.
  Lewis heirs lessee v Waterhouses Executors. Cause is continued.
  Lewis heirs lessee v Waterhouses Executors. Cause is continued.
  Simeon Geniss[Gennis?] compl v Woodson Francis respt. Equity. Dismissed, judgment entered agt respondant for all costs.
p.198 John McClennahan v John Spears. Defendants death heretofore suggested, plf by atty brought names of James Spears and John Miller admrs of the intestate at time of his death; scire facias issue to admrs to appear at next Term.
  Benjamin Rodgers v John Wood. Since last Term, plf ordered suit dismissed; dft directed judgment be entered against him for all costs.
  Court adjourned untill Tommorrow.   Charles F Keith

p.199 Tuesday 29th Septr. Present the honorable Charles F Keith, Judge, &c.
  William R Hines v Seaburn Sellars. Order plaintiff give security. William

SEPTEMBER 1829

Marshal enters himself security for the plaintiff.

William Young & Co plff in Error v Armstead Bedwell admr of Elias Bedwell decd. Opinion of Court that this appeal in error be dismissed and cause remanded to County Court below for final judgment, and that the plaintiff pay the costs expended in this Court in bringing up sd appeal. Plf recovers his costs against dft.

Peter Daniel, James Rodgers, John Lea, Asahel Johnson, William Smith Senr jurors of the original pannel came not; they forfeit $5 each.

p.200 Samuel Frazier Esq licensed to practice as an attorney took oath of an attorney and therefore is allowed to practice in this Court.

Rezin Rawlings to legal heirs & devisees of Wm S Leuty deceased. Deed dated 15 Septr 1829 for 236 acres, also a deed for 158 acres ackd by the maker thereof.

Rawlings extrs to Henry Sisheart. Deed dated 25 Septr 1829 for 490 acres ackd by Rezin Rawlings & John Locke exrs of the estate of Daniel Rawlings decd.

Michael F Buster v James Kelley. Jury Jeremiah Bolin, Wm Madlock, Sampson Sellars, Matthias Hines, John McClennahan, Alexr McPherson, John Johnson, Thomas Woodward, Wm Gillispie, Ralph B Locke, Robt M Hooks, Vaden H Giles find for plf and that the judgment of the County Court is in all things correct.

p.201 Waterhouses executors v William & Allison Howard. On affidavit of Richard Waterhouse one of the plaintiffs, this cause is continued untill next Term.

David Johns by his next friend Jonathan Fry v Anson Dearmon. On affidavit of Jonathan Fry, this cause is continued untill next term of this Court.

Orlando Bradley v James Kelley & John Clack. Cause continued.

John A Rodgers v Valentine Houpt. Jury Hiram Miller, Wm B Marshall, Wm Locke, Wm F Gerrald, Joseph Johnson, Jesse Matthews, Joseph McDaniel, David Roper, Jas Montgomery, Wm Smith Sr, Wm Matlock, John Dole. Plf recovers agt dft his debt $79.77, damages and costs of suit.

p.202 William P Lorance v Lewis Howle. Jury Vaden H Giles, Scott Powel, Benjn Cembrill[?], Thomas Lucas, John Johnson, Jeremiah Bolen, Ralph B Locke, John B Campbell, Augustin Bridwell, Jonathan Collins, Nathaniel W Wilson, Wm Matlock. Plf recovers agt dft damages $40.50 besides his costs of suit.

State v John P Long. Dft in proper person; recognizance $500, William Gillespie $250, condition John Long attend Court to answer charge of an affray.

James Coulter to heirs & devisees of Wm S Leuty decd. Deed dated 17th April 1829 for 190 acres ackd by James Coulter the maker thereof.

p.203 Gideon Morgan Jr lessee v Samuel McDaniel & others. Lessee of plf not appearing, lessee is nonsuited; dft recovers agt lessee their costs of defence.

Jackson Howarton v Robert Love. Writ of enquiry. Jury Vaden Giles, Scott Powel, Benjn Kimbrill, Thos Lucas, John Johnson, Jeremiah Bolen, Ralph B Locke, John B Campbell, Augustin Bridwell, Jonathan Collins, Nathl W Wilson, Wm Matlock. Plf recovers agt dft damages $500 besides his costs.

Jesse Matthews v William F Gerrald. Plf in proper person dismissed suit; judgment against him for costs.

p.204 Adam Seaboult v Jesse Matthews. Cause is continued. Dft to take deposition of John Seaboult of Cherokee Nation before Hugh Montgomery & James S Williams or either of them, also deposition of Wm F Gerrald.

Jacob Price v John Bedwell, Leroy Bedwell & Squire Bedwell. Plaintiff directs his suit be dismissed; dfts agree that judgment be rendered against them for all costs in this behalf expended.

Samuel Chun v John Condley. Jury James Stewart, Jos Johnson, Wm Smith, Asahel Johnson, James Kelley, William D Collins, Abraham Davis, Thomas Marshall,

SEPTEMBER 1829

George Frazier, William Fowler, Hiram Miller, Sampson Sellers who retired under charge of the sheriff.

p.205 Abner Underwood for the use of John Parker. Item is X's out.

State v John Stanley, William Stanley, Micajah Prewitt, John Yates. Grand jury brought in a presentment against the defendants for an affray.

State v John P Long. Grand jury returned bill/indictment agt dft for an affray endorsed by their foreman "A true bill."

State v Fleming H Fulton. Grand Jury brought in a bill/indictment agt the dft for extortion, endorsed by foreman "A true bill."

Court adjourned till tomorrow 9 Oclock.   Charles F Keith

p.206 Wednesday 30th September. Present the Honorable Charles F Keith, Judge &c.

Beshear for the use of Mitchell v Lewis Howle. Plf prays a rule to shew cause why suit should be dismissed and rule is granted accordingly.

Michael W Buster v James Kelley, Thomas Kelley. Jurors sworn yesterday returned verdict in favour of plf by finding the judgment of the County Court heretofore given in all things correct for sum of $87 besides costs. [The name of James Berry as a security was X'd out]

State v John P Long. Dft in proper person says he is guilty. Dft fined $20 and is in custody untill sd fine and costs are paid.

p.207 State v John Madden. Dft in proper person. Perjury. Cause is continued. Dfts recognizance $1000; William Brown and James P Haynes his securities $500 each. Bond of Thomas B Swan, condition he appear March next to prosecute and give evidence against John Madden.

Grand Jurors bill/indictment against Stephen Mayfield for murder endorsed by Rezin Rawlings their foreman, "A true bill."

Joseph C Stocton & William Long summoned to attend as jurors came not, fined $5 each.

p.208 State v Stephen Mayfield. Defendant in proper person says he is not guilty. Jury Abijah Baugus, Wm Gwin, John Ferrell, Danl D Armstrong, Andw Casteel, James C Mitchell, Saml Ferguson, Saml Howard, Jas Ferrell, Thos Hains, Jas P Miller, Benjn Kimbrell. Sheriff Saml R Hackett takes charge of jury and not suffer them to disperse nor converse with any other person.

John Madden v Thomas B Swan. Commissions generally are awarded to take depositions of respective witnesses.

Court adjourned untill Tommorrow morning.   Charles F Keith

p.209 Thursday 1st Octr. Present the Honorable Charles F Keith, Judge, &c.

State v John P Long. John P Long and William Gillispie in proper person and sd Wm Gillispie confessed judgment jointly with dft for fine of $20 & all costs.

Samuel Chen v John Condley. Asahel Johnson one of the jurors is withdrawn and the rest from rendering verdict are discharged. John Condley in proper person agreed that judgment be entered against him for $90 and also costs.

State v George Ransom. Nole prosequi entered.

p.210 State v Flemming H Fulton. Extortion. Dft in proper person. Cause is continued untill next term. Recognizance of dft $500, Arthur Fulton $250. Jesse Thompson recognizance $250 condition he appear March next to give evidence.

State v Stephen Mayfield. Jurors heretofore sworn find dft Stephen Mayfield

SEPTEMBER 1829

not guilty of murder, but they find him guilty of the felonious slaying of John Millins in manner and form as charged in the bill of indictment and the defendant is remanded to prison.

p.211 Grand jurors brought bill/indictment against James Burton & Matthias Green endorsed by Rezin Rawlings foreman "A true Bill."

The Grand Jurors brought a bill/Indictment against James Burton & Matthias Green endorsed thereon by Rezin Rawlings their foreman "A True Bill."

James Kelley v Robert Bell. Cause is continued. Plf to take deposition of Preston W Davis of Turnersville, Robinson County, TN.

State v James Burton & Matthias Green. Same v Same. Dfts in these two causes in proper persons say they are not guilty. Dft James Burton puts himself on his country. Jury Matthias Hines, Peter Fine, Saml Merricks, William Johnson, John Warmack, Thos Blankenship. Paskill Simpson, Abner Triplett, John McCarrol, Thomas Henry, Henry Henry, James Woodward who find dft James Burton guilty as charged; dft is remanded to prison.

Court adjourned till tomorrow 9 Oclock.   Charles F Keith

p.212 Friday 2 Octr 1829. Present the honorable Charles F Keith, Judge, &c.

John Madden v Matthew English. Plf claims priviledge the law extends to poor persons; Court appoint George W Churchwell counsel for sd plaintiff.

Matthias Hines v Anderson W Smith. Plf claims benefit extended by law to poor persons; Court appoint James P Lowrie counsel for sd plaintiff.

Jacob Bashear for use of David L Mitchell v Lewis Howle. Rule heretofore entered to dismiss certiorari is argued; certiorari dismissed. Plf recovers against Lewis Howle and his securities Richard Nelson and Jesse Thompson his costs of suit.

Elijah C Rice v George W Mayo & Thomas McCallie. Plaintiff by his attorney directed his suit be dismissed; Dfts recover agt plf their costs of defence.

p.213 Balden H Fine compl v John Miller & Jesse Attwood respt. Jury of reference returned their award: find verdict in favour of complainant; respondent John Miller pays all costs in this cause heretofore expended. Jesse Thompson, Orville Paine, Thomas C Wroe, Jacob Wassum, Briton Peters, Moses Thompson, Jacob Brown. Whereupon Balden H Fine directed his Bill of Injunction be dismissed and John Miller one of the respondents in proper person assumed the payment of all costs. John Locke clerk. Therefore bill dismissed and complainant recovers agt dft John Miller the costs as confessed about his bill in this behalf expended.

p.214 State v Matthias Green. Dft in proper person withdraws his plea of not guilty and puts himself on the mercy of the Court.

State v James Burton & Matthias Green. Dfts in proper persons say they are not guilty. Jury John Johnson, Pleasant Hollowman, Thomas Kelley, Beaty Perry, Wm Lewis, Benjamin Kimbrill, Wm Matlock, Vaden H Giles, Andw Casteel, Alfred Beckhold, Wm Gwin, John Ferguson find dfts guilty, find value of property stolen to be $8, so they say all.

Thomas Cox & Abraham Cox to William S Leuty. Deed dated 1 Decr 1828 for fractional quarter in Hiwassee district containing 50½ acres in Rhea County ackd.

p.215 Thos & S Cox to Thomas J Campbell. Deed dated 10 Septr 1829 acknowledged.

Locke & Chilton exrs/estate of Wm S Leuty decd v Thos & S Cox. [X'd out]

State v Richard Bradford & others. Grand Jurors brought into Court a bill of Indictment against Richard Bradford and others endorsed by Rezin Rawlings foreman "A true Bill." Richard Bradford in proper person says he is not guilty.

100

SEPTEMBER 1829

Jury Jeremiah Bolen, Asahel Johnson, Thomas Marshall, Sampson Sellers, Matthias Hines, John Dolen, Wm B Marshall, Hiram Miller, Wm Johnson, Jas Kelly, Jas Carrol, John Warmack retire under charge of the sheriff not to disperse or converse with other persons, and bring them into Court Tommorrow.
       Court adjourned untill Tommorrow morning.   Charles F Keith

p.216 Saturday 3d October. Present the honorable Charles F Keith, Judge, &c.
       State v Richard Bradford. Dft in proper person. Jury sworn yesterday find defendant guilty. Richard Bradford for his crime of conspiracy fined $30 and remain in prison four callender months from this date, and pay all costs in this behalf expended, and that he be kept in custody untill sd fine and costs be paid or secured by good bond and security.
       State v Stephen Mayfield. Defendant for his crime to be branded in the left hand with the letter M between the hours of 12 and 1 o'clock this day in open court, that he be imprisoned in the common jail six callendar months from this day, and pay all costs in this behalf expended, and be kept in close custody till said costs be paid, and that sheriff carry said sentence into execution.
p.217 State v James Burton & Matthias Green. Benjamin McCarty prosecutor. Dfts sentenced: Dfts each receive ten lashes on their bare backs on Monday 5th Octr between hours of 12 and 2 oclock and remain in custody untill the costs are paid, and the sheriff to see this sentence executed.
       State v James Burton & Matthias Green. Isaac Baker prosecutor. Sentenced that James Burton and Matthias Green on 5th Octr 1829 between 12 & 2 Oclock receive fifteen lashes on their bare backs and to remain in custody untill the costs of this cause are paid, the sheriff to put their sentence into execution.
       William P Sawrmer[?] v Lewis Harrell[Hannah?]. Rule heretofore granted dft to shew cause for new trial is discharged.
p.218 State v Samuel R Hackett. Dft discharged without payment of costs from attachment agt him and suit dismissed.
       William R Hinds v Sampson Sellers. Cause is continued.
       Matthias Hinds v Anderson W Smith. Leave granted plf to file declaration.
       Thomas Jack to Rezin Rawlings. Deed proven by Thos Jack for three lots in southern liberties of Washington in Rhea County.
       Rezin Rawlings to Jefferson B Love. Deed acknowledged by Rezin Rawlings for three lots in southern liberties of Washington in Rhea County.
       Jurors from further attendance at this Term are discharged.
p.219 Jesse Matthews ads State. Bill of cost. Justice Gamble .50
       Constable Russell arrest 50 cts, 3 subpoenas 75 cts $1.25
       State Tax $1
       Clerk filing and docketing record 100 cts; indictment 60 cts process 100 cts 1 subpoena 12½ cts, 22 witnesses probate 137½ cts Judgment 100 cts. for costs 25 cts. taxing costs 40 cts. Copy of costs 50 cts.
       Sheriff Orville Paine 1 subpoena .25
       Attorney General $1.25
       Witness for state Samuel Gamble 2 days $1.00
           "   William F. Gerrall 2 days ferriage 25 cts $1.25
           "   Charity Rigg 2 days ferriage 25 cts $1.25
           "   Mary White 2 days 24 miles ferriage 25 cts $3.21
           "   Susan Harp 2 days 30 miles ferriage 25 cts $3.45

SEPTEMBER 1829

Ditto   William Brumley 2 days ferriage 25 cts $1.25
"   Nancy F. Gerrald 2 days ferriage 25 cts $1.25
"   Taylor Eldridge 2 days 24 mile ferry 25 cts $3.21
"   John McClenahan 2 day ferriage 25 cts $1.25
"   John McClenahan 2 days ferriage 25 cts $1.25
"   Jane Lawson 2 days 25 miles ferriage 25 cts $3.25
"   Anderson F. Gerrald 2 days ferriage 25 cts $1.25
"   Joseph Harp 2 days 15 miles ferriage 25 cts $2.85
"   John Harp 2 days ferriage 25 cts $1.25
"   Alexander Philpot 2 days ferriage 25 cts $1.25
"   Polly Mahan 2 days ferriage 25 cts $1.25
"   Jesse Halloway 2 days ferriage 25 cts $1.25
"   Alexander Rice 2 days ferriage 25 cts $1.25
"   Mason McClenahan 2 days ferriage 25 cts $1.25
"   Joseph Sebourn 2 days ferriage 25 cts $1.25
Josiah Star 1 day ferriage 25 cts .75

It is therefore considered by the Corut that the County of Rhea pay said costs and that the Clerk certify the same to the County Court of sd County.

p.220 Jesse Matthews, William Miller & William White ads State. Petit Larceny. Court ordered this bill of cost to be put on record, the attorney general having certified it correctly. Justice Gamble .50. Constable Russell 3 arrests, 3 subpoenas $2.25; Clerk process 100 cts filing & docketing record 100 cts entering 10 recognizances 250 cts. Indictment 60 cts 27 subpoenas 337½ cts. 24 witnesses probate 150 cts. Judgment 100 cts for cost 25 cts taxing cost 40 cts Copy of costs 50 cts $12.12½. Sheriff John Lea 26 subpoenas $4.50
Sheriff Orville Paine 1 subpoena .25
Attorney General $1.25
Witness for state William F. Gerrall 2 days ferriage 25 cts $1.25
ditto   Charity Rigg ditto diotto $1.25
"   Mary White 2 days 24 mile ferriage 25 cts $3.21
"   Susan Harp 2 days 30 mile ferriage 25 cts $3.45
"   William Brumley 2 days ferriage 25 cts $1.25
"   Nancy F Gerrald 2 days ferriage 25 cts $1.25
"   Taylor Eldridge 2 days 24 mile ferriage 25 cts $3.21
"   John McClenahan 2 days ferriage 25 cts $1.25
"   Jane Lawson 2 days 25 mile ferriage 25 cts $3.25
"   William B Russell 2 days ferriage 25 cts $1.25
"   Martin Rigg 2 days ferriage 25 cts $1.25
"   Samuel Gamble 2 days $1.00
"   Andrew F. Gerrald 2 days ferriage 25 cts $1.25
"   Joseph Harp 2 days 15 mile ferriage 12½ cts $2.72½
"   John Harp 2 days ferriage 25 cts $1.25
"   Adam Seabolt 2 days ferriage 25 cts $1.25
"   Alexander Philpot ditto ditto $1.25
"   Polly Mahan   "   "   1.25
"   Jesse Holloway "   "   1.25
"   Alexander Rice "   "   1.25
"   Mason McClenahan "   "   1.25
"   Joseph Sebourn "   "   1.25
"   Joseph Star 1 day ferriage 25 cts .75

MARCH 1830

John McClenahan 2 days ferriage 25 cts $1.25
p.221   Considered by the Court that the County of Rhea pay said costs and that the Clerk certify the same to the County Court of said County.
John Doland v Thomas Marshall. Dft came not. Plf recovers of dft, but because it is not known what amount, let a jury come at next term of this court to enquire of the damages that the palintiff hath sustained by reason of the dft speaking the words in the plaintiffs declaration mentioned.
Court adjourned until Court in Course.   Charles F Keith

p.222   Monday 22d March 1830. At a Circuit Court of law and equity in the courthouse in the Town of Washington on the fourth Monday of March, present presiding on the bench the honorable Charles F Keith one of the Circuit Judges commissioned and assigned to hold the Circuit Courts within the Seventh Judicial Circuit.
Sheriff Saml R Hackett returned the Venire facias: Wm McDonald, Samuel Howard, John Hughes Sr, James Preston, George Gillispie, Jno Walker, John Hill, Isaiah Sellers, Larkin Butram, John Wasson, Levi W Ferguson, Samuel Looney, Robert Cooley, Thomas Hunter, Matthias Shaffer, Eli Ferguson, Jesse Roddy, Randolph Gibson, Joseph Love, Rezin Rawlings, John Bolin, Robert Gamble, Samuel Gamble, Richard Waterhouse. Sheriff returned that Peletiah Chilton was not found.
Grand Jury John Hill, John Wasson, Samuel Howard, William McDonald, Rezin Rawlings, Robert Gamble, Randolph Gibson, John Walker, James Preston, Eli Ferguson, Thomas Hunter, Levi W Ferguson, John Hughes Senr. Court appointed John Hill foreman of the Grand Jury.
p.223   Constable Robert W Caldwell was sworn to attend the Grand Jury.
Remaining of the original pannel George Gillispie, Larkin Butram, Samuel Looney, Robert Cooley, Matthias Shaffer, Jesse Roddy, Joseph Love, John Bolin, Samuel Gamble and Richard Waterhouse.
William Seymore to William Johnson. Deed dated 3 Jany 1829 for four lots in southern liberties of Washington #17, 18, 35, 36 proven by Thomas Price & John Day.
From affidavits of John Levi, Peter Daniel, Asahel Johnson, conditional judgment entered agt them at last Term as delinquent jurors is discharged.
William K Hines v Sampson Sellers. Rule granted dfts atty to cause plf to give security for the prosecution of this cause dismissed.
Abner Underwood for the use of John Parker v Simeon Geven. Dft came not. Jury John Hill, John Wasson, Saml Howard, Wm McDonald, Rezin Rawlings, Robt Gamble, Randolph Gibson, John Walker, Jas Preston, Eli Ferguson, Thos Hunter, Levi W Ferguson find for plf $34.37 besides his costs.
p.224   William Long v John Locke. Order Carson Caldwell to bring into Court the papers in the cause William Long against William Gwin now in his possession.
Court adjourned untill Tommorrow morning.   Charles F Keith

Tuesday 23d March. Preent the Honorable Charles F Keith, Judge &c.
Lewis Ross v John Spears & James Cowen. No steps has been taken in this cause for the two terms past, therefore on motion of the dft James Cowan by counsel, suit dismissed. Dft recovers agt complt his costs.

MARCH 1830

From affidavit of William Smith, the forfeiture agt him at last Term for his delinquency as a juror is set aside.

p.225 From affidavit of James Rodgers, conditional judgment entered against him at last Term of this Court is set aside on his payment of the costs.

Lewis' heirs lessee v Waterhouses executors. Two causes. By mutual consent, causes are continued. Dft to take depositions of John Shults of Tennessee and Valentine Shults of Alabama.

Peter Davis v George W Riggle. Plf in proper person acknowledges full satisfaction of his debt. Defendant in person directed his appeal dismissed and confesses judgment for all costs in this cause heretofore expended.

p.226 William R Hines v Sampson Sellers. Jury Geo Gillispie, Saml Luney, Matthias Shaffer, Jos Love, Larkin Butram, Robt Cooley, Jesse Roddy, Orville Paine, William Locke, Jno McClenahan, Thomas B Swan, Thomas Hains. Dft recovers agt plf his costs.

William Frenchs executors v George Mainas. Deed dated 26. Feby and 4 March 1829 for 138 acres heretofore ackd by James Cowan one of the makers thereof was this day ackd by William Smith the other maker thereof.

Orlando Bradley v James Kelley & John Clack. Plf came not; dfts recover agt plf their costs of defence in this behalf expended.

p.227 James Kelley v Robert Bell. Jury John Hill, John Wasson, Saml Howard, John Walker, Wm McDonald, Rezin Rawlings, Robt Gamble, Randolph Gibson, Jas Preston, Eli Ferguson, Thos Hunter, Levi W Ferguson. Plf no further prosecuting his suit, jury from rendering verdict is discharged and plf nonsuited. Dft recovers agt plf his costs about his defence in this behalf expended for which execution may issue.

Adam Seaboult v Jesse Matthews. Jury[above]. Dft recovers his costs.

Matthias Hines v Anderson W Smith. Plf came not; nonsuited. Dft recovers against the plaintiff his costs by him about his defence in this behalf expended.

p.228 Abraham Miller v John H Worbell. Plf by atty dismissed his appeal and confessed judgment for all costs.

William Long v John Locke. Plf is permitted to release William Lewis as his security; whereupon came John Long and Ruben Freeman to undertake for said plaintiff. Jury Geo Gillispie, Saml Looney, Matthias Shaffer, Joseph Love, Samuel Gamble, Larkin Butram, Robt Cooley, Jesse Roddy, Jno Bolin, Richd Waterhouse, Saml Garwood, Wm D Collins find for plf $24 besides his costs.

James P Lowrie Esq attorney generall having failed to appear at this Court, the Court appointed William L Welker attorney generall protempore.

p.229 Samuel Jamison v William Fitz Gerrald. Plf came not; nonsuited; defendant recovers against plaintiff his costs about his defence expended.

Court adjourned untill Tommorrow morning.   Charles F Keith

Wednesday 24th March. Present the honorable Charles F Keith, Judge &c.

John Dolen v Thomas Marshall. From affidavits of dft and Thomas J Campbell the judgment by default entered last Term is set aside on defendant paying costs; leave given dft to plead. Plaintiff recovers against dft his costs.

Samuel Jammison v William Fitz Gerrald. Nonsuit is set aside.

John Madden v Matthew English. By mutual consent cause is continued.

p.230 State v John Madden. from affidavit of Thomas B Swan, cause is continued. Dfts recognizance $500, James P Haynes and William Brown securities. Bond of Thomas B Swan, condition he appear at September Term to prosecute & give evidence against John Madden, charge of perjury. Bonds of David Able, Edwd Stewart, Robert S Mahan,

MARCH 1830

George Gordon, William English $250 each, condition they appear Septr Term to give evidence against John Madden for perjury.
p.231　John Madden v Thomas B Swan. Cause is continued.
　　State v Flemming H Fulton. Dft in proper person says he is not guilty. Jury Geo Gillispie, Saml Looney, Matthias Shaffer, Saml Gamble, Larkin Butram, Robt Cooley, Jesse Roddy, John Bolin, Richd Waterhouse, Hazard Bean, William Howard, Jas Stewart find dft not guilty. State recovers against Lewis Pollard the prosecutor the costs about this prosecution in this behalf expended.
　　State v Jonathan Stanley. Dft in proper person says he is not guilty. Jury[above except James McCanse for Richd Waterhouse] find dft not guilty.
p.232　George Gillispie complt v Allen Gillispie & Adam Broyls. Continued.
　　Waterhouses extrs v William & Allison Howard. Jury Geo Gillispie, Larkin Butram, Saml Looney, Robt Cooley, Matthias Shaffer, Jesse Roddy, Saml Gamble, John Bolin, Jas McCanse, Jos Love, Samuel Garwood, Josiah Howser say dfts are guilty as complainant hath complained. Plfs recover agt dfts damages $78.80 & costs.
　　[Following item is X'd out: Grand Jurors return presentments against James Pickett, Ira Gothard, William Fretwell, Willis West, George Gothard, John Yates, James Lea, Bartley Benson, Robert Benson and Robert Boulton.]
　　John McClenahan v John Spears. Alias Sci fa awarded plf.
p.233　Johns by his next Friend Jonathan Fry v Anson Dearman. Cause is continued.
　　William D Collins v Jesse Matthews. Jury John Hill, John Wasson, Samuel Howard, William McDonald, Robt Gamble, John Walker, Randolph Gibson, Wm Locke, Jas Preston, Thomas Hunter, Rezin Rawlings, Thomas Henry. Defendant recovers agt plf.
　　Asa Bowden for use of Abraham Davis. Alias capias returned not executed; plurias awarded plf returnable at next Term of this Court.
　　On application of Grand Jury a subpoena is awarded commanding Fletcher French to appear before Grand Jury and give evidence in relation unlawful gaming, who was sworn and sent before Grand Jury. Upon which testimony grand jury returned presentments against James Pickett, Ira Gothard, Wm Fretwell, Willis West, George Gothard, John Yates, James Lea, Bartley Benson, Robert Benson & Robert Bolton.
p.234　Court adjourned until tomorrow morning.　　　　　　　　Charles F Keith

Thursday March 25. Present the same judge as on yesterday.
　　Johns by his next Friend Jonathan Fry v Anson Dearmon. Plaintiff to take deposition of Thomas Johns of Georgia.
　　James Berry to Thomas McCallie. Power of attorney dated 24 March 1830 from James Berry to Thomas McCallie proven by Thomas J Campbell and Return[Retwin?] J Miegs the subscribing witnesses.
　　William Smith v William G Brownlow. Time is given to plead.
p.235　Miles Vernon, Francis Rockhold, Joseph McCorcle complainants v Samuel McDaniel respondent. Upon affidavit of Miles Vernon three months allowed for taking depositions on behalf complainants, cause set for hearing at next Term; complainants pay costs of this continuance.
　　Jury from further attendance are discharged.
　　James Kelley v Robert Bell. On affidavit of plf nonsuit entered this Term is set aside on plfs paying costs of this term togeher with costs expended by order of last term for taking depositions. Dft recovers agt plf. Revive order of last Term for plf to take deposition of Preston W Davis.
　　Jesse Poe admr v William Lewis et al. Cause is continued.

MARCH 1830

p.236   State v Isaac Garrison. Dfts recognizance, John Garrison and John Garrison his securities, condition Isaac Garrison appear Septr next to answer charge of the State against him for grand larceny. Richard Waterhouse bond, condition he attend Septr next to prosecute and give evidence against Isaac Garrison. Cyrus Waterhouse, Darius Waterhouse, Barbary Johnston, Robert Johnston, Jacob Garrison and Eli Ferguson bond, condition they attend Septr Term to give evidence against Isaac Garrison.

p.237   State v William Fretwell. Recognizance of Timothy F French, condition he attend Septr next to give evidence against Wm Fretwell for unlawful gaming.

    State v Willis West. Recognizance of Timothy F French[as above].

    State v George Gothard. Recognizance of Timothy F French[as above].

    State v John Yates. Recognizance of Timothy F French[as above].

p.238   State v Robert Bolton. Recognizance of Timothy F French[as above].

    State v Robert Benson. Recognizance of Timothy F French[as above].

    State v Bartley Benson. Recognizance of Timothy F French[as above].

    State v James Lea. Recognizance of Timothy F French[as above].

p.239   State v James Pickett. Recognizance of Timothy F French[as above].

    State v Ira Gothard. Recognizance of Timothy F French[as above].

    Richard G Waterhouse to Asahel Rawlings. Deed dated 2 January 1827 for 632 acres in Hambleton County proven by Joseph Garrison and remaining witness.

    State v John P Long. Cause is continued untill next term of this Court.

    Account for keeping Richd Bradford in jail $71.25. Keeping Matthias Green $33. Keeping James Barton $33. Keeping George Ransom $25.23. Keeping Jonathan Copeland $7. Bill inspected and allowed.

p.240   William T Lewis heirs lessee v Waterhouses executors. Plf by atty Thomas J Campbell directed this suit be dismissed and confessed judgment for all costs.

    William T Lewis heirs lessee v Waterhouses executors. Plf by atty Thomas J Campbell directed this suit be dismissed and confessed judgment for all costs.

    Jane Price to George W Churchwell. Deed dated 16 Octr 1828 for land in Arkansas Territory proven by Richard Waterhouse the remaining witness.

    Ephraim Price & Jane Price to George W Churchwell. Deed dated 16 Octr 1828 for land in Arkansas Territory proven by Richard Waterhouse the remaining witness.

p.241   State v George Ransom. Grand Larceny. Costs certified by attorney general. State tax $1; Justice .50; Constable Craig warrant 50 cts 3 subpoenas 75 cts $1.25; Clerk receiving & filing record 100 cts entry 20 cts 11 recognizances 275 cts indictment 60 cts 24 subpoenas 300 Jury 12½ cts, judgt 100 cts, note 25 cts continuance 40 cts 2 orders 50 cts 20 witnesses probates 125 cts, 3 aff 37½ cts, judgt 100 cts, taxing costs 40 cts copy of costs 50 cts, $13.35. Shff Hackett 18 subpoenas 450 cts 2 not found 25 cts 2 calls 8 cts. Jury 12½ cts $4.95½. Ditto Carr, 1 subpoena 25 cts .25. Ditto Woodward 2 subpoenas 50 cts .50. Ditto Brown 1 subpoena 25 cts 1 Non st 12½ .37½. Attorney general $2.50. $25.93.

Witnesses on part of the state: John Billingsley 3 days 74 miles $5.96

    Matthew Hubbard 3 days $1.50

    John Crabtner[?] 1 day .50

    Benjn Whitehead 1 day 42 miles $2.68

    John Condly 3 days $1.50

    Elizabeth Furguson 1 day .50

    James Swan 1 day .50

    Spills B Dyer 3 days $1.50

    John Miller 3 days $1.50

John Parker jailor, for keeping George Ransom 53 days at 37½ pr day $19.97½.

SEPTEMBER 1830

    For 4 turnkeys @ 3 each $2
    Six days [illegible] @ 2/3 pr day $2.25
    2 turnkeys @ 3/ each $1
Considered by Court that the State of Tennessee pay the above costs.
    Court adjourned till court in course.   Charles F Keith

p.242   Monday 27th September. A Circuit Court of law and equity held for Rhea County in the Town of Washington on fourth Monday, and presiding on the bench the Honorable Charles F Keith on of the Circuit Judges assigned to hold Circuit Courts within the seventh Judicial Circuit.
    Sheriff Samuel R Hackett returned venire facias: Carson Caldwell, John Cozby, John McClure, Matthias Saffer, Vaden H Giles, Isaac Roddy, Beal Gaither, Azariah David, Crispien E Shelton, Samuel Gamble, Arthur Fulton, Matthew Hubbart, Joseph McCorkle, Archibald D Paul, James Swan, Jesse Thompson, George Gillespie, James McDonald, Daniel Walker, Daniel M Stockton, James A Darwin, Peach Taylor, Hoil Butram, William Smith, Robert Elder. George Preston of original venire was not found.
    Grand Jury: George Gillespie, Beal Gaither, Arthur Fulton, John McClure, James A Darwin, Azariah David, Daniel Walker, Matthew Hubbart, Archibald D Paul, Vaden H Giles, Isaac Roddy, Crispien E Shelton, Peach Taylor. Court appoint George Gillespie foreman of Grand Jury.
    Constable William B Lauderdale was sworn to attend on Grand Jury.
    From affidavits of Carson Caldwell, Robert Elder, William Smith, James Swan and John Cozby they are excused from further attendance as jurors at this Term.
p.243   Jonathan Fine to Matthias Broyles. Deed dated 24 Septr 1829 for 167 acres proven by James Berry and Samuel R Hackett.
    Ralph B Locke v Thomas Henry. Appeal. Parties filed written agreement whereby plf agrees to dismiss his appeal and dft confesses judgment for costs.
    Court adjourned untill tomorrow morning nine oclock.   Charles F Keith

Tuesday 28th Septr. Present the Honorable Charles F Keith, Judge &c.
    Excuse James McDonald from further attendance as a juror at this Term.
    William Smith v William G Brownlow. Pleadings to be amended.
    John Madden v Thomas B Swan. Cause is continued. Dft to take deposition of Horatio Belt & also deposition of Matthew English.
p.244   James Kelly v Robert Bell. Cause is continued.
    Samuel Jamison v William Fitzgerald. Jury George Gillispie, Arthur Fulton, James A Darwin, Daniel Walker, Archibald D Paul, Isaac Roddy, Beal Gather, John McClure, Azariah David, Matthew Hubbard, Vaden H Giles, Crispian E Shelton assess plfs damage to $50 besides his costs.
    Levin Stokes v Alexander Coulter. Parties in proper persons agree to refer matters in dispute to award of Thomas Harris and Orville Paine.
p.245   Samuel Jamison v William Fitzgerrald. Jury Joseph McCorcle, Hoil Butram, Abram Cox Sr, Michael Kelly, Matthias Shaver, John Oldham, Robert Stockton, John McClanahan, James Stuart, Jeremiah Jack, John Day, Jesse Thompson find dft guilty

SEPTEMBER 1830

on the first count and not guilty on the second. Plf recovers of dft $20.
    Henry Griffith v Orville Paine. Jury George Gillispie, Arthur Fulton, James A Darwin, Daniel Walker, Archibald D Paul, Isaac Roddy, Beal Gather, John McClure, Azariah David, Matthew Hubbard, Vaden H Giles, Pruit Taylor respited till tomorrow.
    John Madden v Matthew English. Plf & dft in proper persons; plf dismissed his suit; dft confessed judgment for one half the costs.
p.246   State v John Madden. Recognizance of John Madden, James P Hayns and Matthew English securities, condition Madden appear at March term. Thomas B Swan bond, condition he appear at March Court to prosecute and give evidence against Madden.
    State v Stephen Mayfield. Jailor John Parker presented following account: for keeping Stephen Mayfield in jail 292½ days $109.68⅛; to 6 turn keys @ 3/each $3; sworn in open court. Total $112.68⅛. John Locke, clerk, by his deputy James Berry. J.P.Lowry Att.Genl of 11th Sol. Dist.
p.247   Thomas Haslerig to Orville Paine. Power of attorney from Thomas Haslerig to Orville Paine dated 5 April 1830 proven by James Stuart and John Parker.
    Court adjourned till tomorrow morning.   Charles F Keith

Wednesday Sept 29th. Present the Honorable Charles F Keith, Judge, &c.
    John McClanahan v John Spears executors. PLurias Sci Fa awarded plf.
    Samuel McDaniel et al v Elihu S Barcklay. Alias Sci Fa awarded plf.
    Waterhouses executors v James Hannah, John Davis, Daniel D Armstrong. Alias Sci Fa awarded plfs against James Hannah and John Davis.
    State v Micajah Privott. Cause is continued.
    State v William Stanley. On motion of James P Lowry attorney general, order alias Plurias capias awarded.
    State v John Yates. On motion of James P Lowry atty genl, alias plurias capias awarded.
p.248   State v John C Miller. Indictment. Joseph Dyer by atty Spencer Jarnagin confessed judgment for all costs.
    State v John C Miller. Scire facias. Joseph Dyer by atty Spencer Jarnagin having confessed judgmt, atty genl dismissed scire facias. State recovers of Joseph Dyer all costs.
    State v Joseph Dyer security for John C Miller. Dft by atty Spencer Jarnagin who produced to Court an act of General Assembly releasing sd Dyer from payment of the forfeiture heretofore taken against him on his paying the costs as well of scire facias as the original prosecution in behalf State against him.
p.249   State v William Fretwell, Willis West, George Gothard, John Yeats. Alias Ccapias issues. Recognizance of Timothy F French, condition he appear at next Term to give evidence in behalf State against defendants.
    State v Ira Gothard. [as above]
p.250   State v James Pickett. [as above]
    State v James Lea. [as above]
    State v Bartley Benson. [as above]
p.251   State v Robert Benson. [as above]
    State v Robert Bolton. [as above]
    Henry Griffith v Orville Paine. Jury heretofore sworn say they cannot agree; order mistrial be entered and jury discharged and cause continued.
p.252   David Johns by his next friend Jonathan Fry v Anson Dearman. Cause is continued at the instance of plaintiff on affidavit of Samuel Gamble.

SEPTEMBER 1830

William Smith v William G Brownlow. Dfts demurrer overruled. Cause continued. Dft to take deposition of William C Anderson of Davidson County, James C Mitchell of McMinn County, and Hugh Beaty of Bledsoe County.

State v Isaac Garrison. Grand jury indictment agt dft for grand larceny endorsed by their foreman George Gillispie a true bill, and dft says he is not guilty. Jury James Gibson, Larkin Butram, Absalom Foster, Robert Cooly, James Baily, James Coulter, William M Stephens, Matthias Shaver, Thomas B Swan, Samuel Howard, Birtel Stephens, David W Brown say dft is not guilty.

p.253 Leavin Stokes v Alexander Coulter. Arbitrators heretofore appointed make return: defendant shall pay to plaintiff $3, and defendant shall pay all costs; Orville Paine, Thomas (x) Davis, Jesse Thompson.

State v Samuel Humberd. Grand jury returned indictment against defendant for perjury endorsed "a true bill" by their foreman George Gillispie. Dft being charged pleaded not guilty. Cause is continued until next Term. Samuel Humberd and
p.254 Adam Humberd and William Humberd dfts securities. William Yates, Jacob Butram, James Wilson, Larkin Butram, Hail Butram recognizances, condition they appear March Court to give evidence in behalf State against the defendant.

State v John Oldham, John Baker, James Griffith, Charles Rector, William Hare, John Richardson, Isaac Conley[Canby?], Robert Stockton, Leroy Furguson. Grand Jury indictment endorsed by George Gillispie their foreman "a true bill" against John Oldham, John Baker, James Griffith, Charles Rector, William Hare, John Richardson and "not a true bill" against Leroy Furguson. Dfts say they are not guilty. On affidavit of Samuel Humbert this cause is continued till next term. Recognizances of John Oldham, John Baker, James Griffith, Charles Rector, John
p.255 Richardson, condition they appear March next. Bond of Samuel Humbert, Benjamin Davis, Mary Davis, Leroy Furguson to make appearance at March term, sd Samuel Humbert to prosecute and give evidence and sd Benjamin Davis, Mary Davis, and Leroy Furguson give evidence in behalf the State.

State v Robert Stockton. Dft came not; forfeited his recognizance $1000 unless at next term he shew sufficient cause to the contrary.

John Dolan v Thomas Marshall. Cause continued; dft pays costs. Plaintiff &
p.256 defendant in proper persons refer matters in dispute to award of William Matlock, Daniel Briggs, James Wilson, John Farmer, Beal Gather, Thomas Price and Miles Vernon.

Jesse Matthews v Robert Murphy. Jesse Matthews petitions for writs of certiorari and supersedeas; writs issue.

Jesse Poe, admr v William Lewis & Thomas Huddleston. Dft William Lewis who appealed from county court is discharged, and he recovers of plaintiff his costs about his defence in this behalf expended.

State v William B Marshall. Dft in proper person. Offence with which defendant is charged, if committed, was committed in Claiborne County TN; order dft be recognized to appear before Circuit Court for Claiborne County to be held at Tazewell October next. Bond of William B Marshall; David Buster and David Marshall his securities. Recognizance of John Bullard[Ballard?], condition he appear to prosecute and give evidence against Wm B Marshall.

Grand and traverse jurors discharged from further attendance at this term.

State v James Burton & Matthias Green. Bill of costs: Justice 2 warrants $2; constable 2 arrests $1; Constable R H Jordan 2 arrests and 2 supboenas $1.50;
p.258 state tax $1; Clerk process $1; filing record $1; entry 20 cts; 2 recognizances 50 cts; indictment 60 cts; 5 subpoenas 62½ cts; 6 witnesses probate

109

37½; jury 12½; order 25 cts; judgment 100 cts for costs 25 cents, taxing costs 40 cents, copy of costs 50 cents; Sheriff Hackett 5 subpoenas $1.25; jury 12½. Call 4 cents 2 commitments 100 cents, 2 whippings 100 cents, Attorney General $5. Witnesses for State Isaac Baker 3 days 150 cts, A Forster 2 days 100 cents, Benjamin McCartey 3 days 150 cents, Robert H Jordan 2 days 100 cents. The above bill of costs is legally taxed Sept 29th 1830. J P Lowry, atto general. Clerk to certify sd bill to County Court for their allowance.

The following bills of costs were presented to the court certified by the attorney general to be legally taxes; order same be spread upon the record and certified to County Court for their allowance to wit:

State v James Burton. Justice .50. Warrant 50 cts 2 subp 50 cts $1; State tax $1. Clerk process 100 cts, filing record 100 cts, entry 20 cts, indictment 60 cts, 2 recognizances 50 cts, 5 sup 62½ cts; 4 witnesses probate 25 cts, jury 12½ cts order 25 cts, taxing costs 40 cts, copy of costs 50 cts...$6.70. Sheriff five subpoenas 125 cts, jury 12½ cts, call 4 cts, commitment 50 cts, whipping 50 cts ...$2.61½. Attorney General $5. Witnesses for State Isaac Baker 2 days $1; A Foster 1 day .50; Benjamin McCarty 2 days $1; Robert H Jordon 1 day .50. Costs legally taxed Sept 29th 1830. J P Lowry attorney general.

p.259   State v Matthias Greene. Justice .50; State tax $1. Clerk [details omitted here; total $6.70]. Sheriff 5 subp 125 cts, call 4 cts, commitment 50 cts; whipping 50 cts...$2.29. Attorney General $5. Witnesses for State Benjamin McCarty 3 days $1.50; Isaac Baker 3 days $1.50; A Foster 2 days $1; R H Jordon 2 days $2. The above bill of costs is legally taxed Sept 29th 1830. J. P. Lowry Attorney General.

State v Richard Bradford. Tax $1; justice .50; Constable warrant 50 cts, 8 subpoenas 200 cts. Clerk[details omitted] $11.45. Sheriff Hackett 23 subp 575 cts; 2 commitments 100 cts, call 4 cts. $6.16½. Attorney General $5. Witnesses for State Daniel Walker 3 days $1.50; Richard Waterhouse 3 days $1.50; James Barnett 3 days $1.50; John Barnett 3 days $1.50; Lucinda Parker 3 days $1.50; Peggy Ransom 3 days $1.50; Joannah Parker 3 days $1.50; James Parker 3 days $1.50; James Hubbert 3 days p.260 $1.50; Abner Triplett 3 days $1.50; Elizabeth Temple 3 days $1.50; John Miller 3 days $1.50; Anson Dearmon 3 days $1.50. The bill of costs hereto annexed Sept 29th 1830. J P Lowry, attorney general.

State v Stephen Mayfield. Indictment for murder. Justice .50; Constable 50 cts 2 subpoenas 50 cts $1. State tax $1. Clerk [details omitted here] $9.22. Sheriff Hackett 16 subpoenas 400 cts, 3 arrests 37½; call 4 cts, jury 12½ cts; 2 commitments 50 cts each...$5.50. Sheriff Brown 2 subpoenas 50 cts. Attorney general $5. Witnesses for State, Sally Kilgore 2 days 40 miles $3.60; Henry Miller 2 days $1; John Walker 2 days $1; Margaret Buck 2 days $1; Richard Waterhouse 2 days $1; Blackstone Waterhouse 2 days $1; Thomas Smith 2 days $1. Above bill of costs in legally taxed. Sept 29th 1830. J P Lowry attorney general.

p.261   Samuel Humbert v John Baker, James Griffith, John Richardson, Robert Stockton, John Oldham, Leroy Furguson, Charles Rector. Separate writs of capias and respondenum having been by mistake of clerk issued against the dfts as also against Isaac Condley and William Hare, with assent of Court sd writs are consolidated into one cause which is to stand as though but one writ had been issued jointly.

Court adjourned till tomorrow.   Charles F Keith

Thursday 30th Septr. Present the Honorable Charles F Keith, Judge, &c.

MARCH 1831

William Smith v William G Brownlow. Dft to take deposition of Clinton Armstrong of Hawkins County.

Asa Rowden for use of Abraham Davis v John Spencer & Jesse B Spencer. Leave given defendant to plead at next term.

George W Frazier v Richard & Blackstone Waterhouse. Plffs by atty suggested that since last term the plaintiff has departed this life.

p.262 Miles Vernon, Francis Rockhold & Joseph McCorcle v Samuel McDaniel. Parties by attorneys; plffs produced letters from Spencer Jarnagin to Hon Hugh L White, and Hugh L White to Circuit Court, concerning treaties of 1817 and 1819 between United States and Cherokee Indians, and moved court to transfer this cause for final hearing to Circuit Court of Knox County. Clerk to make out a transcript of proceedings and transmit same together with original pleadings, proofs &c to Circuit Court of Knox County.

p.263

Samuel Kean v Thomas C More. Dft injoined from having execution of his judgment at law against complainant till next term of this Court; that complainant by next term file with clerk and master the evidence of his title to the southeast quarter of Section 17 of Twp 57 north of the base line of range 20 west of 5th principal meridian situate in the tract of land appropriated in the late territory now State of Missouri by act of Congress for Military Bounties, also to file a deed of conveyance executed by laws of Missouri to convey to dft sd land.

State v Isaac Garrison. Jury having found dft not guilty, Blackstone Waterhouse the prosecutor in this cause pay costs thereof.

Court adjourned till Court in course.   Charles F Keith

p.264 Circuit Court of law and equity held for Rhea County in Washington on fourth Monday, 28th day of March, presiding on the bench the Honorable Charles F Keith one of the Circuit Judges assigned to Hold the circuit Courts within the Seventh Judicial Circuit.

Sheriff Henry Collins returned the venire facias: William Carter, William Howard, Benjamin Jones, George Gillespie, James Preston, Adam Caldwell, Jesse Roddye, Samuel Igow, Benjamin McKinzie Senr, Rezin Rawlings, Thomas McCallie, John Day, Thomas Kelly, Matthias Shaffer, Peach Taylor, George W Riggle, James McCanse, James Lillard, Joseph McCorkle, Jesse Thompson, James Swan, Stephen [Winton], James Wilson, David Houndshell, James A Darwin.

Answered to their names: Wm Carter, Benjn Jones, Jas A Darwin, Jesse Thompson, Saml Igow, Wm Howard, Benjn McKinzie Sr, James Wilson, Jas Swan, Jas Preston, Stephen Winton, Jas McCanse, George W Riggle, James Lillard, Thomas McCallie, Rezen Rawlings, Peach Taylor, Matthias Shaffer.

Grand jurors: James Preston, Wm Carter, Benjamin Jones, Jas A Darwin, Jesse Thompson, Saml Igow, Wm Howard, Benjamin McKinzie Sr, Jas Wilson, Jas Swan, Stephen Winton, Jas McCanse, Geo W Riggle. Court appointed James Preston foreman of jury.

p.265 Constable Anson Dearmon sworn to attend said Grand Jury.

From affidavit of James Lillard, Court being satisfied that Thos McCallie is deputy postmaster, they are excused from further attendance as jurors this term.

John Dolen v Thomas Marshall. Referees to whom was referred all matter of dispute returned their award: Find for plaintiff $30 damage and cost. James Wilson,

MARCH 1831

Beal Gaither, Miles Vernon, William Matlock, John Farmer.
Rezin Rawlings to William McDonald. Deed dated 16 Nov 1830 for 100 acres on Richland Creek ackd.

p.266 Sally McKenley v Benjamin McKenly. Plf by counsel Thos J Campbell. Sheriff returned subpoena that dft Benjn McKenzie[sic] is not found in his county; therefore order alias subpoena awarded. Publication to be made for four weeks for said Benjn McKenley to appear next Term to answer plaintiffs petition.

John & Catharine Chatten to John D Chatten. Power of Attorney dated 2 March 1831 acknowledged by John Chatten and Catharine Chatten his wife. Sd Catharine formerly Catharine Davis being examined appart from her husband declared she executed sd Power/Attorney of her own accord.

James P Lowrie attorney general not being present, Court appointed John W M Brazeal attorney general protem.

p.267 William Smith v William G Brownlow. Permit dft to withdraw several pleas by him pleaded; plf directed suit be dismissed; dft recovers against plaintiff his costs about his defence in this behalf expended.

Court adjourned till tomorrow 9 O'clock.
                                                              Charles F Keith

Tuesday 29th March. Present the honorable Charles F Keith, Judge &c.
The following jurors answered to their names yesterday: Peach Taylor, Matthias Shafer, Rezin Rawlings of the original panel, and on this day, the following appeared when called: John Day, George Gillispie, David Hownshell, Adam W Caldwell and the following failed to appear: Joseph McCorcle and Thomas Kelly.

Excuse John Day from further attendance as a juror at this term.
Fine Sheriff Henry Collins $5 for failing to attend at Court.
Constable Anson Dearmon fined $5 for failing to attend at Court.

p.268 Polly Gilbert and Richard Gilbert v Daniel Walker admr of Charles Walker decd and guardian of Polly Gilbert. Cause is continued; plf to take deposition of Elizabeth Sheilds of Sevier County TN.

David Johns by his next friend Jonathan Fry v Anson Dearmon. Plaintiff nonsuited; dft recovers of plf his costs about his defence expended.

Alexander D Keys is admitted to practice as an attorney of tis court.
Henry Johns v Isaac Dail. Appeal. Plaintiff recovers of dft $4.50 the amount of the judgment together with his costs.

p.269 John B Thompson v Wright Smith. Dft confesses judgment; suit dismissed.

On application of James Preston foreman of Grand Jury subpoena issued for Samuel Craig to appear to give evidence of unlawful gaming.

Declaration of John Pardoe, formerly a subject of King of Great Britain, swears he has resided in United States seven years, that it is his intention to renounce allegiance to kings and become a citizen of the United States.

State v James Robinson. Grand jury returned bill of indictment against dft for passing or offering counterfeit bank notes endorsed by foreman James Preston Not a True Bill.

John Pardoe v Beaty Perry. Alias capias awarded against defendant.

p.270 State v Richmond Clift. Nolle prosequi entered. Dft and Joseph B Johnston confessed judgment for half of the costs, and Thomas Henry and Henry Henry confessed judgment for the other half.

George Gordon to Robert Craven. Deed dated 6 Novr 1830 for 120 acres proven by Matthew English and William S Gillenwaters, subscribing witnesses thereto.

MARCH 1831

    Henry Griffith v Orville Paine. Jury Matthias Shafer, David Hounshell, Adam W Caldwell, Andrew Jack, Miles Vernon, Jesse Poe, William Matlock, Leroy Furguson, John McClanahan, John Smith, John Oldham cannot agree; mistrial entered.
    Court adjourned till tomorrow.   Charles F Keith

p.271   Wednesday 30th March.   Present the honorable Charles F Keith, Judge, &c.
    Asa Rowden for the use of Abraham Davis v John Spencer & Jesse B Spencer. Cause is continued till the next Term.
    State v Joseph Lambert. Nolle prosequi entered.
    State v Daniel D Armstrong & Jesse Matthews. Recognizance of William Carter, condition he attend day to day the present term to give evidence in behalf of the State in the above cause and not depart.
    Grand Jury returned bill/indictment against William H Crawford for grand larceny endorsed by James Preston foreman a true bill.
    State v John Oldham & others. On motion of atty general, a plurius capias is awarded to Roane County against defendant William Hare in this cause.
p.272   State v John Madden. Horatio Belt a witness for State came not; forfeits $125 unless he shew cause to contrary at next term of this court.
    State v John Madden. Jesse McFalls [as above]
    State v John Madden. Perjury. Defendant in proper person pleaded not guilty. Jury William Locke, Matthias Shafer, David Hounshell, Peach Taylor, John McCallen, Orville Paine, William B Russell, John McClanahan, Thomas C Wroe, Rezin Rawlings, Danl M Stockton, Abraham Davis find dft not guilty.
p.273   State v John Oldham and others. Cause continued on affidavit of Samuel Humberd the prosecutor. Dfts John Oldham, John Baker, John Richeson, James Griffith, and Charles Rector bond $3000, condition they attend Septr Court to answer charge of State against them for a riot. Bond of Samuel Humberd, David Hounshell, George Preston, Hugh Lawson, Robert Stockton, Bird Deatherage, and William Earp, Samuel Humberd $500, and the others $250 each, condition they appear at Septr Court to prosecute and give evidence in behalf State in above cause.
p.274   State v Micajah Privot. John Parker appearance bail for defendant surrendered dft Micajah Privot who is ordered into custody of the Sheriff. Jury James Preston, William Carter, Benjamin Jones, James A Dearmon, Jesse Thompson, Saml Igo, William Howard, Benjamin McKenzie Sr, Jas Wilson, Jas Swan, Stephen Winton, James McCanse find dft guilty; fined $10 and pay costs of prosecution.
    State v Samuel Humberd. Perjury. Cause continued. Samuel Humberd, William
p.275   Humberd and Adam Humberd appearance bond. Bond of William Yates, George Preston, Hail Butram, Larken Butram, Jacob Butram, and James Wilson, condition they appear Septr Term, Wm Yates to prosecute and give evidence, the others to give evidence in behalf State in the above cause against the defendant.
    State v Robert Stockton. On affidavit of defendant the forfeiture taken against him at last term is set aside upon his paying all costs.
    State v Daniel D Armstrong. Affray. Dft in proper person says he is guilty; fine $20; remain in custody till fine and costs of prosecution are paid.
p.276   State v Jesse Matthews. Affray. Dft in proper person says he is not guilty; jury John McClanahan, John Miller, John Smith, Daniel M Stockton, Thomas C Wroe, Edmon Bran, James Montgomery, Abraham Davis, William Lewis, John B Campbell, Philip Harwood, Abraham Miller find dft guilty. Fine $20; remain in custody till fine and costs of prosecution are paid.

MARCH 1831

      John Madden v Thomas B Swan. Plf dismissed suit; dft confessed judgment; plf recovers of dft all costs accrued in this cause for which judgmt is confessed.

      State v James Robinson. Grand Jury having returned Not a true bill against dft, defendant is discharged from confinement.

p.277

      The commissioners appointed to examine the county entry takers office presented report: receipts sufficient to cover money received; locations all of record. Samuel Frazier, Thomas McCallie.

      Samuel Humberd v Isaac Condley and Same v William Huse[Han?]. On application of plaintiff, a plurius capias awarded.

      Court adjourned till tomorrow at 9 O'clock.   Charles F Keith

p.278   Thursday 31st March. Present the honorable Charles F Keith, Judge &c.

      Campbell & Locke admrs of estate of John Hudson decd to Charles A Scott & Robert W Ashlin. Bill/Sale dated 9 June 1827 for sundry Negro slaves ackd by Thos J Campbell and John Locke the administrators of sd estate.

      Charles S Scott to John Locke. Bill/sale dated 7th Decr 1830 for Negro man Sam proven by Thos J Campbell and Allen Kennedy subscribing witnesses thereto.

      Richard Manley to John Locke. Bill/sale dated 21 April 1828 for Negro woman Jane proven by Thomas Henry and George Henry two subscribing witnesses.

      Joseph Love & Jefferson B Love to John Locke. Bill/Sale dated 23d April 1829 for Negro girl Mary ackd by Joseph Love one of the makers thereof.

p.279   On motion of Attorney Generall, Clerk of Court produced receipts of Treasurer of East Tennessee and Trustee of Rhea County. Received of John Locke Clerk of Circuit Court of Rhea County his return from 1 October 1829 to 1 October 1830 together with the sum of $23.93 after deducting his commissions being the full amount of revenue by him collected; Miller Francis treasurer of East Tennessee. Received of John Locke Clerk of Circuit Court of Rhea County $23.37½ the amount of fines and forfeitures by him collected from first Decr 1829 to first Decr 1830. John Cozby Trustee of Rhea County.

      Samuel McDaniel et all v Elihu S Barclay. Sci Fa. Defendant came not; plf is granted execution against dft for $35.23 amount of writ; also costs expended.

p.280   Waterhouses executors v James Hannah, John Davis & Daniel D Armstrong. Sci Fa. Dfts came not; plf granted execution agt dfts for $20.56 and their costs.

      State v William Fretwell. Order alias plurias capias awarded. Recognizance of Timothy F French condition he attend Septr next to give evidence.

      State v Willis West. [as above]

p.281   State v George Gothard. [as above]

      State v John Yates. [as above]

      State v Ira Gothard. [as above]

p.282   State v James Pickett. [as above]

      State v James Lea. [as above]

      State v Bartlett Benson. [as above]

p.283   State v Robert Boulton. [as above]

      State v Robert Benson. [as above]

      The 30th Regiment of Tennessee Militia v Edmond Bean. Came to be decided, the rule heretofore entered in this cause to dismiss the petition of Edmond Bean, and the same being argued, sd petition dismissed, and Edmond Bean to pay costs. See records of Friday, appeal granted in this cause.

p.284   State v William H Crawford. Dft in proper person says he is not guilty.

MARCH 1831

Jury Daniel M Stockton, Jas Montgomery, Robt N[?] Gillispie, Matthias Shafer, Wm M Gillispie, Geo Henry Jr, Peter Fine, Peach Taylor, Thos Henry, John McClanahan Sr, Jesse Matthews, John Smith say dft is guilty of feloniously stealing two bank bills the property of Mumford Smith the value of $12; further say that for his offence he suffer three years imprisonment in the penitentiary house of this State from date hereof; defendant granted rule to shew cause why a new trial should be granted.

James Kelly v Robert Bell. Jury James Preston, Benj Jones, Jesse Thompson, James A Darwin, Wm Howard, Jas Wilson, Stephen Winton, Saml Igo, Jas McCanse, Geo W Riggle, Wm Carter, Jas Swan, who say dft did undertake as plf alledged; assess plfs damage to $50 besides costs.

p.285 George W Frazier v Blackstone Waterhouse. Death of plaintiff having been suggested at last term and no step to revive for two terms, this suit abates.

State v Stephen Ford and Nathan Blackwell. Horse Stealing. Dfts discharged from recognizance; considered by Court that dfts be discharged.

Jurors from attendance at this Term are discharged.

Court adjourned till tomorrow 9 Oclock.   Charles F Keith

p.286 Friday 1st April. Present the Honorable Charles F Keith, Judge &c.

Charles A Scott & Robert W Ashlin to John Locke. Bill/Sale dated 9 June 1827 for five Negro slaves proven by Thomas J Campbell one of the subscribing witnesses who says he saw Willis H Chapman the other witness thereto sign his name.

Thirtieth Regt of Militia & Henry Collins Judge Advocate v Edmund Bean. Dft prays appeal in nature of Writ of Error to next Superior Court to be held at Knoxville; entered bond with Thomas J Campbell his security, and same is allowed.

State v Jesse Matthews. John McClenahan and Eli Sharp confess judgment for the fine and costs haeretofore rendered in this cause.

Leutys executors v Joseph Harwood et al. Defendant Joseph Harwoods death is admitted; order scire facias issue against legal representatives of sd Joseph p.287 Harwood decd; Malachi Harwood & Philip Harwood the other dfts by their atty prayed rule to shew cause why they should be discharged from their undertaking as security in this behalf; cause is continued until next term.

State v William H Crawford. Dft in proper person; rule heretofore to shew cause why a new trial should be granted is discharged on motion and by consent of dft. Considered by Court upon verdict of jury that dft William H Crawford suffer confinement in penitentiary house in this State for three years commencing on 31st March 1831 as afsd and pay costs in this behalf expended which which execution may issue, further considered that sheriff of Rhea County execute judgment of Court and p.288 impress two guards to his assistance in conveying dft William H Crawford to the penitentiary house together with three horses for the purposes aforesaid.

Samuel Kean v Thomas C Wroe. Equity. Complainant filed in Clerks office a deed of conveyance executed by Henry Parkes and Jane Parkes to sd complainant assuring to him in fee the tract mentioned in interlocuty decree, also deed from complainant and wife to sd dft for same land. On consideration, order dft be perpetually injoined from having execution of his judgment by him recovered at law against sd complainant, that title to the lot 43 in town of Athens in McMinn County on which dft lived on 2 Decr 1825 when the contract of exchange was made between sd parties be divested out of sd dft and his heirs and vested in sd complainant and his heirs forever, and that title to southeast quarter of section 17 two 57 north in range 20 west in tract appropriated by act of Congress for military bounties in

115

SEPTEMBER 1831

late Territory now State of Missouri which sd complainant has filed in Clerks office be at disposal of defendant.
Court adjourned until Court in Course.   Charles F Keith

p.289   At a Circuit Court of law and equity held for Rhea County in town of Washington on fourth Monday and 26th day of September when was present the Honorable Charles F Keith one of the Circuit Judges commissioned to hold the Circuit Courts within the Seventh Judicial Circuit.
   Sheriff Henry Collins returned the venire facias: Asahel Johnson, Samuel Garwood, Crispen E Shelton, Samuel R Hackett, Rezin Rawlings, Samuel McDaniel, Joseph McCorkle, Robert Cooley, Isaac Masoner, John McClure, Vaden H Giles, Samuel Gamble, George Gillispie, Peach Taylor, John Cozby, Matthias Shaver, James McDonald, James A Darwin, James Wilson, Isaac Roddy, James Swan, Stephen Winton, Matthew Hubbert, Daniel M Stocton, James Preston.
   Answered to their names: Saml McDaniel, Robt Cooley, Danl M Stocton, Rezin Rawlings, Isaac Roddy, Peach Taylor, Jas A Darwin, Jas McDonald, Jas Preston, Vaden H Giles, Jos McCorkle, Mattw Hubbert, Asahel Johnson, Matthias Shaver, Stephen Winton, Saml R Hackett, George Gillispie, Crispin E Shelton, Jno Cozby, Jno McClure.
   Grand Jury: James Preston, Vaden H Giles, Joseph McCorkle, Matthew Hubbert, Asahel Johnson, Matthias Shaver, Stephen Winton, Saml R Hackett, Isaac Masoner, Geo Gillispie, Crispin E Shelton, John Cozby, John McClure.
   Court appoint James Preston foreman of sd Jury.
   Constable John Lillard sworn to attend on grand Jury.
p.290   Robert Parks to Dempsey Bandy. Deed dated 17 Sept 1831 for 50 acres proven by William Fouler and William Johnson subscribing witnesses thereto.
   Samuel Ferguson to Samuel Frazier. Deed, 10 Step 1831, for 193 acres ackd.
   Excuse jurors Saml Gamble & Jas Swan from further attendance at this term.
   Following jurors of original pannell answered to their names: James A Darwin, Isaac Roddy, Daniel M Stocton, Peach Taylor, Robert Cooley, Samuel McDaniel, James Wilson, Rezin Rawlings, James McDonnald.
   Peletiah Chilton to Franklin Locke & Newton Locke. Transfer of certificate of survey dated 3 January 1831 for 100 acres ackd by Peletiah Chilton.
   Peter Fine v Peter Merrick. Appeal. Plaintiff in proper person dismissed suit and confessed judgment for all costs.
p.291   Salley McKinley against Benjamin McKinley. Divorce. Defendant having failed to enter his appearance according to rules of Court is called to come into Court and answer complainants petition or same will be taken for confessed and set for hearing Exparte.
   Abijah Baugus v John W Masses. Plf by atty enters rule to shew why certiorari should be dismissed.
   Henry Griffith v Orville Paine. Jury Saml Garwood, Saml McDaniel, Daniel M Stocton, Rezin Rawlings, Robt Cooley, John Riggle, Mattw English, Wm Noblett, Abraham Davis, Thos Godbehere, Robt McCracking, Hazzard Bean could not agree; they are respited from rendering verdict untill tommorrow morning.
   Court then adjourned untill Tomorrow morning.   Charles F Keith

SEPTEMBER 1831

p.292   Tuesday 27th Sept. Present the Honorable Charles F Keith, Judge &c.

Abijah Baugus v John W Masses. Certorari. Suggested dft has departed life.

John Madden v Matthew English. Dft prays rule to shew cause why taxation of costs should be corrected.

Salley McKinley v Benjamin McKinley. Divorce. Dft having failed to enter appearance according to rules is now called to answer complainants petition, or same will be taken as confessed and set for hearing exparte.

John Witt v William Jewel. Cause is continued.

James P Lowrie attorney general not being present at this Court, Court apptd John W McBrazeal attorney general protem.

Samuel Humberd v John Baker et all. Cause is continued.

p.293   Jesse Matthews v Robt Murphey. Certorari. Plf not appearing is nonsuited. Defendant recovers against plaintiff his costs about his defence expended.

Polly Gilbert et all v Daniel Walker. Cause is continued.

Rowden for Davis v John & Jesse B Spencer. Cause is continued on dft paying all costs of present term.

Benjamin Perkins v Robert McCrackin. Jury James A Darwin, Peach Taylor, James Wilson, James McDonald, John Smith, James Poe, Philip Harwood, Malekiah Harwood, Wm Jewel, Michael Stiner, Levi Griffith, Wm O Collins. Dft recovers agt plf.

p.294   Henry Griffith v Orville Paine. Jury heretofore respited find defendant guilty and assess the plaintiffs damages to $70 besides costs.

Accounts proven and filed by John Parker jailor of Rhea County: for keeping William H Crawford in jail from 20 Feb to 1 April at 2/3 per day $19.12½; for two turnkees $1; for 4 turnkees $2. Sworn September 27th John Locke, Clerk. To keeping James Robinson from 29 October to 29 March at 2/3 $56.25; to 2 turnkees $1. Sworn 27 Sept, John Locke, Clerk.

p.295   John Dolen v Thomas Marshall et all. Plfs atty moved for judgmt agt dft and his securities David Marshall, James Sutton, and Vinson Blanton on a forfeited delivery bond. Considered by Court that plf recover agt Thomas Marshall and his securities David Marshall, James Sutton, and Vinson Blanton $67.46½ together with costs of levy and delivery bond and also costs of this motion.

Court adjourned untill tomorrow.   Charles F Keith

Wednesday 28th Septr. Present the Honorable Charles F Keith, Judge &c.

Discharge juror Samuel McDaniel from further attendance at this Term.

Rawlings extrs to Lauderdales extx. Deed dated 26 May 1824 for 47 acres acknowledged by the makers thereof.

p.296   Salley McKinley v Benjamin McKinley. Divorce. Dft called to answer plfs petition or same will be taken for confessed and set for hearing exparte.

State v George Gothard & Willis West. Defendants in proper person say they are not guilty. Jury Jas A Darwin, Isaac Roddy, Daniel M Stocton, Peach Taylor, Jos Rice, Geo W Kennedy, Ruben Freeman, Saml Humberd, William Humberd, Wm N Gillispie, Abraham Davis, John Baker find dfts guilty. Dfts fined each $10 and pay costs.

State v William Fretwell. Sheriff took defendant in custody. Dft in proper person says he is guilty of unlawfull gaming. Fined $10 and costs.

p.297   State v Samuel Humberd. Perjury. Dft in person. Cause is continued. Bond of Samuel Humberd with William Humberd and William Clowers, condition he appear on March Term to answer charge against him. Bonds of James Wilson, Jacob Butram, George Preston, Hail Butram, and Larkin Butram, condition they attend March next to

SEPTEMBER 1831

p.298   testify and give evidence in State against Samuel Humberd.

John McClenahan v James Spears & John Miller. Dfts demurrer not sufficient in law; cause stands revived against sd defendants.

State v Thomas Brandon, Beveridge Brandon, William Wirick, Fredrick Wyrick, & Parmer Brandon. Grand Jury returned bill of indictment against dfts endorsed by James Preston their foreman a True Bill. Dfts in proper persons say they are not guilty, not being ready for trial were remanded to prison.

p.299   State v David Houndshel. Deft made default, forfeited his recognizance. State recovers $250 unless dft shew suffcient cause to contrary at next Term.

State v Hugh S Balden. Dft made default, forfeited recognizance $250 unless sufficient cause to contrary be shewn to next Term of this Court.

State v Benjamin Davis. Dft summoned witness on behalf State against John Oldham and others, came not; State recovers agt dft $125 unless sufficient cause of his disability to attend be shewn at next Term of this Court.

p.300   State v Mary Davis. Dft was summoned a witness on behalf State against John Oldham made default, forfeits $125 [as above]

State v John Oldham & others. On affidavit of John Baker, James Griffith and John Richeson cause is continued untill next Term. Whereupon Elisha Sharp and Abraham Davis make bond, condition John Oldham appears March next to answer charge of State against him for a riott. Recognizance of John Baker $500, Elisha Sharp and Abraham Davis $250 each, condition John Baker appear March next to charge of State

p.301   against him for a riott. Recognizance of Charles Rector, William McCarter security, condition Charles Rector appear to answer charge of state agt him for a riott. [Same: James Griffith, James Wilson security. Same John Richardson, Beal Gaither and George Preston security]. Recognizance of George Preston, condition he

p.302   appear March next to testify against John Oldham and others. [Same: Robert
p.303   Stocton, William Earp, Barton McPherson, Daniel Clower, Bird Deatheridge, and Hugh Balden].

State v Hugh L Balden. Dft in proper person. State recovers agt dft.
State v Thomas Haynes. Grand Jury bill/indictment endorsed a True Bill.
State v Lewis Knight & Rebecca Knight. Grand Jury bill/indictment against dfts endorsed by James Preston their foreman a True Bill.

p.304   State v William Stanley. Attorney General enters Nolle prosequi.
State v John Yates. Alias plurias capias awarded returnable next Term.
State John Yates. Recognizance of Timothy F French, condition he attend March next to testify & give evidence against defendant for unlawful gaming.
State v Ira Gothard. [as above]

p.305   State v James Pickett. [as above]
State v James Lea. [as above]
State v Bartley Benson. [as above]
State v Robert Benson. [as above]

p.306   State v Robert Boulton. [as above]

Deed of Trust Fredrick Wyrick to Wm Matlock proven by William Humberd as follows, date 27 Septr 1831 between Fredrick Wyrick and William Medlock, $1 and a note executed by Wyrick to George W Churchwell for $50 dated 28 Septr 1831 due six months after date, sold set of blacksmith tools consisting of bellows, vice, screw plates, tongs, hammers and all necessary tools and appendages anville &c hand vice, gun rods, cherrys &c chisels &c do screws for the plates which tools sd Wyrick has

p.307   now in possession. Medlock as trustee to advertise and sell sd tools upon ten days advertisement at A Baugges house in Rhea County, sd tools to secure pay-

118

SEPTEMBER 1831

ment of sd note to Churchwell; if not paid when due, sd trustee is to sell as afsd.
State v Elizabeth McCarroll. Grand Jury bill/indictment agt dft endorsed by James Preston their foreman a True Bill; defendant in proper person says she is not guilty. Jury Daniel M Stocton, Robert Cooly, James Wilson, John Baker, Daniel D Armstrong, John McClenahan, John T Merriott, Abraham Davis, John Barnett, Jesse Matthews, Edmund Bean, William Pile to try cause on tomorrow.

Isaac Blevins, Mumford Smith, Wade H Adkins, John Smith, David Leuty, Wm Gwin, Jacob Brown, Thomas J Lewis, Anderson W Smith, Arthur Fulton summoned to attend this day as jurors came not. Fined $5 each.

Court adjourned unill Tommorrow morning.   Charles F Keith

p.308   Thursday 29th Sept. Present the Honorable Charles F Keith.
State v Elizabeth McCarroll. Dft in proper person. Jury heretofore impannelled find defendant not guilty of murder and felony as charged.

William Lewis to John J Lewis. Power of Attorney dated 28 Sept 1831 ackd.

Thos J Lewis & William C Lewis to John J Lewis. Power of Attorney dated 26 Septr 1831 proven by Robert Hannah and Malechiah Harwood.
p.309   State v Lewis Knight & Rebecca Knight. Defendants in propper person say they are not guilty. Jury John Ferrell, Robt Pharis, Rezin Rawlings, John Day, Wm Johnson, Elisha Sharp, Malakiah Harwood, Asahel R Chilton, Saml F Martin, Jas Poe, James McDonnald, John B Campbell find dfts not guilty.

Jacob Brown summoned as a juror but made default; fined $5.

William Gillian and Wm Rice Junr summoned to attend this day as jurors came not; fined $2 each.

Court adjourned untill tomorrow morning.   Charles F Keith

p.310   Friday 30th Sept. Present the Honorable Charles F Keith, Judge &c.
John McClennahan v James Spears & John Miller. Cause continued.

State v Thomas Haynes. Dft in proper person says he is not guilty; owing to defendants poverty Court appoints James Bradford and Return J Meigs his advocates; not being ready for Trial, defendant is remanded to prison.

Samuel B Hackett to John Locke. Bill/sale dated 14 June 1830 for Negro man Tom acknowledged in open court.

James Wilson a juror of original pannell is released from further attendance at this term.
p.311   Charles K Gillispie v James Preston. Plf by atty directed his suit be dismissed. Dft recovers against plaintiff his costs about his defence expended.

State v Thomas Brandon, Parmer Brandon, Fredrick Wyrick, Wm Wyrick. Dfts in proper persons say they are not guilty. Jury Wm D Collins, Danl D Armstrong, John Miller, Andley P Defriese, Wm N Gillispie, Jos McDaniel, Edmund Bean, John Ferrell, Malakiah Harwood, John McClennahan, John B Campbell, Robert Williams find dfts not guilty as charged in the first part of bill/indictment against them, and find dfts guilty as charged in the second count of sd indictment. Dfts remanded to prison.

Grand and Traverse jurors from further attendance at this term are discharged except those impanelled in the case of the State v [illegible]
p.312   State v David Marshal. Dft was summoned a witness behalf State against Thomas Brandon and others came not. State recovers agt dft $125 unless sufficient cause of his disability to attend be shewn at next term of this Court.

SEPTEMBER 1831

State v Jesse McFall. Alias scire facias issued.
State v Horatio Belt. Alias scire facias issued.
Catharine Barnes v Silas F Barnes. Dft was not found; publication to be made notifying sd Silas F Barnes to appear next term of this Court to answer plffs petition, or same will be set for hearing exparte and decree accordingly.
p.313 State v Thomas Haynes. Petit Larceny. Dft in proper person says he is not guilty. Jury Jesse Tyson, Abijah Bogges, Robt Pharis, Elisha Sharp, Thomas Kelley, James Smith, William Gwin, James McDonald, William Long Jr, Allen Holland, Thomas Harris, John Taff, put in case of sheriff untill tommorrow morning.
Court adjourned untill tommorrow.

Charles F Keith

Saturday 1st October. Present the Honorable Charles F Keith, Judge &c.
State v Thomas Haynes. Dft in person; jury respited untill this day say they find dft guilty of taking stealing and carrying away the goods of William Martin to the value of $8 as alledged in bill of indictment. For his offence he suffers confinement in the publick jail and penitentiary house of the State from date hereof twelve calendar months and the court do no remission of his punishment.
p.314 And pay the costs in this behalf expended for which execution may issue; further considered by Court that Sheriff be impowered to summon a sufficient guard not exceeding two with a sufficient number of horses not exceeding three as assistance in safely conveying sd defendant to jail and penitentiary house.
State v John Madden. Attorney generall reported following bill of costs correctly taxes: Clerk 2 copies 200 cts; indictment 60 cts; entry 20 cts; 24 sub 425 cts; aff 37½ cts [other costs here omitted, total $25.33] Shff Paine .66½. ditto Hackett 4 sub 100 cts 4 calls 16 cts. citto Cox 1 sub 25 cts; ditto T H Fulton 4 sub 100 cts. ditto J Bird arest & bail 125 cts 2 sub 50 cts. ditto J Kilgore 6 sub 150 cts. ditto R S Gilliland 2 sub 50 cts. ditto J Be Mason 4 sub 100 cts. ditto R A Brown 3 sub 75 cts. ditto U Oregin 1 sub 25 cts. Attorney general $2.51. Witness Edward Stewart 5 days $2.50; Wm Brown 3 days 150 miles $9; Benjamin Longacre 2 days 84 miles $5.36; David Able 3 days 132 miles $8.28. Joel Long 5
p.315 days 200 miles $13. George Gordon 4 days 166 miles $10.64. Robt S Mahan 5 days 234 miles $14.36. John Ferguson 2 days 242 miles $11.93. Henry S Murrell 1 days 42 miles $2.68. William English 5 days $2.50. Matthew English 3 days $1.50.
State v Crawford. Costs in this cause as follows. State Dr to Henry Collins Shff. To expenses of conveying Wm H Crawford from Rhea County to penitentiary himself and two guards say 140 miles each going and 140 miles returning with the use of three horses $61.60. Sworn in Open Court Henry Collins, Shff. 1st Octr 1831. John Locke, Clerk.
Leuty executors v Harwood et all. Scire facias returned that it could not be made known as no legal representative of the deceased existed and no further steps taken to recover this Cause, same be abates. Dfts recover agt plffs their costs in their defence expended.
From affidavit of John Smith the fine against him as a delinquent juror is set aside on his payment of the costs expended. Execution may issue.
p.316 From affidavit of Jacob Brown, fine agt him as delinquent juror[as above]
From affidavit of Arthur Fulton, [as above]
From affidavit of William Gwin, [as above]
John Madden v Matthew English. Taxation on scire facias issued in this cause stands corrected by stroking out twenty five cents for an order and fifty

120

MARCH 1832

cents a part of the costs charged on issuance of the execution.

p.317   Salley McKinley v Benjamin McKinley. Divorce. Petition of plf for divorce from dft heard, it appearing that dft had been more than two years wilfully absent from plf; therefore decreed that bonds of matrimony heretofore sustained between Salley McKinley and Benjamin McKinley be dissolved; Salley McKinley wholy released from obligations thereof; decreed that Jesse Tyson by who as next friend of petitioner the suit has been prosecuted, pay all costs that have accrued therein and that he recover the same of and from sd Benjamin McKinley for which execution may issue respectively.

State v Thomas Brandon, Parmer Brandon, Fredrick Wyrick, William Wyrick. Dfts in proper person. Each dft fined $25 and remain in close confinement in common jail for three months; thence remain in custody untill sd fines & costs are paid.

State v John Oldham et all. Alias plurias capias awarded against William Hare and Oldham.

Saml Humberd v William Hare et al. Alias plurias cap awarded agt dft.

p.318   Samuel Humberd v Isaac Condley. Alias plumas cap ad response awarded plf against defendant.

State v Anderson W Smith, Mumford Smith and David Leuty. From affidavit of defendants the fines entered against them at this Term as delinquent jurors is set aside on payment of the costs.

All causes not specially acted on at this Term is continued untill next term of this Court. Court then adjourned untill Court in Corse.   Charles F Keith.

p.319   Court of law and Equity held for Rhea County in Washington on fourth Monday and twenty sixth day of March, there was presiding on the bench the Honorable Edward Scott, one of the Circuit Judges assigned to Hold the Circuit Courts within the Seventh judicial Circuit.

Sheriff Henry Collins returned the venire facias Jesse Martin, Robert Bell Junr, James Roddye, James Walker, Abel Massey, William Carr, James Lillard, John Hill, John Stewart, James Preston, Jesse Roddey, William Kennedy, William Woodward, Wright Smith, Landon Rector, Samuel R Hackett, Thomas Kelley, Isaack Roddye, George Preston, Thomas Carter, George Gillispie, Azariah David.

On call of sheriff the following answered to their names: Jesse Martin, Robt Bell Junr, Jas Roddey, James Walker, Abel Massey, William Carr, James Lillard, John Hill, John Stewart, James Preston, Jesse Roddy, William Kennedy, William Woodward, Landon Rector, Thomas Kelley, Isaac Roddye, George Preston, Thomas Carter, George Gillispie, Azariah David.

Grand jurors: Geo Gillispie, Able Massey, Geo Preston, Jas Roddy, Wm Woodward, John Stewart, James Preston, Wm Kennedy, Thomas Carter, Jesse Roddy, Landon Rector, Robert Bell Jr, Isaac Roddey. Court appointed George Gillispie foreman.

Constable Jonathan Fry sworn to attend on the grand jury.

p.320   Excuse James Walker & Jno Hill from further attendance as jurors this term.

Remained of original pannel who answered to their names Azariah David, James Lillard, Thomas Kelley, William Carr, Jesse Martin.

Catharine Barnes v Silas F Barnes. Divorce. Dft called to plead and answer the complainants petition or same would be taken for confessed and set for heaving

MARCH 1832

exparte, and decreed accordingly.
  Levi Geren v William Cozby. Under the law to help poor persons obtain their rights, order Samuel Frazier attorney for plaintiff.
  Court adjourned untill tomorrow morning.   Edw Scott

Tuesday 27th March. Present the Honorable Edward Scott Judge &c.
  Catharine Barnes v Silas F Barnes. Divorce. Dft having failed to appear to answer complainants petition, same will be taken as confessed.
p.321 Parmer Brandon to George W Churchwell. Deed dated 30 Sept 1831 for severall tracts of land this day proven by John Parker and John Smith.
  Samuel L Childers licensed to practice as an attorney is permitted to take the usual oath and thereupon is allowed to practice in this Court.
  George Gillispie compl v Allen Gillispie & Adam Broyls respts. Decreed that the injunction be dissolved upon the respondent Adam Broyles giving bond and sufficient security to the Clerk of Court to refund in the event on final hearing the decree of the Court be against them. Further, respt Adam Broyls recover vs George Gillispie compl, Thomas J Gillispie & Robert N Gillispie his securities $369.73 the amount of the judgt at law enjoined together with six percent interest from the 5th of May 1829 the date of the rendition of sd judgment at law.
  Levi Geren v William Cozby. Plf by atty directed his suit be dismissed. Dft recovers agt plf his costs by him about his defence expended.
p.321½ State v Jesse McFalls. Dft in proper person. Conditional judgt set aside; state recovers agt dft & George Preston his security all costs.
  Asa Rowden for use of Abraham Davis v John Spencer & Jesse B Spencer. Covenant. Jury Azariah David, James Lillard, Thomas Kelley, Wm Kerr, Jesse Martin, Jacob Runolds, John Wise, Wm Center, Hugh Carroll, John Majors, Warren West, Isaac Dail find dfts have not kept their covenant; assess plfs damages to $35.72 & costs.
  Jefferson B Love to Joseph Love. Deed dated 30 August 1829 for three lots in southern liberties of Washington #6, 13, 24 acknowledged by the maker thereof.
  John McClenahan to John Locke. Power of Attorney dated 27 March 1832 acknowledged in open court by the maker thereof.
p. Samuel Humberd v David Houndshell. Dft was summoned a witness in behalf Samuel Humberd against John Oldham et all but made default; Samuel Humberd recovers agt dft $125 unless sufficient cause of his disability to attend be shewn at next term of this Court after notice of this judgment; scire facias issues.
  Samuel Humberd v Mary Case. [as above]
  Samuel Humberd v Hugh L Bauldon. [as above]
  John Witt v William Jewel. Parties by attornies mutually submitted all matters in dispute to determination of John Able and Robert Bell Jr.
p.322 Den on demise of Richard Waterhouse et all v Richard Fen with notice to Mumford Smith tennant in possession. Ejectment. Lessee of plf by his attorney and directed this suit be dismissed. Whereupon Mumford Smith tennant in possession by attorney confessed judgment for all costs.
  Samuel Humberd v David Houndshell. Forfeiture entered against dft for his delinquency as a witness is set aside on his payment of costs accruing thereon.
  Samuel Humberd v Hugh L Baulden. Forfeiture set aside; plf recovers agt dft his costs in this behalf expended.
p.323 John McClenahan v John Spears representatives. Certiorari. Parties by their attorneys. Execution is this cause quashed; judgment of County Court is reversed;

MARCH 1832

dfts recover against plaintiff their costs about their defence expended.
William Locke to John Locke. Deed dated 23 March 1832 for 109 acres ackd.
Grand Jurors brought presentment against John Wood and Spells B Dyer, a bill/indictment against Abraham Miller, and a bill of Indictment against Joseph Thompson, signed by jury and their foreman as true presentment and bills.
Court then adjourned untill tommorrow.   Edw Scott

p.324 Wednesday 28th March 1832. Present the honorable Edward Scott, Judge &c.
Catharine Barnes v Silas F Barnes. Divorce. Dft failing come answer the complainants petition, exparte hearing ordered.
Franklin Locke qualified as a deputy Clerk in this Court.
State v Joseph Thompson. Dft in proper person says he is not guilty. Cause is continued and defendant is remanded to prison.
State v John Oldham et al. Attorney generall enters Nole prosequi. John Oldham, John Baker, James Griffith, Charles Rector, Robert Stocton, John Richardson, William Hare, and Isaac Condley confessed judgment for all costs.
p.325 State v Horatio Belt. Dft came not; State granted execution against dft for $125 the amount in scire facias together with costs of prosecuting the writ.
State v Samuel Humberd. Attorney general enters Nole prosequi. Came William Yates, John Baker, and John Oldham, securities, confess judgment for all costs.
State v Robert Benson. Dft in proper person says he is not guilty. Jury Levi H Knight, Thomas H King, John B Campbell, Edward McCain, Pleasant C Comes, Wm Lewis, Stephen Moore, Thomas B Swan, John Moyers, Hugh T Blevins, Anson Dearmon, Wm C Stocton say dft is guilty; dft fined $5 and to pay costs of this prosecution, and be in custody untill the fine and costs are paid.
p.326 State v Abraham Miller. Defendant in proper person says he is not guilty; cause is continued. Recognizance of dft & William S Russell recognizance, condition defendant Abraham Miller appear Sept Term to answer charge of State against him.
State v Robert Boulton. Dft in proper person says he is not guilty. Recognizance of Robert Boulton, John Parker, Crispian E Shelton, condition Robert Boulton attend September to answer a charge of the State against him for gaming.
From affidavit of Jesse Roddy, order Clerk certify to Clerk of Rhea County to issue sd Roddy a jury ticket for March Term 1831 for days he proves attendance.
p.327 State v Daniel M Stocton. Attorney generall enters nole prosequi whereupon William Wand confessed judgment for all costs.
State v John Yates. Two cases. Process awarded against defendant.
State v Ira Gothard. Process awarded agt defendant returnable next Term.
State v James Pickett. Process awarded agt dft returnable next Term.
State v James Lea. Process awarded against dft returnable next Term.
State v Bartley Benson. Process awarded agt defendant returnable next Term.
p.328 Samuel Humberd v John Oldham et al. Plf by atty directed his suit be dismissed. John Baker, Charles Rector, John Richardson, James Griffith, Robert Stocton, John Oldham, Isaac Condley, William Hare, and Leroy Ferguson by attorney and in person confessed judgment for all costs.
George W Thompson v Edmund Beard. Cause is continued.
State v David Houndshell. Forfeiture heretofore entered is set aside and dft in proper person confessed judgment for all costs expended.
Grand Jurors returned bill of indictment against William Long endorsed by their foreman Not a true bill.

123

SEPTEMBER 1832

p.329 State v Mary Davis. Dft came not. State recovers against dft $125 the amount specified in the writ, also costs expended in prosecuting writ.

State v Spills B Dyer. Dft in proper person says he is not guilty. Jury Abraham Miller, Thomas B Swan, Jonathan F Robinson, Jesse McFalls, Samuel Tucker, Abijah Harris, George W Riggle, Wm Johnson, Thos C Wroe, James Kelley, John Moyers, Jacob Runalds find the defendant not guilty.

The grand & travers jury from further attendance this term are discharged.
Court adjourned untill Tomorrow morning. Edw Scott

p.330 Thursday March 29. Present on the bench the Hon Edward Scott Judge &c.

Catharine Barnes v Silas F Barnes. Divorce. Silas F Barnes abandoned the petitioner Catharine Barnes for the space of two years before the filing of her petition for divorce without reasonable cause and had not since taken her under his protection. Decreed by Court that bonds of matrimony heretofore existing between petitioner Catharine Barnes and sd Silas F Barnes dissolved; further, John Parker the next friend of the petitioner, pays costs in this behalf expended, and sd John Parker to recover the costs afsd from Silas F Barnes for which execution may issue.

p.331 State v John Yates, Ira Gothard, Jas Pickett, Bartley Benson. Recognizance of Fletcher French, condition he appear Sept Term to give evidence on behalf State in each of the foregoing causes.

State v Benjamin Davis. Defendant came not. State recovers against dft $125 the amount in the writ specified and also the costs in this behalf expended.

Court adjourned until Court in Course. Edw Scott

p.332 Monday 24th September. At a Circuit Court of law and Equity held for Rhea County, on the bench the honorable Charles F Keith, assigned to hold Circuit Courts within the Seventh judicial Circuit.

Sheriff Henry Collins returned venire facias: William Carter, Crispin E Shelton, William Smith, Mattw Hubbert, James C Mitchell, Edward Templeton, Orville Paine, Jno Day, Samuel R Hackett, Gideon B Thompson, Wm McCarter, Michael W Buster, James Moore, Jas McCanse, James Holloway, John Cozbey, John W Hill, Asahel Johnson, Adam Cole, Reuben McKinzie, Alexander Philpot, Robert Elder, Samuel Looney, Richard Waterhouse; Elijah Wyatt was not to be found.

Grand jurors: Wm Smith, Reuben McKinzie, Saml R Hackett, Mattw Hubbert, Jas McCanse, Asahel Johnson, Jas Holloway, Adam Cole, John Day, Alexander Philpot, John Cozbey, Robert Elder, James C Mitchell. Court appt William Smith foreman of jury.

Constable Anson Dearmon sworn to attend on the grand jury.

Remaining of original pannel who answered to their names Orville Paine and Gideon B Thompson.

Remaining of the original pannel who failed to answer to their names: Wm Carter, Crispin E Shelton, Edward Templeton, William McCarter, Michael W Buster, James Moore, John W Hill, Samuel Looney, Richard Waterhouse.

p.333 Polly Gilbert & Richard Gilbert v Daniel Walker, admr of Charles Walker, deceased and guardian of Polly Gilbert. Complainants by counsel directed their cause be dismissed. Dft in propper person confessed judgment for all costs.

SEPTEMBER 1832

[Item X'd out: Doctor Gideon B Thompson and Orville Paine excused from further attendance as jurors for the present day.]
John Witts lessee v Richard Fen with notice to James Carter. Plf by atty; from affidavit of Wm Gilbreath, John Gilbreath and Mary Jane Gilbreath are admitted to defend in the roomm of sd Richard Fen and also in the room of sd James Carter tennant on whom notice hath been served, on his agreement to confess lease entry and ouster in the plaintiffs declaration supposed and retry on title only at trial. William Gilbreath and Spencer Jarnigan undertake for sd John & Mary Jane Gilbreath.
Brinkley Hornesby to Thomas McCallie. Deed 24 Sept 1832 for 160 acres ackd.
John Pardoe v Beaty Perry. Plf by atty directed his suit be dismissed. Dft recovers against plaintiff his costs by him about his defence expended.
p.334   Lewis Ross v John McClenahan. Petition and certiorari quashed.
George W Thomson v Edmun Bean. William F Gillenwaters undertakes for plf.
Joseph Thompson v John B Swan. [Item X'd out: Plf moved dft give security]
John Witt v William Jewell. Plf in propper person; referees returned their award, certified by John Locke: plf recovers nothing and pay half costs, dft pay other half. Signed by John Able, Jesse Day, referees.
Court adjourned untill Tomorrow.   Charles F Keith

p.335   Tuesday 25th Sept. Present the Honorable Charles F Keith, Judge &c.
Samuel McDaniels lessee v Miles Vernon et all. Cause is continued.
Michael W Buster v Daniel M Stocton. Plf not appearing, suit no further prosecuted. Dft recovers against plaintiff his costs of defence.
George W Thomson v Edmun Bean. Jury Wm Smith, Reuben McKinzie, Saml R Hackett, Jas McCance, Asahel Johnson, Jas C Mitchell, Jas Holloway, Adam Cole, Alexr Philpot, Robt Elder, Edwd Templeton, Vaden H Giles find for dft who recovers against plaintiff his costs of defence.
Lewis Knight & Rebecca Knight v Andrew Wassum & others. Matters in this cause not triable in this court; remanded to county Court whence it came.
Joseph Thompson v John B Swan. Cause is continued.
p.336   Joel W Hickey v Wright Smith. Plaintiff failing to appear is nonsuited; dft recovers against plaintiff his costs about his defence expended.
John Patterson v Mary Cranmore. Jury Reuben McKinzie, Sam R Hackett, Mattw Hubbert, Jas McCanse, Asahel Johnson, Jas C Mitchell, Jas Holloway, Adam Cole, John Day, Alexr Philpot, Jno Cozbey, Robt Elder. Plf no further prosecutes; dft recovers against plaintiff her costs about her defence in this behalf expended.
Court adjourned untill Tomorrow morning.   Charles F Keith

Wednesday 26th Sept. Present on the bench the Honorable Charles F Keith judge &c.
Lewis Ross v John McClenahan. Cause continued untill next term.
Benjamin B Cannon Esquire licensed to practice as an attorney took oath and is admitted to practice in this Court.
p.337   State v Robert Boulton. Dft in proper person. Jury William Carter, Edward Templeton, Jas Moore, John W Hill, Wm Gwin, T H Hensley, Mattw Gardenhire, Pleasan C Comes, Robt Cooley, Alexr Vines, Abraham Miller, John McClenahan say dft is not guilty as charged in the bill of indictment.
State v Joseph Thompson. John Owen summoned as a witness behalf State against John Thompson came not. Forfeits $255 unless sufficient cause of his

SEPTEMBER 1832

disability to attend be shewn at next Term of this Court.
    State v Abraham Miller. Nolle prosequi entered.
    State v John Wood. Attorney general suggests to Court that since the last continuance of this cause the defendant departed this life.
p.338   State v Ira Gothard. Dft in proper person says he is guilty; fined $10 and costs. Robert Boulton confessed judgment jointly with defendant.
    State v James Lea. Dft in proper person says he is not guilty. Jury Wm Carter, Edwd Templeton, Jas Moore, John W Hill, William Gwin, T H Henseley, Matthew Gardenhire, Pleasant C Comes, Robert Cooley, Alexander Vines, Abraham Miller, John McClenahan find dft guilty. Dft fined $5 and costs. Whereupon Hugh Carroll, Timothy F French, Ira Gothard, Robert Boulton, George C Archeart, Abner Witt, Jonathan Fry, Jesse Sampley & Thomas Kelley confessed judgment jointly with dft for fine & costs.
p.339   State v Bartlet Benson. Unlawfull gaming. Cause is continued untill next term. Recognizance of dft, William Carter and Timothy F French his securities. Bond of Timothy F French, condition he appear March Term to testify against Bartlett Benson for gaming.
    Abijah Baugus v John W Masses alias Sarah Masses. Plf by attorney directed this cause be dismissed. Sarah Masses confessed judgment for all costs.
p.340   Mercy Stewart v Abraham Miller. Plaintiff by attorney dismissed suit; plf recovers against defendant all costs.
    Sabra Duncan & others v Jonathan Fine. Plaintiffs by attorney dismissed suit. Defendant in proper person confessed judgment for all costs.
    Grand Jurors bill of indictment against Cornelius Harriss endorsed by their foreman Not a true bill; dft is discharged.
    Grand jurors bill of indictment against Joseph Gibbens endorsed by foreman a true bill; dft in propper person says he is not guilty; remanded to prison.
    Grand jurors bill of indictment against John McGill endorsed by their foreman a True bill; dft says he is not guilty; remanded to prison.
p.341   State v Cornelious Buttram. Dft in proper person says he is not guilty. Jury Wm Snelson, Wm Kerr, Jas Mitchell, John Miller, Matthias Broyles, Joseph McDaniel, Edwd Templeton, Geo Dearmon, Thos C Wroe, Archibald D Paul, Caleb Dobbs, Thos Carter find dft guilty; to be confined in penitentiary house of this state for Three Years next ensuing; remanded to jail.
    Court adjourned until tomorrow morning.   Charles F Keith

Thursday 27 Sept. Present on the bench the Honorable Charles F Keith Judge &c.
    State v John Yates. Affray. Order process against dft returnable next term.
p.342   State v John Yates. Gaming. Gaming. Order process awarded against defendant returnable next Term. Recognizance of Timothy F French, to appear March term to testify and give evidence in cause the State against John Yates for gaming.
    State v James Pickett. Gaming. [as above]
    State v Elizabeth McCarroll. Murder. Report of costs: Justice .50; Constable Craig warrant .50 11 subpoenas 275 cts. Constable Collins 7 subpoenas 175 cts. State tax $1. Clerk expences [details here omitted] $12.93¾. Sheriff Collins 2 subpoenas 50 cts, jury 12½¢, call 04 cts. Attorney general $2.50. Witnesses for State: Polly Houpt 2 days $1; Jane Griffith 2 days $1; Rebecca Tipton 2 days $1; p.343   Elizabeth Goad 2 days $1; Margaret Buck 2 days $1; Edmun Howerton 2 days $1; Abraham Miller 2 days $1. David Leuty for keeping 1 jury of 12 men all night @ 75 cts each $7. John Parker jailor for keeping Elizabeth McCarroll in jail 29 days

SEPTEMBER 1832

at 37½¢ per day and 4 turn keys at 50 cents each $11.75. Bill of costs is legally taxed, Samuel Frazier, attorney Generall. State to pay bill of costs.

State v Lewis & Rebbecca Knight. Grand Larceny. Bill of costs. Justice 50¢. Constable Craig warrant 50 cts 4 subpoenas 100 cts. State tax $1. Clerk [expenses here omitted] $9.71¼. Attorney general $2.50. Sheriff Collins 7 sub 175 cts, jury 12¢, call 4 cts. Shff Darwin 1 subpoena 25 cts. Witnesses on part of the State Andrew Erwin 2 days $1; Joseph Garrison 2 days $1; John Still 2 days $1; James Ferguson 2 days $1; Robert B Miller 2 days $; Joseph Mullins 2 days $1; Ann Mullins 2 days $1; John Miller 2 days $1; Condley Smith 2 days $1. Above bill of costs is legally taxed, Samuel Frazier attorney General. State pays foregoing costs.

p.344 State v David Marshall. Dft came not; state is granted execution against dft for $250 in scire facias specified, costs of serving writ, and prosecution.

State v John McGill. Dft in proper person says he is not guilty. Jury John Miller, Pleasant Hollomon, Alexander Rice, Caleb Dobbs, Jesse Matthews, John Dolen, Terry H Hensley, Thomas Kelley, John McClenahan, Edward Templeton, James Mitchell, Matthias Broyles could not agree; court directed sheriff to take charge of jury and return them into Court tomorrow; defendant was remanded to prison.

Court adjourned untill tomorrow.   Charles F Keith

Friday 28th September. Present on the bench the Honorable Charles F Keith, Judge.
p.345 State v James Robinson. Passing Counterfeit bank bill; bill of costs: State tax $1; Justice .50; constable warrant .50. Clerk [details here omitted] $6.78¼; Sheriff Collins call 04 cts. Attorney General $1.25; Witness for State William Rodden 1 day 130 miles $6.20. To John Parker jailor for keeping James Robinson from 29 Octr to 29 March at 2/3 $56.25; to 2 turnkeys $1. Sworn to in Court 27 Sept 1831 John Parker. John Locke clerk. Above bill of costs is legally taxed; Samuel Frazier attorney Generall. State to pay foregoing bill of costs.

State v Joseph Lambert. Passing Counterfeit bank bill. Bill of costs: Justice 50 cts. State tax $1. Clerk [details here omitted] $6.89; Sheriff Collins call 04 cts; Sheriff Paine warrant 50 cts. Attorney general $2.50. Above bill of costs is legally taxed, Samuel Frazier attorney general. State to pay costs.

p.346 State v William Stanley. Affray. Bill/costs: state tax $1. Clerk [details here omitted] $11.92½. Attorney generall $2.50. Sheriff Hackett 54 cts; Sheriff Collins $1.08; Sheriff Cox $1. Foregoing bill of costs is legally taxed, Samuel Frazier Attorney general. Certified to Court of Pleas & Quarter Sessions for Rhea County for allowance.

Henry Collins Sheriff to George W Stuart. Deed dated 27 Sept 1832, 266 acres proven by Spencer Jarnigan and John Locke.

State v John McGill. Passing counterfeit bank bill. Defendant in proper person. Jurors heretofore empanneled declared they could not agree. Mistrial entered. Defendant remanded to jail there to remain untill he shall be discharged by due course of law. John O Sims recognizance, condition he appear March term to p.347 give evidence behalf State against John McGill. Recognizances of Thomas W Muncy and Abner Witt, condition they appear March next to testify and give evidence in behalf State against John McGill.

Grand jurors bill of indictment against Thomas O Wroe and others signed by their foreman Not a true bill.

Grand and travers jurors of original panel are discharged from further attendance at this Term.

127

SEPTEMBER 1832

George Gillispie v Allen Gillispie & others. Injunction. Cause continued.
Samuel Humberd v Mary Case. Plf awarded alias scire facias.
State v Joseph Gibbens. Indictment: assault and batry with intent to commit a rape. Dft in proper person says he is not guilty. Jury John P Long, Pleasant C Comes, Henry Henry, Jackson Howerton, Allen Holland, George Henry, George W Dearmon, William Johnson, Robert Cooley, Robert Mitchell, Adam W Caldwell, John McClure declared they could not agree; therefore the sheriff takes charge of the jury, and
p.348 will return them into Court tomorrow morning.
Recognizance of Joseph Gibbins, condition he appear tomorrow.
Jesse Matthews, Eli Sharp, Alexander Rice bond $500 jointly, condition Joseph Gibbins appears tomorrow to answer charge of state against him.
Court adjourned untill tomorrow morning.   Charles F Keith

Saturday 29th Sept. Present the Honorable Charles F Keith, Judge, &c.
State v John McGill. State Dr to David Leuty to keeping 12 men all night, supper, bedding, and breakfast @ 4/6d each $9.
State v Joseph Gibbins. Washing 29th Sept 1832. State to David Leuty to keeping 12 men all night to supper, bedding and breakfast at 4/6 each $9.
Foregoing accounts are allowed, ordered to be attached to their respective bill of costs.
p.349 William N Love to Jefferson B Love. Deed dated 30 July 1832 two lots in southern liberties in Washington proven by R R Gist and Abraham Miller.
State v Cornelious Buttram. Horse Stealing. Upon finding of jury aforesaid, deft Cornelious Buttram to be confined in State penitentiary three years commencing 26 Septr 1832, pay costs in this behalf expended for which execution may issue; sheriff to summon sufficient guard and horses to safely convey dft to penitentiary.
State v Joseph Gibbins. Dft in proper person, jurors heretofore empanneled say dft is not guilty.
All causes in this Court not otherwise disposed of stand continued untill next term of this Court. Court adjourned untill Court in Course.   Charles F Keith

p.350 Monday 25th March. At a circuit Court of law and equity held for Rhea County in the town of Washington on the fourth Monday, present, presiding on the bench, the Honorable Natthaniel W Wiliams, one of the Circuit judges assigned to hold Circuit Courts within the Seventh Judicial Circuit.
Sheriff Henry Collins returned the venire facias: Matthias Shaver, James Swan, Peach Taylor, John Hill Senr, George Gillespie, Samuel Gamble, Vaden H Giles, John Pardoe, James C Mitchell, Thomas J Alexander, William Matlock, Joshua Renfro, Isaac Baker, Jeremiah Chapman, John McCallon, Elisha Sharp, George Preston, John Randles, James Wilson, Avara Hannah, Jesse Thompson, Beal Gaither, John Cozbey. Arthur Fulton and John Huff not to be found.
Grand Jury: George Gillespie, Thomas J Alexander, John McCallon, Beal Gaither, Matthias Shaver, James C Mitchell, John Hill Senr, George Preston, Jeremiah Chapman, James Swan, Vaden H Giles, John Pardoe, Jesse Thompson. Court appointed George Gillespie foreman.

MARCH 1833

    Constable Anson Dearmon sworn to attend on the grand jury.
    Excuse Joshua Renfro from further attendance as a juror at this Term.
    Remaining of original panel who answered their names: Elisha Sharp, Peach Taylor, William Matlock, Avary Hannah, John Cozbey.
p.351   Remaining of original panel who failed to answer their names John Huff, Isaac Baker, John Randles, Samuel Gamble, James Wilson.
    John Snow v James Smith. Cause is continued.
    Sarah McCoy v William Snelson. Matters in dispute submitted to the determination of James Swan, John Huff, James Wilson, Wm Wand, Pleasant Holloman, William Green, and John Farmer whose award is to be the judgment of the Court.
    Court adjourned until Tomorrow morning.   Nath W Williams

Tuesday 26th March. Present on the bench the Honorable Natthaniel W Williams.
    Excuse Elisha Sharp from further attendance as a juror at this Term.
    Joseph Thompson v John B Swan. Debt. Cause is continued.
    Lewis Knight & Rebecca Knight v Jacob Rassums heirs. Cause is continued.
p.352   Alfred Marsh v Theophilus Smith & Johnson Minton. Plf failing to appear is nonsuited; dfts recover against plaintiff their costs of defence.
    Alfred Marsh v Theophilus Smith & Johnson Minton. [as above]
    John McClenahan v William B Russell. Forfeiture. Dft who before this time was summoned a witness on behalf of John McClenahan in cause Lewis Ross against sd John McClenahan this day came not. John McClenahan recovers agt dft $125 unless sufficient cause of his disability to attend be shewn at next term of this Court.
    John Wills lessee v John Gilbreath & Mary Jane Gilbreath. Ejectment. From affidavit of the lessee of the plaintiff this cause is continued untill next term. Plf to take deposition of Thomas Hopkins in his residence in McMinnville, Warren County, giving William Gilbreath of Knox County notice of time and place.
p.353   Lewis Ross v John McClenahan. Certiorari. Jury Peach Taylor, Wm Matlock, Avara Hannah, Samuel Gamble, John Baker, Joseph Thompson, James Dyre, James Stuart, Andrew Wassum, John Able, Johnson Ceviret, Asahel Chilton who find in favor of the defendant $8.18. Dft recovers against plaintiff sd sum and also his costs.
    Samuel McDaniels lessee v Miles Vernon et all. Ejectment. Cause being heretofore continued from term to term to abide the final determination of a cause in Chancery wherein Miles Vernon the dft in this cause and others were complainants and the lessee of the plf Samuel McDaniel respondent. Decree of the Supreme Court in afsd cause was in favor of respondent. Therefore on motion of lessee of plf by his atty, he recovers agt dfts his term yet to come in messuage lands & tenements in his delcaration and also his costs about his defence expended.
    Samuel Humbard v Mary Case. Scire facias. Dft made default. Plf granted execution for sum $125 together with costs of suing and prosecuting this writ.
p.354   Henry Bullard v Robert McCracken. Exparte. Plf by atty moved Court for judgment against dft for monies by him paid as security on a judgment and execution obtained at instance of George Maines against present dft before William Smith, Esquire, an acting justice of the peace for Rhea County. Jury Thomas McCallie, James Montgomery, John McClenahan Jr, Anderson H Smith, Wm Seymore, Hugh Rhea, Martin Rigg, Addison Riggs, Wm Bice, Willie Lewis, John H Beck, John Cozbey. Plf recovers against dft $13 with interest thereon and also his costs.
    Court adjourned untill tomorrow morning.   Nath W Williams

MARCH 1833

Wednesday 27 March. Present the Honorable Natthaniel W Wilson, Judge &c.
State v John Yates. Afray. Process awarded agt dft returnable next Term.
State v John Yates. Gaming. Recognizance of Timothy F French, condition he appear Sept next to testify on behalf State against John Yates for unlawful gaming.
p.355 State v James Pickett. Gaming. [as above]
Lewis Ross v John McClenahan. Certiorari. Plf prays new trial; entered.
Thomas C Wroe to Samuel Kean & Margarett Kean. Deed dated 25 March 1833 for 160 acres acknowledged by Thomas C Wroe the maker thereof.
Alfred Marsh v Theophilus Smith & Johnson Minton. Two causes. Plf having suffered a nonsuit, obtained leave and withdrew evidence.
Asa Glascock v Lewis Pollard. Plf has taken no steps to prosecute for more than three terms last past, this cause is stricken from roles of this Court; dft recovers against plaintiff all costs in this behalf expended.
p.356 Richard & Blackstone Waterhouse executors of Richard G Waterhouse v Henry Collins & John Stuart, administrators of estate of Thomas Price deceased. Dfts in proper persons say they cannot gainsay plfs action for $1500 their debt together with $907.92 damages of detention, to be levied when the assets of the estate of their intestate shall come to their hands to be administered. Plfs recover agt dfts debt and damages and allso their costs of suit.
State v Robert Ellerson. Atty general enters nole prosequi. James Elerson and James Bradford confessed judgment for all costs.
State v Susanah Richards. Forfeiture. Dft bound in recognizance $100 to testify in a cause State against Nicholas Romines this day made default. State recovers agt dft $100 unless sufficient cause of her disability to attend be shewn at next term; scire facias issues accordingly.
State v Nicholas Romine. Grand jury indictment against defendant endorsed by George Gillespie their foreman Not a true bill; dft discharged.
p.357 State v John McGill. Dft in proper person says he is not guilty. Jury Hirum Henry, John Baker, Aron Maloney, Joseph Rice, Addison Rigg, Daniel D Armstrong, John F Owens, Lewis Knight, George Maners[?], Hugh Carroll, Alexander Vines, Thomas Henry find defendant not guilty; discharged.
State v Reuben Freeman. Exparte. Dft summoned as a juror came not; fine $5.
A F Herrick summoned as a juror came not; fine $5.
William Gwin summoned as a juror came not; fine $5.
James L Cobb summoned as a juror came not; fine $5.
p.358 State v Elizabeth Mullins & Catharine Millins. Grand Jury bill/Indictment agt defendants for Petit Larceny endorsed by foreman George Gillespie a true bill.
State v Edmund Howerton, Henderson Cumpton & William Johnson. Grand jury bill of indictment against the defendants for assault endorsed by their foreman George Gillespie a true bill.
State v James Stewart. Grand Jurors bill of indictment against dft for assault and battery with intent to commit a rape endorsed by their foreman George Gillespie a True Bill.
Court adjourned untill tomorrow morning. Nath W Williams

Thursday 28th March. Present the Honorable Natthaniel W Williams Judge &c.
Clerk of this Court produced receipt of Treasurer of East Tennessee for revenue by him collected for year last past: Recd of John Locke Clerk of Circuit Court of Rhea County $38.005. Miller Francis Treas of E Tennessee.

MARCH 1833

p.359   State v Thomas Branom. Attorney general reported following bills of costs legally taxed: justice 12½¢. Constable Baugges warrant 50 cts 6 subpoenas 37½¢. State tax .25. Clerk [details here omitted] $4.37½. Sheriff Collins 01 cts. Sheriff Russell 1 subpoena 6½¢. Attorney General $1.25. Witnesses for State A Baugges 3 days 25 ferriages .43¾, Sollomon McCall 3 days 25 ferriages 43¾¢. Thomas Branom in custody of John Parker jailor 12 Sept 1831 released 31 Decr (was confined) 111 days at 37½¢ per day & 8 turn keys $4. $45.62½.

State v Parmer Brandon. Costs same as above $8.84¾. Jailors fees same as above $45.62½. $54.47½.

State v William Wyrick. Court costs same as above; jailors fees same.

State v Frederick Wyrick. Court costs same as above. Dft was commited into the custody of John Parker jailor 28th Sept 1831 and released 31 Decr 96 days at 37½ per day $36. 8 turnkeys $4. $48.84¾. Above bills of costs are legally taxed. Samuel Frazier attorney general. State of Tennessee pays foregoing bill of costs.

p.360   Cornelious Harris ads State. Grand Larceny. Attorney general reported to Court the following bill of costs as being legally taxed: Justice .50. Constable McFalls warrant and 2 subpoenas $1. Clerk $9.37½. Sheriff Preston 26 subpoenas $6.62½. Attorney general $1.25. Witness on part of state Isaac Cresman 1 day 25 ferriages .75; Noah Buttram 1 day, ferriages .75; Claibourn Bondrin 1 day .50; Richard Bondron 1 day .50. Foregoing bill of costs are correctly taxed, Samuel Frazier, attorney general; State of Tennessee pay foregoing bill of costs.

Robert Boulton ads State. Gaming. Following bill of costs legally taxed: State tax $1. Clerk $13.77½. Sheriff Collins $2.74½. Sheriff Hackett $1.08. Attorney General $2.50. Witness for State Timothy F French 5 days $2.50. Foregoing bill of costs are correctly taxed, Samuel Frazier, attorney General.

p.361   State v Bartely Benson. Gaming. Dft in proper person says he is not guilty. Jury Peach Taylor, William Matlock, Avara Hanah, John Cozbey, Saml Gamble, Abraham Wright, William G English, Reuben McKinzie, Addison Rigg, Jno Witt, Robert Boulton, Job F Owins say dft is not guilty as charged in bill of indictment.

State v Elizabeth Mullins & Catharine Mullins. Petit Larceny. Defendants in proper person say they are not guilty. Jury Thomas C Wroe, Wade H Atkins, Robert N Hooke, Wm Matlock, Avara Hannah, William G English, Andrew Casteal, James Kelley, Robert Williams, Joseph Rice, Reuben McKinzie, Adison Rigg find the defendants not guilty in manner and form as charged.

Lewis Ross v John McClenahan. Certiorari. The rule for new trial is made absolute; cause is continued untill the next term of this Court.

p.362   Joseph Gibbons ads State. Assault & battery with intent to commit a rape. Attorney General reported the following bill of costs as legally taxed: Justice 50 cts. Constable Russell $3.50. State Tax $1. Clerk [details here omitted] $8.38¼. Sheriff Collins 3 subpoenas 75 cts, jury 12½¢, call 04, .91½. Sheriff Russell 5 subpoenas 1.25, 1 nonest on subp 12½, $1.37½. Sheriff D Gibbons 4 subp $1 3 nonests 37½¢, $1.37½. Attorney General $2.50. Witness for State William Miller 3 days $1.50. State of Tennessee Dr $22.05½. To David Leuty for keeping 12 men all night to supper bedding breakfast at 75¢ each $9. Foregoing bill of costs are legally taxed $31.05½. Samuel Frazier, atto General. State to pay foregoing bill of costs.

State v James Stewart. From affidavit of Catharine McClaine this cause is continued untill next term. Recognizance of James Stewart, $1000, James A Darwin and Robert N Gillespie securities, to answer charge of assault and battery with intent to commit a rape. Recognizance of Catherine McClaine, $500, condition she
p.363   attend next term to prosecute and give evidence in behalf state agt dft.

MARCH 1833

State v Edmund Howerton, William Johnson & Henderson Cumpton. Riot. Dfts in proper person. From affidavit of Edmund Howerton one of the dfts Henderson Cumpton is permitted to plead seperately to bill of indictment. Causes are continued untill next term. Recognizance of dfts $500 each, Lewis R Collins & Crispin E Shelton securities $250 each. Bond of John McCarroll, condition he appear Sept term to prosecute and give evidence in behalf State in above cause.

Jurors from further attendance at this term are discharged.

Gideon B Thompson summoned to attend this day as a juror came not; fine $5 together with contempt charges.

p.364 State v Nicholas Romines. Petit Larceny. Account proven in Open Court as filed by John Parker jailor: for keeping and finding Nicholas Romines in jail on charge of petit larceny from 7 Decr 1832 to 27 March 1833 at 37½¢ per day $41.62½. For two turnkeys .50 each $1. $42.62½. John Parker, jailor. John Locke, Clerk.

State v Elizabeth Mullins & Catharine Mullins. To John Parker jailor for keeping and finding Catharine Mullins in common jail on charge of Petit Larceny from 11 Decr 1832 to 27 Decr 1832 at 37½¢ per day $6. For two turnkeys $1. The above account is just and true. John Parker, Jailor. John Locke, Clerk.

The Court then adjourned untill tomorrow morning.   Nath W Williams

p.365 Friday 29th March. The Honorable Nathaniel W Williams Judge &c.

John McGill ads State. Indictment for passing counterfeit bank note. Bill of costs: Justice .50. Constable warrant .50. Clerk [details here omitted] $10.35. Sheriff Collins $2.08; Sheriff Preston .50; Sheriff Russell $1. Attorney General $5. Witnesses on part of State. William F Gillenwaters 3 days $1.50; William G English 3 days $1.50. William Walker 2 days $1. Thomas W Munsey 5 days $2.50. George C Areheart 3 days $1.50. Abner Witt 6 days $3. John O[C?] Sims 6 days 280 miles $17.30. John Witt 3 days 52 miles $5.08. $56.31. To John Parker jailor for keeping and finding John McGill in the common jail from first Sept 1832 to 27 March 1833 209 days at 37½¢ per day $78.37½. For six turnkeys $3. State of Tennessee Dr to David Leuty to keeping 12 men all knight supper bedding & breakfast at 75¢ each $9. $143.68½. The foregoing bills of costs are legally taxed. Samuel Frazier, Atto General. State of Tennessee pay foregoing bills of costs.

p.366 Robert Cooley v Margarett Rucer [Reecer?] et all. Writs of certiorari & supercedas awarded Cooley returnable next term of Court.

Lewis Knight & Rebecca Knight v Jacob Wassums heirs. Hearing next Term.

State v John Owins. Dft not appearing, State has execution agt dft for $250 the forfeiture specified, and the costs of writ.

State v James P[?] Cobb. Exparte. Fine $5 against him this term is set aside on payment of costs.

State v A F Herick. Exparte. Dft by Thos J Campbell his attorney. Fine of $5 against him as a delinquent juror is set aside on payment of costs.

p.367 State v William Gwin. Exparte. [worded as above]

State v Reuben Freeman. Exparte. [worded as above]

State v Gideon B Thompson. Exparte. [worded as above]

The Revenue Commissioners filed in this office their settlements with the entry taker for Rhea County and the same was ordered to be made a file in this office. Causes that have not been acted upon is continued untill next term.

Court adjourned untill Court in Corse.   Nath W Williams

SEPTEMBER 1833

p.368 At a circuit Court of law and equity for Rhea County in Washington on fourth Monday of September, present the Honorable Charles F Keith one of the judges assigned to hold the Circuit Courts within the seventh judicial circuit.

Sheriff Henry Collins returned venire facias: George Gillespie, Prior Neil, Stephen Winton, Matthias Shaver, Crispin E Shelton, Daniel Wallker, Vaden H Giles, Noah Buttram, Peach Taylor, James A Darwin, Arthur Fulton, Samuel Howard, Elisha Sharp, William Matlock, David Ragsdale, John Cozbey, Jerremiah Farmer, John Able, Matthias Shaver, Samuel Gamble, William Smith, John McClure, William Kerr, Alfred Marsh. John Holland and Carson Caldwell of original pannel was not to be found.

Grand jury: George Gillespie, Prior Neil, Stephen Winton, Matthias Shaver, Crispin E Shelton, Daniel Wallker, Vaden H Giles, Noah Buttram, Peach Taylor, James A Darwin, Arthur Fulton, Samuel Howard, Elisha Sharp.

Court appoint George Gillespie foreman of grand jury.

Constable Anson Dearmon sworn to attend on the grand jury.

There remained of original pannel who answered to their names John Cozbey, John Able, Jerremiah Farmer, Matthias Shaver, David Ragsdale, William Matlock.

Remaining of original pannel who failed to answer to their names John McClure, William Kerr, Alferd Marsh.

p.369 William Smith is a poast master for Rhea County; he is excused from further attendance as a juror at this term.

Excuse Samuel Gamble from further attendance as a juror at this term.

John Snow v James Smith. Plaintiff in proper person dismissed this cause and confessed judgment for all costs.

John Witts lessee v John Gilbreath & Mary Jane Gilbreath. Ejectment. Cause is continued untill next term of this Court.

Julius F Devinport & Mary Devinport to Moses Whitaker. Deed dated 23 Sept 1833 for 110 acres in State of Virginia ackd by Julius T Devinport. Mary Devinport examined apart from her husband says she signed sd deed without compulsion.

James H Wilkerson licensed to practice as an attorney took the oath and thereupon is admitted to practice in this Court.

p.370 William Coats v Lucretia Coats. Divorce. Subpoena and copy of complainants petition issue upon complainants giving bond and security according to law.

Joseph McDaniel v Lewis Knight. Debt. Plfs atty moved Court for a rule to cause dft to give security on or before second day of next Term; granted.

Court adjourned untill tomorrow morning.   Charles F Keith

Tuesday 24th September. Preent on the bench the Honorable Charles F Keith, Judge.

Joseph McDaniel v Lewis Knight. Debt. Dft by atty moved for rule to cause plf to give security on or before second day of next term; granted.

Abijah Bogges v John Twiford. Petition. Writs of certiorari & supersedas awarded dft returnable to next term of this Court.

Henry Collins, Shff, to John Carter. Deed, 16 Sept 1833 for 160 acres ackd.

p.371 Lewis Ross v John McClenahan. Certiorari. Jury Isaac Blevins, Jeremiah Farmer, Matthias Shaver, David Ragsdale, John B Campbell, William Gwin, John Twiford, Abraham Miller, Abijah Bogges, Wm Kerr, Carson Caldwell, Zackariah Compton find for dft $8.70½; dft also recovers agt plf his costs of defence.

William N Morriss v Lewis Knight. Cause is continued.

John McClenahan v William B Russell. Scire Facias. Plf in proper person dismissed his suit. Defendant confesses judgment for all costs.

SEPTEMBER 1833

Joseph Thompson v John B Swan. Jury Geo Gillespie, Alfred Marsh, Stephen Winton, Pryor Neil, Matthias Broyles, Crispin E Shelton, Daniel Walker, Vaden H Giles, Noah Buttram, Peach Taylor, Samuel Howard, Elisha Sharp find for defendant $14.94½; dft also recovers agt plf his costs about his defence expended.
p.372 Robert McCormack v John D Chatten. Pauper. Suit is instituted under the provisions of law to help persons in obtaining their rights, appointed Samuel Frazier attorney for plaintiff; plaintiff by attorney directed his suit to be dismissed. Defendant recovers against plaintiff his costs about his defence expended.

Sarah McCoy v William Snelson. Referees James Swan, John Huff, James Wilson, Pleasant Hollomon, Wm Hand, Wm Green, John Farmer to whom was referred the determination of this cause returned their award: William Snelson pay plf $7.37½ damages and all Court costs in sd suit expended.

Robert Cooley v Margarett Reecer & Andrew Casteel. Certiorari. Dfts by atty pray rule to shew cause why petition should be dismissed; rule granted.
p.373 Joseph McDaniel v Lewis Knight. Appeal. Jesse Matthews in proper person undertakes for plaintiff. Jury Isaac Blevins, Jeremiah Farmer, Matthias Shaver, David Ragsdale, John B Campbell, William Gwin, John Twiford, Abraham Miller, Abijah Bogges, William Kerr, Carson Caldwell, William Ferguson say dft oweth plf nothing. Dft recovers of plaintiff his costs by him about his defence expended.

State v Nathan Lowder, Isaac Robins, & John Hackler. Grand Jury bill of Indictment against dfts endorsed by George Gillespie their foreman Not a true bill.

James Knight & Rebecca Knight v Jacob Wassums heirs. Cause continued, Lewis Knight paying all costs of present term. Wassums heirs recover agt L Knight their costs at this term expended. Parties to take deposition of Thomas B Smith giving each other notice of time and place, notice to be served on Jacob & Andrew Wassum, and their notice to be served on Lewis Knight.
p.374 Joseph Thompson v John B Swan. Debt. New trial granted plaintiff.

Court adjourned until tomorrow morning. Charles F Keith

Wednesday 25th September. Present the Honorable Charles F Keith, Judge &c.

State v James Steuart. Defendant in proper person says he is not guilty. Jury John Cozbey, John Able, Jeremiah Farmer, David Ragsdale, Wm Matlock, Wm D Collins, Wm Bullion, John B Campbell, John Twiford, John Burnett, Joseph Thompson, Wm N Gillespie say dft is not guilty. Prosecutrix to pay cost of this malicious & frivolous prosecution. State to recover of Catherine McClain costs expended.

State v Cornelious Buttram. Account of John Parker jailor for keeping dft in jial on charge of grand larceny from 16 June 1832 to 29 sept 1832 at 37½¢ per day $40.12½. Three turnkeys $1.50.
p.375 Jas & Wm Park assignee of A Cox v David Leuty. Dft in proper person confessed judgement for $224.80 debt & $2.24 damage. Plfs also recover costs of suit.

Thos McCallie et all v John Parker. Complainants by John Hook their counsel moved for judgment agt respondent, he having made no defence; set for hearing at next Term of this Court.

State v John Yates. Affray. Dft in proper person says he is guilty. Fined $5, pay prosecution costs & be in custody untill fine & costs are paid or secured.
p.376 State v John Yates. Gaming. Dft in proper person saith he is guilty. Fined $10, pay costs, and be in custody untill fine and costs are paid or secured.

State v James Pickett. Capias returned Not Found; process issue.

State v John Wood. Death of dft previously suggested, cause abates.

SEPTEMBER 1833

 State v Edmond Howarton, Henderson Compton & Wm Johnson. Dfts in proper person say they are not guilty. Continued on affidavit of dfts that Thomas J Campbell their counsell is absent. Recognizance of dfts $500 each, Thomas Haws and
p.377 William Compton their securities. Recognizance of John McCarroll $250 condition he appear next Term to prosecute and give evidence in cause State v Edmond Howarton & others. Sarah McCarroll, Henry McCarroll, & Wm Ferguson bond, condition they appear next Term to give evidence in behalf the State.

 Kean v Wroe. Order Clerk deliver to complainant the deed deposited in his office executed by Henry Perkins & wife to sd complainant.

 Edward Brown to James Gambell. Deed of Trust dated 25 Sept 1833 for land in Roane County proven by Robert N Gillespie and John Parker.
p.378 Robinson v Wm Cozbey. Plf not appearing to prosecute her suit, on motion of defendant by attorney, plaintiff non prossed, dft recovers against plaintiff.

 State v Abraham Weasse & Isaac Wease. Grand Jury bill of indictment agt dfts for conspiracy endorsed by foreman a True bill. Dfts in proper person say they are not guilty. Jury John Able, Matthias Shaffer, David Ragsdale, William N Gillispie, Wm Kerr, Wm Locke, John McCarroll, George Henry Jr, Joseph Thompson, Thomas C Wroe, Wm Compton, Azariah Barton say dfts are not guilty.
p.379 Morriss v Knight. Subpoena awarded defendant commanding Isaac Roddy and Joseph McCorcle at next term to bring a States warrant against William N Morriss for arson issued by them at the instance of said defendant.

 Grand and Traverse jurors are discharged from further attendance this term.

 State v William Brown. Crime charged was committed in Monroe County TN; order Sheriff transmit dft from jail in Rhea County to jail in Monroe County, and Clerk transmit a transcript of proceedings had in this Court to next Circuit Court to be holden for Monroe County. Whereupon William Whitten bond, void on condition he appear Monroe Circuit Court Novr next to prosecute and give evidence against Wm Brown on a charge of Forgery.
p.380 Robert Cooley v Margarett Reecer & Andrew Casteel. Margarett Recir and Andrew Casteel recover against Robert Cooley their costs of defence.

 Joseph Thompson v John B Swan. Rule for new trial is discharged.

 Margarett Reecer v Robert Cooley & others. Margarett Reecer by attorney moved for judgment on the bond given for writs of certiorari & superceedas, but Court refused, writ of prosedendo issued to Isaac Roddy, acting justice of peace for this County; original papers filed in this Cause transmitted to sd justice.

 State v Sarah Sutton. Dft having been summoned to appear as witness behalf State against James Steuart came not; dft forfeit $250 unless sufficient cause of her disability to attend be shewn at next term of this Court.
p.381 Elizabeth Mullins & Catharine Mullins ads State. Petit Larceny. Bill of costs: Justice .50; Constable Thompson $2.25, State tax $1. Clerk [details here omitted] $6.51½. Sheriff Collins $2.29½. Attorney General $5. Witnesses on part of State Simeon Jackson 2 days $1; Peggy Ransom 4 days $2. To John Parker jailor for keeping and finding Catharine Mullins in the common jail committed on charge for petit larceny from 11 Decr 1832 to 27 Decr 1832 being 16 days at 37½¢ $6; for two turnkeys $1.

 State v Catharine McClaine. Dft before this time was bound in recognizance $500 to appear at this term and prosecute and give evidence against James Steuart came not. State recovers against dft $500 unless sufficient cause ofher disability to attend be shewn at next term of this Court; scire facias issue.
p.382 Nicholas Romines ads State. Bill of Costs. Justice .50; Constable Cozbey

135

SEPTEMBER 1833

$1.50; State tax $1. Clerk [details here omitted] $5.57½. Sheriff Collins .04; attorney general $5; witnesses on behalf of State, Thomas Romines 1 day .50; Mary Romines 3 days $1.50; James Atchley 3 days $1.50; Timothy F French 3 days $1.50. To John Parker jailor for keeping and finding Nicholas Romines in jail on charge of petit larceny from 7 Decr 1832 to 27 March 1803 at 37½¢ per day $41.62½; two turnkeys $1.

  State v Thomas Haynes. Petit Larceny. Bill of costs: justice .50; Constable $1.25; witness attendance before justice .75; state tax $1. Clerk [details here omitted] $5.67½. Attorney general $5. Sheriff Collins .16½. Witnesses on part of
p.383 the State: Moses Blevins 3 days 25¢ ferriages $1.75; Samuel F Martain 3 days & ferriage $1.75. Clerk writ of Farie facias .40. Thomas Haynes committed into custody of John Parker jailor 2 Sept 1831 and was confined 33 days at 37½ cts per day $12.37½; six turnkeys $3. Foregoing bill of costs is truly taxed, Samuel Frazier, attorney general.

  State v Cornelious Buttram. Grand Larceny. Bill of costs. Justice .50. Constable warrant & subpoenas $1.50. State tax $1. Clerk [details here omitted] $6.47½. Sheriff Collins .16½. Attorney general $5. Witnesses on part of State: Charley Crisman 1 day & ferriage .66; Wm Parmer 1 day & ferriages .66. To John Parker jailor for keeping Cornelious Buttram in jail from 14 June 1832 to 29 Sept 1832 at 37½ per day $40.12½. Three turnkeys $1.50.

p.384 Henry Collins & John Stewart admrs of Thomas Price v heirs at law of Thomas Price & Richard & Blackstone Waterhouse executors of Richard G Waterhouse. By consent of parties this bill was brought on for hearing this day, it is ordered by Court that Clerk & master of Court expose land mentioned in sd bill to public sale to highest bidder or so much thereof as may be sufficient to satisfy the debt in sd bill mentioned and such other debts as account thereof may find to be due from sd Thomas Price decd and unpaid first giving forty days notice of sd sale. Further ordered that clerk and master take an account of sd debt of Waterhouses executors and of such other debts as may be exhibited by plf to him, and report thereof to the next Term of this Court as also his sproceedings touching the sale of the premises in the bill mentioned. Further ordered that when sale be made sd clerk and master may pay sd dfts Richard & Blackstone Waterhouse the sum due to them by virtue of the judgment in bill mentioned, and the sd Richard & Blackstone Waterhouse shall stand in place of the money arising on sd sale, and the plaintiffs pay the cost os this cost out of the proceeds of the sale.

  Court adjourned untill tomorrow morning.   Charles F Keith

Thursday 24th September. Present same judge as on yesterday.
  Court adjourned till Court in Course.   Charles F Keith

p.385 Monday 24th March 1834. At a court of law and Equity held for Rhea County in Washington on the fourth Monday of March 1834, presiding on the bench the Honorable Charles F Keith one of the Circuit Judges commissioned to hold the Circuit Courts within the Seventh judicial Circuit.

  Sheriff Samuel R Hackett returned venire facias: Bryant McDonald, Benjamin

MARCH 1834

Jones, Samuel Garwood, Jackson Howerton, Thomas Haws, Levi W Ferguson, Baty Breeding, John R Hill, Farley Brady, Brinkley Hornesbey, Edward E Wasson, John Challen, Jesse Martin, Robert Cravins, Pleasant N Lea, Robert A Gillespie, Richard Waterhouse, Robert Pharriss, William H Stocton, James Blevins, John W Smith, Daniel Cates, Abraham Cox Junr.

    Grand Jury: Richard Waterhouse, Pleasant N Lea, Robert Pharris, Baty Breeding, John Chatten, Jackson Howerton, Robert Cravins, Bryant McDonal, Thomas Haws, Jesse Martin, Brinkley Hornsbey, William H Stocton, Robert Gillespie.

    Court appointed Richard Waterhouse foreman of the Grand Jury.

    Constable William B Cozbey sworn to attend on sd grand jury.

    From affidavits of Farley Brady, John W Hill, Edward E Wasson are excused from further attendance as jurors at this term.

    Remaining of original pannel who failed to answer to their names: Benjamin Jones, Samuel Garwood, Levi W Ferguson, James Blevins, John W Smith, Daniel Cates, Abraham Cox Junr.

p.386   Thomas N Vandyke licensed to practice as an attorney in the Circuit Courts took the oath of an attorney and is admitted to practice in this Court.

    Williamson Smith et all complt v William Hogan et al respdt. Complainants by counsel Return J Meigs dismissed their bill; the respondent recovers against the complainants their costs by them about their defence expended.

    Court adjourned untilll tomorrow morning.   Charles F Keith

Tuesday 25th March. Present on the bench the honorable Charles F Keith, Judge.

    Asahel Johnson assinee of Edward Templeton v William Grigsbey & Abner Witt. Cause is continued untill next term on affidavit of the defendants.

    William N Morriss v Lewis Knight. Cause is continued untill next term.

p.387   Anson Dearmon for the use of Gideon B Thompson v William W Pile et all. Rule granted plf to shew cause why proceedings in this cause should be quashed; rule discharged.

    John Wills lessee v John & Mary J Gilbreath. Ejectment. Cause is continued; commission is awarded plaintiff to take deposition of John Gamble on sd lessee of plf giving William Gilbreath five days previous notice. Commission awarded lessee of plaintiff to take deposition of Thomas Hopkins of Warren County TN.

    Anson Dearmon for use of Gideon B Thompson v William W Pile et all. Plf by atty prayed rule for dfts to give security; granted. Dfts by attorney move for rule to cause plf to give security; whereupon Robert N Gillespie undertakes for plf.

p.388   Spills B Dyre v Jacob Wassum. Matters in dispute referred to determination of Matthew Hubberd, Arthur Fuellen, John Ferguson, Carson Caldwell.

    Thomas J Alexander v George Hanson. Matters in dispute submitted to determination of Jackson Howerton, Carson Caldwell, Orville Paine & James A Darwin.

    Lewis & Rebecca Knight v Jacob Wassums heirs. Caveat. Cause is continued, Lewis Knight paying all costs of present term. Plf to take depositions of Anthony Debrill, John W Simpson, Lewis Evans, Simon Doyle, Henderson McFarland of White

p.389   County, TN, giving Jacob or Andrew Wassum notice. Henry Owins, Jacob Beck & John Garrison come into court, Henry Owins and John Garrison undertake for dfts.

    Chunn Gillespie & Co v John Wasson. Dfts record before the justice in this cause brought to tis Court. Chumr Gillespie, Alexander Wassam.

    Thomas McNeill v James Steuart. Pauper case. Plf filed instructions to dismiss his suit on dfts confessing judgment for all costs. Dft in proper person

MARCH 1834

confessed judgment for costs; Plf recovers agt dft his costs of suit.
      Benjamin Maxfield assinee v John Howell et all. Return J Meigs undertakes for plaintiff. Commission awarded defendant to take deposition of James H Ragen of McMinn County TN.
p.390   Robert N Gillespie v William W Pile. Cause stricken from roles of Court.
      Court adjourned untill tomorrow Morning.   Charles F Keith

Wednesday 26 March. Present on the bench the honorable Charles F Keith, judge &c.
      Henry Collins and John Steuart admrs of Thomas Price deceased v John H Price, William C Price, Thomas J Price, Jas F Price, Charles M Price, Minerva C Price, Isaac R Price, Louisa E Price, Eliza N Price, and Hugh W Price heirs at law of sd Thomas Price deceased, and Richard Waterhouse and Blackstone Waterhouse executors of the will of Richard G Waterhouse. Interlocutory decree of last term in all things confirmed. Wright Smith purchased the premises in the bill, legal title to sd premises vested in the heirs of Richard G Waterhouse; power to sell same vested by will in Richard Waterhouse and Blackstone Waterhouse as executors thereof, therefore adjudged by Court that title rested in John H Price, William C Price, Thomas J Price, James F Price, Charles M Price, Minerva C Price, Isaac R Price, Louisa E Price, Eliza N Price and Hugh W Price be divested out of them in
p.391   favor of Wright Smith and be vested in him. To the end that the legal title of Richard Waterhouse Blackstone Waterhouse, Myra Waterhouse, Cyrus Waterhouse, Darius Waterhouse, Euclid Waterhouse, Ann Waterhouse, Vesta Waterhouse and Franklin Waterhouse legatees and heirs of Richard G Waterhouse may be divested out of them it is further ordered and decreed that Richard Waterhouse and Blackstone Waterhouse exrs of will of sd Richard G Waterhouse execute a warranty deed to sd Wright Smith of the premesis in the interlocutory order mentioned, bounded as follows [omitted].
      State v Edmond Howarton and others. From affidavit of Henderson Compton cause is continued. Recognizance of Edmond Howarton, Henderson Compton, & William Johnson, Lewis R Collins and Anson Dearmon securities, condition Edmond, Henderson, and William appear Septr term to answer charge of state against them. Recognizance
p.392   of John McCarroll, condition he appear Septr term to prosecute and give evidence against Edmond Howarton. Recognizance of William Ferguson, Henry McCarroll and Sarah McCarrol, condition they appear Septr to give evidence against Howarton.
      Robert Williams v Anson Dearmon. Pauper case. Plf came not. Dft recovers against plf his costs about his defence expended.
      Chunn Gillespie & Co v John Wasson. Continued untill next term.
p.393   Robert McCormack v John D Chatten. Pauper case. From affidavits of Jonathan Fry and Jacob Prillerman shewing that this action is frivolous and malicious, suit is dismissed; dft recovers agt plaintiff his costs of defence.
      Owen David v Lewis Boulton. Trover. From affidavit of Timothy F French this cause is continued untill next term of this Court.
      Robert N Gillespie v William W Pile. Writs of certiorari & superseedus awarded plaintiff.
      State v Susan Richards. Scire facias. Dft came not. State awarded execution against dft for $100 together with costs of suing and of writ.
      State v James Pickett. Gaiming. Process issue returnable next term.
p.394   State v Sarah Sutton. Scire facias. Sci Fa returned Not found; alias scire facias issues returnable to next term of this Court.
      State v Catharine McClaine. Scire facias. Return of Sheriff Not made Known;

MARCH 1834

Alias Scire Facias issued returnable at next term of this Court.

Edmund Waggoner v Timothy F French. Wm Bryant, plfs counsel, to show his authority to next term of this court.

On application of grand jury, subpoena is awarded commanding Abraham Cox to appear and give evidence in relation of unlawful gaming who was sworn in open Court and sent before sd grand jury; Grand jury returned presentment against Thomas C Pile and Lewis Knight.

On application of grand jury, subpoena is awarded commanding John Traynor to appear and give evidence in relation to unlawful gaming; sworn, sent before grand jury; grand jury returned presentment agt Lewis R Collins & Thomas W Munsey.

On application of grand jury, subpoena is awarded commanding David Leuty &
p.395 Abraham Miller to give evidence in relation to unlawful gaming; sworn sent before grand jury who returned presentment against William Evans and David Roddy.

Grand & traverse jury from further attendance at this term are discharged.

On application of attorney general, Clerk of this Court produced treasurer of East Tennessees receipt for revenue by him collected for year last past: recd of John Locke Esqr from 1 Octr 1832 to 1 Octr 1833 $17.79½. Miller Francis, treasurer.

Revenue Commissioners Thomas McCallie and Samuel Frazier, receipt.

State v John Yates. Gaiming. John Parker jailor of Rhea County account: for keeping and finding John Yates in common jail on charge of affray and unlawful gaiming from 6 Augt 1833 to 26 Septr 1833 $19.13½.

p.396 State v Cornelious Buttram & Thomas Haynes. Larceny. It appearing to Court from evidence that Defendants has no property in any part of the State out of which the costs can be collected; state pays costs $90.45.

Thomas McCallie & Hooke v John Parker. Sd deft is indebted to complainants $302.78 with interest thereon; order that dft within three months pay complainants afsd sum and $30.27 interest with costs of suit, or deed of mortgage be foreclosedm proceeds thereof to pay sd complainants their debt, interest and costs.

Court adjourned untill tomorrow morning.   Charles F Keith

p.397 Thursday 27th March. Present on the bench the Honorable Charles F Keith.

Anson Dearmon for use of Gideon B Thompson v William W Pile et all. Demurrer. Plaintiffs demurrer to plea of defendants overruled.

All causes on docket not otherwise disposed are continued.

Court adjourned till court in course.   Charles F Keith

p.398 Monday 22d September. At a circuit Court of law and Equity for Rhea County on fourth Monday of September, present on the bench the Honorable Charles F Keith one of the circuit judges assigned to hold Circuit Courts within the Seventh judicial Circuit.

Sheriff Samuel R Hackett returned the venire facias: George Gillespie, William Smith, John McClure, John Cozbey, Carson Caldwell, Azariah David, Matthias Shaver, James McCanse, John Pardoe, Vaden H Giles, Samuel Gamble, Isaac Baker, Peach Taylor, John McCallon, Robert Cooley, Arthur Fulton, Joseph McCorkle, John Randles, James Wilson, James Blevins, Jesse Thompson, William Kerr, Stephen Winton,

SEPTEMBER 1834

Edward E Wasson and Matthew Hubbert. Isaac Roddy and David Hounshell not found.

Grand jury: John Cozbey, John McClure, Stephen Winton, Peach Taylor, Edward E Wasson, Carson Caldwell, James McCanse, John Pardoe, Vaden H Giles, John Randles, Azariah David, George Gillespie, James Blevins.

Court appointed John Cozbey foreman of the grand jury.

Constable Anson Dearmon sworn to attend on said grand jury.

Excuse Arthur Fulton, James Wilson, Jesse Thompson from further attendance as jurors at this Term.

Remaining of the original pannel who failed to answer to their names William Smith, Matthias Shaver, William Kerr, John McCallon.

p.399 Chun Gillespie & co v John Wasson. Cause continued untill next term.

Spills B Dyre v Jacob L Wassum. Rule made at last term stands revived.

James J Long v Anson Dearmon. Pauper case. Suit instituted under law to help poor persons obtain just rights, appoint Thomas J Campbell attorney for plaintiff.

Josheph Thompson v Moses Thompson & Elam Reese. Pauper. Appoint Thomas J Campbell attorney for plaintiff.

State v Sarah Fulton. From affidavit of defendant, forfeiture heretofore entered in this cause is set aside without costs.

William Ballard v Charles Witt. Record failing to shew that an appeal had been granted from judgment rendered therein; on motion of dft by atty, this cause stricken from roles of this Court and papers delivered over to justice.

State v James Clement, Joseph C Dyre & Levi Borin. Grand jurors returned a bill/indictment agt dfts for note endorsed by John Cozbey, foreman, a true bill.

p.400 On application of Thomas Snelson & others, subpoena awarded to cause Alexander H McCall and Absolam Foster subscribing witnesses to a deed of partition appear at present term and prove the same in open Court.

John Witts lessee v John & Mary Jane Gilbreath. Ejectment. Cause continued. Dft recovers agt plf costs at this term expended. Plf to take deposition of John Gamble giving William Gilbreath notice. Sd lessor also to take deposition of Thomas Hopkins giving William Gilbreath notice.

Court adjourned untill tomorrow morning.   Charles F Keith

Tuesday 23d September. Present on the bench the honorable Charles F Keith, Judge.

Benjamin Maxfield v John Howell et all. Record before the justice failing to shew that an appeal had been granted from the judgment rendered therein, cause stricken from roles of this Court.

Dearmon for Thompson v William W Pile et all. William H Minott undertakes for defendants.

p.401 Asahel Johnson assinee of Edward Templeton v William Grigsbey & Abner Witt. Jury Matthew Hubbert, Isaac Baker, Joseph McCorkle, John Miller, Joseph Thompson, Richard Waterhouse, Robert Gillespie, William Humberd, Zachariah Cross, Martin Russell, William W Pile, William N Meriott find for plf $85.56 besides costs.

Martin Low v John Witt. Jury Stephen Winton, Peach Taylor, Edward E Wasson, Carson Caldwell, James McCanse, John Pardoe, Vaden H Giles, John Randles, Azariah David, George Gillespie, James Blevins, John Wasson. Plf recovers agt dft $25 debt, $1.11½ damages and also his costs of suit.

James & William Park & Co v Alphord Hutchison. Cause is continued.

Richard Waterhouse v Jacob L Wassum. Cause is continued.

SEPTEMBER 1834

Excuse Matthias Shaver from further attendance as a juror at this term.
p.402   Joseph Thompson v John Miller. Dft prayed rule to cause plf to give security, same is ordered.

Jesse Sampley v Henry Griffith. Jury Matthew Hubbert, Isaac Baker, Joseph McCorkle, John Miller, Joseph Thompson, Richard Waterhouse, Robert A Gillespie, Wm Humberd, Zackariah Cross, Martin Russell, William W Pile, William N Meriott. Plf recovers agt dft $1.50 and also his costs.

Anson Dearmon for use of Gideon B Thompson v William W Pile, Thomas C Pile & Allan Holland. Defendants in proper persons acknowledge they are indebted to the plaintiff $23.86 besides costs.

Deed or article of Partition dated 1 March 1834 between heirs and legal representatives of James Snelson decd for land proven in open court by Alexander H McCall one of the subscribing witnesses.

Deed or article of partition dated 1 March [blank] between heirs and legal representatives of James Snelson for land proven by Alexander H McCall one of the subscribing witnesses thereto.
p.403   Deed or article of partition dated 1 March [blank] between heirs and legal representatives of James Snelson decd for land proven by Alexander H McCall.

William A Morriss v Lewis Knight. From affidavit of Rebecca Knight cause is continued untill next term, dfts paying all costs.

Owen David v Lewis Bolton. Jury Matthew Hubbert, Isaac Baker, Joseph McCorkle, John Miller, Richard Waterhouse, William Humberd, Zachariah Cross, Martin Russell, William D Meriott, Samuel Gamble, Jesse Poe, John Wasson find dft guilty of trover and conversion. Plaintiff recovers agt dft $32.10 damages & his costs.

Martin Russell v Lewis Knight. Suit instituted under law to help poor persons in obtaining their rights apptd Samuel L Childress attorney for plaintiff; certiorari is awarded him to Clerk/Court of pleas & quarter Sessions Rhea County.
p.404   Benjamin Maxfield v John Howell et all. From petition of John Howell, order writs of certiorari & supersedias awarded upon petitioners giving bond.

John H Dick attorney for James Smith v William Smith exr. Plf dismissed his suit; dft recovers against plaintiff his costs about his defence expended.

State v William C Henley. Grand jury bill of indictment agt dft for larceny endorsed by John Cozbey foreman Not a true bill. Dft discharged.

Thomas J Alexander v George Ransom. Referees returned their award. Carson Caldwell, one of the commissioners, refusing to serve, parties agreed that Anson Dearmon should serve in his place who, with Commissioners Jackson Howerton, Orville Paine, James A Darwin met at the house of Thomas J Alexander on 20 September. After hearing allegations and evidences of both parties, we adjudge that Thomas J Alexan-
p.405   der recover against George Ransom $12.75 debt and allso his costs.

Court adjourned till tomorrow morning.   Charles F Keith

Wednesday 24th Sept. Present the honorable Charles F Keith.

James D Rhea and Charles K Gillespie licensed attornies were sworn and admitted to practice in this court.

Owen David v Lewis Boulton. Dft by counsel moved for a new trial; disallowed. Plaintiff recovers of Timothy F French the dfts security the sum of $32.10 damages assessed by the jury together with all costs.
p.406   Asahel Johnson v William Grigsbey et als. Plaintiff recovers of Jesse Witt and Robert Boulton the securities named in bond jointly with the defendants the sum

141

SEPTEMBER 1834

of $85.56 and all costs.

Jesse Sampley v Henry Griffith. Plaintiff recovers of John Crawford security for appeal jointly with defendant the sum of $1.50 together with all costs.

Martha Russell v Lewis Knight. It does not appear from the record that
p.407 final judgment had been rendered in the court below. Appeal is dismissed; County Court to prosecute to final judgment in the cause; appellant in error pay costs of sd appeal in error for which execution may issue.

State v Edmund Howerton & others. Nolle prosequi entered.

State v Catherine McClain. On affidavit of dft, forfeiture heretofore entered against her is set aside.

p.408 State v T C Pile & Lewis Knight. Nolle prosequi entered.

State v Lewis R Collins & Thos W Muncy. Presentment of the grand jury in this cause is quashed.

State v Wm Evans & David Roddy. Presentment of Grand jury is quashed.

State v James Clements et als. Order alias capias to issue.

p.409 State v James Pickett. Alias capias is ordered to issue.

Edmd W Waggoner v F Birch. Plfs attorney having produced satisfactory authority for prosecuting this suit, the rule made at last Term is discharged.

Lewis Knight & wife v Jacob Wassums heirs. From affidavit of Rebbecca Knight one of the plaintiffs the rule of last Court requiring plfs to give security is suspended until next term and cause is continued.

Geo Gillespie v Allen Gillespie et all. Complainant in proper person confessed judgment for all costs. Bill dismissed; respondants recover agt complainant.

State v James Clement et all. Recognizance of Abner Triplet, condition he appear March next to prosecute and give evidence in behalf State agt dft.

p.410 Abraham Miller jailor presents account for keeping Wm C Henly in prison from 22 June untill 23 September 1834, 93 days, $34.87½. Two turn keys $1. Sworn before John Randles an acting justice of the peace for Rhea County. A. Miller.

Jacob L Wassum v Swan et all. Plf by atty dismissed cause & confessed judgment for all costs.

Jacob L Wassum v Swan et als. Plf by atty dismissed suit. Dfts recover of plf all costs.

p.411 Thos McCallie & Robt N Hook v John Parker. Charles F Keith judge sitting in chancery. John Parker had failed to pay debt and interlocutory decree; clerk and master had exposed to public sale the mortgaged premises in complts bill mentioned, after giving required notice, on Saturday 9th August at courthouse door, Thomas McCallie bid $300 which being highest & best bid sd McCallie became the purchaser of sd mortgaged premises to wit Lot 11 in Washington. Proceeds of the sale to be
p.412 applied first to payment of costs of this cause and the remainder to payment of complainants debt, and that complainant recover of respondant the remainder of sd debt for which he may have execution.

Priscilla Moses et als v Sarah Moses et als. Petition of Sarah Moses and Miles Vernon seen by court, order James Lillard appointed receiver who shall enter bond with security in sum $1000 before the clerk and master of this Court for the faithful performance of his duty as receiver; further ordered that dft John Parker forthwith deliver to James Lillard the possession of the land referred to in the
p.413 pleadings in this cause, that a copy of this order be served upon said Parker, and that James Lillard manage sd lands, mills, retaining the rents subject to the court, and Parker shall not deliver possession upon demand; the sheriff shall immediately put Lillard into possession of sd lands & mills except the

142

MARCH 1835

tenements occupied by Priscilla Moses.
    State v Henderson Compton. Nolle prosequi entered.
    State v William Johnson. Nolle prosequi entered.
p.414 All jurors are discharged.
    Court adjourned untill court in course.   Charles F Keith

p.415 Monday 23d March. At a Circuit Court of law and equity for Rhea County on the fourth Monday of March, was present on the bench the honorable Charles F Keith, assigned to hold Circuit Courts within the Seventh Judicial Circuit.
    Sheriff Samuel A Hackett returned the venire facias: Samuel Garwood, Bryant A McDonald, Thomas J Gillespie, Andrew McCaleb, Archibald D Paul, Robert Locke, James Montgomery, John Day, Samuel Frazier, Akiah Parker, John Chatten, Jesse Martin, William Blythe, John Wasson, James A Darwin, James Roddye, Matthew English, Brinkley Hornsby, Alexander Brown, John Taff, Samuel Looney, William Matlock, Abijah Bogges, Abner Witt. Benjamin Jones said writ was not executed.
    Grand jury: James A Darwin, Andrew McCaleb, Samuel Garwood, William Blythe, John Wasson, James Roddye, Abijah Bogges, Alexander Brown, John Chatten, Samuel Frazier, Jesse Martin, Akiah Parker, Alexander Brown[James Montgomery?].
    Court appointed James A Darwin foreman of the grand jury.
    Constable William B Cozbey sworn to attend on said grand jury.
p.416 There remained of original pannel who answered to their names William Matlock, Robert Locke, Bryant R McDonald, Brinkly Hornsby, Abner Witt, John Taff, Samuel Looney, Archibald D Paul.
    Remaining of original pannel who failed to answer to their names Thomas J Gillespie, John Day and Matthew English.
    Chunn Gillespie & Co v John Wasson. Appeal. Cause continued.
    Robert N Gillespie v William W Pile. Certiorari. Cause is continued.
    Tellitha Walker v James Walker. Plf by atty prayed rule to cause dft to give security for prosecution; granted. Thereupon the intermarriage of plaintiff to Richard Wollerd since the commencement of this suit is suggested; plf to give security for prosecution in their joint names.
    Court adjourned untill tomorrow morning.   Charles F Keith

p.417 Tuesday 24th March. Present on the bench the Honorable Charles F Keith.
    On application of Samuel Frazier solicitor of eleventh solicitorial district John Locke clerk of this Court produced a receipt from the Treasurer of East Tennessee showing John Locke's return from 1 Oct 1833 to 1 Oct 1834 certified, with $23.53 the full amount due for said year. Miller Francis, Treas. E.T.
    Robert F McCormack v Jonathan Free. On motion of dft, a rule is granted to shew cause why proceedings in this cause should be quashed.
    Levi H Knight v Randolph Gibson. Dft by atty is granted a rule to cause plf to give security. Plf by atty is granted a rule to cause dft to give security.
    Richard Waterhouse v Jacob L Wassum. Plf by atty allowed to amend warrant.
    James & William Parks v Alfred Hutchison. Cause is continued.
p.418 John Witts lessee v John & Mary J Galbreath. Ejectment. Jury Wm Matlock,

Robt Locke, Robt N Gillespie, John Day, Bryant R McDonald, John Taff, Saml Looney, Archd D Paul, Preston G Eads, Saml Martin, Brinkley Hornsby, Wm Long find dfts not guilty of trespass. Dfts recover against the lessor of plf their costs.

John B Campbell v John D Traynor. Plf by written direction dismissed this cause. Dft recovers against plf his costs in this behalf expended.

William N Morriss v Lewis Knight. Jury James A Darwin, Andw McCaleb, Samuel Garwood, Wm Blythe, John Wasson, Jas Roddye, Abijah Bogges, Alexander Brown, John Chatten, Samuel Frazier, Jesse Martin, Akiah Parker.

Court adjourned untill tomorrow morning. Charles F Keith

p.419 Wednesday 25th March. Present the honorable Charles F Keith, Judge.

John Witts lessee v John & Mary Jane Gilbreath. Ejectment. Lessor of plf by his attorney prays rule 1to shew why new trial should be had; granted.

David Hounshell v John McClenahan. Plf by atty prayed a rule to shew cause why petition for certiorari should be dismissed; granted.

Bedy Ferrell admx of Jas Ferrell deceased v Anson Dearmon. Pauper. Suit instituted under law to help poor persons in obtaining their rights; court apptd F[J?] N Vandyke attorney for plaintiff.

James J Long v Anson Dearmon. Pauper case. Cause is continued.

Spills B Dyre v Jacob L Wassum. Appeal. Matters of dispute submitted to determination of Arthur Fulton, Carson Caldwell, and Matthew Hubbert.

p.420 Johnson Minton v Abner Weatherly. Certiorari. Jury Drury Godsey, Robert Locke, Bryant R McDonald, John Taff, Saml Looney, Archd D Paul, John Day, George Ramsey, Wm Long, John Dunlap, Peulaski Poe, Brindkey Hornsby find for defendant.

Lewis Patterson v Richard Waterhouse & Thos C Wroe. Jury Drury Godsey, Robt Locke, Bryant R McDonald, Brinkly Hornsby, John Taff, Samuel Looney, Archd D Paul, John Day, Geo Ramsey, Wm Long, Eli Ferguson, Pulaski Poe find for plf $52.08 besides costs.

William N Morriss v Lewis Knight. [item is X'd out]

p.421 State v James Pickett. Gaiming. Nolle prosequi entered.

State v James Clements, John C Dyer et al. Riot. Samuel Craig summoned as a witness on behalf the State came not; forfeits his recognizance. Attorney general enters a nolle prosequi in this cause.

Joseph Thompson v John Miller. Rule heretofore granted to cause plf to give security for prosecution of this suit is discharged; plf is admitted to prosecute as a pauper. On motion of plf by atty, warrant is amended.

State v William McCartie. Grand jury returns bill of Indictment agt dft for grand Larceny endorsed by James A Darwin, foreman, a true bill.

p.422 Jacob Wassums heirs v Lewis & Rebecca Knight. From affidavit of Rebecca Knight, rule heretofore granted for dfts to give security is discharged, and dfts are admitted to defend as paupers. Jury John McKinley, John Wood, Jackson Howerton, James N Smith, Thos C Pile, Wm Howard, James Kelley, Jas P Collins, Wm Guin[Gain?], Herun Henry, Henry Greffit, Wm Humberd say the writing produced by the plaintiffs purporting to be the will was not the will of Jacob Wassum deceased. On motion of the plffs by their attornies the verdict is set aside on payment of all costs. Dfts recover against plaintiffs their costs at this term expended.

State v Thomas McNutt. Grand Jury returns presentment against dft endorsed by their foreman a true presentment.

Robert F McCormack v Jonathan Free. Rule heretofore entered to shew cause

MARCH 1835

why warrant should be quashed being argued, rule is discharged. On motion of plf by atty, leave is granted him to amend the warrant so that it may show what kind of property was trespassed upon.
p.423   Court adjourned until tomorrow morning.   Charles F Keith

Thursday 26th March. Present on the bench the honorable Charles F Keith, Judge.
    Abner Triplett v John Condley. Suit was instituted under law to speed poor persons in obtaining their rights, appoint Spencer Jarnigan attorney for plaintiff.
    Levi H Knight v Randolph Gibson. Brinkley Hornesby, Abijah Bogges, and John Wasson undertake for defendant.
    John Wills lessee v John & Mary J Gilbreath. Rule for new trial discharged.
    State v John Condley. Grand jury returned preentment agt dft for usury.
p.424   William A Morriss. Jury heretofore empannelled from rendering verdict respited, say they find dft guilty and assess plfs damage to $4000 besides costs. Came plaintiff in proper person & enters remitter $3750 of sd payment.
    State v William McKerler. Larceny. Dft in proper person says he is not guilty. Cause is continued. Recognizance of Wm McKerler; John A Hook, Jesse McKerler & George Burdet securities. Recognizance: Robt Locke, condition he appear Sept
p.425   next to prosecute and give evidence in behalf State against Wm McKerler for grand larceny. Hugh T Blevins, Thomas Wamack, Jas Blevins, Joshua W Hunter, John McKindley recognizance to give evidence in behalf State agt William McKerler.
    State v Thomas McNutt. Affray. Recognizance of James Montgomery, condition he appear Sept Term to give evidence on behalf State against Thomas McNutt.
    Grand & travers jurors are discharged from further attendance at this Term.
p.426   Waterhouses executors v James Swan. Subpoena returned not executed. Alias subpoena to issue returnable here at next term of this Court.
    State v John Yates. Gaiming. Costs: State tax $1. Clerk [details here omitted] $17.05; Sheriff Collins $3.16. Sheriff Paul $1; Sheriff Hackett $1; Sheriff [illegible] $5; Witness for state Timothy F French 7 days $3.50.
    State v John Yates. Affray. Bill of costs: State tax $1. Clerk[details here omitted] $18.48¼. Sheriff Collins $2.95; Sheriff Hackett $1.62½; Shff Preston $1;
p.427   Shff Cox $1; Attorney general $5. Witness for State Micaja Prewit .50.
    William C Hanly[?] v State. Larceny. Bill/costs. State tax $1. Justice .50. Constable Fry .50. Clerk [details here omitted] $7.26½. Shff Hackett .79; Shff Wm B Cozby .75; attorney general $1.25. Witness for State Bosbely Fowler $3.66. William Rains $1.25; James Singleton .75; Thomas Coulter $2.25; Abraham Miller to keeping and finding dft in jail from 22 June until 23 Sept $34.87½; two turn keys $1.
p.428   Waterhouses executors & Gideon Thompson v William Kelley et all. Equity. Alias subpoena ad respondes awarded complainants returnable here nat term.
    Waterhouses executors v Theoderick B Rice et al. Equity. Dft having made not defence, Court grants judgment accordingly.
    Abner Triplette v John Condly. By consent time is given to plead.
    David Hounshell v John McClenahan. Petition for certiorari dismissed.
    Cooper Canthus[Cawthen?] & Co v Abraham Cox et al. Abraham Cox Junr appointed guardian to minor heirs of John Howell.
p.429   Joseph Thompson v Moses Thompson. Cause continued.
    Benjamin Maxfield v John Howell. Notice issues to plaintiff directed to Sheriff of McMinn County to appear next term of this court and prosecute his suit.
    Bedy Ferrell exr v Anson Dearmon. Time given to plead, not to delay trial.

SEPTEMBER 1835

John Thompson v John McAllen & Francis Bon. Time is given plaintiff until next term to file his declaration.
Court adjourned untill Court in Course.   Charles F Keith

p.430   Monday Sept 28th. At a Circuit Court held for Rhea County on fourth Monday of September, on the bench the Honorable Charles F Keith a judge assigned to hold circuit courts within the seventh judicial Circuit.
   Sheriff Samuel R Hackett returned the venire facias: Robert Cravens, James Roddye, Jesse Thompson, Andw McCaleb, Thos J Gillespie, Elisha Sharp, Isaac Baker, John Smith, Joseph Kee junr, Stephen Winton, John McCallon, David Hounshell, Abraham Cox Junr, Thomas Lucas, Robert Elder Sr, Jackson Howerton, James Purser, Jacob Prillamon, William S Russell, John Cozbey, John Day, Levi Ferguson, Abraham Miller, John Roddye, Samuel Gamble.
   The following persons answered to their names: John Cozbey, Jesse Thompson, Thomas J Gillespie, Stephen Winton, Robert Cravins, Andrew McCaleb, Thomas Lucas, Jacob Prilliman, John Rodye, Elisha Sharp, John Smith, Jackson Howerton, James Purser, Samuel Gamble, William P Russell, Joseph Kee junr, James Roddye, Abraham Cox junr, Robert Elder Senr, John McCallon, Levi Ferguson.
   Grand jurors: John Cozbey, Jesse Thompson, Thomas J Gillespie, Stephen Winton, Robert Cravins, Andrew McCaleb, Thomas Lucas, Jacob Prilliman, John Roddye, Elisha Sharp, John Smith, Jackson Howerton, James Purser.
   Court appoint John Cozbey foreman of the grand jury.
   Constable Johnathan Frie sworn to attend on said grand jury.
p.431   From affidavits of Abraham Cox jr, James Roddye, Robert Elder Sr, and John McCallen they are excused from further attendance as jurors at this term.
   There remained of original pannel who answered to their names Samuel Gambel, Levi Ferguson, William S Russell, Joseph Kee Junior.
   Remaining of original pannel who failed to answer to their names Isaac Baker, Jon Day, Abraham Miller.
   Chunn Gillespie & Co v John Wasson. Appeal. Cause is continued.
   Robert W Gillespie v William W Pile. Certiorari. Cause is continued.
   John Thompson v John McCallon and Francis Bon[Box?] admrs Michael Box[Bon?] decd. By mutual consent, time is given plaintiff to file his declaration.
   James & William Park & Co v Alpherd Hutchison. Cause is continued. Dft to take deposition of John Murphree of Hamilton County.
p.432   Matthew Timon v Anderson Vernon. Appeal. Record before the justice failing to shew that appeal had been prayed or granted from the judgment rendered therein, cause stricken from roles of this Court and papers remanded to the justice.
   Charles McClung v William Smith. Debt. Spencer Jarnigan suggested that since last continuance of this cause plf departed this life. By mutual consent cause is revived in names of Matthias McClung and Hugh L McClung exrs of plf.
   Spills B Dyre v Jacob L Wassum. Appeal. Rule of refference made last term is revived and Levi W Ferguson is chosen by the parties as additional refferee.
   William N Morriss v Lewis Knight. Thomas McCallie appearance bail for dft surrenders him; defendant ordered into custody of sheriff.

SEPTEMBER 1835

p.433   President, directors and company of the Union Bank of Tennessee v Richard Waterhouse, Thomas McCallie Robert N Gillespie and Allen Kennedy. Debt. Jury Saml Gamble, Levi H Knight, Levi Ferguson, Wm S Russell, Joseph Kee, Cain Able, Thornton J Creed, Isaac Blevins, Willliam W Pile, Samuel Craig, William Ferguson, William Kelley find for plaintiff his debt $400, and find the judgment of the County Court for $418.46½ to be correct. Plaintiffs recover of dfts sd sum, also $20.94¼ being interest at 12½% to this time, also their costs of suit.
        Resignation of John Locke former Clerk of Court was presented and excepted. Court then adjourned untill tomorrow morning.   Charles F Keith

Tuesday, 29th Sept. Present on the bench the Honorable Charles F Keith, judge.
        Court proceeded to fill the vacandy occasioned by resignation of John Locke
p.434   and appoint Franklin Locke Clerk/Court who took the oaths. Signed: Charles F Keith. John Locke, Franklin Locke, Wright Smith, Orville Paine.
p.435   Oaths of Clerk of Court [same signatories]
p.436   John Daniel v Nancy Hyse. Order writs of certiorari and supersedeas awarded dft returnable here at next term, petitioner Hyse giving bond.
        Cain Able v Timothy F French. Certioran. Petition granted plf.
        Matthew Timons v Anderson Vernon. Petition for certiorari granted dft.
        Edmund M Waggoner v Timothy F French. Case. Cause is continued.
        Beedy Ferrell admx v Anson Dearmon. Cause is continued.
        Thomas N Frazier a licensed attorney was sworn & admitted to practice in this Court.
p.437   Richard Waterhouse v Jacob L Wassum. Appeal. Jury Saml Gamble, Levi Ferguson, William P Russell, Joseph Kee Jr, Isaack Baker, Jas Kelley, James C C Kelley, Abraham Cox, Thos C Pile, Wm W Pile, Palaskey Poe, Abijah Bogges. Dft recovers agst plaintiff his costs by him about his defence expended.
        Joseph Thompson v John Miller. Appeal. Jury John Cozbey, Thos J Gillespie, Steephen Winton, Robt Cravins, Andrew McCaleb, Thomas Lucas, Jacob Prilliman, John Roddy, Elisha Sharp, John Smith, Jackson Howerton, James Purser. Plaintiff recovers of dft $27 and also his costs about his suit expended.
        Robert J McCormack v Johnathan Fry. Appeal. James Eakin undertakes for plf.
p.438   Richard Wallerd & Telitha Wallerd v Jams Walker. Appeal. Plfs in proper person dismiss suit. Dft recovers of plf his costs of defence.
        Jacob Wassums heirs v Lewis & Rebbecca Knight. Caveat. From affidavit of Andrew Wassum one of the plfs, Henry Owens one of the securities for prosecution of this suit is released. Whereupon Henry Collins undertakes for plaintiffs. Jury Saml Gamble, Levi Ferguson, Abijah Bogges, William Russell, Joseph Kee Jr, Isaac Baker, James C Kelley, Abraham Cox Sr, William R Pile, Pulaskey Poe, John Walker, William Ferguson find instrument of writing produced to be the last will and testament of Jacob Wassum deceased.
        Court adjourned untill tomorrow morning.   Charles F Keith

p.439   Wednesday 30th September. Present the Honorable Charles F Keith, judge.
        State v Samuel Craig. Scire facias. Dft in proper person confessed judgment; State recovers of defendant costs in suing and prosecuting this writ.
        Abner Triplet v John Condley. Trespass on the case. Suit under the law to help poor persons obtain their just rights. Dft recovers agt plaintiff his costs.

SEPTEMBER 1835

Levi H Knight v Randolph Gibson. Appeal. Defendant recovers against plf his costs of defence.

p.440 State v William McCartie. Grand Larceny. Dft in proper person says he is not guilty. Jury Levi H Knight, Joseph Perry, Wm W Pile, Henry Collins, William R Sullivan, Samuel Gamble, Levi Ferguson, Jacob S Wassum, James Swan, Isaac Baker, John Walker, Joseph Kelough say defendant is not guilty.

State v Thomas McNutt. Affray. Dft in proper person. Cause is continued. Recognizance of Thomas McNutt, condition he appear March term to answer charge of the State against him. Recognizance of William B Cozby, condition he appear March
p.441 term to answer chage of State for an affray. Recognizance of James Montgomery, condition he appear March term to testify in behalf State against Thos McNutt.

State v John Condley. Usury. Dft in proper person. Cause is continued. Recognizance of John Condley; Anson Dearmon his security.

John H Beck v William Smith. Case. Cause is continued.

p.442 Benjamin Maxfield v John Howell. Cause is continued.

Thomas Gibbs v Benjamin F Locke. Appeal. Jury Levi H Knight, Joseph Perry, Wm W Pile, Henry Colllins, Samuel Gamble, Levi W Ferguson, Jacob Prilliman, James Swan, Isaac Baker, John Walker, John Smith, Isaac W Ginn find for plaintiff $49.50 besides costs by him about his suit expended.

James Cain v George Gillespie. Appeal. Plf came not. Dft recovers of plf his costs in this behalf expended.

William McSpadon v Cedron Pile, Thomas C Pile, John Roddy. Appeal in two cases. Two causes are continued untill next term.

p.443 Jacob Wassums heirs v Lewis Knight & Rebecca Knight. Caveat. Jury having heretofore found the paper produced to be the will of Jacob Wassum, therefore considered by the Court that the Clerk transmit sd paper together with a copy of the finding of the jury and also this judgment to Clerk of the County Court to be recorded. Lewis Knight pays the costs of this cause.

Levi H Knight v Randolph Gibson. Appeal. Cause is reinstated on giving security to prosecute and payment of the costs of this term. William Humbert undertakes for plaintiff. Dft recovers of plf his costs of defence at this term, and cause is continued until next term of this court.

State v Edward P Burnett & Ely P Haden. William Grose who was bound in recognizance to appear this day to prosecute came not. State recovers against sd William Grose $50 unless sufficient cause of his disability to attend be shewn at
p.444 next term; sci facias issues. Nolle prosequi entered by attorney general.

Robert T McCormack v Jonathan Fry. Appeal. Vaden H Giles to bring to next term the warrant, judgment & execution issued by him in case of John Roddy against Robert T McCormack. Defendant to take deposition of William Wood of McMinn County.

Abraham Cox v John Roddy. Appeal. Cause is continued.
Abraham Cox v JOhn Roddy. Appeal. Cause is continued.
Abraham Cox v John Roddy. Appeal. Cause is continued.
Abraham Cox v John Roddy. Appeal. Cause is continued.
p.445 Abraham Cox v John Roddy. Appeal. Cause is continued.

James J Long v Anson Dearmon. Pauper case. Cause is continued.

John Smith & John Brown v John Locke & Thomas J Campbell executors of Robert Bell deceased. Defendants by attorney Spencer Jarnigan filed pleas.

Ross & Slover v Neville & Dyre. Appeal. Defendants by their attorney Spencer Jarnigan filed their plea.

Richard Waterhouse & Blackstone Waterhouse executors of Richard G Water-

SEPTEMBER 1835

house v Nancy Ann Kelley admx of Thomas Kelley deceased. Appeal. Jury Thos C Pile, Cedron Pile, Jacob Riggle, Anson Dearmon, Lewis Knight, Jacob C Thompson, John Steuart, Daniel Walker, Andrew Wassum, Anderson Walker, Wm B Cozbey say dfts have
p.446   not paid. Plaintiffs recover of dfts $546.00½ the judgment of the County Court, also $21.34 interest at rate of 12½% from 7 May 1835 to this time, also costs of this cause.

Richard Waterhouse & Blackstone Waterhouse exrs of Richard G Waterhouse deceased for use of Gideon B Thompson v David Caldwell. Debt. Continued.

Grand jurors return bill of indictment against Spills B Dyre for assault & Battery endorsed by John Cozby their foreman Not a true bill.

Jurors afsd from further attendance at this term are discharged.

Court adjourned untill tomorrow morning.   Charles F Keith

p.447   Thursday 1st Octr. Present on the bench the Honorable Charles F Keith.

Abraham Cox v John W Smith. Appeal. Plf by atty dismissed suit. Dft in proper person confessed judgment for all costs.

George C Graves & William Burd v Richard Waterhouse. Debt. Jury John Stuart, Thos C Pile, John Roddy, Levi H Knight, Jacob P Wassum, John Walker, Saml Gamble, Lewis Knight, Levi Ferguson, Wm S Russell, Joseph Kee, Isaac Baker say dft has paid the debt except $282; assess plfs damage to $23.23 besides costs.

Abraham Cox v John Roddy et al. Time is given to plead.
p.448   Thomas Gibbs v Benjamin Locke. Plf by atty moved for judgment against the defendants security for his appeal. Plf recovers against John Locke the security named in the bond jointly with the defendant $49.50 and all costs.

Waterhouses executors v Carson Caldwell et al. Cause is continued.

Matthew D Cooper, Maddison Caruthers & William McNail vs Eliza Cox, Rachel Cox and the other heirs of Thomas Cox and others. Equity. James Gragg, one of the defendants, is not an inhabitant of this state but a citizen of Alabama, order publication be made in newspaper published in Athens commanding sd James Gragg to appear and answer complainants bill or same will be taken pro confesso.

John Smith & John Brown v John Locke & Thos J Campbell exrs of Robert Bell decd. Time to reply is granted as on affd of plaintiff so as not to delay trial.
p.449   George Gordon v Matthew English et al. Plf by atty dismissed suit. Defendants recover against plaintiff their costs in this behalf expended.

Silas Condley v Alexander Rice. Plf failing to appear, plf is nonprossed; defendant recovers against plaintiff his costs about his defence expended.

Cain Able v Timothy F French. Dfts petition dismissed; plf recovers against defendant his costs about his suit expended.

Calvin Morgan & Sons v John Roddy. Came Calvin Morgan, Franklin Morgan and Rufus Morgan merchants by their attorney A D Rigs[?] with a Promissory note. John Roddy in proper person cannot gainsay demand of Calvin Morgan & Sons and confessed
p.450   judgment. Plf recovers debt and costs.

Priscilla Mapes, Polly Ann Mapes, Joseph C Mapes, James M Mapes, Jeremiah N Mapes, and Sally E Mapes v Sarah Mapes, Miles Vernon and John Parker. Equity. Com-
p.451   plainants have failed to make out their case, order that complainants bill be dismissed, that Pricilla Mapes pay the costs of this cause. Further order that James Lillard receiver apptd in this cause forthwith deliver to Miles Vernon or his agent the premises named in complainants bill and account to him for the rents and profits he may have received since his appointment as receiver.

SEPTEMBER 1835

Joseph Thompson v Moses Thompson and another. Order that an account be taken before the Clerk and Master, between the complainant and respondents, charging the respondant Moses Thompson with the value of the waggons mentioned in complainants bill together with the value of the use and occupation of sd waggon
p.452 and oxen. Charge for use is to be made only up to the time of their death; clerk & master is further directed to credit respondent in said account with the amount of the money paid by respondent to Richard Waterhouse on account of complainant with interest up to time of this decree. Clerk has power to summon witnesses and hear testimony in taking said account.

John H Becks assignee v William Smith. Plfs demurrer argued and overruled.

Richd G Waterhouses exrs v Carson Caldwell and others. Plfs demurrer to 2d and 3d pleas of dft is sustained.

p.453 William McSpadden v Cedron Pile & others. Plf by atty dismissed his suit. Dfts recover of plf their costs in this behalf expended.

William McSpadden v Cedron Pile and others. Plf by atty dismissed his suit. Dfts recover of plf their costs in this behalf expended.

Dunhams admrs v Bells exrs. Allow time for plaintiffs to reply to defendants plea as on affidavit of plaintifff so as not to delay trial.

All jurors not before discharged are now discharged from further attendance at this term.

Cooper, Caruthers & Co v heirs of Thomas Cox and others. Sheriff returned
p.454 subpoena executed on Abraham Cox Junr as guardian of Eliza Cox, Rachel Cox, Elizabeth Jane Cox, and John Cox and the sd guardian failing to appear and answer complainants bill, order bill be taken pro confesso against sd Eliza Cox, Rachel Cox, Elizabeth Jane Cox, John Cox, minor children and heirs of Thomas Cox decd.

Court adjourned untill Court in Course.   Charles F Keith

Monday 28th March 1836. At time prescribed by law for holding the Circuit Courts for Rhea County and Third judicial Circuit, the Honorable judge of Third judicial Circuit failing to appear and open sd Court, ordered by Clerk that the Sheriff in persuance of the Statutes adjourn sd Court over untill tomorrow morning.

Tuesday 29th March. On this day the Honorable judge of the third judicial Circuit failing to appear, order Court be adjourned untill tomorrow morning.

Wednesday, 31st March. The judge of the Third judicial Circuit failing to appear to open & hold a Circuit Court for Rhea County, the Clerk of Court in persuance of the
p.455 Statutes proceeded to take the following recognizances, forfeitures, &c.

State v John H Burnett. Robery. Recognizance of dft, John Neil security.

State v John B Campbell. Recognizance of dft, Richard Waterhouse his security, on charge of assault & battery with intent to commit murder. Recognizances of James H Steuart, John Glen & Wm Rhea, condition they appear July next to prosecute and give evidence in behalf of the State agt John B Campbell.
p.456 State v John B Campbell. Disturbing Public worship. Recognizance of John

150

MARCH 1836

B Campbell, Richard Waterhouse his security, condition dft appear July next at Court. Recognizance of Jacob Brown, to prosecute and give evidence in behalf State against John B Campbell for disturbing public worship.

State v John B Campbell. Recognizance of John B Campbell, Richd Waterhouse his security, condition dft appear July next to answer a charge against him for keeping a tipling house. Recognizance of Blount Morriss, to testify & give evidence on behalf of the State against John B Campbell for keeping a tipling house.

State v John Condley. Recognizance of Anson Dearmon, condition John Condley appear before Circuit Court July next.

p.457 State v Margarett Ellerson. Recognizance of Margarett Ellerson, Jacob L Wassum and Darius Waterhouse her securities, condition dft appear July next to answer charge of the State for assault & battery. Recognizance of Austin Evans, Arthur L Fulton & Jacob L Wassum his securities, condition Austin Evans appear July to prosecute and give evidence in behalf State against Margarett Ellerson.

State v Austin Evans. Recognizance of Austin Evans, Arthur L Fulton and Jacob Wassum his securities, condition Austin Evans appear July next to answer charge of State against him for assault & battery. Recognizance of Margarett Ellerson and Jacob L Wassum & Darius Waterhouse her securities, condition she appear July next to prosecute and give evidence in behalf State against Austin Evans for assault & battery.

State v George Lowder. Recognizance of George Lowder, Nathan Lowder and Henry Hackler his securities, to appear July next to answer charge of State against him for assault & battery with intent to commit murder.

State v Thomas McNutt. Recognizance of James Montgomery, condition he appear July next to testify & give evidence in behalf State against Thomas McNutt for an affray.

INDEX

ABEL, Cain 2 5 8 9 12 14-16 19 27 47 79 Philip 15
ABLE, Cain 45 47 48 64 65 67 79 80 95 96 147 149 David 104 120 John 54 58 60 122 125 129 133-135
ACKMAN, Thomas 1
ADAMS, Joseph 28 Robert 1 10
ADKINS, Wade 119
AGEY, James 81
ALABAMA 14 15 17 18 19 21 26 28 31 32 33 40 44 45 46 48 54 57 104 149
ALEXANDER, John 47 72 Thomas 128 137 141 William 17 22 39 43 49 50 52 55 56 79
ALLEN, Benjamin 16 George 60 63 66 74 Isaac 44 James 20 John 28 29 31 32 42 60 63 66 74 Mathew 49 51 53
ALLISON, Benjamin 15 16 17 19 21 22 35
AMERINE, Henry 58 59 65
AMMERINE, Henry 65
ANDERSON, Isaac 81 Constable 91 J 32 33 Joseph 25 26 27 28 35 42 44 47 48 50 51 52 54 57 73 87 89 96 Thomas 7 9 49 75 76 77 William 17 23 24 46 48 57 60 93 109 -- 95
ANDERSON COUNTY 22 24 42 46
ANTHONY, John 18
APPLEGATE, Samuel 37 38 40 41 43
ARCHEY, Isaac 59
AREHEART, George 126
ARKANSAS TERRITORY 106
ARMS, Elly 50
ARMSTRONG, Barefoot 52 89 Benjamin 83 Clinton 111 Daniel 25 26 41 52 53 56 57 59 62 63 65 66 79 81 90 91 93 95 99 108 113 114 119 130 Elihu 25 39 40 49 52 John 73 Martha 92 Robert 56
ARNETT, William 77
ARNOLD, Daniel 75 78 79 81 91 George 41 William 27
ARRINGTON, Able 58 60
ASHLIN, Robert 114 115
ATCHLEY, James 136 Joshua 20 Martin 43 Thomas 61 62
ATCHLY, Martin 39
ATCKLEY, Joshua 7
ATCKLY, Joshua 8
ATKINS, Wade 131
ATTWOOD, Jesse 100
ATWOOD, Jesse 81 96

AYRHEART, Harry 7
AYRHEART, Henry 4 6
BAILEY, James 1 3 20 21 22 34 John 55
BAILY, James 3 109 John 56
BAKER, George 18 Isaac/Isaack 34 50 65 101 110 128 129 139 140 141 146 147 148 149 J 55 John 34 58 60 109 110 113 117 118 119 123 129 130 Samuel 34
BALCH, Alfred 57
BALDEN, Hugh 118
BALDWIN, William 9 22 61 62
BALLARD, John 109 William 140
BANDY, Dempsey 116
BARCKLAY, Elihu 108
BARCLAY, Elihu 114 William 10 11 12 13
BARNES, Catharine 120-124 John 56 57 Silas 120-124 Solomon 56 57
BARNETT, James 110 John 36 37 39 40 42 43 81 86 90 110 119
BARNS, Catherine 93 James 36 42 47 John 47 48 61 Silas 95 Solomon 61
BARR, John 62
BARROW, Martin 42
BARSON, Robert 41
BARTON, Azariah 135 James 106
BASHEAR, Jacob 100
BATES, Ezekiel 75 76 84 86
BATEY, Hugh 48
BAUGGES, A 118 131 Constable 131
BAUGUS, Abijah 82 85 86 89 90 99 116 117 126 Giles 85
BAULDEN, Hugh 122
BAULDON, Hugh 122
BAULTON, Robert 96
BAYLES, William 47 51 53 56
BAYSON, Jacob 2
BEAN, Edmond/Edmun/Edmund 15 16 18 21 39 40 53 78 87 88 90 95 96 114 115 119 125 Hazard/Hazzard 105 116 Leonidas 87 Louisa 87 -- 76 78
BEANE, Edmund/Edmd 28 123
BEARD, Robert 34 37 38 40 41 43 -- 77
BEATY, Hugh 40 109
BEAVERS, Sheriff 91
BECK, Jacob 37 38 40 41 43 92 94 95 137 James 79 81 John 129 148 150
BECKHOLD, Alfred 100
BEDFORD COUNTY 18
BEDWELL, Armstead 98 Elias 98 John 98 Leroy 98 Squire 98

INDEX

BEEN, Edmund 17
BEERMAN, William 14
BELCHER, John 2 5
BELL, Elizabeth 25 John 93 Robert 1-3 5 7-9 11 15 21 22 25 33 36 45 47 48 52 53 55-57 66-68 95 100 104 105 107 115 121 122 148 149 -- 150
BELT, Horatio 107 113 120 123
BENNET, Vincent 1 4 6 11
BENNETT, Peter 3 9
BENSON, Bartlett 114 126 Bartely/Bartley 105 106 108 118 123 124 131 Isaac 55 95 Matthias 15 39 45 47 Robert 41 105 106 108 114 118 123
BENTON, Nancy 28 47 50
BERRY, Hugh 3 8 9 21 James 21 41 46 51 54 59 71 76 82 92 94 99 105 107 108 -- 75 86 89 90 92
BESHEAR, Jeremiah 60 62 65 Samuel 60 -- 99
BEVELY, Salley 93
BICE, William 129
BILLINGSLEY, John 106
BIRCH, F 142
BIRDSONG, John 15 23
BLACK, John 19
BLACKLEY, James 4 6 7
BLACKWELL, Colonel 75 78 79 81 91 Joab 31 32 Joel 80 Nathan 115
BLACKWOOD, William 34 35 41
BLAKELEY, Thomas 17 18 19 22
BLANKENSHIP, Thomas 100
BLANTON, Vinson 117
BLEDSOE, Lewis 3
BLEDSOE COUNTY 13 15 18 28 31 32 34 41 42 43 45 54 56 66 68 109
BLEVINS, Hugh 123 145 Isaac 119 133 134 147 James 137 139 140 145 Moses 136
BLITHE, William 62 64 65
BLOUNT COUNTY 5 28 40 45
BLUNT COUNTY 42
BLYTHE, Elijah 92 Stephen 3 William 66 143 144
BODDY, John 42
BODELY, John 42
BODLEY, John 28 29 31
BODLY, Charles 32
BOGGES, Abijah 120 133 134 143-145 147
BOGGS, Abijah 67
BOLEJACK, Mathew 53 54 55

BOLEN, Jeremiah 98 101
BOLIN, Jeremiah 97 98 John 103 104 105
BOLINGER, Andrew 67 85
BOLTON, Lewis 141 Robert 105 108 Thomas 9 23
BON, Francis 146 Michael 146
BOND, Benjamin 34 35 39 41 44 58 60 62 63 65 68
BONDRIN, Claibourn 131
BONDRON, Richard 131
BOOKER, William 2 5
BORIN, Levi 140
BOUGERS, Abijah 83
BOULTON, Lewis 138 141 Robert 105 114 118 123 125 126 131 141
BOWDEN, Asa 105
BOWMAN, Esaias 2
BOX, Francis 146 Michael 146
BRABSON, Robert 51 53 56 57 59 60 61 65 72 73 76 77 80 85 86 Thomas 56 77 80
BRABSTON, Robert 57
BRADFORD, Hamilton 18 James 97 119 130 Richard 91 100 101 106 110
BRADLEY, Orlando 60 64 66 88 90 93 98 104 William 6 21
BRADLY, Orlando 56
BRADY, Charles 10 12 34 35 36 37 40 42 43 Farley 137 William 11
BRAKEBILL, Henry 68
BRAMLY, Austin 29
BRAN, Edmon 113
BRANDON, Beveridge 118 Carter 95 Lewis 95 Parmer 118 119 121 122 131 Philip 95 Thomas 118 119 121
BRANOM, Thomas 131
BRASLETON, Isaac 57
BRAZEAL, John 112
BRAZEALE, William 44
BRAZELTON, Isaac 25 27 30 32 39 Shepherd 27 32 45 52
BRAZLETON, Isaac 41 43 73
BREAKBILL, Henry 68
BREAZEALE, William 44 Willis 2 8
BREEDEN, Byram/Byrun 8 11 14 16 44
BREEDING, Baty 137 Bryant/Byrum 37 41
BRENNLY, Austin 28
BRIDWELL, Augustin 98
BRIGGS, Daniel 109
BRIGHTWELL, Leonard 95
BRITWELL, Leonard 62

153

INDEX

BROOKS, Leonard 71 72 Ludwin 15 Mary 1 7 11 Providence 14
BROWN, Alexander 143 144 David 109 Edward 135 George 52-55 63 67 Isaiah 92 Jacob 8 14 40 63 65 81 90 95 96 100 119 120 151 Joel 85 95 John 5 6 148 149 Sheriff 110 120 Thomas 1 2 5-8 40 45 William 94 99 104 120 135 -- 83 106
BROWNLOW, William 105 107 109 111 112
BROWNLY, Austin 29 Catharine 29
BROYLES, Adam 122 Matthias 107 126 127 134
BROYLS, Adam 105 122
BRUDEN, Byrum 8
BRUMBY, Austin 28 29 Catharine 29
BRUMLEY, Austin 31 William 102
BRUMLY, Austin 29 Catharine 28
BRYSON, Jacob 3 5 8 9 15 16
BRYAN, John 44 Rachel 44
BRYANT, William 139
BRYSON, Abraham 9
BUCK, Margaret 110 126
BUICE, William 75 76
BULLION, William 134
BULLOCK, Leonard 24
BULLARD, Henry 129 John 109
BULLOCK, Patsy 24
BURD, William 149
BURDET, George 145
BURK, Jacob 28 John 66
BURK COUNTY, NC, 6
BURNETT, Edward 148 John 134 150
BURNS, Alexander 3 6 7
BURTON, James 100 101 109 110 John 27
BUSH, David 7
BUSTARD, Michall 36
BUSTER, David 109 Michael 85 88 90 93 98 99 124 125 William 51 56 57
BUTRAM, Hail/Hoil 107 109 113 117 Jacob 109 113 117 Larkin 103 104 105 109 113 117
BUTTRAM, Cornelious 126 128 134 136 139 Noah 131 133 134
BUYSE, William 75
CAHABA COUNTY, AL, 32 33 61
CAHAUBA COUNTY, AL, 25
CAHILL, Elisha 83 James 83 94
CAIN, James 148
CALDWELL, Adam 9 12 15 39 41 52 88 111 112 113 128 Alexander 95 C 86 Carson 14 27 32 33 49 50 61 62 73 78 84 85 86 103 107 133 134 137 139 140 141 144 149 150 David 12 13 32 38 40 41 49 50 71 72 88 90 149 Robert 103 -- 7
CALISON, James 37
CALLETT, Reuben 48
CALLISON, James 1 3 6 7 35
CAMBLE, Thomas 54
CAMPBELL, Andrew 3 8 David 49 63 67 68 72 Elizabeth 15 James 2 6 23 John 17 98 113 119 123 133 134 144 150 151 Mrs 2 8 T 42 Thomas 17 27 39 41 42 44-48 50 53 56 60 62 63 72 76-80 86 94 100 104-106 112 114 115 132 135 140 148 149 Victor 89 William 56 81 -- 114
CAMPBELL COUNTY 18
CANBY, Isaac 109
CANNON, Benjamin 125 Jacob 56 James 3 4 7 10 11 Thomas 22
CANON, David 20 22
CANTHUS, -- 145
CARDWELL, William 28
CARNAHAN, Al;exander 27
CARP, Josiah 43
CARR, John 55 56 William 121 -- 106
CARRELL, James 68
CARROL, James 101
CARROL COUNTY, GA 82 85 86 90
CARROLL, Hugh 122 126 130 William 39
CARTER, James 125 John 133 Landon 2 8 18 19 20 22 29 47 49 Thomas 121 126 William 66 78 86 96 111 113 115 124 125 126 -- 2 3 4 6 8 11 12 14 16 21 26 41 47 48 49 58 68
CARUTHERS, Maddison 149 -- 150
CARY, Thomas 89 90
CASE, Mary 122 128 129
CASEY, Thomas 93
CASTEAL, Andrew 131
CASTEEL, Andrew 73 82 99 100 134 135 Joseph 73
CATCHING, Seymour 1 6
CATCHINGS, Seymour 7 8
CATES, Daniel 137
CATSWORTH, David 43
CAWOOD, John 9
CAWTHEN, -- 145
CAYWOOD, John 8
CEMBRILL, Benjamin 98
CENTER, William 122

INDEX

CEVIRET, Johnson 129
CHALTEN, John 93
CHAPMAN, Delmore 81 Jeremiah 79 128 Willis 115 Wyllys 61 86 87
CHARLES, Thomas 45
CHATTEN, Catharine 112 John 92 93 94 95 112 134 137 138 143
CHATTON, John 95
CHELTON, Chrispian 90 Peletiah 68 95 96
CHEN, Samuel 99
CHEROKEE COUNTY 10
CHEROKEE NATION 19 98 111
CHICKASAW NATION 16 20
CHILDERS, Samuel 122
CHILDRESS, Samuel 141
CHILDS, Roland 19 20 Rowland 9 11 12 17 -- 14
CHILTEN, John 96
CHILTON, Asahel 119 129 Chrispian 22 Palatiah/Peletiah 37 38 40 43 88 96 103 116 -- 100
CHINE, W 91
CHRISTIAN, George 13
CHUN, Samuel 98 -- 140
CHUNN, -- 137 138 143 146
CHURCHWELL, G 86 94 George 61 92 100 106 118 122 -- 119
CLACK, John 68 90 93 98 104 Micajah 92 93 95 96 Rolla 89
CLAIBORNE COUNTY 109
CLARK, H 29 Susan 16 Thomas 1-4 8 9 12 14 16 18-20 22 23 26 28 29 33 39 41 44 46 50-53 55 56 59 62 -- 2 3 4 6 8 11 12 14 16 21 26 33
CLARKE, Thomas 46 49
CLAYTON, Daniel 19 26 27
CLEMENT, Isaac 62 James 140 142
CLEMENTS, Hezekiah 81 James 142 144
CLERK, Thomas 47 50 58 -- 8 11 58
CLIFT, Richmond 112
CLOWER, Daniel 118
CLOWERS, William 117
CLYTON, Daniel 31
COATS, Christopher 31 34 38 Lucretia 133 William 133
COBB, James 61 88 130 132
COBBS, James 61
COCKE, George 66 William 44 49
COCKE COUNTY 25 44 54
COFFEE, Asbury 88 Pleasant 30

COLE, Adam 58 60 124 125 N 87 Nathan 81 83 86 89 91
COLLIER, Robert 54
COLLINS, Constable 126 Henry 1 3 4 7 17 18 19 22 23 26 32 52 55 56 64 65 68 72 78 89 111 112 115 116 120 121 124 127 128 133 136 138 147 148 James 14 17 19 21 23 24 27 144 John 14 46 Jonathan 88 89 90 94 98 Lewis 37 38 40 41 43 64 132 138 139 142 Sheriff 126 127 131 132 135 136 145 Williams 89 91 98 104 105 117 119 134
COLTER, Alexander 28
COLUMBIA COUNTY, GA 2 5
COMES, Pleasant 123 125 126 128
COMPTON, Henderson 135 138 143 William 135 Zackariah 133
CONDLEY, Anne 40 Isaac 110 114 121 123 John 16 40 98 99 144 145 147 148 151 Silas 149
CONDLY, John 12 106 145
CONGACRE, Benjamin 65
CONLEY, Ann 37 38 41 43 Isaac 109 John 37 38 41 43
CONOLLY, John 13
COOLEY, Robert 84 103 104 105 116 125 126 128 132 134 135 139
COOLY, Robert 109 119
COOPER, Kennedy 97 Matthew 149 -- 145 150
COPELAND, Jonathan 106
CORBY, John 1
CORLEY, John 1
CORLY, John 14
COTACO COUNTY, AL 25
COTTEN, John 2
COULTER, Alexander 61 62 63 66 72 76 80 83 85 88 89 90 107 109 James 14 15 20 22 39 41 43 54 57 58 60 64 66 67 68 75 76 77 85 92-95 98 109 Thomas 19 145
COURSON, Joseph 68
COWAN, Andrew 42 James 30 40 79 80 82 93 103 104
COWEN, James 103
COX, A 134 Abraham 84 100 137 139 145-150 Abram 107 Edward 1 6 Eliza/Elizabeth 149 150 John 150 Rachel 149 150 S 100 Sheriff 127 145 Thomas 26 29 54 68 81 84 86 93 95 100 149 150 -- 95
COZBEY, Constable 135 John 124 125 128

INDEX

129 131 133 134 139 140 141 146 147 William 135 137 143 149
COZBY, James 13 14 23 26 30 43 46 John 13 17 18 20 26 33 39 41 43 49 55 56 61 62 63 67 68 71 75 76 84 85 86 92 96 107 114 116 149 Robert 7 8 20 61 William 122 145 148
CRABTNER, John 106
CRAFT, Jesse 90
CRAIG, Constable 106 126 127 James 40 45 Samuel 35 79 92 93 112 144 147
CRANMORE, Mary 125
CRAVEN, Robert 112
CRAVENS, Robert 146
CRAVINS, Robert 137 146 147
CRAWFORD, John 89 95 142 Jonathan 28 31 35 36 41 43 44 47 50 54 71 Matthias 28 44 47 William 113-115 117 120 -- 120
CREED, Thornton 79 81 147
CREEL, Elijah 27 81 -- 33 44 51 53 56 59 62
CRESIN, David 26
CRESMAN, Isaac 131
CRESUP, Fletcher 14 James 14 John 14
CRISMAN, Charley 136 Isaac 97
CROOM, David 22
CROSS, Zachariah/Zackariah 140 141
CRUM, David 1 7 14 16 18 19 24 27 30 31 33 50 53 56 58 -- 7
CRUN, David 46
CRUTCHER, Thomas 57
CRUTCHFIELD, William 83
CUMBERLAND COUNTY, KY 40
CUMPTON, Henderson 130 132
CUNNINGHAM, James 8 32 33 Jonathan 27 31
CYPHERS, George 78
DAIL, Isaac 112 122
DALLAS COUNTY, AL 25 28 32 33 40 45 54
DALLIS COUNTY, AL 44
DANFORTH, Joseph 36 Josiah 6 14 40 41 47 48 50 53 56 58 62 65 72 78 80
DANIEL, JOhn 147 Peter 34 38 40 43 61 98 103
DANIELS, Peter 37 62
DANNIEL, Peter 61 62
DANTFORTH, Josiah 27
DARWIN, James 67 68 72 84 85 88 89 90 107 108 111 115 116 117 131 133 137 141 143 144 Sheriff 127

DAVID, A 33 Azariah 1-5 8-12 14 16 18 20 22-24 26 28 29 33 39 41 43-47 49-53 71-73 80 84 86 107 108 121 122 139 140 Owen 15 16 17 19 21 22 53 54 138 141 -- 11 16
DAVIDSON, J 91 Jesse 4 6 7 79 William 12
DAVIDSON COUNTY 8 18 40 45 57 109
DAVIS, Abraham 80 98 105 111 113 116-119 122 Benjamin 109 118 124 Catharine 112 George 91 Henry 83 86 95 Jacob 64 John 108 114 Margaret 61 Mary 109 118 124 Miles 79 80 Peter 104 Preston 100 105 Robert 30 Thomas 109 -- 117
DAVISON, Pleasant 48
DAWSON, Pleasant 40
DAY, Jesse 4 17 84 85 125 John/Jon 15 62 66 67 68 75 84 86 88 89 90 93 94 103 107 111 112 119 124 125 143 144 146
DEAN, Edward 41
DEARING, Anslm/Anslen 88
DEARMAN, Anson 105 108
DEARMON, Anson 78 79 81 84 88 90 91 93 98 105 110 111 112 123 124 129 133 137 138 139 140 141 144 145 147 148 149 151 George 126 128 James 113 -- 140
DEATHERAGE, Bird 113 118
DEBRILL, Anthony 137
DEETLOW, James 57
DEFREESE, Hiram 14
DEFRIESE, Andley 119 Hiram 21
DEN, John 21 24 26 62 74 89 -- 49
DENFORTH, Josiah 30
DENNIS, Michael 27
DEPREESE, Hiram 14
DERICK, Jacob 85
DEVINPORT, Julius 133 Mary 133
DICK, John 141
DIRE, Spilsby 37
DIXSON, William 18
DOBBS, Caleb 126 127
DOLAN, John 109
DOLAND, John 103
DOLE, John 98
DOLEN, John 101 104 111 117 127
DONALD, Mathew 59
DONEL, Peter 41
DONELSON, Stockley/Stockly 19 59 60
DONNALD, Mathew 60

INDEX

DONNELL, Peter 40
DORAN, James 66
DOXEY, Daniel 86 87 91
DOYLE, Simon 137
DRINON, Thomas 9
DRUM, David 12
DUDLEY, John 40
DUFF, Josiah 60 63
DUNCAN, David 18 94 Jeremiah 3 26
Sabra 126
DUNHAM, -- 150
DUNLAP, Hugh 8 30 40 45 54 John 144
Richard 33 Will 83 William 77 83 89
-- 3
DUNLOP, W 30 William 68
DUTLEY, John 45
DYER, John 144 Joseph 85 94 95 108
Spells 123 Spels 43 Spills 106 124
Spils 68 Spilsby 36
DYRE, Edmund 14 James 129 Joseph 140
Spile 42 Spills 137 140 144 146 149
Spillsby 14 Spilsby 40 -- 148
EADS, Preston 144
EAKIN, James 147
EARP, Josiah 36 37 40 42 46 William
113 118
EASLEY, Warham/Warkum 6 11 12
EASLY, Wacham/Warham 4 7
EAVES, Thomas 90
EDINGTON, James 21
EDWARDS, Waller 35 Walter 37 38 40 41
43 59 Walton 32
ELDER, Robert 33 71 72 107 124 125 146
ELDERS, Robert 146
ELDRIDGE, Taylor 102
ELERSON, James 130
ELLERSON, Margarett 151 Robert 130
EMMERSON, Thomas 7-10 13-15 17-20
ENGLISH, Mathew/Matthew 64-67 73 77 78
90 94 100 104 107 108 112 116 117 120
143 149 William 105 120 131 132
ERWIN, Alexander 35 Anderson 35 Andrew
32 127 Benjamin 36 37 40 42 43 Samuel 3
EVANS, Andrew 62 63 65 Austin 151 Evan/
Even 11 20 23 24 54 57 60 64 Lewis 137
William 139 142
EVENS, Andrew 35 Even 54
EVERETT, John 24 25 Newel 24 25
EVINS, Andrew 35
EWIN, Samuel 22

EWING, Nathan 57 Samuel 22
FARIS, Richard 1 Robert 45 47
FARMER, Jeremiah/Jerremiah 133 134 John
84 91 109 112 129 134
FAULER, William 72
FELTS, Cader 62
FEN, Richard 5 24-26 30-32 35-38 44 48
52 53 58 62 66 68 72 74 89 122 125 -- 6
FERGUSON, Aaron 82 Alexander 13 14 30
36 38-41 43 46 76 89 Aron 30 Eli 33
79-81 103 104 106 144 Elias 16 20 29
30 33 34 43 45 James 33 36 54 127
John 6 30 37 38 40 41 43 45 47 48 52 64
65 100 120 137 Leroy 72 76 78 123
Levi 103 104 137 146 147 148 149
Martin 62 Moses 30 40 42 43 55 56 65
68 78 Robert 3 5 6 16 33 56 Samuel 30
36 37 40 42 43 99 116 Toliver 81 93
William 75 134 135 138 147
FERRELL, Bedy/Beedy 144 145 147 James
99 144 John 91 99 119
FIKE, Josiah 84 86
FINCH, -- 2
FINE, Balden 95 100 Baldwin 93 96
Jonathan 17-19 22 27 29 30 36-38 40 41
43 45 47 48 50 53 55 56 58 61 62 64-68
72 75 76 78 80 84-86 94 107 126 Peter
100 115 116
FINVICE, Ferdinand 2
FISHER, Absolam 58
FITZGERALD, William 107
FITZGERRALD, Anderson 76 81 102 Andrew
102 Archibald 76 92 95 Nancy 102
Samuel 76 97 William 98 104 107
FLOYD, William 33 36 37 40 42 43
FLUVANAH COUNTY, VA 51
FORBES, Alexander 6 26 28 32 38 Rachel
26 28 32 38
FORBUSH, Alexander 56
FORD, Stephen 115
FORGERSON, Elias 27
FORGUSON, Robert 19
FORSTER, A 110
FORT DEPONTE 19
FOSTER, A 110 Absolam/Absolam 58 109
140 George 16 James 15 16 18 20 30
John 92 Salley 92
FOULER, William 73 116
FOWLER, Bosbely 145 William 72 99
FRANCIS, Joseph 27-31 34 41 42 Miller

INDEX

1 4 7 11 14 25 28 33 41 43-48 51 62 72 85 89 96 114 130 139 143 Samuel 34 William 14 Woodson 1 6 7 10 13 15-17 20 22-24 26 29 33 39 40 44-46 49 50 52 55 58 61 64 67 71 78 82 85 97
FRANK, William 8
FRAZIER, Beriah 26 45 47 49 52 75 76 77 George 91 95 96 99 111 115 Samuel 98 114 116 122 127 131 132 134 136 139 143 144 Thomas 147 William 63
FREE, Jonathan 143 144
FREELDS, John 19
FREELS, John 11 12 13 15
FREEMAN, Reuben/Ruben 76 81 89 104 117 130 132
FRENCH, Fletcher 105 124 Timothy 106 108 114 118 126 130 131 136 138 139 141 145 147 149 William 7 8 15 18-20 22-25 30 93 104 -- 2 4 11 12 14 16 27 43 46
FRETWELL, William 105 106 108 114 117
FRIE, Johnathan 146
FRIELDS, John 17
FROST, Joseph 2 3 4 5 9 11 12 17 19 20 -- 14
FRULS, John 11
FRY, Constable 145 Johnathan/Jonathan 90 93 98 105 108 112 121 126 138 147 148
FUELLEN, Arthur 137
FULKERSON, F 66 Frederic/Fredrick 3 4 7 8 10 11 12 21 26 29 32 34 51 55 56 57 67 68 79 80 88
FULTON, Arthur 20 23 24 33 36 37 40 42 43 45 47 49 50 84 88 90 99 107 108 119 120 128 133 139 140 144 151 Fleming/Flemming 99 105 John 17-19 Sarah 140 Sheriff 120
FURGUSON, Elizabeth 106 Leroy 109 110 113 Moses 36 37
GADDY, H 91
GAINS, James 19 Richard 13
GAITHER, Beal 107 112 118 128
GALBREATH, James 1 2 18 John 143 Mary 143
GALEWOOD, Richardson 44
GALLANT, James 34 40 43
GALLENT, James 36 37 42
GAMBELL, Charles 62 James 135 Robert 47
GAMBLE, Charles 1 2 4 6 7 8 15 16 23 66 71 76 David 76 James 76 John 2 28 48 49 53 57 137 140 Justice 101 Margaret 76 Robert 1 2 13 17 20 23 26 33-36 41-45 48 52 55 56 61-63 76 86 88 103-105 Samuel 39 45 47 58 60 64 66 76 82 84 86 101-105 107 108 116 128 129 131 133 139 141 146-149 William 15 23 24 49 -- 77 82
GANTT, Samuel 40 45
GARDENHIRE, Matthew 125 126
GARDINER, John 15
GARLAND, Jesse 19 32 John 41 Ruth 32 Ruthey 19
GARRET, William 44
GARRIS, Jacob 61
GARRISON, Isaac 106 109 111 Jacob 61 62 106 John 106 137 Joseph 72 106 127 Robert 21 27 30 46
GARWOOD, Samuel 97 104 105 116 137 143 144
GASS, John 18
GATEWOOD, Richard 28 47 50 Richardson 31 35
GATHER, Beal 107 109
GAVINS, William 66
GENISS/GENNIS, Simeon 97
GEORGIA 2 5 16 18 56 61 82 85 86 105
GEREN, Levi 122 Silas 21
GERRALL, William 101 102
GEVEN, Simeon 103
GIBBENS, Joseph 126 128
GIBBINS, Joseph 128
GIBBONS, D 131 Joseph 131
GIBBS, Thomas 148 149
GIBSON, Jacob 13 James 109 Randolph 26 103-105 143 145 148 --rdon 51 -- 45
GILBERT, Polly 112 117 124 Richard 112 124
GILBREATH, John 125 129 133 137 140 144 145 Mary 125 129 133 137 140 144 145 William 125 129 137 140
GILCHRIST, John 16
GILES, Vaden 71 97 98 100 107 108 116 125 128 133 134 139 140 148
GILESPIE, George 39 41 50 53 55 61 63 71 72 73 77
GILLASPIE, George 86
GILLENWATERS, William 23-25 112 125 132
GILLESPIE, Allen 142 Charles 141 George 1 2 10-12 15 23 24 29 32 35 41 44 49 55 75-77 81 107 111 128 130 133 134 139

INDEX

140 142 148 Robert 131 135 137 138 140 141 143 144 146 147 Thomas 143 146 147 William 37 98 134 -- 137 138 140 143 146
GILLIAN, John 32 Major 81 86 89 95 William 119
GILLIHAN, John 5 6 46 Major 5 6 7 9 10 11 12 Margaret 6 -- 7
GILLILAND, Sheriff 120
GILLISPIE, Allen 105 122 128 Charles 119 George 56 57 78 80 84-86 103-105 107-109 112 116 121 122 128 Robert 115 122 Thomas 122 William 98 99 115 117 119 135
GIST, R 128
GIVEN, Simeon 87
GIVENS, William 68
GLASCOCK, Asa 130
GLASGOW, James 8
GLAZE, George 81
GLEN/GLENN, John 72 150
GLOVER, Jacob 39
GOAD, Elizabeth 126
GODBEHAST, Thomas 43
GODBEHERE, Thomas 37 38 40 41 116
GODSEY, Drury 144
GOLDSBY, Charles 90
GOOD, William 26
GOODWIN, William 38
GORDON, George 2 18 65 73 75 76 78 105 112 120 149 Jesse 78
GOTHARD, George 105 106 108 114 117 Ira 105 108 114 118 123 124 126
GRAGG, James 149
GRANTHAM, Amos 97
GRAVELLY, Mary 3 4 7 9
GRAVES, George 149
GRAY, Edward 39 41 43 52 61 62 79 80 82 John 18
GRAYSON, Jesse 60 63
GREAT BRITAIN 112
GREEN, Berry 19 40 James 2 48 Joshua 88 90 Matthias 100 101 106 109 William 129 134
GREEN COUNTY 7 46 56 57
GREEN COUNTY, GA 16
GREENE, Berry 45 Matthias 110
GREENE COUNTY 18 57
GREENWOOD, John 84 85 87 Nancey/Nancy 84 85 87

GREFFIT, Henry 144
GRIFFITH, Elijah 72 George 20 Henry 108 113 116 117 141 142 James 109 110 118 123 Jane 126 Levi 117 Levy 90
GRIGSBEY, William 137 140 141
GROAT, George 79
GROCE, Jacob 54
GUNN, James 20
GUTHERIE, James 18
GWIN, William 99 100 103 119 120 125 126 130 132 133 134
H--, Thomas 95
HACKET/HACKETT, John 19 59 60 Samuel 92 96 97 99 101 103 107 116 119 121 124 125 136 139 143 146 Sheriff 106 110 120 127 131 145 William 10 30
HACKLER, Henry 151 John 134
HACKWORTH, Nichodemus 7 9
HADEN, Ely 148
HAGE, James 57
HAINES, Archibald 28 29 Luster 28 29
HAINS, Archibald 42 Lester 42 Luster 42 Matthias 96 Miller 44 Thomas 99 104
HAKWORTH, Nichodemus 8
HALE, Douglass 18 Richard 72 78 Roswell 48
HALEY, David 4
HALL, George 6 John 26 95 Roswell 7 10-13 17 20 23 24 26 Russell 17 Samuel 12
HALLOWAY, Jesse 102 Major 78
HAMBLETON COUNTY 42 43 59 68 106
HAMILTON, Thomas 27 30 34
HAMILTON COUNTY 26 66 146
HAMILTON DISTRICT 13 23
HAN, William 114
HANAH, Avara 131
HANCOCK, John 60 William 79
HANCOCKE, William 86
HAND, William 134
HANDY, John 5
HANKINS, Wright 54 57 61 77
HANLY, William 145
HANNA, Avard 88 90 David 36 Joshua 37 Robert 21 23
HANNAH, Avara 128 131 Avary 65 88 129 Avory 64 David 35 37 40 42 43 89 94 James 49 52 108 114 John 8 Lewis 101 Robert 21 24 119
HANSOM, George 137
HANTRIG, Richard 55

INDEX

HARE, William 109 110 113 121 123
HARIMORE, John 50
HARMAN/HARMON, William 58 60
HARP, John 102 Joseph 102 Susan 101 102
HARRELL, Lewis 101
HARRIMORE, John 50
HARRIS, Abijah 9 124 Cornelious 131 Thomas 107 120
HARRISS, Cornelius 126
HARROW, Martin 36 42 43 47
HARVEY, Jeremiah 27
HARWOOD, Joseph 7 8 20 35 57 115 Malacyah/Malachi/Malechiah 91 115 117 119 Philip 91 113 115 117 Turner 4 7 -- 120
HASELRIG, Richard 75 92 Thomas 97 -- 75 86 89 90 92
HASLERIG, Richard 56 Thomas 108
HASTRIG, Richard 54
HATCH, Benjamin 44 Sally 44
HAUPT, Valentine 97
HAUSER, Josiah 81
HAWKINS COUNTY 97 111
HAWS, Thomas 135 137
HAYNE, James 76
HAYNES, Archibald 31 32 James 71 83 86 87 92 97 99 104 John 10 90 Luster 31 32 Thomas 118 119 120 136 139
HAYNS, James 108
HAZLERIG, Richard 83
HENDERSON, Lilburn 11 William 14 17
HENLEY/HENLY, William 141 142
HENRY, Charles 7 46 Ezekiel 1 3 7 15 George 28 46 53 54 79 80 114 115 128 135 Henry 61 74 77 81 87 91 100 112 128 Herun 144 Hirum 130 James 22 90 John 3 15 16 46 Thomas 58 60 100 105 107 112 114 115 130 William 3 46
HENSELEY/HENSLEY, T 125 126 Terry 127
HERICK/HERRICK, A 130 132
HERSKEL, -- 83
HICKEY, Joel 125
HIGDON, Charles 28 29 31 42 Jesse 42 John 29
HILL, Gerusha 92 93 Jerusha 85 87 Jesse 80 John 6-9 11 20 26 27 30 33 37-41 43 45-48 51 53 79 80 82 92-95 103-105 121 124-126 128 137 William 56 72 73 74 79 85 86 87 92 93 94 -- 7
HILTON, Betiah 41
HINDMAN, Thomas 34 35 41

HINDS, Matthias 101 104 William 101
HINES, Maleijah 85 Matthias 98 100 101 William 97 103 104 Willis 54
HOGAN, William 137
HOGE, Robert 18
HOGUE, James 66
HOLCOMB, B 91 R 91
HOLDERMAN, -- 33 44 46 51 53 56 59 62
HOLLAND, Allan/Allen 120 128 141 Isaac 33 John 29 38 54 74 93 94 133 William 48
HOLLOMAN, Pleasant 129
HOLLOMON, Pleasant 127 134
HOLLOWMAN, Pleasant 100
HOLLOWAY, Barnett 42 Bermilian 40 Bermillion 43 Bremillian 37 James 124 125 Jesse 102
HOLOWAY, Bermilian 36
HOLT, Erby 43 Irby 40 JOseph 18
HOOD, John 2 4
HOOK, John 134 145 Robert 142
HOOKE, Robert 131 -- 139
HOOKS, Robert 98
HOOTERFILS, Philip 28
HOPE, William 61
HOPKINS, Joseph 8 Polly 1 2 5 6 Robert 8 13 14 Thomas 2 5 6 11-13 16 17 20-23 28 30 32 34 38 44 47 48 51-53 55 57 61 63 66 67 80 81 129 137 -- 7 14 44
HORNBUCKLE, William 12 13
HORNESBY, Brinkley 125 137 145
HORNSBY, Brinkley/Brinkly 143 144 William 37 38 40 41 43 45 47 48 71 72 79
HOSKINS, Samuel 71 77
HOTH, Irby 40
HOUNDSHEL, David 118
HOUNDSHELL, David 80 111 122 123
HOUNSHELL, David 77 113 140 144 145 146
HOUPT, Polly 126 Valentine 90 93 98
HOUSTON, Robert 56
HOWARD, Abraham 10-12 20 23-25 39 46 47 50 54 83 93 Abram 2 Allison 47 67 68 72 76 78 80 81 83 86 93 96 105 John 2 8 Mariah 93 Martha 2 5 Mison 47 Samuel 58 60 86 99 103 104 105 133 134 William 45 47 55 56 64 66 83 90 96 105 111 115 144 -- 79 87 89 90
HOWARTON, Edmond 135 138 Grief 15 39 Jackson 72 73 94 95 96 98 Jeremiah 20

INDEX

36 37 43 60 77 81 Lucy 60 Micajah 95 96
HOWEL, Blackstone 88 Lewis 88
HOWELL, John 138 140 141 145 148 Lewis 94
HOWERTON, Edmun/Edmund 126 130 132 142 Grief 75 Jackson 3 71 72 88 92 93 128 137 141 144 146 147 Jeremiah 15 20 40 42 60 73 Micajah 71 88 93
HOWET, Nancy 23 Thomas 23
HOWIT, Nancy 23 Thomas 23
HOWLE, Lewis 98 99 100
HOWNSHELL, David 112
HOWSER, Josiah 105
HUBBARD, James 25 Mathew 54 58 60 64 67 Matthew 64 65 66 67 106 107 108
HUBBART, James 28 Matthew 68 107
HUBBERD, Matthew 137
HUBBERT, James 6 110 Justice 91 Mathew/Matthew 1-3 84-86 89 91 116 124 125 140 141 144
HUDDLESTON, Thomas 17 19 109
HUDSON, John 61 62 86 114 Thomas 3 8 12
HUFF, John 68 128 129 134
HUGHES, John 97 103 Polly 67 Thomas 67
HUGHS, Abraham 90 Caswell 58 60 John 52 63 64 67 Polley 55 Polly 52-54 58 60 63 64 67 Thomas 52-55 58 60 63 64
HUMBARD, Samuel 129
HUMBERD, Adam 109 113 Samuel 109 113 114 117 118 121 122 123 128 William 109 113 117 118 140 141 144
HUMBERT, Samuel 109 110 117 William 148
HUMPHREY, Carlisle 24 Eustace 28 Thomas 32 -- 25
HUMPHREYS, Carlisle 5 6 8 12 15 21 22 25 Rice 18 19 -- 27 28 30
HUMPHRIES, Carlisle 51
HUNTER, Andrew 62 65 Jacob 18 Joshua 145 Thomas 71 72 73 103 104 105
HURNBOSE, Isaac 41
HUSE, William 114
HUTCHISON, Alfred 143 Alpherd/Alphord 140 146 Anderson 22 24 25 33
HYDE, William 3 9 12 15
HYSE, Nancy 147
IGO, John 89 Samuel 67 68 79 113 115
IGOW, Samuel 111
ILLINOIS 2 32 33 65
INDIANA 2

INGLE, William 15 92 93 94 95
ISAM, Henry 65
JACK, Andrew 113 Jeremiah 107 John 1-3 17 19 79 80 Thomas 11 30 36 37 40 42 43 68 75 80 101
JACKS, Jasen 14
JACKSON, Andrew 8 12 18 John 25 30 65 Simeon/Simon 79 88 93 95 96 135 William 79
JACKSON COUNTY, AL 31 48
JACOBS, -- 71 72 79
JAMES, Jesse 31 Lewis 62 Tandy 23 Thomas 7 8 15 47 48 56 57 59-61 65 72
JAMISON, Samuel 104 107
JAMMISON, Samuel 104
JARNAGIN, Spencer 60 75 80 82 89 94 108 111
JARNIGAN, Spencer 125 127 145 146 148
JARNIGEN, Spencer 17
JASPER COUNTY, GA 2
JEFFERSON COUNTY 21
JEFFERSON COUNTY, AL 32 33
JERNAGEN, Spencer 75
JEWEL, William 117 122
JEWELL, William 125
JOHNES, Jeremiah 13
JOHNS, David 90 93 98 108 112 Henry 90 112 Thomas 90 105 William 45-47 -- 105
JOHNSON, Allen 3 Aquilla 5 9 Asahel 98 99 101 103 116 124 125 137 140 141 Benjamin 76 Caswell 86 95 Hezekiah 6 John 46 97 98 100 Joseph 1 3 7 8 12 13 14 20 98 Marck 65 Peter 57 Thomas 11 William 1 2 23 26 29 32 34 35 37 38 40 41 43 49 50 55 75-79 94 100 101 103 116 119 124 128 130 132 135 138 143
JOHNSTON, Asahel 97 Barbary 106 Joseph 112 Robert 106
JONES, Benjamin 22 52 61 62 75 76 92 93 95 96 111 113 115 137 143 Elisha 6 9 Elizabeth 61 Jeremiah 14 Jesse 28 29 31 42 John 3 6 8 11 William 61
JORDAN, R 109 Robert 110
JORDEN, Robert 80 81
JORDON, Robert 110
KARSNER, Benjamin 41
KEAN, Margarett 130 Samuel 111 115 130 -- 135
KEE, Joseph 146 147 149
KEELER, Joseph 15

161

INDEX

KEENUM, George 92 93 95
KEITH, Charles 23-26 29 30 32-35 39 41 42 44-52 55-67 75 77-90 92-97 99-101 103-105 107 108 110-117 119-121 124-128 133 134 136-147 149 150
KELERU, John 57
KELLEY, James 49 58 63 64 71 72 85 88 90 98 99 100 104 105 124 131 144 147 Nancy 149 Thomas 12 45 48 73 99 100 120-122 126 127 149 William 145 147
KELLY, James 5 9 12 13 20 23 24 26 30 50 62 90 93 101 107 115 Michael 107 Thomas 1 3 4 5 6 10 12 13 16 17 19 20 21 22 24 26 32 37 39 40 41 43 45 63 111 112 William 34 46 -- 6 14
KELOUGH, Joseph 77 148
KENEDY, Allen 50 53 George 53 John 46 William 40 50 54
KENNEDY, Allen 32 46 52 64 65 68 114 147 Daniel 79 George 46 117 Gilbert 68 72 76 John 46 William 20 33 37-39 41 43 45-49 53 67 68 77 97 121
KENNER, Peter 18
KENNON, Thomas 85 90
KENTUCKY 2 21 40 45 61 72
KENUM, George 96
KERR, Robert 79 William 122 126 133 134 135 139 140
KEYS, Alexander 112
KILCREASE, John 20
KILGORE, Sally 110 Sheriff 120 William 64 65 Willson 52 64
KILLON, Robert 55
KIMBLE, James 45
KIMBRELL, Benjamin 99
KIMBRILL, Benjamin 98 100
KINCANNON, Andrew 88
KING, James 16 17 John 40 45 Thomas 123 -- 10
KINNON, Thomas 73
KINNUM, George 96
KNIGHT, James 134 John 36-38 41-43 46 L 134 Levi 123 143 145 147-149 Lewis 86 87 90 91 118 119 125 127 129 130 132 133 134 137 139 141 142 144 146-149 Rebecca 118 119 125 127 129 132 134 137 141 142 144 147 148 -- 135
KNOX, John 16 25 -- 10
KNOX COUNTY 7 8 13 18 21 27-29 33 40 42 44 45 48 52 53 56 59 82 111 129

KONNER, Benjamin 41
KULBETH, William 1
LABY, John 33
LAMAN, Thomas 6
LAMBERT, Joseph 113 127
LAMKIN, James 25 27 William 25 27
LANGSTON, Richard 2 5
LAUDERDALE, James 2 92-95 William 4 27 31 35 75 76 77 107 -- 117
LAVENDER, John 35 36 38 40 42 43
LAWRENCE, William 88 94
LAWSON, Hugh 113 Jane 102 Richard 66
LEA, James 105 106 108 114 118 123 126 John 45-48 52 75 79 84 86-88 91 93 97 98 Pleasant 137 Pryor 33 William 52 53 60 68 -- 95
LEE, John 22 Ramsey 12
LEFTWICH/LEFTWICK, John 12 41 47
LEMONS, Levi 24
LEUTY, David 33 61 63 68 73 78 81 88 89 90 91 94 96 119 121 126 128 131 132 134 139 John 64-67 Margarett 61 William 4 6 9 14 15 16 19 44 67 79 93 98 100 -- 115 120
LEVI, John 103
LEWIS, Charlotte 3 7 Elizabeth 31 George 4 6 7 10-12 26 Henry 93 Isaac 29 52 53 56 James 14 31 John 4 10 52 55-57 61 62 64-67 75-77 119 Margaret 3 Maryann 7 Moses 15 Thomas 119 W 38 57 Wiley 85 86 William 3 4 6 7 9 10 17 24 26 29 31 32 34 48 49 51-53 56 59 62 65-68 76 78-83 87 88 91 100 104-106 109 113 119 123 Willie 129 -- 34 44 72 84 92 97 104
LEWISS, William 59
LILLARD, James 67 88 90 111 121 122 142 149 John 75 76 116
LINCOLN, Jesse 18
LINCOLN COUNTY, NC 9
LINLY, William 7
LISENBY, William 73 77
LISSENBRY, John 61
LITTLE, Joshua 81 Thomas 78
LOCKE, Benjamin 90 148 149 Franklin 116 123 147 John 16 19-21 23 24 26 30 33 36 50 58 64 73 81 82 84-87 91 93 96 98 100 103 104 108 114 115 117 119 120 122 123 125 127 130 132 139 143 147-149 Newton 116 Ralph 76 98 107 Robert 14

INDEX

16 17 19 23 24 33 39 40 44 47 49 64-66
80 95 96 143-145 William 28 50 66 77
88 93 95 98 104 105 113 123 135 --
100 114
LOE, Samuel 54
LOGAN, Samuel 1 3
LONG, James 140 144 148 Joel 120 John
97 98 99 104 106 128 William 9 12 46
49 53 84 96 99 103 104 120 123 144
LONGACRE, Benjamin 120
LOOKE, Robert 10
LOONEY, John 86 Samuel 103-105 124 143
144
LOONY, Samuel 52
LORANCE, William 98
LORD, Hezekiah 14
LOVE, Charles 65 Isaac 9 16 17 19 40
42 Isaac 36 37 39 43 46 Jefferson 101
114 122 128 John 3 4 5 7 12 51 95 96
Joseph 33 55-57 61 62 67 71-73 79-81 83
97 103-105 114 122 Robert 1 3 15 53 88
96 98 William 12 53 128
LOVELADY, John 27 31 34 35
LOW, Martin 140 Samuel 31 35 43 50
LOWDER, George 151 Nathan 134 151
LOWE, Samuel 47
LOWREY, Charles 74 John 73 William 74
LOWRIE, Charles 66 James 84 86 89 100
104 112 117 John 61-64 66 74 77 82
William 66 84 95
LOWRY, J 108 110 James 108 William 77
88 89
LUCAS, Thomas 98 146 147
LUIS, William 9
LUNEY, Samuel 104
LURTY, David 33
LUTY, William 9 47 79
LYKES, Drury 56
LYON, William 1 8 18-24 29 44 46 -- 2
4 11 12 14 16
MACOY, John 2 11 38 40
MADDEN, John 89 90 94 95 99 100 104 105
107 108 113 114 117 120
MADDISON COUNTY, MS TERRITORY 3
MADISON COUNTY, AL 14 17 46
MADLOCK, William 98
MAGHEE, George 35
MAHAFFE/MAHAFFEE, Martin 3
MAHAN, Alexander 72 John 49 50 Polly
102 Robert 40 104 120

MAHONE, Isaac 68 76 John 49 52
MAINARD, Edey 87 Henry 87
MAINAS, George 46 104
MAINES, George 25 86 93 129
MAINOR, George 78
MAINYARD, Eady/Edy 84 85 Henry 84 85
MAJORS, Abraham 34 Absalon 15-21 23
Absolam 65 Cornelius 77 John 122
Peter 34 37 38 40 41 43 82 88 89 91
MAKEN, Isaac 27
MALONEY, Aron 130
MALONY, Hugh 8
MANERS, George 130
MANEYARD, Henry 83 Nancy 83
MANLEY, Fleming 80 Richard 114
MANLY, Richard 28
MAPES, James 149 Jeremiah 149 Joseph
149 Polly 149 Pricilla/Priscilla 149
Sally 149 Sarah 149
MARBERRY, Benjamin 49 52
MARION COUNTY 27 42 43 48 55 56 66 68
78
MARLIN, Robert 16
MARSH, Alferd/Aldred 129 130 133 134
MARSHAL, Abraham 2 David 119 Joseph 2
Solomon 2 5 William 98
MARSHALL, David 109 117 127 Joseph 5
Thomas 98 101 103 104 109 111 117
William 98 101 109
MARTAIN, Samuel 136
MARTIN, James 34-45 48-51 55 58 61 62
67 81 Jesse 26 52 71 121 122 137 143
144 John 2 17 19 Joseph 19 Miss 84
Patrick 7 8 15 20 45 47 48 52 67 68 92-
94 Samuel 90 119 144 William 120
MASLEY, Joshua 57
MASON, Sheriff 120
MASONER, Isaac 116
MASSES, John 116 117 126 Sarah 126
MASSEY, Abel/Able 121
MASSUM, Jacob 66
MATHEWS, Jesse 66
MATLOCK, William 97 98 100 109 112 113
118 128 129 131 133 134 143
MATTHEWS, Alexander 27 30 Jesse 68 73
74 89 91 98 101 104 105 109 113 115 117
119 127 128 134
MAXFIELD, Benjamin 138 140 141 145 148
MAXWELL, Thomas 60 63 66
MAYFIELD, Stephen 99 101 108 110

INDEX

MAYO, George 100
McALISTER, William 6 9
McALLEN, John 146
McANDLASS, John 12 13
McANDLESS, John 94
McBRAZEAL, John 117
McCAIN, Edward 123
McCALEB, Andrew 143 144 146 147
McCALL, Alexander 1 9 10 53 57 59 60 140 141 Joseph 49 Mary 53 Sollomon 131 -- 4
McCALLA, -- 76
McCALLED, Thomas 63
McCALLEN, John 113 146
McCALLER, Thomas 63 65
McCALLIE, Thomas 63 65 87 90 93 100 105 111 114 125 129 134 139 142 146 147 -- 78 90 93 96
McCALLON, John 128 139 140 146
McCALLY, Daniel 7
McCAMPBELL, John 2 8 16 18 20 21 24
McCANCE, James 60 83 88 89 125
McCANDLESS, Richard 75 76
McCANNON, Cornelius 28 29 31 32 42
McCANSE, Benjamin 55 James 40 42 43 49 50 73 77 88 91 95 105 111 115 124 125 139 140
McCARLY, J 44
McCARREL, John 73
McCARROL, Bryant 95 John 86 89 90 100 Sarah 138
McCARROLL, Elizabeth 119 126 Henry 135 138 John 132 135 138 Sarah 135
McCARTER, William 118 124
McCARTEY, Benjamin 110
McCARTIE, William 144 148
McCARTY, Benjamin 101 110 James 9 John 30 40
McCLAINE, Catharine/Catherine 131 134 135 138 142
McCLANAHAN, John 107 108 113 115
McCLANNAHAN, John 28 67
McCLELLAN, John 5 6 21 Matthew 13 14
McCLELLAND, John 57 Samuel 43
McCLENAHAN, John 89 102-105 115 118 119 122 125 126 127 129 130 131 133 144 145 Mason 102
McCLENDON, Willis 18
McCLENNAHAN, John 62 63 72 95 97 98 119
McCLUNG, Charles 1 3-7 10-12 14 18 19 28-30 33 39 40 43-46 48 49 52 146 Hugh 14 15 146 Matthias 146 -- 11 16
McCLURE, John 37 46 51 71 72 77 78 84 85 91 107 108 116 128 133 139 140 Peggy 46 Robert 18 88
McCONEL, James 36
McCORCLE, Joseph 60 88 105 107 111 112 135
McCORKLE, Joseph 107 111 116 139-141
McCORMACK, Robert 134 138 143 144 147 148 William 68 73
McCORMICK, William 12 13 66
McCORY, John 37
McCOY, Annanias 25 John 41 43 Sarah 129 134
McCRACKEN, Robert 86 129
McCRACKIN, Robert 117
McCRACKING, Robert 116
McCRARY, Joel 54 56 William 40
McCRAY, William 20 23 26 43
McDANIEL, James 93 Joseph 51 57 60 62 64 65 68 72 77 86 95 98 119 126 133 134 Pierce 89 90 Samuel 29 45 47 55-57 64 65 75 88 93 98 105 108 111 114 116 117 125 129
McDANNIELL, Samuel 48
McDONALD, Bryant 92 93 136 143 144 Edward 80 84 85 James 26 45-47 55 57 84-86 107 116 117 120 William 103 104 112
McDONNALD, James 45 47 55 66 86 116 119 William 58
McDONNELL, Samuel 45
McDONOUGH, John 79 89 90 91
McDOWEL, -- 75 86 89 90 92
McDOWELL, Samuel 83
McENTIRE, Archibald 36 38 42 43
McFALL, Jesse 120
McFALLS, Constable 131 Jesse 113 122 124
McFARLAND, Henderson 137
McGEE, James 30
McGHEE, Malcum/Marcum 16 20
McGILL, John 126 127 128 130 132 William 15 16 20
McGONERY, James 33
McINTIRE, Archibald 40
McJOHNSON, S 94
McKEDDY, Thomas 34
McKENLEY, Benjamin 112 Sally 112
McKENNEY, John 18

164

INDEX

McKENNON, Thomas 77
McKENSIE, Benjamin 58
McKENZIE, Benjamin 76 112
McKERLER, Jesse 145 William 145
McKINDLEY, John 145
McKINLEY, Benjamin 116 117 121
  John 144 Salley 116 117 121
McKINSIE, Benjamin 57 60 64 72 97
McKINZIE, Benjamin 111 Reuben 124 125
131
McLEMORE, John 67
McMEANS, Isaac 6 9 11
McMILLAN, Alexander 45 Robert 24
McMILLEN, Alexander 2 40 Robert 15 23
McMILLION, Alexander 21
McMILLON, Alexander 18
McMINN, Joseph 16 33
McMINN COUNTY 42 48 56 64 66 68 75 81
82 85 89 109 115 138 145 148
McNAIL, William 149
McNEILL, Thomas 137
McNUTT, Thomas 91 92 144 145 148 151
McPHADDEN, David 21
McPHERSON, Alexander 95 98 Barton 10
11 12 13 118 Daniel 7 11 14 16 85 86
90 R 91 -- 7
McRAE, William 24 27 28
McREYNOLDS, Samuel 18
McSPADDEN/McSPADON, William 148 150
MEAD, Marston 1
MEANS, Robert 14
MEANY, Robert 1
MEDLEN, Britton 62
MEDLOCK, William 118
MEIGS, Return 3 4 7 10 14 18 19 41 137
138 Timothy 3 4 7 10 Return 119
-- 11 16
MELEGAN, Cornelius 62
MELONEY, David 26
MEMEMS, Isaac 5
MENAS, George 30 -- 27
MENES, George 43
MERIOTT, William 140 141
MERRIATT, Thompson 78
MERRICK, Peter 116 William 76
MERRICKS, Samuel 100
MERRIMON, William 76
MERRIOT, Jane 76 Thompson 82
MERRIOTT, John 119 Mary 76
MERRYMAN/MERYMAN, William 72

MILES, Jane 28
MIEGS, Return 105 Retwin 105
MILLER, Abraham 61 62 67 68 95 97 104
113 123-126 128 133 134 139 142 145 146
Henry 110 Hiram 98 99 101 James 72 75
78-80 86 90 95 96 99 John 34-36 41 44
79 80 85 93-97 100 106 108 110 113 118
119 126 127 140 141 144 147 Robert 127
William 76 79 80 89 97 131
MILLICAN, William 14
MILLIGAN, Cornelius 64 65 66
MILLINS, Catharine 130 John 100
MILLS, Jane 28
MINICK, Peter 73
MINOTT, Thompson 82 William 140
MINTON, Johnson 129 130 144
MISSISSIPPI 43 44
MISSISSIPPI TERRITORY 2 3
MISSOURI 111
MITCHEL, James 43
MITCHELL, Charles 34 35 37 38 40 41 43
David 100 J 13 James 1-3 8 10 16 17
20 23 29-33 36 37 40-43 46 47 53 55 60
61 63 65 67 80 81 83 85 89 90 99 109
124-128 Robert 128 -- 21 26 99
MONROE COUNTY 42 44 66 91 135
MONTEETH/MONTEITH, Robert 82 91
MONTGOMERY, Elizabeth 91 Hugh 93 98
James 23 24 36 37 40 42 43 58 60 67 68
81 83 86 88 90 92 93 95 96 98 113 115
129 143 145 148 151 Jeremiah 91 John
24 25 27 28 35 Johnson 32 Joseph 47
Samuel 91
MOOR, John 24 56 William 56
MOORE, Isaac 82 Jacob 68 James 34 36
37 40 42 78 124 125 126 John 3 6 10 12
13 17 19 20 22 24 27 30 35-38 40 41 43
44 47 48 52 53 Jonathan 22 Robert 7 8
48 Stephen 123 Thomas 4 5 William 67
68 -- 7
MOOREHAD, Armstead 45
MOORHEAD, Armsteed 40
MORE, Thomas 111
MORGAN, Calvin 149 Franklin 149 George
71 72 79 Gideon 98 Lewis 66 67 Mary
1 2 5 7 8 Rufus 149 Washington 66 67
Willis 1 4 7 10 -- 7 71
MORGAN COUNTY 42
MORGANS, -- 72 79
MORLEY, William 23

INDEX

MORRISON, Edward 15 17 18 20 21 23
Polley/Polly 15 17 18 20 21 23
MORRISS, Blount 151 William 133 135 137 141 144 145 146
MOSES, Priscilla 142 143 Sarah 142
MOYERS, Cornelius 73 78 79 John 123 124 Peter 22
MULLINS, Ann 127 Catharine 131 132 135 Elizabeth 130 131 132 135 Joseph 127
MUNCY, Thomas 127 142
MUNROE COUNTY 44
MUNSEY, Thomas 139
MURFREE, Samuel 50
MURPHEY, Edward 21 Hugh 19 20 21 89 Robert 96 117 Samuel 6 18 21 22 48 54 81 86 89 -- 25
MURPHREE, Allen 22 Hugh 76 James 26 John 7 53 146 William 3 5-9 11 14 17 19 21 22 26-29 32 33 35 42-44 46-48 50-52 54 57 73 87 89 96   -- 7 25
MURPHY, Edward 24 Hugh 9 18 24 John 3 8 9 Robert 109 Samuel 5 9 12 22 24 95 -- 7
MURRELL, Henry 120
MYERS, John 18
NAIL, James 5 43 45 73 77 Matthew 7 Nicholas 13 14
NARIMORE, John 47
NARREMORE, John 31 35
NEAL, Basil 2 5 James 17 24
NEIL, John 150 Prior/Pryor 133 134
NEILSON, Joseph 81   -- 44 53 59 62
NELSON, Joseph 27 M 78 Matthew 21 86 Nancy 31 35 Richard 100   -- 51 56
NETHERLAND, George 93   -- 95
NEVILLE, -- 148
NEWKIRK, James 83
NEWMAN, Cornelius 18
NEWTON, George 33
NIGHT, John 40
NIVENS, Wilson 6
NOBLET, William 37 38 40 41 43
NOBLETT, Thomas 78 William 58 60 77 116
NOBLIT, William 73
NORRIMORE, J 31
NORTH CAROLINA 6 9 54
NOTON, Thomas 2
NOWLIN, James 36
OATS, David 27 35
OATSWELL, David 37

OBRYANT, James 78 John 78
OHAROW, Martin 40
OHARRA, Martin 38
OHIO 3 57
OLDHAM, John 107 109 110 113 118 121 122
OREGIN, U 120
ORM/ORME, Polly 31 35
ORMES/ORMS, Elly 31 35 54
OUTLAW, Alexander 2 5 8 11 12 14-16 18-20 25 26 44 48 51 54
OVERTON COUNTY 18 30
OWEN, John 125
OWENS, Henry 1 7 12 14 16 18-22 24 26 27 30 31 33 46 50 53 56 58 147 John 130 -- 7
OWINGS, Henry 9
OWINS, Henry 137 Job 131 John 132
OXSHEER, Samuel 31 43 44
OXSHIRE, Samuel 28 35
PAIN, Joseph 3 Orvell 39 Thomas 28
PAINE, Joseph 3 O 91 Orvill 48 Orville 64 67 72 75-83 86 88 91-93 97 100 101 104 107-109 113 116 117 124 125 137 141 147 Philip 9 Sheriff 120 127
PALL, Moses 68
PANQUE, William 51
PARDOE, John 112 125 128 139 140
PARK, James 134 140 146 William 134 140 146
PARK--, John 32
PARKER, Akiah 143 144 Elisha 9 23 James 110 Joannah 110 John 14 23 24 28 40 90 93 94 96 99 103 106 108 113 117 122-124 126 127 131 132 134-136 139 142 149 Lucinda 110 Patsy 23 Salley 93   -- 90
PARKES, Henry 115 Jane 115
PARKHIL/PARKHILL, David 1 3 6 9 17 20
PARKING, John 40
PARKS, James 143 Robert 14-17 19 26 45-48 54 58 60-62 64-67 72 77 93 116 144
PARMER, William 136 143
PARSONS, Enoch 5 6 26
PATTEN, -- 75 86 89 90 92
PATTERSON, John 125 Lewis 144 Robert 10 11 12 47 48 49
PAUL, Archibald 107 108 126 143 144 Moses 15 29 37 39-41 43 67 Sheriff 145
PAYNE, Alfred 88 Joseph 5

166

INDEX

PEACE, James 6
PEARSON, Holderman 23 27 30
PECK, Peter 55
PENDERGRASS, Nimrod 9
PENTERGRASS, Nimrod 6
PEPER, Chase 89
PERKINS, Benjamin 117 Henry 135
PERRY, Beaty 100 112 125 Joseph 148
PETERS, Briton 100 Joseph 28 47 50
PHANON, Martin 35
PHARIS, James 91 R 91 Robert 58 64 65 66 67 97 119 120
PHARISS/PHARRISS, Robert 58 60 137
PHARROW, Martin 35
PHILIPS/PHILLIPS, Robert 92 93 94 95
PHILPOT, Alexander 102 124 125 Richard 3 8 18 19 31
PICKETT, James 105 106 108 114 118 123 124 126 130 134 138 142 144
PIERCE, William 93
PILE, Cedron 148-150 T 142 Thomas 139 141 144 147-149 William 119 137-141 143 146 147 148
PIPER, Thomas 40
PITMAN, Jefferson 2 5
POE, James 117 119 Jesse 39 43 49 55 56 58 60 78 79 105 109 113 141 Parson 77 Pulaski/Palaskey/etc. 67 144 147
POLLARD, Lewis 105 130
PONK, James 2
PORCK, James 2
PORTER, Miner 14
POWEL, S 23 Samuel 27 Scott 98
POWELL, James 89 Samuel 22
POWERS, James 61
PREGMORE, Ephraim 60
PRESTON, George 107 113 117 118 121 122 128 James 1 3 10 20 34 50 55 56 57 63 73 77 91 103 104 105 111 112 113 115 116 118 119 121 Sheriff 131 132 145
PREWIT, Micaja 145
PREWITT, Micajah 99
PRICE, Charles 138 Henry 84 Eliza 138 Hugh 138 Isaac 138 Jacob 98 James 138 Louisa 138 Minerva 138 Samuel 88 Scion 56 63 Sion 47 51 53 Thomas 29 32 55 56 63 73 77 88 103 109 130 136 138 William 138
PRIGMORE, Ephraim 63
PRILLAMON, Jacob 146

PRILLERMAN, Jacob 138
PRILLIMAN, Jacob 146 147 148
PRINE, Robert 41 47
PRIVOT/PRIVOTT, Micajah 108 113
PURDY, Robert 1 5 7
PURRISS, Henry 59
PURSER, James 146 147
RACUSUS, -- 10
RAFFERTY, Richard 21
RAGEN, James 138
RAGLAND, Gideon 64 65
RAGLIN, Gideon 52
RAGSDALE, David 9 60 62 65 84 133 134 135
RAINS, William 145
RAMSAS, -- 10
RAMSEY, A 48 Andrew 45 Francis 28 George 144 John 3 4 12 13 17 19 22 24 26 32 45 William 6 12 14 19 20 24 -- 1 5 6 7 12 13 14
RAMSY, John 21
RANDLE, John 92
RANDLES, John 128 129 139 140 142
RANDOLPH, Mary 76 William 54 71 78 85 90
RANDOLS, John 92
RANSOM, George 94 95 96 99 106 141 Peggy 110 135
RASSUM, Jacob 129
RAWLING, -- 6
RAWLINGS, Asahel 16 21 23 106 Daniel 2 6 8 14 16 18-20 22-25 27 29 33 35 36 38 40 41 43 45-47 54 58 98 John 82 Mary 46 Polly 46 Rezin 7 9 33 35 38 40 41 43 46 58-60 63 67 78 81 84 89 97-101 103-105 111-113 116 119 Sally 46 -- 2-4 8 11 12 14 16 21 26 98 117
RAY, Hugh 73
RECIR, Margarett 135
RECTOR, Charles 109 110 113 123 Cumberland 4 6 7 34 39 41 55 56 57 64 65 66 Landon 34 36 37 40 42 43 58 121
REDMOND, John 65 76 77 80
REECE, Rodger/Roger 28 66 68 92
REECER, Margarett 132 134 135
REED, James 14 15 18 19 Lemuel 4-7
REES, Roger 33 37 40
REESE, Elam 140 Jesse 45 Roger 41 47 67 William 40 45
REMBERT, Alexander 17

INDEX

RENFRO, Joshua 128 129
RENTFROW, John 45 48 53 63
REPPETO/REPPITO, William 63 64 67
REVELY, Salley 93
RHEA, Hugh 4 6 14 129 James 141
William 150
RICE, Alexander 102 127 128 149 Elijah 27 77 78 90 94 100 George 78 John 4 6 7 13 14 19 20 21 22 24 25 27 29 33 46 49 50 54 60 64 71 78 Joseph 22 33 54 78 117 130 131 Roger 68 Theoderick 145 William 79 119 -- 25 27 28 30
RICHARDS, Curtis 72 76 Susan 138 Susanah 130
RICHARDSON, John 109 110 118 123
RICHESON, John 113 118
RICHMOND COUNTY, GA 2
RIDDLE, James 13 14 49 Willliam 81
RIGG, Addison/Adison 130 131 Charity 101 102 Martin 102 129 Townley/Townly 77 79 80
RIGGEL, George 10 11 12 28 50 Henry 10 12 Jacob 7 10 12
RIGGLE, George 17 19 30 32 33 43 45 47 49 58 104 111 115 124 Jacob 149 John 71 72 97 116 Solomon 50 57
RIGGS, Addison 129 Townley 62 64 68 72 Townly 60 63 68 Townsley 57
RIGHT, Isaac 53
RIGS, A 149
RILEY, Samuel 15 16 18 20 30
RIPPETO/RIPPITE/RIPPITO, William 53-55
RITCHARDS, Curtis 72
ROADES, John 48 53
ROAN COUNTY 42
ROANE, Archibald 1 4 9 10 James 51 53 57 59 60
ROANE COUNTY 4 5 6 11 13 14 17 30 40 44 45 46 48 49 57 66 113
ROBERTS, Samuel 87 -- 76 78 90 93 96
ROBERTSON, John 26 55 Nelson 26 William 20 21 22 23 26
ROBINS, Isaac 134
ROBINSON, Alexander 42 H 33 James 112 114 127 John 1 4 7 12-14 22 27 29 33 45 55-57 63-65 Jonathan 67 124 Lucy 1 Mark 15 Nelson 32 T 66 William 4 19 32 -- 7 14 16 135
ROBINSON COUNTY 100
ROBISON, John 4 6 46 William 2 -- 11

ROCKBRIDGE COUNTY, VIRGINIA 38
ROCKHOLD, Francis 68 88 105 111
RODDEN, William 127
RODDEY, Isaac 121 James 121 Jesse/Jessy 11 12 121
RODDY, David 139 142 Isaac/Isack 6 88 90 96 107 108 116 117 135 140 James 121 Jesse 10 11 39 41 52 65 71 72 92 93 95 96 103-105 121 123 John 58 60 67 68 92 95 96 147 148 149 Moses 9 15
RODDYE, Isaac/Isaack 121 James 121 143 144 146 Jesse 20 29 111 John 146
RODES, John 45 48
RODGERS, Archibald 88 Benjamin 97 James 1 4-7 9 11 13-16 22 24 26 30 33 54 58 79 88 97 98 104 John 90 93 97 98 William 83 84 95
RODY, Jesse 6 John 58
RODYE, John 146
ROGERS, James 18 19 20 22 29 34 43
ROMINE, Jasper 27 Nicholas 130
ROMINES, Mary 136 Nicholas 130 132 135 136 Thomas 136
ROPER, -- 44
ROSS, David 13 20 22 24 27 30 Frederick 51 Lewis 28 30 40 41 44 62 65 66 68 71 72 76 77 82 103 125 129 130 131 133 -- 23 48 52 53 148
ROWDEN, Abraham 90 Asa 21 33 111 113 122 -- 117
ROY, Hugh 77
RUAL, Roger 38
RUCER, Margarett 132
RUCKER, John 25 27
RUNALDS, Jacob 124
RUNNION, John 6 9
RUNNELLS, Jacob 56
RUNOLDS, Elijah 81 Jacob 122
RUSE, Roger 38 43
RUSH, Isaac/Isac 32 34 36 37 40 42 43
RUSSELL, Alexander 13 14 Andrew 1 Constable 101 131 James 1 John 1 17 19 20 27 29 31 34 35 42 Martha 142 Martin 140 141 Sheriff 131 132 William 75 88 96 102 113 123 129 133 146 147 149
RUTHERFORD, James 81
RYAN, C 58 Charles 36 37 42 43 60 65 66
RYON, Charles 1 3 17 34 40
SAFFER, Matthias 107
SAINT, Hugh 10

168

INDEX

SAMPLEY, Jesse 126 141 142
SAPP, John 1 13 14
SAPPINGTON, James 77 85
SAWRMER, William 101
SAYLOR, Henry 5
SCOTT, Charles 114 115 E 22 Edward 4-8 10-13 15-17 20 21 27 40 45 121-124 Jesse 63 65 Thomas 36 37 40 42 43
SEABOLT, Adam 102
SEABOULT, Adam 74 98 104 John 98
SEBOURN, Joseph 102
SELLARS, Sampson 98 Seaburn 97
SELLERS, Isaiah 103 Sampson 99 101 103 104
SEVIER, Abraham 30 George 18 Valentine 18
SEVIER COUNTY 112
SEYMORE, William 86 103 129
SHAFER, Matthias 112 113 115
SHAFFER, Henry 96 Matthias 103 104 105 111 135
SHARP, E 91 Eli 76 81 115 128 Elisha 65 118 119 120 128 129 133 134 146 147 Stockley 3
SHAUTZ, Jacob 33 Kineson 33 Valentine 33
SHAVER, Matthias 107 109 116 128 133 134 139 140 141
SHEILDS, Elizabeth 112
SHELBY, Valentine 32
SHELL, John 2
SHELTON, Chrispian 22 66 107 123 Crispen/Crispin 23 116 124 132 133 134 Crispian/Crispien 84-86 88 107 David 49 52 68 71 81 97 Palatial 27 William 28 29 30 31 34 42
SHERILL, Jesse/Jessee 3 9 14
SHERLEY, Benjamin 51 53 59 62 -- 33
SHERLY, Benjamin 27 46
SHERRELL, Elizabeth 28 Jesse 16 28 44 47 Samuel 28
SHIPLEY, William 82 86
SHIRLEY/SHIRLY, Benjamin 24 56 -- 30
SHOOLLS, Martin 11 Valentine/Vallentine 5 6 13
SHOOTTS, Martin 13
SHULTS, John 104 Valentine 104
SHULTZ, Jacob 32 Kinason 32
SIMMS, Job 28 Little 45 Littlepage 25 26 28

SIMPSON, John 22 137 Paskill 100
SIMS, Job 32 33 John 127 Little 3 17 18 21 32 33 Littlepage 14 40
SINGLETON, James 145 John 58 61 62
SISHEART, Henry 98
SKIDMORE, John 3 6 7 11 23 -- 7
SKILERN, John 57
SLAVES: Henry 76 Jack 11 Jane 114 Leah 93 Mary 114 Nicholas 76 Sam 114 Tom 119 Viney 76
SLOVER, Jacob 71 72 79 Martha 84 94 -- 148
SMALL, Robert 53 86 93 96
SMITH, Abraham 10 13 14 23 24 Alexander 21 22 24 33 Anderson 100 101 104 119 121 129 Arthur 85 90 91 Condley 127 Francis 1 4 7 10 George 46 James 46 49 56 120 129 133 141 144 John 2 11 15 21 22 25 43 44 46 48 49 51 53 68 74 79 80 91 93 113 115 117 119 120 122 137 146 147 148 149 Joseph 91 Joshua 41 Mumford 15 22 47 61 62 63 115 119 121 122 Randolph 2 7 Right 93 Robert 40 45 Samuel 63 81 Theophilus 129 130 Thomas 110 134 William 4 10-12 15-22 24 29 30 43 54-56 59 62 64-66 75-77 81 83 84 86 93 97 98 104 105 107 109 111 112 124 125 129 133 139-141 146 148 150 Williamson 137 Wright 23 49 61 62 80 95 112 121 125 138 147 -- 7
SNELSON, James 1 10 12 29 32 34 35 58 59 60 141 Thomas 59 140 William 81 85 90 91 126 129 134
SNOW, John 129 133
SOUTH CAROLINA 3
SPEAR, John 30 41 76 82
SPEARS, James 97 118 119 John 34 35 44 72 89 95 97 103 105 108 122
SPENCER, Jesse 111 113 117 122 John 111 113 117 122
SPERGIN, Abraham 90
SPRING, Henry 91
STANDEFER, James 21 60 W 29 30 William 18 19 21 22 25 27 28 75
STANLEY, John 99 Jonathan 105 William 99 108 118
STAPLETON, John 3
STAR, Joseph 102
STARNES, George 1 Leonard 18 Nicholas 13

INDEX

STARNS, George 1 2 3 45 Jane 7 Nicholas 14 20 45
ST. CLAIR COUNTY, AL 32 33
STEPHENS, Birtel 109 William 109
STEPLETON, John 5
STEUART, James 134 135 137 John 138 149
STEWART, Edward 49 58 60 104 120 Hugh 10 James 41 43 47 48 60-63 66 72 75 76 79 80 85 87-91 93 94 98 105 130 131 John 61 88 90 121 136 Mercy 126
STILL, Andrew 60 63 John 127
STINER, Michael 91 117
STOCKTON, Daniel 35 64 107 113 115 Robert 107 109 110 113
STOCTON, Daniel 64-67 84 86 116 117 119 123 125 Joseph 99 Robert 118 123 William 123 137
STOKES, George 96 Leavin/Levin 107 109
STONE, William 60 63
STONER, Hannah 19 Michael 8 11 13 14
STOUT, Abraham 25 26 Benjamin 50 88
STOVER, Jacob 43 68
STRONG, Joseph 8 10 23 26 30
STUART, David 2 5 11 16 17 25 44 54 Edward 34 49 53 George 127 James 3 12 22 26 61 81 107 108 129 John 44 130 149 Thomas 1 2 3 4 -- 7 14
SULIVAN, Polly 62
SULIVAN COUNTY 90
SULLIVAN, William 148
SUSENBERY, John 61
SUTTON, James 117 Sarah 135 138
SWAGGERTY, Abraham 6 14 17 44
SWAN, James 36 38 40-43 58 60 71-73 78 81 85 90 106 107 111 115 116 128 129 134 145 148 John 20 58 62 63 65 125 129 134 135 Samuel 71 83 86 87 97 Thomas 68 83 86 87 90 94 95 96 97 99 104 105 107 109 114 123 124 -- 142
SWANS, Samuel 76 92 Thomas 76 92
TABER/TABOR/TABOUR, John 49 50 52 60
TAFF, John 120 143 144
TAMBLE, Samuel 65
TAUL, Micha 40 45
TAYLOR, Archibald 67 68 Henry 4 6 8 10 15 John 15 91 Peach 71 73 84 88 107 111 112 113 115 116 117 128 129 131 133 134 139 140 Pruit 108 Robert 14 49 54
TEMPLE, Elizabeth 110 Edward 45 88 94
124 125 126 127 137 140
TERRY, Samuel 18
THOMAS, William 4 7 20 56 Woodson 15
THOMPSON, A 55 Absolam 64 72 76 Absolem 58 Absolum 57 60 Constable 135 George 75 78 80 123 Gideon 124 125 132 137 139 141 145 149 Jacob 149 James 2 3 5 6 34 68 77 80 86 146 Jesse 2 3 13 14 23 25-27 33 41 43 55 56 68 75 77 84 86 99 100 107 109 111 113 115 128 139 140 146 John 2-6 9 11 12 16-20 35 43 45 54 64 85 112 125 146 Joseph 2 3 5 8 26 29 30 47 48 51-53 56 57 59-61 65 72 76 77 123 125 129 134 135 140 141 144 145 147 150 Josheph 140 Moses 5 20 29 33 34 49 50 52 55-57 64 65 77 81 92 94 95 100 140 145 150 Thomas 19 34 41 85 86 Verdingberg 49 -- 14 140
THOMSON, George 125 Jesse 24 John 24 Joseph 26
THORNTON, John 57
TIGNER, Thomas 23
TILLERY, Samuel 52
TILLY, Austin 31 34 35 Catherine 31
TIMON/TIMONS, Matthew 146 147
TINDAL, Susan 62
TINDLE, Joshua 62
TINVICE, Ferdinand 2
TIPTON, James 86 Rebecca 126
TOFF, John 71 72 84
TOWNSEND, Taylor 5
TRIGG, William 11
TRAYNOR, John 139 144
TRIMBLE, James 40 Samuel 65
TRIPLET, Abner 142 147
TRIPLETT, Abner 100 110 145
TRIPLETTE, Abner 145
TRUMAN, Reuben 9
TUCKER, James 61 Samuel 124
TULEN, Willis 18
TURNEY, Hopkins 71
TUTEN, Willie 15
TUTTLE, Henry 3 8 14
TYSON, Jesse 92 93 94 95 120 121
TWIFORD, John 133 134
UMPHRIE, W 33
UNDERWOOD, Abner 5 9 21 23 24 99 103 Thomas 72
UNION BANK OF TENNESSEE 147
UPTON, James 20 22 23 24 40 Jesse 28

INDEX

29 32 42 William 82
VANDYKE, Alexander 1 Eliza 1 J 144 Jefferson 1 Mary 1 Thomas 5 7 Nixon 1 Thomas 1 137
VARNER, Edward 20 35 James 15
VAUGHN, Sheriff 91
VERNER, Edd 32
VERNON, Anderson 146 147 Miles 58 59 65 88 93 94 105 109 111-113 125 129 142 149
VINES, Alexander 125 126 130
VIRGINIA 38 48 51
WAGNER, Matthias 89 95 Thomas 91
WALDONS RIDGE 30
WALKER, Anderson 149 Charles 112 124 Daniel 10 11 17-19 22 25 27 29 31 32 41 51 57 63 64 66 68 73 75-77 84-86 89 91 107 108 110 112 117 124 134 149 David 54 Freeman 2 George 1 4 6 8 11 14 17 19-21 23 24 26 27 30 33 43 51 53 56 64 James/Jams 121 143 147 John 53 55 56 59 62 77 82 90 91 92 95 103 104 105 110 147 148 149 Jonathan 2 3 4 5 Mary 64 Patsy 21 Richard 2 Robert 2 39 40 41 43 71 72 Samuel 44 48 Tellitha 143 William 49 60 64 65 132
WALL, William 12
WALLACE, James 37 John 14
WALLERD, Richard 147 Telitha 147
WALLKER, Daniel 133
WALTON, Henry 19 36 37 40 42 43 45 47 48 68 William 76 83 ridge 30
WAMACH/WAMACK, John 90 Thomas 145
WAND, William 123 129
WAPIN/WAPUM, Jacob 5 6
WARD, Duke 48
WARMACK, John 100 101
WARREN COUNTY, KY 40 44
WARREN COUNTY, TN 57 62 88 129 137
WASHINGTON, Frederick 16 23
WASHINGTON COUNTY 77 80
WASSAM, Alexander 137
WASSEN, John 40 66
WASSINN, Jacob 3 5
WASSOM, Jacob 3 58
WASSON, Edward 137 140 John 17 36 37 52 58 71 103 104 105 137 138 140 141 143 144 145 146
WASSUM, Andrew 125 129 134 137 147 149 Conrad 41 Coonrod 35 Jacob 6 9-11 20 21 33 41 66 75 76 100 132 134 137 140 142-144 146-149 151 John 42 66 67 71 -- 7
WASSUN, John 43
WATERHOUSE, Ann 82 83 138 Blackstone 76 78 80-82 89 94 96 110 111 115 130 136 138 148 149 Cyrus 81 106 138 Darius 82 83 106 138 151 Euclid 82 83 138 Franklin 82 83 138 Myra 81 83 138 Polly 2 Richard 1-6 8 10 11 14-17 19-32 34-36 38-40 42-46 48-56 58-63 65-68 72-78 80-83 86 89 94 96 98 103-106 110 111 122 124 130 136-138 140 141 143 144 147-151 Syms 83 Vesta 82 83 138 -- 7 9 32-34 44 66 80 82 84 88 92 95-97 104 106 108 114 145 149
WATHER, George 46
WATSON RIDGE 39
WAUGH, Justice 91
WAYNE COUNTY 40 54
WEASE, Isaac 135
WEASSE, Abraham 135
WEATHERLY, Abner 144
WEAVER, S 91
WELKER, William 104
WELKES, Henry 62
WELLS, Drinnen 61
WEST, Isaac 3 5 30 54 Warren 122 William 65 Willis 105 106 108 114 117
WHALEY, John 71 73 86 90
WHARTON, Stephen 51
WHITAKER, Moses 133
WHITE, Eliza 78 George 7 8 11 16 Hugh 18 40 45 82 111 Jesse 2 4 6 13 14 19-23 26 32 John 65 Mary 101 102 Peter 11 Samuel 46 William 78 89 -- 7 11 14 16 59
WHITE COUNTY 62 88 137
WHITEHEAD, Benjamin 106
WHITES CREEK 87
WHITFIELD, Bons 44 Edith 44 Edmond 48 51 54 Edmund 44 Elizabeth 44 Gains 44 Hepzibah 44 Needham 44 48 William 44 -- 14 17 19 21 22
WHITTEN, William 135
WILHELM/WILHELMS, Andrew 12 13 27
WILIAMS, Natthaniel 128
WILKENSON, Lewis 40 43
WILKER, Henry 62 William 82 83
WILKERSON, James 133 Lewis 30 35 45 48

171

INDEX

Luis 47
WILKES, William 80
WILKINSON, John 14 Lewis 36 37 42 47
WILLIAMS, Benjamin 2 David 46 54 George 3 James 44 93 98 John 2 4 8 12 14 18-20 22 23 44 47 51 Joseph 20 39 54 71 79 80 82 Nathaniel/Natthaniel 26-29 52 53-55 67 68 71-75 77 129 130 132 Robert 119 131 138 Samuel 12 T 81 Thomas 5 6 8 10 12 18 23 26 50 82   -- 11 16 68
WILLINGHAM, John 2
WILLS, John 129 137 145
WILLSON, James 36 42 43 William 65
WILSON, Dice 89 James 7 10 29 33 37 40 52 84 85 89 91 109 111 113 115-119 128 129 134 139 140 N 91 Nathaniel 83 90 98 Sheriff 91 William 71 77 80 81
WILSON COUNTY 38
WINFORD, Alexander 2
WINLOW, John 44
WINTON, John 44 George 5 7 17 19 32 Stephen 49 65 71-73 84-86 91 111 115 116 133 134 139 140 146 147
WIRICK, William 118
WISE, John 122
WITT, Abner 126 127 137 140 143 Charles 140 Jessee 22 54 79 141 John 55 56 86 117 122 125 131 133 140 143 144
WOLLERD, Richard 143
WOOD, John 82 97 123 126 134 144 William 148
WOODHOUSE, Richard 23
WOODS, John 73 William 88
WOODWARD, Charles 14 37-41 43 54 James 100 John 15 24 34 37-41 43 Thomas 2 6 15 23 29 30 32 47 98 Willliam 16-19 121 -- 106
WOOLEY, William 62
WOOTON, Lucy 44
WORBELL, John 104
WORLEY, Hiram 32 William 24 30 46 51 53 56 59
WORLY, Hiram 27 William 27
WRIGHT, Abraham 82 131 Isaac 56 William 75
WROE, Thomas 100 113 115 124 126 127 130 131 135 144 -- 135
WYATT, Elijah 124
WYLY, Robert 97
WYRICK, Frederick/Fredrick 118 119 121 131 Martin 10 12 William 119 121 131
YATES, John 99 105 106 108 114 118 123 124 126 130 134 139 145 William 109 113 123
YEATS, John 108
YORK, Allen 82 83 85 86 89 90 Josiah 82 86 Thomas 54 62 65 82 86 William 5 8 11 14 15 16 18 20 22 24 30 33 43 51 -- 3
YOUNG, William 98

Other Heritage Books by Carol Wells:

Abstracts of Giles County, Tennessee: County Court Minutes, 1813-1816 and Circuit Court Minutes, 1810-1816

CD: Tennessee, Volume 1

Davidson County, Tennessee County Court Minutes, Volume 1, 1783-1792

Davidson County, Tennessee County Court Minutes, Volume 2, 1792-1799

Davidson County, Tennessee County Court Minutes, Volume 3, 1799-1803

Dickson County, Tennessee County and Circuit Court Minutes, 1816-1828 and Witness Docket

Edgefield County, South Carolina Probate Records, Boxes One through Three Packages 1-106

Edgefield County, South Carolina Probate Records, Boxes Four through Six Packages 107-218

Edgefield County, South Carolina: Deed Books 13, 14 and 15

Edgefield County, South Carolina: Deed Books 16, 17 and 18

Edgefield County, South Carolina: Deed Books 19, 20, 21 and 22

Edgefield County, South Carolina: Deed Books 23, 24, 25 and 26

Edgefield County, South Carolina: Deed Books 27, 28 and 29

Edgefield County, South Carolina: Deed Books 30 and 31

Edgefield County, South Carolina: Deed Books 32 and 33

Edgefield County, South Carolina: Deed Books 34 and 35

Edgefield County, South Carolina: Deed Books 36, 37 and 38

Edgefield County, South Carolina: Deed Books 39 and 40

Edgefield County, South Carolina: Deed Book 41

Edgefield County, South Carolina: Deed Books 42 and 43, 1826-1829

Genealogical Abstracts of Edgefield, South Carolina Equity Court Records

Natchez Postscripts, 1781-1798

Rhea County, Tennessee Circuit Court Minutes, September 1815-March 1836

Rhea County, Tennessee Tax Lists, 1832-1834, and County Court Minutes Volume D: 1829-1834

Robertson County, Tennessee Court Minutes, 1796-1807

Rutherford County, Tennessee Court Minutes, 1811-1815

Sumner County, Tennessee Court Minutes, 1787-1805 and 1808-1810

Williamson County, Tennessee County Court Minutes, July 1812-October 1815

Williamson County, Tennessee County Court Minutes, May 1806-April 1812

www.ingramcontent.com/pod-product-compliance
Lightning Source LLC
Chambersburg PA
CBHW070917180426
43192CB00038B/1741